Mastering the TEKS in
WORLD GEOGRAPHY

Mark Jarrett, Ph.D.

Stuart Zimmer

James Killoran

Jarrett Publishing

HMH/JP SPECIAL EDITION

The authors wish to thank the following educators for their comments, suggestions, and recommendations which proved invaluable to this manuscript.

Greg Byers
Social Studies Coordinator, Alief ISD
Former President, Texas Social Studies
Supervisors Association (TSSSA)

Montra Rogers
Secondary Social Studies Content Specialist,
Houston ISD

Marci Smith Deal
Social Studies Coordinator,
Hurst-Euless-Bedford ISD
Former President, Texas Social Studies
Supervisors Association (TSSSA)
Steering Committee Member, Texas
Alliance for Geographic Education

Polly Schlosser
Instructor of Curriculum and Instruction,
University of Texas at Dallas
Former Secondary Social Studies
Coordinator, Plano ISD
Former President, Texas Council for the Social
Studies (TCSS) and TSSSA "Supervisor of the Year"

Tracey Hurst
Texas High School Project
Former Advanced Academics Director,
Richardson ISD

Dr. Mary McDonald
Associate Professor of Geography,
University of Hawaii

Layout, maps, graphics, and typesetting: Burmar Technical Corporation, Sea Cliff, N.Y.

This book is dedicated...

to the memory of my father, Paul Jarrett (1919–2013)   — *Mark Jarrett*

to Joan, Todd, and Ronald
and my grandchildren Jared and Katie   — *Stuart Zimmer*

to Donna, Christian, Carrie, and Jesse
and my grandchildren Aiden, Christian, and Olivia   — *James Killoran*

ISBN 9780544469105
Printed in the United States of America
First Edition
7 8 9 10   1026   18
4500708488

TABLE OF CONTENTS

ABOUT THE AUTHORS

Mark Jarrett is a former Social Studies teacher and attorney. Dr. Jarrett has served as a test writer for the New York State Board of Regents, and has taught at Hofstra University. He was educated at Columbia University, the London School of Economics, the Law School of the University of California at Berkeley, and Stanford University, where he received a Ph.D. in history. Dr. Jarrett has received several academic awards including the Order of the Coif at Berkeley and the David and Christina Phelps Harris Fellowship at Stanford. His dissertation analyzed British Foreign policy in the aftermath of the French Revolution. His law practice included representation on issues of American Constitutional law, natural resources, and intellectual property rights.

Stuart Zimmer is a former Social Studies teacher. He has written *Government and You* and *Economics and You*. He served as a test writer for the N.Y. State Board of Regents in Social Studies, and has written for the National Merit Scholarship Examination. In addition, Mr. Zimmer has published numerous articles on teaching and testing in Social Studies journals. He has presented many educational workshops at local, state, and national teachers' conferences. In 1989, Mr. Zimmer's achievements were recognized by the New York State Legislature with a Special Legislative Resolution in his honor.

James Killoran is a former Assistant Principal. He has written *Government and You* and *Economics and You*. Mr. Killoran has extensive experience in test writing for the N.Y. State Board of Regents in Social Studies and has served on the Committee for Testing of the N.C.S.S. His article on social studies testing has been published in *Social Education*, the country's leading social studies journal. In addition, Mr. Killoran has won a number of awards for outstanding teaching and curriculum development, including "Outstanding Social Studies Teacher" and "Outstanding Social Studies Supervisor" in New York City. In 1993, he was awarded an Advanced Certificate for Teachers of Social Studies by the N.C.S.S. In 1997, he became Chairman of the N.C.S.S. Committee on Awarding Advanced Certificates for Teachers of Social Studies.

ALSO BY JARRETT, ZIMMER, AND KILLORAN

Mastering the TEKS in United States History Since 1877
Mastering the TEKS in World History
Mastering the Grade 8 TAKS Social Studies Assessment
Mastering the Grade 10 TAKS Social Studies Assessment
Mastering the Grade 11 TAKS Social Studies Assessment
Texas: Its Land and Its People
Mastering New York's Intermediate-Level Social Studies Standards
Mastering New York's Grade 7 Social Studies Standards
Mastering New York's Elementary Social Studies Standards: Grade 5 Edition
The Key to Understanding U.S. History and Government
Mastering U.S. History
Learning About New York State
The Key to Understanding Global History
Mastering Global History
A Quick Review of U.S. History and Government
A Quick Review of Global History
Ohio: The Buckeye State
Mastering Ohio's Grade 5 Social Studies Achievement Test
Mastering World Regions and Civilizations
Mastering Ohio's Grade 8 Social Studies Achievement Test
Mastering Ohio's Graduation Test in Social Studies
North Carolina: The Tar Heel State
Michigan: Its Land and Its People
Mastering the GHSGT in Social Studies

WELCOME TO THIS SPECIAL EDITION

With the publication of this co-branded book, Jarrett Publishing Company enters into an exciting new phase — a partnership with Houghton Mifflin Harcourt ("HMH"), the nation's premier provider of social studies textbooks and online resources.

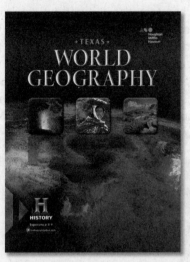

Why a Partnership?

Why shouldn't the best provider of social studies content in depth and the best provider of focused instruction, test preparation and review get together?

Our *Mastering the TEKS* series of books already provide you with the best overview of the social studies TEKS and the best preparation for the STAAR tests. With the statewide adoption process under Proclamation 2015, you will now have more resources available than ever before, including those published by Houghton Mifflin Harcourt. These resources include not only their textbooks, but also their online programs and compelling videos.

With so many resources at your disposal, you now need — more than ever — the guiding thread that only *Mastering the TEKS in World Geography* can provide. This book will ensure that you cover all of the TEKS in world geography. It will also familiarize you with the types of questions that you will later have to answer when you take the EOC in U.S. History. At the same time, our book is fun to read and easy to use! You can read it *before*, *during*, or *after* you look at other materials. It presents all the key concepts and facts that you need to know, in a clear and concise style.

In general, *Mastering the TEKS in World Geography* takes advantage of the latest developments in learning theory to help you learn more easily. Some of the special features of this book are described on pages 2 and 3 below. These features include material before and after the main text of each chapter. A list of TEKS, a list of key terms, places and concepts, a summary of *Important Ideas*, and a series of *Essential Questions* are found at the beginning of each chapter. At the end of each chapter, there are graphic organizers, study cards and practice questions similar in style to those found on STAAR tests. The book is also chock full of student activities, including *Applying What You Have Learned* activities and *Acting as an Amateur Geographer*.

With *World Geography*, published by Houghton Mifflin Harcourt, you also have a wealth of resources to learn more about world geography. HMH's *World Geography* is divided into ten regional units. Each unit begins with a preview of today's issues, followed by an atlas. The unit atlas always includes a physical map and a political map of the region, as well as several specialized maps showing patterns of physical and human geography, such as languages and religions in the region, and population density. The unit atlas concludes with a regional data file, listing each country, its flag and capital city, its area, its population, average life expectancy, annual GDP (gross domestic product), average literacy rate, and other important statistics. Next comes the first chapter of the unit — on the region's physical geography. This chapter is divided into three sections: landforms and resources, climate and vegetation, and human-environment interaction. The second chapter in the unit will tell you about the region's human geography. This chapter is divided into smaller regions or countries, such as the United States and Canada, or the regions of Mediterranean, Western, Northern and Eastern Europe. The final chapter in each unit is entitled "Today's Issues," and explores special topics relevant to the region today, such as pollution in Europe, regional conflict in Russia, oil wealth in Southwest Asia (also known as the "Middle East"), population in South Asia, and earthquakes and volcanoes in the Asia-Pacific region. Each of these chapters ends in a "Case Study," examining topics such as the European Union and peace in the Middle East.

A Comparison: How These Books Cover World Geography

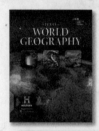

Mastering the TEKS	HMH's World Geography
UNIT 1: INTRODUCTION Chapter 1: How to Answer Multiple-Choice Questions Chapter 2: How to Answer Data-Based Questions Chapter 3: Understanding Maps: "The Language of Geography" Chapter 4: Problem-Solving and Research Skills	**UNIT 1: THE BASICS OF GEOGRAPHY** Chapter 1: Physical Geography: Looking at the Earth Chapter 2: Physical Geography: A Living Planet Chapter 3: Physical Geography: Climate and Vegetation Chapter 4: Human Geography: People and Places
UNIT 2: PHYSICAL GEOGRAPHY Chapter 5: World Gazetteer: A Look at the Seven Continents Chapter 6: Processes Shaping Planet Earth Chapter 7: People and Nature	**UNIT 2: THE UNITED STATES AND CANADA** Chapter 5: Physical Geography of the United States and Canada Chapter 6: Human Geography of the United States Chapter 7: Human Geography of Canada Chapter 8: Today's Issues • The Fight Against Terrorism • Urban Sprawl
UNIT 3: HUMAN GEOGRAPHY Chapter 8: Aspects of Culture Chapter 9: Cultural Regions Chapter 10: Demography Chapter 11: Migration	**UNIT 3: LATIN AMERICA** Chapter 9: Physical Geography of Latin America Chapter 10: Human Geography of Latin America • Mexico • Central America and the Caribbean • Spanish-Speaking South America • Brazil Chapter 11: Today's Issues • Rain Forest Resources • Giving Citizens a Voice • The Income Gap

Mastering the TEKS	HMH's *World Geography*
	UNIT 9: EAST ASIA Chapter 27: Physical Geography of East Asia Chapter 28: Human Geography of East Asia • China • Mongolia and Taiwan • The Koreas: North and South • Japan Chapter 29: Today 's Issues • The Ring of Fire • Trade and Prosperity • Population and the Quality of Life
	UNIT 10: SOUTHEAST ASIA, OCEANIA, AND ANTARCTICA Chapter 30: Physical Geography of Southeast Asia, Oceania, and Antarctica Chapter 31: Human Geography of Southeast Asia, Oceania, and Antarctica • Southeast Asia • Oceania • Australia, New Zealand and Antarctica Chapter 32: Today 's Issues • Aboriginal Land Claims • Industrialization Sparks Change • Global Environmental Change

Power Combo: Strategies for Using These Resources Together

As you can see, these two books are not organized in quite the same way. *Mastering the TEKS in World Geography* takes a conceptual — or thematic — approach to world geography. It is organized around various themes or topics that affect all regions, such as processes shaping Earth's landforms, demography, culture, migration, cultural convergence and divergence, and economic growth. HMH's *World Geography* is organized around regions, such as Latin America, Africa, Southwest Asia, and East Asia. You can see these different approaches by comparing the tables of contents of the two books, shown in the chart above. Because these books take different approaches to world geography, they can be very effectively used to reinforce one another. If you are using this book as your primary classroom resource, you will be able to use HMH's *World Geography* for additional explanations and for examples from all regions of the world to illustrate the concepts you are learning about. The correlation charts at the beginning of each chapter of this special edition will help you to draw the right connections. If your class is taking a regional approach to world geography and you are using HMH's *World Geography* as your primary classroom resource, then you should use this book, *Mastering the TEKS in World Geography*, to clarify and reinforce your understanding of key concepts as you encounter them in the course of your study of each region. For example, if you are studying volcanoes in the Pacific Ring of Fire, you can read further about the forces shaping Earth in Chapter 6 of this book. If you are studying population growth in China or India, you can refine your understanding of demographic concepts by reading Chapter 10 of this book. If you are learning about demographic and economic indicators, such as "GDP/per capita," you should be sure to read Chapter 18 of this book. If you are studying the impact of globalization, you should read Chapter 19 of this book.

What is the best way to use these different resources together? It is best to keep the main purpose of each resource in mind. The aim of this book is to help you, as its title suggests, to "Master the TEKS." This book explains and clarifies, with a laser-sharp focus, each of the TEKS in World Geography. This book further provides you with valuable study tools, including review cards and practice questions.

The aim of HMH's *World Geography* is to help you understand and appreciate the vast panoi world geography in greater depth. This textbook permits you to explore topics of special interest to you your class. The special features of this book can help you to understand world geography more fully.

Many teachers and students believe that the best way to use these resources together is to start with *Mastering the TEKS* and to read the language of the TEKS themselves at the front of each chapter. Then read the *Important Ideas*. Write down any terms from the *Geographic Terminology* section you don't already know, and then fill in their definitions or identifications as you read further. After you have whetted your appetite for a deeper understanding of the topic, you should then turn to HMH's *World Geography*. You might want to compare the information found in the two books on the same topic, or even make a Venn diagram or chart comparing this information.

Here are some other ideas for using both resources together:

❑ You can turn the TEKS at the start of each chapter into a chart. On the left side, copy the TEKS. On the right side, rewrite each TEKS in your own words as something you will do. Then use both books to help you achieve each objective. For example:

History 1B	Trace the spatial diffusion of phenomena such as the Columbian Exchange or the diffusion of American popular culture and describe the effects on regions of contact.	I will be able to show how something like American popular culture (popular music, clothing styles, films, television programs, and fast-food restaurants) spread to new areas, such as Europe, Africa and Asia, and also be able to describe the effects that this spread had on those places.

❑ Create your own chart with the *Important Ideas* listed on the second page of each chapter. Then use information from both books to explain or illustrate each idea.

Important Ideas	Your Explanation
A. Processes of spatial exchange, or diffusion, have influenced events in the past and continue to shape the present.	A.
B. During the Columbian Exchange, new plants, animals, ideas and even diseases were exchanged between the peoples of the Americas and those of Europe, Asia and Africa. More recently, aspects of American popular culture have spread throughout the world. Such spatial diffusions have affected regions of contact.	B.
C. Cultural divergence occurs when different cultural influences cause an area to divide into separate parts. Cultural convergence occurs when different cultures exchange ideas and become more similar.	C.
D. Cultural diffusion today is leading to cultural convergence on a global scale, creating a common global culture. This can be seen in the spread of democratic ideas, the English language, technology, and global sports.	D.

❏ After reading the *Important Ideas* at the beginning of each chapter of this book, make predictions about what you expect to learn from the information in both books. Then read through the related chapters and see if your predictions are accurate.

❏ Use the *Geographic Terminology* at the beginning of each chapter to create your own glossary. Use information from both books to define or identify the terms you list.

❏ Classify the information found in each book. Decide which names, terms, places and events are *political*, which of these are *economic*, and which are *social*.

❏ Develop your own note-taking style for both books. With your teacher's permission, you might highlight important sections of this book, underline important places and facts, and make your own comments in the margin. Marginal comments could be headings for different sections of the text, or short sentences summarizing main events and ideas.

❏ You might also write a *summary* or create an *outline* on a separate sheet of paper. Many students find it helpful to make an *informal outline*: each main point begins a separate line; supporting facts and details are indented. You could also create a *concept map* with your topic or main idea in the center and supporting facts and details in surrounding bubbles. Or make *combination notes* with an informal outline on the left and your own diagrams and illustrations on the right.

❏ Use information from both books to create an *illustrated map* showing the most important facts and concepts about each topic or region you are studying.

❏ Think about an important *decision* or *current issue* for the region you are studying. Then use information from both books to make the best decision or to make your own case in the historical debate.

❏ Make your own *concept map* of the topic or region you are studying. Use information from both books to add supporting ideas and details. Then compare your concept map with the one in this book at the end of each chapter.

❏ *Compare* how the two books treat one or more of the topics you are studying. Look at the topic in this book. Then use the correlation chart at the beginning of each chapter to find the corresponding pages in HMH's *World Geography* that treat the same topic. Be sure to identify both similarities and differences:

Topic: _____

Similarities	
Differences	

Remember: Knowledge is Power!

■ These books will help you to master important facts and ideas about world geography that every American citizen should know. Someday as a voter, you will have a chance to help determine our nation's future. A knowledge of world geography is essential for understanding current events. How can you decide how American leaders should relate to other countries unless you know where these countries are and something about their physical and human geography and history?

■ These books can also teach you important skills for analyzing information and solving problems. You can use these skills later in life, both at home and at work.

■ A knowledge of world geography will also help you make predictions about the speed and effects of globalization, which may influence your choice of career and other lifestyle choices, including where to spend your future vacations.

■ These books will help you to perform your very best in class and on the future EOC test in U.S. History, which you will take later in high school. This may improve your job prospects and increase your opportunities for a higher education.

By using *Mastering the TEKS* and HMH's *World Geography*, you can do well in class and lay a foundation for performing your very best on later statewide tests. The key is to use *Mastering the TEKS* as your guide and to use HMH's *World Geography* to explore particular topics and regions in greater depth. You will be amazed at how much you can learn!

UNIT 1

INTRODUCTION

This year you will learn about world geography. **Geography** is one of the world's oldest fields of study. In ancient times, travelers reported about the *physical features* (*mountains*, *forests*, *deserts*, and *seas*) and peoples of other lands they had visited. The word "geography" itself comes from two ancient Greek words — the word for *Earth* (*geo*) and the word for *writing* (*graphy*).

Modern geography includes the study of the Earth's surface and how the location, climate, physical features and resources of a place affect its people. Geographers examine how people interact with their environment, and how people, goods, and ideas move from place to place. They are concerned with how Earth's surface shapes human processes.

WHY STUDY WORLD GEOGRAPHY?

These days it is more important to learn about world geography than ever before. You will learn concepts and relationships that almost everyone agrees you should know. You will learn where America is situated in relation to the rest of the world and about the challenges of globalization. You will learn about other cultures around the globe with which you will be coming into increasing contact in the years ahead — through the Internet, Facebook, Skype, text messaging, global trade, and jet travel. Knowledge of world geography will help you to better understand and respect these cultures.

You will learn how these various cultures developed, about their institutions, and how they relate to one another. You will also see how location and physical features often affect the people living in a place.

By learning about world geography, you will better understand your own opportunities in our increasingly global economy. You will also better understand the current threats to our physical environment. As a voter, you will make more informed decisions; in choosing a career, you will make better choices. You can also enjoy learning about other places that you may visit someday. Knowledge of world geography has simply become indispensable for success in our shrinking world. After taking this course, you will be better prepared for college, for the job market and for the duties of citizenship.

HOW THIS BOOK WILL HELP YOU MASTER WORLD GEOGRAPHY

This book will help you to learn every one of the World Geography TEKS. The TEKS have been organized in this book in a way to make them easier to learn. At the beginning of each chapter, you will see the TEKS that it covers. Some TEKS appear in more than one chapter. The first unit of the book will help you improve your social studies skills. You will learn how to answer test questions, how to read maps and graphs, how to conduct research, and how to make decisions and solve problems.

THE ORGANIZATION OF CONTENT CHAPTERS

In later units, you will learn and review the World Geography TEKS. Each content chapter has several unique features, designed to help you learn and recall important concepts and facts more easily:

IMPORTANT IDEAS

Each chapter is introduced by a list of "Important Ideas." This is an advanced organizer that briefly summarizes the main concepts you will learn in the chapter.

GEOGRAPHIC TERMINOLOGY

At the start of each content chapter there is also a list of important geographic terms used in the chapter. These are the terms that you will find in **bold** print throughout the chapter.

ESSENTIAL QUESTIONS

At the beginning of each content chapter you will find one or two *Essential Questions*. These *Essential Questions* establish overarching themes for each chapter. They raise interesting questions about our world that the chapter will answer.

APPLYING WHAT YOU HAVE LEARNED

Each section of text includes one or more *Applying What You Have Learned* activities. These activities encourage you to think about what you have read. You can complete these activities alone or in a small group.

ACTING AS AN AMATEUR GEOGRAPHER

These "hands-on" activities will ask you to think like a geographer as you complete geography-related projects.

LEARNING WITH GRAPHIC ORGANIZERS

These exercises ask you to complete a graphic organizer summarizing the major ideas and concepts in the chapter.

STUDY CARDS

Study Cards identify the major ideas and facts at the end of each chapter. You can use these cards alone to quiz yourself, or with a group of classmates. You are encouraged to expand the number of *Study Cards* by adding additional cards of your own.

CHECKING YOUR UNDERSTANDING

Each content chapter ends with practice test questions. The answer to the first question is always fully explained. All these questions are in a format similar to those on the ***STAAR End-of-Course Assessment*** that you will later be taking in U.S. History.

UNIT ORGANIZATION

Each group of related content chapters are organized into a unit. Each unit concludes with a *Concept Map* showing how all the information in the unit is related, and a series of exercises for you to complete, called *Pulling It All Together*.

IMPORTANT TOOLS FOR REMEMBERING INFORMATION

World geography concerns how people relate to their physical environment and to each other. In studying world geography, you will learn many new terms and concepts. With so much information, it's sometimes hard to identify exactly what is and what is not important. This section will help you to do that.

IMPORTANT TERMS

Terms refer to specific things that actually happened or existed — such as particular features, places, or groups. When you learn a new term, you should focus on its main features. These main features may include:

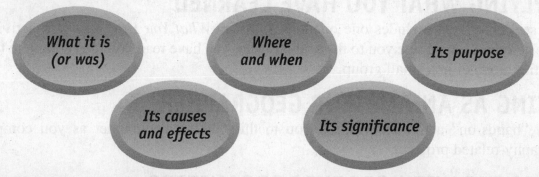

What it is (or was)

Where and when

Its purpose

Its causes and effects

Its significance

KEY CONCEPTS

Concepts are words or phrases that refer to categories of information. They allow us to organize large amounts of information. For example, Judaism, Christianity, and Islam share certain common characteristics. The concept "religion" acts as an umbrella, grouping these specific examples together by identifying what they have in common. Questions about concepts usually ask for a definition or an example of the concept. Thus, when you study a concept, you should pay careful attention to:

Its definition

Examples of the concept

HOW TO USE YOUR STUDY CARDS

At the end of every content chapter, there are two to eight *Study Cards*. These *Study Cards* highlight the most important information you should know about a particular term, concept or idea in the chapter. You should make a habit of building a collection of these cards by copying by hand or photocopying them.

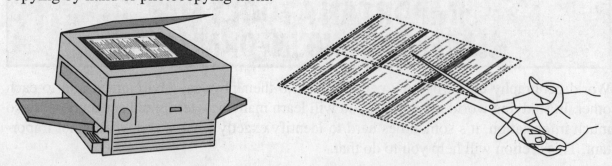

After you duplicate the cards, use the back of each card to create your own illustration. Why should you draw your own illustration? Turning written information into a picture can help you to better understand the term or concept. Many people are visual learners. By "seeing" the term or concept, you create an impression in your mind that will help you to remember the term better.

There are many ways to use *Study Cards* to recall information, especially for a test. One method is to sort your cards into two stacks, based on how well you recall the information on each card.

First, gather your cards into one pile. Try to recall the information on the card on top of the stack. If you can recall it, place the card in the "Know It" stack. If you have trouble recalling the information, place the card in the "Don't Know It" stack.

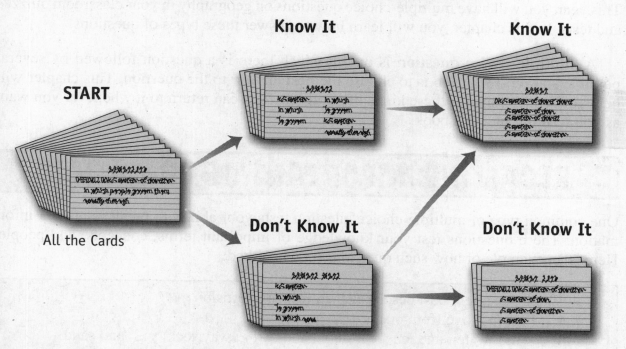

Review the cards in the "Don't Know It" stack every time you study. Study the cards in the "Know It" stack every other time you study. As you move closer to the day of a unit test or final exam, you should see the number of cards in the "Don't Know It" stack shrink. This will give you even more time to study the ones you know the least.

This book will provide you with all you need to know about world geography. With this book as your guide, you will be very well prepared to face many of the most important challenges presented by our shrinking world.

HOW TO ANSWER MULTIPLE-CHOICE QUESTIONS

CHAPTER 1

TEKS COVERED IN CHAPTER 1

- ■ **Social Studies Skills 21** The student applies critical-thinking skills to organize and use information acquired from a variety of valid sources....
- ■ **Social Studies Skills 22(B)** Generate ... generalizations ... supported by evidence.

This year, you will have multiple-choice questions on geography in your classroom quizzes and tests. In this chapter, you will learn how to answer these types of questions.

A **multiple-choice question** is one in which there is a question followed by several possible answers. Your job is to choose the **best** answer to the question. This chapter will help you learn to answer these kinds of questions. You can return to it whenever you want as you read through this book.

RECALLING IMPORTANT INFORMATION

One common type of multiple-choice question tests your ability to recall important information. These questions test your knowledge of important terms, concepts, and people. Here is an example of how such questions may be asked:

> **1**   Which statement best describes the process of erosion?
> **A**   People move from one area to another.
> **B**   Wind, water, and ice wear down and carry away rock, soil, and sand.
> **C**   Large plates in Earth's lithosphere shift their position.
> **D**   New ideas spread from one region to another.

As you can see, this question tests your ability to recall information describing a specific term — erosion.

UNLOCKING THE ANSWER

🗝 What do you think is the answer to **Question 1**? _____

🗝 Explain why you selected that answer. _____

_____

_____

_____

_____

_____

HOW TO USE THE "E-R-A" APPROACH

Whatever type of multiple-choice question you are asked, we suggest you follow the same three-step approach to answer it. Think of this as the "**E-R-A**" approach:

EXAMINE The Question	**R**ECALL What You Know	**A**PPLY What You Know

Let's take a closer look at each of these steps to see how they can help you select the right answer.

STEP 1: EXAMINE THE QUESTION

Start by carefully reading the question. Be sure you understand any information the question provides. Then make sure you understand what the question is asking for.

The question on page 6 asks you to select the best description of the process of erosion. Which answer choice best describes erosion?

STEP 2: RECALL WHAT YOU KNOW

Next, you should identify the topic that the question asks about. Take a moment to think about what you know about that topic. Mentally review all the important concepts, facts, and relationships you can remember.

> *In this case, you should think about what you can remember from your study of physical geography. You should recall that erosion occurs when wind, water or ice wear down a land form and carry its particles away.*

STEP 3: APPLY WHAT YOU KNOW

Finally, take what you can recall about the topic and apply it to answer the question. Sometimes it helps to try to answer the question **before** you even look at the answer choices. Then look to see if any of the choices is what you thought the answer should be. Review all the choices to be sure you have identified the best one. Eliminate any choices that are obviously wrong. Then select your final answer.

> *To answer this question, you need to recall what erosion is. Then you have to apply this information by selecting the best description of the process of erosion from the four answer choices.*
>
> ★ *Choice A describes migration, the movement of people from one place to another.*
>
> ★ *Choice C defines tectonic plate movement, the shifting of large plates on Earth's crust.*
>
> ★ *Choice D describes cultural diffusion, the movement of ideas.*
>
> ✪ *Choice B is the best answer. It is the only answer choice that correctly describes erosion.*

Do not be concerned if you don't know all the terms in this question. You will learn more about them in later chapters. For now, you should focus on learning the "**E-R-A**" approach — the process for finding the correct answer to a multiple-choice question:

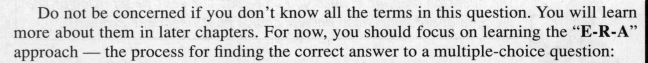

| **EXAMINE** The Question | **RECALL** What You Know | **APPLY** What You Know |

GENERALIZATION

A **generalization** identifies characteristics that several specific facts or examples share. In order to understand generalizations better, look at these three statements about particular ancient civilizations:

Egyptian civilization developed along the Nile River.	**Mesopotamian civilizations developed between the Tigris and Euphrates Rivers.**	**Chinese civilization first arose along the Hwang Ho.**

What do these three specific facts show in general? They show that the first civilizations arose along major rivers. This statement is called a **generalization**.

Some questions will test your ability to see the relationship between specific examples and generalizations about them. Here is how these questions may appear:

2 The city-states of ancient Greece grew rich from trade. The West African Kingdom of Ghana became wealthy by taxing the gold and salt trade. Today, Saudi Arabia is rich from selling its oil. Which generalization do these examples support?
  F Trade often leads to conflict and war.
  G Trade between places can lead to wealth and prosperity.
  H Merchants in ancient Greece and West Africa traded with each other.
  J Strong rulers often conquer neighboring peoples.

UNLOCKING THE ANSWER

What generalizations can you make based on the three examples in the question? _____

_____

_____

_____

What do you think is the answer to **Question 2**? _____

As you can see, this question asks you to make a generalization based on three examples. To answer questions about generalizations, you should use the "**E-R-A**" approach. Let's see how this approach can be used to answer this question.

USING THE "E-R-A" APPROACH

◆ **Step 1: EXAMINE The Question.**
First, read the question carefully. Be sure you understand what it asks for. Does it ask you to make a generalization from examples? Or does it ask you to apply a generalization to a specific situation? In this case, the question gives several examples: trade in ancient Greece, West Africa, and Saudi Arabia. Study these examples to be sure you understand what they show.

◆ **Step 2: RECALL What You Know.**
Now think about what you have learned about generalizations. What do these examples have in common? Notice that in all three cases, societies grew rich from trade. This is an important generalization.

◆ **Step 3: APPLY What You Know.**
Finally, apply what you know to find the correct answer. Look over the choices. Eliminate any choices that are not generalizations or that do not apply to both examples. Then chose the best generalization from the remaining choices. In this example, all of the choices are generalizations. But only one of these generalizations applies to all three of the examples in the question.

★ **Choice F is wrong.** There is nothing in the examples that relates war to trade.

★ **Choice H is wrong.** The examples do not provide any information that tells us that ancient Greece and West Africa traded with each other.

★ **Choice J is also wrong.** The examples do not tell about strong rulers or their conquests.

✪ **Choice G is correct.** The first example states that the ancient Greeks prospered from trade. The second example states that Ghana prospered by taxing trade. The third example states that Saudi Arabia is rich from selling its oil, a form of trade. The generalization that trade can lead to wealth can be drawn from these three examples.

Now try answering a question about generalizations on your own:

Use the information in the boxes and your knowledge of social studies to answer question 3 on the next page.

Israel has a dry climate but borders the Mediterranean. Israeli scientists have developed new ways to obtain fresh water by removing salt from sea water.	North of the Arctic Circle, the Inuit people live in homes made of animal skins or blocks of ice. They wear thick animal skins to keep warm.

3   Which conclusion can best be drawn from these two examples?
   A   People prefer to settle in areas with warm climates.
   B   People sometimes migrate to meet their needs for survival.
   C   A shortage of resources can often lead to conflicts.
   D   People adapt to or modify their physical environment.

To answer this question, use the "E-R-A" approach to see how it can help you to find the correct answer.

APPLYING THE "E-R-A" APPROACH

◆ **Step 1: EXAMINE the Question**

What do the examples show? _____

_____

What does the question ask you to do? _____

_____

◆ **Step 2: RECALL What You Know**

What do you recall about this topic? _____

_____

_____

What do you recall about drawing conclusions? _____

_____

◆ **Step 3: APPLY What You Know**

Based on what you know, which is the best answer? _____

Another type of generalization question starts with a general statement or concept, and then asks you to select the best example of it:

4   Which statement identifies an example of erosion?
   F   The Colorado River cut through land to create the Grand Canyon.
   G   The Great Lakes are among the world's largest fresh water lakes.
   H   Climate change may be causing the world's polar ice caps to shrink.
   J   The Hawaiian islands were formed by volcanic eruptions.

CAUSE-AND-EFFECT QUESTIONS

In geography, you will sometimes investigate why an event occurred or its effects. *Cause-and-effect questions* test your understanding of the relationship between a condition or event, its causes, and its effects.

CAUSES

A **cause** is what made something happen. For example, if you turn the switch of a light, you *cause* the light to go on. Often, important developments have more than one cause. For example, the European exploration of the Americas was caused by the arrival of new technologies — like the compass and better sails. It was also caused by the European desire to reach the Spice Islands of Asia by an all-water route.

EFFECTS

An **effect** is what happens because of something. An effect is the result of an event, action or development. For example, when you turn the switch, the *effect* of that action is that the light goes on. Important historical developments often have several effects. For example, the European encounter with the peoples of the Americas led to an exchange of ideas and products, as well as the European conquest of the Americas and the deaths of millions of Native American Indians by disease. These were all effects of Columbus' voyage.

CAUSE
Someone turned on the switch.

EFFECT
The light went on.

Many questions on the *End-of-Course Assessment* will ask about cause-and-effect relationships. To answer such questions, be careful to understand what the question asks for — a *cause* or an *effect*. Then think about the causes or effects of the event you are asked about.

> 5   Which event led to the introduction of new foods to Western Europe?
> A   Columbus' voyages to the Americas
> B   the spread of the Black Death
> C   the outbreak of the Irish Potato Famine
> D   the development of global positioning systems (*GPS*)

To answer this question, use the "**E-R-A**" approach.

Name _____ Date _____

USING THE "E-R-A" APPROACH

◆ **Step 1:** EXAMINE **The Question.**
Read the question carefully. The question asks you to identify a cause. Your task is to identify an event that led to the introduction of new foods to Western Europe.

◆ **Step 2:** RECALL **What You Know.**
Mentally step back and think of everything you can recall that may have led to the introduction of new foods to Europe. You should recall that the "Columbian Exchange" led to the introduction of new foods — such as corn, potatoes, chocolate, and tomatoes — to Western Europe from the Americas.

◆ **Step 3:** APPLY **What You Know.**
Now apply what you know to find the correct answer.

★ **Choice B** is wrong. The Black Death killed many people but did not introduce new foods to Western Europe.

★ **Choice C** is wrong because the Irish Potato Famine was the result, not the cause, of the introduction of new foods to Western Europe.

★ **Choice D** is also wrong. The more recent development of GPS has had many effects, but the introduction of new foods to Western Europe is not one of them.

✪ **Choice A**, Columbus' voyages to the Americas, is the only choice that led to the introduction of new foods to Europe. Thus, it is the best answer.

Now answer another *cause-and-effect question* using the "**E-R-A**" approach.

6	Which has been an effect of the global spread of American popular culture?
F	the introduction of monarchial governments
G	the spread of English as an international second language
H	the resolution of religious differences
J	the spread of free public education

APPLYING THE "E-R-A" APPROACH

◆ **Step 1:** EXAMINE **the Question**

What does the question ask you to do? Does it ask you to identify a cause or an effect?

_____

_____

CONTINUED

◆ **Step 2: RECALL What You Know**

What do you recall about this topic? What do you remember about the recent spread of American popular culture? _____

_____

◆ **Step 3: APPLY What You Know**

Applying what you know, which answer is best? Explain why the other choices are wrong. _____

_____

COMPARE-AND-CONTRAST QUESTIONS

We often compare two or more things to understand them better. To compare, we look at similarities and differences. Items are similar when they have characteristics in common. Items are different when they have dissimilar features. *Compare* and *contrast* questions often use words such as "*similarities*" or "*differences*." A *compare-and-contrast question* might appear as follows:

7   In what way are Christianity and Islam similar?
A   They proclaim a belief in one God.
B   They believe that followers should visit Mecca.
C   They promise salvation to those who worship Jesus.
D   They consider the Q'uran (*Koran*) as their holy book.

Again, use the "**E-R-A**" approach to find the correct answer:

USING THE "E-R-A" APPROACH

◆ **Step 1: EXAMINE The Question.**
Read the question carefully. The question asks you to identify a similarity. Your task is to select the answer choice that identifies a similarity between two world religions — Christianity and Islam.

◆ **Step 2: RECALL What You Know.**
Recall what you know about the beliefs and practices of Christianity and of Islam. Christians believe that Jesus was the son of God. Muslims believe Mohammed was the last prophet. Both believe in one God.

CONTINUED

◆ **Step 3: APPLY What You Know.**

Based on what you can recall, which answer choice identifies a similarity between Christianity and Islam? **Choice B** and **Choice D** are both wrong, since only Muslims believe in visiting Mecca or follow the Q'uran. **Choice C** is also wrong: Only Christians promise salvation to the followers of Jesus. **Choice A** is the best answer. Both Christians and Muslims proclaim a belief in one God.

Now try answering a *compare-and-contrast question* on your own by using the "**E-R-A**" approach.

8	What is an important difference between Hinduism and Judaism?
A Hindus try to be kind to others.	**C** Hindus believe in reincarnation.
B Hindus believe in prayer.	**D** Hindus prohibit murder.

APPLYING THE "E-R-A" APPROACH

◆ **Step 1: EXAMINE the Question**

What does the question ask you? _____

_____

◆ **Step 2: RECALL What You Know**

What do you recall about this topic? _____

_____

_____

◆ **Step 3: APPLY What You Know**

Applying what you know, which is best the answer? _____

_____

_____

In this chapter, you learned how to answer different types of multiple-choice questions by using the "**E-R-A**" approach. As you work your way through this book, you will find many multiple-choice questions. Try to get into the habit of using the "**E-R-A**" approach to answer these questions. In each group of sample questions, the answer to the first question will always be explained to you. This explanation will show you how to use the "**E-R-A**" approach.

HOW TO ANSWER DATA-BASED QUESTIONS

CHAPTER 2

TEKS
COVERED IN
CHAPTER 2

- ■ **Geography 7(C)** Describe trends in world population growth.
- ■ **Social Studies Skills 21** The student applies critical-thinking skills to organize and use information acquired from a variety of valid sources, including electronic technology.
  - • **Social Studies Skills 21(A)** Analyze and evaluate the validity and utility of multiple sources of geographic information such as primary and secondary sources, aerial photographs, and maps.
- ■ **Social Studies Skills 22(A)** Design and draw appropriate graphics, such as maps, diagrams, tables and graphs to communicate geographic features, distributions and relationships.
- ■ **Social Studies Skills 22(B)** Generate summaries ... supported by evidence.

The study of geography requires you to interpret different types of information, or **data**. Geographers often use maps, tables, graphs, diagrams, and written texts. These include primary and secondary sources.

This year your teacher will probably give you tests and quizzes with questions that include data. Data-based questions test your ability:

To understand data

To draw conclusions from data

These questions often test particular social studies skills found in the TEKS. Chapters 2, 3, and 4 of this book identify questions by the social studies skill that is being assessed.

In this chapter, you will examine some of the major types of data often found in such questions:

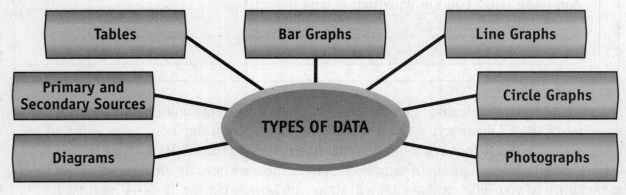

Tables

Bar Graphs

Line Graphs

Primary and Secondary Sources

Circle Graphs

Diagrams

TYPES OF DATA

Photographs

TABLES

A **table** is an arrangement of information in columns and rows. A table is used to organize large amounts of information so that individual facts can be easily found and compared. Examine the table below:

WORLD POPULATION, 1950–2000
(in millions)

Region	1950	2000
Africa	198	819
Asia	1,308	3,698
North and South America	328	840
Europe	366	727

STEPS TO UNDERSTANDING A TABLE

1. **Look at the Title.** The title of the table describes what it shows. This table provides information about the population of several continents in 1950 and 2000.

2. **Examine the Categories.** Each column in the table represents a category in the headings across the top. In this table, three categories are named in the headings: *Region*, *1950*, and *2000*. Each row provides the population of one region during these two periods of time.

3. **Drawing Conclusions from the Data.** By examining a table, it is often possible to identify a trend or to draw a conclusion. For example, geographers believe the population of Europe is not growing as fast as that of other areas. More people lived in Europe in 1950 than in the Americas or in Africa. Today, more people live in the Americas and Africa than in Europe. While the population of Europe doubled over this period, the population of Asia almost tripled.

FINDING SPECIFIC INFORMATION

In order to find specific information, you need to see where the columns and rows meet. For example, suppose you wanted to find the population of Africa in 1950:

★ First, look at the column marked *Region*. Now look down the column until you reach the row for *Africa*.

★ Next, look across the row until you reach the column for *1950*.

★ You can see that in 1950, there were 198 million people living in Africa.

ANSWERING TABLE-BASED QUESTIONS

Use the table on page 17 and your knowledge of social studies to answer the following questions.

1   In which region did the size of the population increase by more than four times between 1950 and 2000?

  A   Africa   **C**   North and South America

  B   Asia   **D**   Europe

2   Which is one reason why the population of Europe did not increase as fast as other regions?

  F   Most Europeans live in small towns.

  G   Europeans began having smaller families.

  H   Other regions were involved in a series of major wars.

  J   Workers from other places migrated to Europe.

BAR GRAPHS

A **bar graph** is a chart made of parallel bars with different lengths. A bar graph is often used to show a comparison of two or more things.

STEPS TO UNDERSTANDING A BAR GRAPH

1. **Look at the Title.** The title tells you what the bar graph shows. For example, the title of this bar graph tells you that the graph shows the population of the world in 1950. In fact, this bar graph presents some of the same information found in the table on page 17, but in a different format.

2. **Examine the Bars or Legend.** Usually the bars of the graph will be labeled. If not, then a legend will tell you what each bar represents. In this graph, each bar represents a different region.

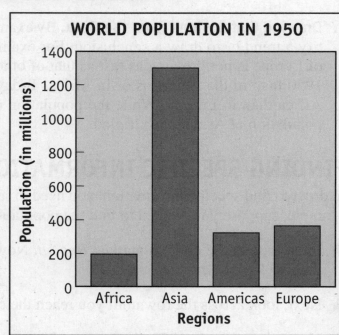

3. Look at the Vertical and Horizontal Axes.

★ The **horizontal axis** runs along the bottom of the bar graph. It often identifies what the bars represent. Here, the horizontal axis indicates the four different regions being compared — Africa, Asia, the Americas, and Europe.

★ The **vertical axis** runs along the left-hand side of the graph. It measures the length of the bars. In this graph, it measures population in millions of people.

FINDING SPECIFIC INFORMATION

To find specific information, you need to examine the length of the different bars carefully. For example, suppose you wanted to find the population of Europe in 1950. Here is what you must do:

★ On the horizontal axis, locate the region for which you are seeking information. In this case, you need to select the bar that represents *Europe*.

★ Then, look at the top of the bar marked *Europe* and compare it with the vertical axis. It should be close to 400. This means that the population of Europe in 1950 was almost 400 million people.

ANSWERING BAR GRAPH-BASED QUESTIONS

Use the bar graph on page 18 and your knowledge of social studies to answer the following questions.

3   What was the approximate population of Africa in 1950?
    A   100 million   **C**   200 million
    B   150 million   **D**   250 million

4   Which of the following best describes the world's population in 1950, based on the information in the graph?
    F   There was little difference in population size between these regions.
    G   Asia was the least populated continent.
    H   There were more people living in Africa than in Europe.
    J   Asia had a greater population than all the other regions combined.

LINE GRAPHS

A **line graph** is a chart composed of a series of points connected in a line. A line graph is often used to show how something has changed over time.

STEPS TO UNDERSTANDING A LINE GRAPH

1. **Look at the Title.** The title identifies the topic. Here, the title is *"World Population."* As its title indicates, the graph shows the total number of people living in the world from 1960 to 2010.

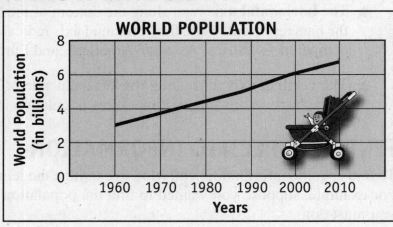

2. **Legend.** A line graph may have several lines. A legend often identifies each line. In this graph, a legend is not necessary. Here, the title indicates what the line shows — the world's population in billions.

3. **Look at the Vertical and Horizontal Axes.**

   ★ **Horizontal Axis.** The horizontal axis runs along the bottom of the line graph. In this line graph, the horizontal axis shows *Years* separated by decades (*every ten years*). The graph begins at 1960. The axis is divided into ten-year intervals.

   ★ **Vertical Axis.** The vertical axis runs along the left-side of the graph. It usually measures an amount. As you move up the vertical axis, the numbers increase. In this line graph, world population is shown in billions. Therefore, the number "4" represents a world population of *4 billion* people.

4. **Check for Trends.** Sometimes a line graph will reveal a trend. A **trend** is the general direction in which things are moving. We can often see a trend by examining the movement of a line.

APPLYING WHAT YOU HAVE LEARNED

Examine the line graph showing the size of the world's population. What *two* trends do you notice?

1. _____

_____

_____

2. _____

_____

_____

FINDING SPECIFIC INFORMATION

To find specific information, you must closely examine the movement of the line on the graph. For example, if you wanted to know the population of the world in 1980, here is what you would need to do:

★ Begin by looking across the horizontal axis marked *Years* until you reach the year *1980*. Then move your finger up until you reach the line showing the world's population.

★ Next, check the vertical axis. You are looking to see the amount reached at this point. The point where "1980" meets the line is between "4" and "5" billion people. Thus, the population of the world in 1980 was about $4\frac{1}{2}$ billion people.

ANSWERING LINE GRAPH-BASED QUESTIONS

Use the line graph on page 20 and your knowledge of social studies to answer the following questions.

5   When did the world's population reach 6 billion people?
    A   between 1970 and 1980   **C**   between 1990 and 2000
    B   between 1980 and 1990   **D**   between 2000 and 2010

6   Which of the following statements best identifies a general trend of world population growth?
    F   World population has increased, but not as rapidly as from 1960 to 1970.
    G   The greatest growth in world population occurred before 1980.
    H   World population has generally decreased since 1960.
    J   World population has more than doubled since 1960.

7   Based on the information in the line graph, which statement most likely predicts the future trend of world population growth?
    A   The world's population will remain the same after 2010.
    B   The world's population will decline after 2010.
    C   The world's population will continue to rise after 2010.
    D   The world's population will increase, then decrease.

CIRCLE GRAPHS

A **circle graph**, sometimes referred to as a **pie chart**, is a circle divided into sections or slices of different sizes. A circle graph is used to show relationships between a whole and its parts.

STEPS TO UNDERSTANDING A CIRCLE GRAPH OR PIE CHART

1. **Look at the Title.** The title tells you what the graph is about. For example, this graph shows *"World Population by Continent in 2010."* It shows the share of the world's population living on each continent.

2. **Examine the Legend.** Sometimes a circle graph will have a legend to indicate what each slice represents. Here, the slices themselves tell what they represent.

3. **Look at the Slices.** Each slice shows the size of something in relation to the whole circle. If you add all the slices together, they total 100%. In this graph, the size of each slice tells you the share each continent has of the world's total population.

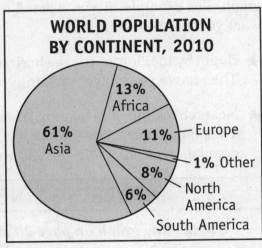

WORLD POPULATION BY CONTINENT, 2010

FINDING SPECIFIC INFORMATION

To find specific information, you need to examine each slice. For example, if you wanted to know Asia's share of the world's population, you need to:

★ Look at the graph and identify the slice of the graph that represents Asia.

★ In this circle graph, the slice marked *Asia* occupies 61% of the graph. It is also the largest slice of the circle graph.

ANSWERING CIRCLE GRAPH-BASED QUESTIONS

Use the circle graph above and your knowledge of social studies to answer the following questions.

8   Which conclusion can be drawn from the graph?
   F   Asia holds more than half of the world's population.
   G   Africa is almost as populous as Asia.
   H   South America and Europe's population are about the same size.
   J   North America is growing at a faster rate than South America.

9   Which statement about the world's population is supported by the graph?
   A   The world's population continues to rapidly increase.
   B   Climate change has greatly affected settlement patterns in the world.
   C   Asia will dominate the world's economy in the future.
   D   The world's population is distributed among several continents.

PHOTOGRAPHS

Photographs show geographers what other places look like. They can be used to record visual information. Old photographs show us how people and places looked in the past. An **aerial photograph** is a picture taken from an airplane or a satellite in outer space. Aerial photographs are especially useful to geographers because they can show the surface features of a large area, almost like a map.

STEPS TO UNDERSTANDING A PHOTOGRAPH

1. Look at the Title or Caption. Most photographs have a title or caption. The title or caption identifies what the photograph shows. In the aerial photograph to the right, there is no title, but the caption is: "*Satellite photo of North and South Korea at night. Bright spots show electricity usage.*"

2. Consider the Background. This photograph, taken from a U.S. space satellite, shows the differences between North and South Korea at night. The light area shows electric lights seen from space. The white lines, showing the borders of the countries, have been added later by the **cartographer** (*mapmaker*).

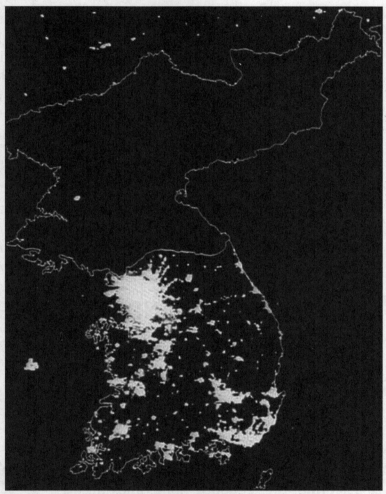

Satellite photo of North and South Korea at night. Bright spots show electricity usage.

In North Korea, the entire country is dark at night. The only illumination is North Korea's capital, Pyongyang. In contrast, South Korea is ablaze with light. This is particularly evident around South Korea's major cities and its capital, Seoul (*located in the northwest of South Korea*).

ANSWERING PHOTOGRAPH-BASED QUESTIONS

Use the photograph on page 23 and your knowledge of social studies to answer the following questions.

10   What conclusion about North Korea can be drawn from this photograph?
   F   North Korea is a modern, technologically advanced nation.
   G   The government of North Korea puts people's comfort above all else.
   H   North Korea has a shortage of electricity.
   J   Most North Korean citizens support their government.

11   Which statement about the Korean Peninsula is best supported by the photograph?
   A   North Korea is a highly developed nation while South Korea is not.
   B   There is a sharp contrast between North and South Korea.
   C   Most cities on the Korean peninsula have plentiful electric power.
   D   All North Koreans enjoy the same social benefits.

DIAGRAMS

A **diagram** is a simplified picture that shows how several things are related or how the different parts of something work. Each part of the diagram is usually identified. Arrows often indicate important relationships, while lines may identify various parts of the diagram. The purpose of a diagram is to help a reader understand how something works or how it is organized.

STEPS TO UNDERSTANDING A DIAGRAM

1. **Look at the Title.** The title tells you what the diagram shows. For example, this diagram is entitled "*A Volcanic Eruption.*" The diagram shows a cross-section of an erupting volcano, bringing magma (*molten rock*) to Earth's surface.

2. **Examine the Legend.** Sometimes a diagram has a legend. The legend then tells what each symbol represents. In this diagram, each part is clearly marked so there is no need for a legend.

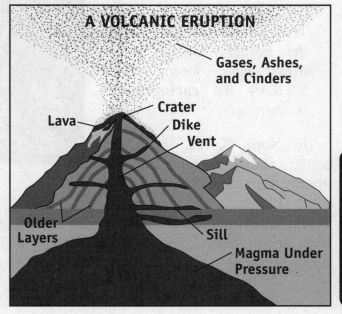

A VOLCANIC ERUPTION

Gases, Ashes, and Cinders

Lava

Crater
Dike
Vent

Older Layers

Sill

Magma Under Pressure

3. Studying the Diagram. The diagram shows how magma comes to the surface as lava when a volcanic eruption occurs. A cone forms around the place where the lava erupts. Lines indicate older layers of the volcano from earlier eruptions.

FINDING SPECIFIC INFORMATION

To find specific information, examine the diagram. For example, suppose you wanted to find out where lava comes from. From the diagram, you can see that the reason for volcanic eruptions is that magma is under pressure below the Earth's surface. When this magma pushes through to the surface, a volcanic eruption occurs. As magma pours out of the volcano, it is called lava. Lava therefore comes from the magma below the Earth's crust.

ANSWERING DIAGRAM-BASED QUESTIONS

Use the diagram on page 24 and your knowledge of social studies to answer the following questions.

12 Based on the information in the diagram, which statement is most accurate?
   F   Volcanoes never erupt at the same time as earthquakes.
   G   The movement of the moon in space affects volcanic eruptions.
   H   Volcanic eruptions can spill gases, ashes and cinders into the atmosphere.
   J   Volcanoes can erupt without magma under pressure.

13 Which conclusion can best be drawn from the information in the diagram?
   A   Most volcanic activity is found in the Pacific rim.
   B   Volcanoes occur when magma escapes to Earth's surface.
   C   Volcanoes are less dangerous than earthquakes.
   D   Volcanoes often cause erosion to neighboring mountains.

PRIMARY AND SECONDARY SOURCES

Geographers and other social scientists rely on both primary and secondary sources.

★ **Primary Sources** are original records about a place or event. They include eyewitness reports, traveler's journals, official records, letters sent by people involved in an event, diaries, and photographs. They can include **artifacts**, things people made and used, such as arrow heads or pottery. Primary sources can also include points of view about an issue or development, if they are written at the time. Almost any type of text or data can be a primary source, if it is written at the time and directly describes something.

★ **Secondary Sources** are the later writings and interpretations of geographers and other writers. Secondary sources like textbooks and articles often provide convenient summaries of the information found in primary sources.

INTERPRETING WRITTEN SOURCES

In interpreting any written document, you must be a critical reader. Sometimes a document will give you information about its writer's background or position. The information will help you understand how the writer's status in society may have affected his or her ideas. The following are the questions you should ask yourself when reading any written document — whether it is a primary or a secondary source.

When and where was the document written?	Why was the document written?	What do I know about the author?

BEING A CRITICAL READER

What is the main idea of the passage?	What facts does the writer present to support his or her views?	What is the tone of the passage?

DETERMINING WORD MEANINGS FROM CONTEXT CLUES

Sometimes you may encounter unfamiliar words or phrases. Context clues will help you figure out what they mean. The surrounding words, phrases, and sentences often provide clues that help you discover the meaning of the unfamiliar word.

Part of Speech. From the words in the sentence, can you guess what part of speech the unfamiliar word is — adjective, noun, verb, or adverb?

Substitute Words. Can you guess the meaning of the word from the tone or meaning of the rest of the passage? What other words would make sense if you substituted them in place of the unfamiliar word?

USING CONTEXT CLUES TO FIND THE MEANING

Related Familiar Words. Is the word similar to any other words you already know? Does that help you to figure out what the word means? Can you determine what the word is by breaking it up into parts — such as a prefix, word stem, or suffix?

Bypass the Word. Can you understand the main idea of the sentence without knowing the meaning of the unfamiliar word? If so, it may not be important to spend time trying to figure out its meaning.

Name _____ Date _____

A SAMPLE PRIMARY SOURCE

For example, read the primary source below. Its author, Leslie Taylor, is a Texan who spends time in the Amazon Rainforest to research plants for medicinal uses:

> "There is no way that you can really experience a rainforest without stepping into one. No photograph, film, movie or book can truly do it justice. The first thing that hits you when you step into the rainforest is the air. It is so heavy with oxygen and humidity that it just envelopes you. There is a heavy, rich stillness to it…. In the heart of a rainforest, little to no wind reaches below the green canopy of trees above you.
>
> The next thing that hits you is the sheer immensity of the trees and the incredible amount of different vegetation that surrounds you. It's an amazing display of nature in her most flamboyant expression of life. Literally everything around you is in some state of living, breathing, growing, decaying, and dying. You can actually watch some plants growing with a naked eye, and huge fallen trees that would take years to return to the earth in a temperate forest are reduced to compost in a month or two. Trees the size of skyscrapers, leaves the size of umbrellas and vines with incredible sizes and shapes seemingly knitting everything together — plants growing out vines are growing up on trees covered with other plants … It can be overwhelming to take it all in. Even if you've trekked a lot of forests, you are still caught off guard by the amazing diversity of different plants in a rainforest."

APPLYING WHAT YOU HAVE LEARNED

★ How can you tell that this a primary source? _____

_____

_____

★ What are the author's feelings about the Amazon Rainforest? _____

_____

_____

_____

★ Which statements in the passage best reveal the author's feelings? _____

_____

_____

_____

_____

ANSWERING READING-BASED QUESTIONS

Use the passage on page 27 and your knowledge of social studies to answer the following questions.

14 Based on the excerpt, which best describes the author's view of the Amazon Rainforest?
  A   Brazilians should remove the rainforest to provide more land for ranching and farming.
  B   The rainforest's beauty is something that cannot be described in words.
  C   Plants grow more slowly in the rainforest than in other climates.
  D   There is very little diversity in the plant life of the rainforest.

SUMMARIZING

A **summary** is a short restatement of a text. To understand a written document, it is often helpful to summarize it. Whenever you make a summary, you restate the main ideas of the passage while leaving out the less important information. You should rewrite some sentences in your own words. You may want to combine two or more sentences expressing the same general idea. Other sentences are just omitted.

Following are several sentences from the passage. Identify which of these sentences are the most important ones that you would include in a summary of Taylor's description.

Sentences	Include in Summary	Leave out of Summary
There is no way that you can really experience a rainforest without stepping into one.		
No photograph, film, movie or book can truly do it justice.		
The first thing that hits you when you step into the rainforest is the air.		
It is so heavy with oxygen and humidity that it just envelopes you.		
There is a heavy, rich stillness to it ...		
In the heart of a rainforest, little to no wind reaches below the green canopy of trees above you.		
The next thing that hits you is the sheer immensity of the trees and the incredible amount of different vegetation that surrounds you.		

CONTINUED

It's an amazing display of nature in her most flamboyant expression of life.		
You can actually watch some of the plants growing with a naked eye ...		
Huge fallen trees that would take years to return to the earth in a temperate forest are reduced to compost in a month or two.		

In the space below, write a summary of Taylor's description. Rewrite, in your own words, the most important sentences using your checklist above. You may wish to combine some of them.

_____
_____
_____
_____
_____
_____
_____
_____
_____
_____
_____
_____
_____
_____
_____

USING MULTIPLE SOURCES

In this chapter, you learned how to interpret different types of sources, and how to answer questions about them. Geographers often use several sources of information at the same time to understand a development or to solve a problem.

These could be several written sources, or a combination of written texts, photographs, tables and graphs. Questions on the *World Geography End-of-Course Assessment* might also include more than one type of data or written source.

When using multiple sources of information, it is important to compare them for similarities and differences. Do they agree in their observations, explanations, or opinions? If they do not agree, can you explain the reasons for any differences? What conclusions can you draw? For example, on page 27, you read a primary source. Now look at a second source about the Amazon Rainforest.

"To say the Amazon is being destroyed misstates what is happening. The Amazon is being changed. At times, deforestation [*cutting down the forest*] results in the creation of farmland, able to sustain a family or families. At other times, deforestation is the first step to building the breadbasket of tomorrow, providing millions of people with new sources of protein and Brazil with foreign currency to support needed social programs. But there are times when deforestation provides nothing more than needless destruction of one of the world's greatest natural resources and the native peoples who inhabit it. Saving the Amazon requires making judgments about development and preservation...."

M. London and B. Kelly, *The Last Forest: The Amazon in the Age of Globalization*

APPLYING WHAT YOU HAVE LEARNED

★ What was the purpose of London and Kelly in writing this introduction to their book? _____

_____

_____

★ How did their purpose differ from that of Leslie Taylor in writing her description on page 27? _____

_____

_____

_____

★ On what points about the rainforest would you expect Leslie Taylor and these authors to be in agreement? _____

_____

_____

_____

_____

Understanding Maps: "The Language of Geography"

This chapter corresponds to Section 2 of Chapter 1 of HMH's *World Geography*, "The Geographer's Tools."

❑ *Before Reading:* In this chapter, you will learn how geographers use different types of maps and globes to represent Earth's surface. You can begin your study of maps by reading the TEKS, *Geographic Terminology*, *Important Ideas*, and *Essential Question* on page 32 of this book.

❑ *During Reading:* Then you might read the rest of this chapter, as well as pages 10–23 of HMH's *World Geography*. Study the maps in the special atlas section, pages A1–A21, of HMH's *World Geography*. There are additional maps and map-skill activities throughout each book.

❑ *After Reading:* Finally, you can apply your knowledge of maps by completing the *Acting as an Amateur Geographer* activities on page 37 (interpreting a rainfall map), page 40 (which asks you to make your own map), and page 41 (which asks you to compare two maps of Iraq), and by completing the "Applying the Skill" sections on pages 135 SK2 and 185 SK2 of HMH's *World Geography*. Be sure to review the two study cards and answer the multiple-choice questions at the end of this chapter.

Topics	*Mastering the TEKS*	HMH's *World Geography*
Interpreting Maps	pp. 32–37	pp. 10–23, 135 SK1–SK2, 185 SK1–SK2
Title	p. 33	
Legend	p. 33	pp. 133 SK1–SK2, 185 SK2
Compass Rose	pp. 31–32	p. 43, SK1–SK2
Scale	p. 34	p. 16
Types of Maps	pp. 35–36	pp. 20–23
Comparing Maps	pp. 36–37	
Latitude and Longitude/ Geographic Grids	pp. 33–34	pp. 6, 17
Map Projections		pp. 18–19
Examples of additional map-skills activities	pp. 69, 71, 74, 157, 250, 304	pp. 37, 76, 84, 204, 206, 215, 220, 222, 245, 248
		Each regional unit opens with a set of maps.

Using Multiple Sources of Information

• Use information from both books to write your own answers to the *Essential Questions* on page 32.
• Look up the terms listed at the bottom on page 32 in both books and make your own glossary or study cards.
• Use information from both books to draw your own "free-hand" maps of different regions of the world.

UNDERSTANDING MAPS: "The Language of Geography"

CHAPTER 3

TEKS COVERED IN CHAPTER 3

- **Social Studies Skills 21(A)** Analyze and evaluate the validity and utility of multiple sources of geographic information such as ... maps.
- **Social Studies Skills 21(C)** Create and interpret different maps to answer geographic questions, infer relationships, and analyze change.

In this chapter, you will learn to speak the language of geography. You will explore how to read maps and interpret map symbols.

AN ESSENTIAL QUESTION

 How do maps help us to represent geographic information?

— IMPORTANT IDEAS —

A. Different types of maps are used to show a variety of different information.

B. Maps can be used to answer geographic questions, infer relationships, and analyze change.

GEOGRAPHIC TERMINOLOGY IN THIS CHAPTER

- Maps
- Legend
- Compass Rose
- Scale
- Thematic Map
- Latitude
- Longitude
- Equator
- Prime Meridian

INTERPRETING MAPS

A famous geographer, Harm de Blij, once called maps "the language of geography." They help geographers communicate information and better understand the relationship of people to the places where they live. A **map** is a flat, two-dimensional representation of space. With maps, geographers can show how places are influenced by their location and how different places affect each other. Maps can be used to answer geographic questions, to make connections, to infer relationships, and to analyze change.

STEPS TO UNDERSTANDING A MAP

Each map is really a diagram of a larger area. It shows where things are located. Every map has certain features you should be familiar with.

TITLE

The title of the map describes the information it presents. For example, the title of the map below is: *Australia*. It shows the continent of Australia with many of its geographical features. These features include major cities, surrounding oceans, mountains, and deserts.

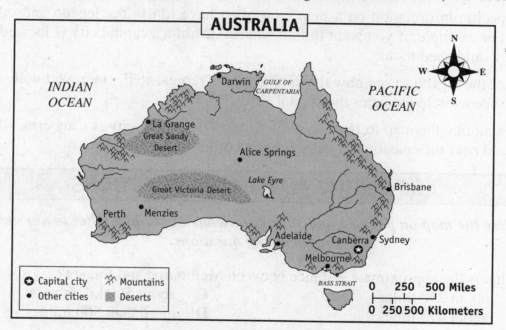

LEGEND

The legend lists the symbols used on the map, including any special colors or shading, and identifies what each symbol represents. For example, according to the legend on the map above:

⊛	This symbol represents the capital of Australia.

⋀⋀	This symbol represents mountains.

•	This symbol represents other cities found in Australia.

▒	This symbol represents deserts.

COMPASS ROSE

The **compass rose** shows where the four basic directions — *north*, *south*, *east*, and *west* — are found on the map. If a map has no compass rose, then you should assume that north is at the top of the map.

SCALE

A map would be impossible to use if it were the same size as the area it shows. **Cartographers** (*mapmakers*) reduce the size of the map to fit onto a page. The scale is used to show how much the map has been reduced. It shows the actual distance between places on the map. Map scales are often shown as a line marked: **Scale of Miles**. For example, on this map one inch represents 500 miles.

FINDING SPECIFIC INFORMATION

To find specific information on a map, you often have to use the legend and other map features. For example, if you want to find where Australia's capital city is located, here is what you would need to do:

★ Look at the legend to see how the capital city is represented. Here, you will see that a star inside a circle indicates the capital city.

★ Then examine the map to find the circled star. The capital city is Canberra, which can be found near the coastline in the southeast corner of Australia.

ANSWERING MAP-BASED QUESTIONS

Use the map on page 32 and your knowledge of social studies to answer the following questions.

1   What is the approximate distance between Melbourne and Sidney?
   A   about 250 miles
   B   about 475 miles
   C   about 500 kilometers
   D   more than 500 miles

2   Based on the map, which statement about Australia is most accurate?
   F   Australia is the largest nation in the Pacific Ocean.
   G   Most of its major cities are located on or near the coastline.
   H   The city of Darwin is less than 500 miles from Brisbane.
   J   Melbourne, Sydney and Canberra are located on the west coast.

INFERRING RELATIONSHIPS

A map shows how different features of a place relate to one another. You can often infer relationships or draw conclusions from the map. For example, for the map on page 32:

★ Based on the map, where are Australia's largest cities located?

★ Where are Australia's deserts located? Are any of its major cities found in desert areas?

★ What relationship can be inferred between the location of Australia's deserts and its cities?

TYPES OF MAPS

There is almost no limit to the kind of information that can be shown on a map. For this reason, there are many types of maps:

★ **Physical maps** show the major physical features of an area, such as its rivers, mountains, vegetation and elevation (*height above sea level*).

★ **Political maps** show the major boundaries between countries or states.

★ **Historical maps** show political boundaries from the past. With a historical map, you should pay close attention to the names of countries, political borders, and the location of cities. These may be different than they are today.

★ **Thematic maps** show information relating to a specific theme, such as the spread of a religion, trade routes, or the industrial growth of a nation.

★ **Population density maps** show where people live in a specific area.

★ **Resource or Product maps** show the major natural resources and agricultural and industrial products of an area.

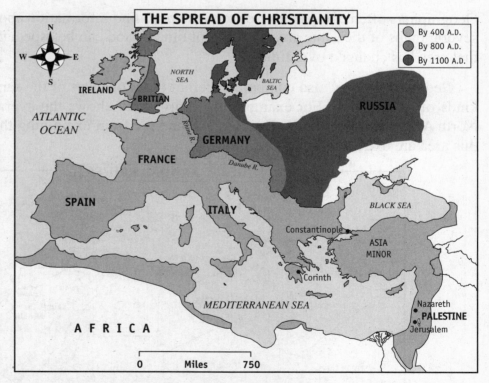

For example, the map to the right deals with the spread of a major religion in the ancient world. The title of the map, *The Spread of Christianity*, shows how Christianity spread across Europe, North Africa, and Southwest Asia.

The legend can be found on the upper right corner of the map. Each shade of gray on the map indicates a further stage in the spread of Christianity. By 400 A.D., Christianity was already established in Italy, France, Spain, Asia Minor and parts of North Africa. By 800 A.D. the Christian religion had spread to include Britain and Germany.

ANSWERING MAP-BASED QUESTIONS

Use the map on page 34 and your knowledge of social studies to answer the following questions.

3 According to the map, when did Christianity first reach Constantinople on the Black Sea?

    A by 400 A.D.
    C between 800 and 1100 A.D.
    B between 400 A.D. and 800 A.D.
    D after 1100 A.D.

4 Which conclusion can best be drawn from this map?

    F Christianity spread eastwards to Germany and Russia.
    G Christianity reached Russia before it reached Spain.
    H Christianity spread from Europe to Palestine.
    J Scandinavians brought Christianity across the North Sea to Britain.

COMPARING MAPS

Geographers often compare two or more maps to find information about an area. A series of several maps of the same area at different time period can be especially helpful to see how that area has changed over time.

Geographers may also compare different types of maps of the same area with different kinds of information. For example, the map below shows the average annual rainfall in North Africa and the Middle East. As you can see from examining the map, many parts of this area are extremely dry:

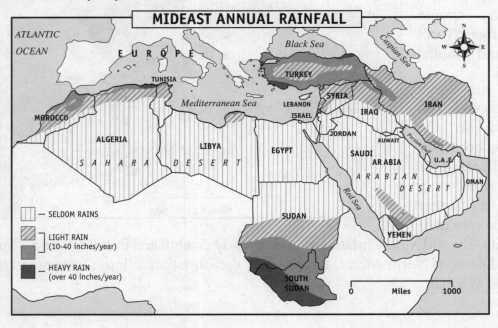

MIDEAST ANNUAL RAINFALL

Now look at the map below. It shows where people live in the same area. You will learn more about population density maps later on in this book. The legend indicates that more people live in the areas with darker shading. By comparing this map with the one on page 35, a geographer can draw conclusions about the relationship of rainfall in an area and where people choose to live.

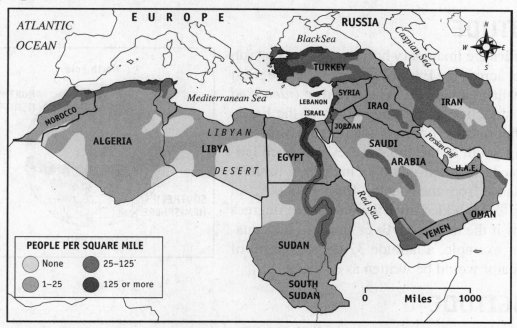

PEOPLE PER SQUARE MILE

- None
- 1–25
- 25–125
- 125 or more

0   Miles   1000

ACTING AS AN AMATEUR GEOGRAPHER

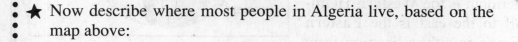

★ Describe the pattern of rainfall in Algeria shown on the first map.

_____

★ Now describe where most people in Algeria live, based on the map above:

_____

★ What relationship do you see between annual rainfall and where many people in the Middle East and North Africa live?

_____

_____

★ Egypt has very little rainfall, yet parts of it are densely populated. Why?

_____

_____

_____

LATITUDE AND LONGITUDE

Geographers have created two sets of imaginary lines — **latitude** and **longitude** — to make it possible to identify every location precisely on Earth's surface.

LATITUDE

Latitudes are imaginary horizontal lines that run parallel across the Earth. The equator is the most important latitude line. The **equator** (*identified as 0°*) stretches around the middle of the Earth. All other latitude lines are identified by how far north or south of the equator they are. Each latitude line is assigned a number in degrees to show its distance from the equator, from 1° to 90°. An "**N**" or "**S**" is added after the number of degrees to show if the line is **north** or **south** of the equator. For example, a latitude 37 degrees north of the equator would be written as 37°N.

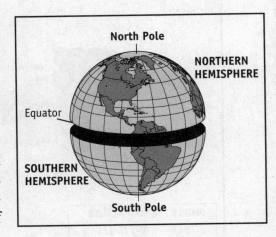

LONGITUDE

Longitudes are imaginary lines that run up and down the Earth. All the longitude lines meet at both the North and South Poles. The **Prime Meridian** (*identified as 0°*) is the most important longitude line, since it divides Earth into two hemispheres. The half west of the Prime Meridian is the **Western Hemisphere**; the half to the east is the **Eastern Hemisphere**. Going in either direction from the Prime Meridian, longitude lines increase from 1° to 180°. Geographers add "**E**" or "**W**" to show if the line is east or west of the Prime Meridian. For example, 100°E.

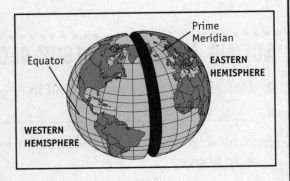

When latitude and longitude lines are shown on a map, they form a grid pattern. By knowing where latitude and longitude lines meet, we can identify the location of any place on Earth.

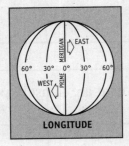

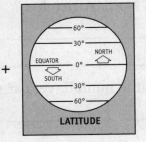

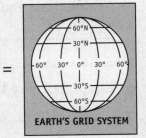

Name _____ Date _____

LEARNING WITH GRAPHIC ORGANIZERS

Complete the graphic organizer below. Define or describe each term.

Legend

_____
_____
_____
_____
_____
_____

Scale

_____
_____
_____
_____
_____
_____

Compass Rose

_____
_____
_____
_____
_____
_____

Longitude

_____
_____
_____
_____
_____
_____
_____
_____
_____

MAPS

SOUTH PACIFIC OCEAN

SOUTH ATLANTIC OCEAN

0   Miles   1000

Latitude

_____
_____
_____
_____
_____
_____
_____
_____
_____

Types of Different Maps

_____
_____
_____
_____
_____
_____

ACTING AS AN AMATEUR GEOGRAPHER

How good a cartographer are you? Let's find out. Make a small map of your home and surrounding neighborhood. Show any schools, stores, hospitals, museums, factories, places of worship or other important buildings. Be sure to include a legend, compass rose and scale of miles. To help you make your map, you might want to look up your community on Google (maps.google/com), Yahoo (maps.yahoo/com), Mapquest (www.mapquest.com) or any similar website. There you can find a satellite view of your community. Use the space below to create your map.

ACTING AS AN AMATEUR GEOGRAPHER

★ Below are *two* maps of Iraq. One map shows annual rainfall and the other shows land use in Iraq.

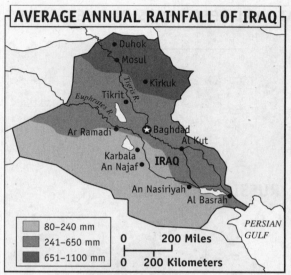

★ Describe the relationship between annual rainfall and the ways in which the land is used in Iraq, based on these *two* maps.

_____

_____

_____

CHAPTER STUDY CARDS

Important Features of a Map

★ **Title.** Describes what the map is about.
★ **Compose Rose.** Shows basic directions.
★ **Scale.** Shows what distances on the map represent.
★ **Legend.** Identifies what any symbols on the map represent.

Types of Maps

★ **Physical Maps** show major physical features: rivers, mountains, elevations.
★ **Political Maps** show major boundaries.
★ **Thematic Maps** show information relating to a particular theme.
★ **Population Density Maps** shows where people in a certain area live.
★ **Resource or Product Maps** show natural resources, and agricultural and other products.

CHECKING YOUR UNDERSTANDING

Directions: Put a circle around the letter that best answers the question.

Use the map and your knowledge of social studies to answer questions 1 and 2.

POPULATION DENSITY AND NATURAL RESOURCES OF THE C.I.S.

1   Which conclusion is most accurate based on the information in the map?
   A   The most densely populated areas are in eastern Russia.
   B   Most cities of one million are located near the Arctic.
   C   Areas near manufacturing centers often have a higher population density.
   D   The most densely populated areas are found near gold mining areas.

SSS 21(C)*

EXAMINE **the question.** This question tests your ability to interpret a map. RECALL **what you know.** You should recall that the legend here shows cities, population density, and major economic activities. APPLY **what you know. Choice A** is wrong. Most heavily populated cities are in the west. **Choice B** is wrong. There are no cities over one million near the Arctic. **Choice D** is also incorrect. No large population centers are near gold mining areas. **Choice C** is the best answer. Most higher population density areas are near manufacturing centers.

_____

* The test will assess various social studies skills along with the mastery of other objectives. In this chapter, we
   have identified some of the questions, indicated by an asterisk, solely by their skills.

Now try answering some additional questions on your own:

2 Based on the map, which economic activities are found in the northernmost parts of Russia, close to the Arctic Ocean?

F manufacturing

G mining and oil

H recreation

J natural gas

> • **EXAMINE** The Question
> • **RECALL** What You Know
> • **APPLY** What You Know

SSS 21(C)*

Use the map of Eastern Europe and your knowledge of social studies to answer questions 3 through 6.

3 A "satellite" is a country under the control of another country. Which nation is identified on the map as a satellite of the Soviet Union (*U.S.S.R*)?

A Turkey SSS 21(C)*

B Yugoslavia

C Greece

D Romania

EASTERN EUROPE IN 1960

Satellites of the USSR

Western Europe

Neutral

0   100   300 Miles

4 The reason that Chile, Cuba, and Mexico are not included on the map is that they were —

F located outside SSS 21(A)* the geographic area shown

G not considered satellites of the U.S.S.R.

H provinces of Poland

J members of the North Atlantic Treaty Organization

5 Based on the map, how are Italy and Greece similar?

A Both are surrounded by water on all but one side. SSS 21(C)*

B Both border on Bulgaria.

C Both are located on the equator.

D Both were once satellites of the Soviet Union.

6 Which of the following statements is accurate according to the map?

F East and West Germany were satellites of the Soviet Union. SSS 21(C)*

G Yugoslavia and Hungary were neutral nations.

H Sofia was the capital city of Bulgaria.

J Minsk was a Soviet city that bordered the Black Sea.

7 Which feature would most likely appear on a physical map?

    A population density

    B capital cities

    C languages spoken

    D mountain ranges

> • **E**XAMINE **The Question**
> • **R**ECALL **What You Know**
> • **A**PPLY **What You Know**

`SSS 21(A)*`

8 Which question could a geographer best investigate with a series of maps?

    F how religious beliefs influence popular customs

    G how economic events affect people's savings rate

    H how the products made in an area change over time

    J how people influence governmental decisions

`SSS 21(A)*`

9 A primary reason that geographers study maps is to —

    A predict changes in government policies

    B infer relationships between people and places

    C understand the time order in which an event unfolded

    D appreciate the value systems of world cultures

`SSS 21(E)*`

Use the map of Bangladesh and your knowledge of social studies to answer questions 10 through 12.

10 Based on the information in the map, most land in Bangladesh is used for —

    F high-tech industries `SSS 21(E)*`

    G agriculture

    H manufacturing

    J logging

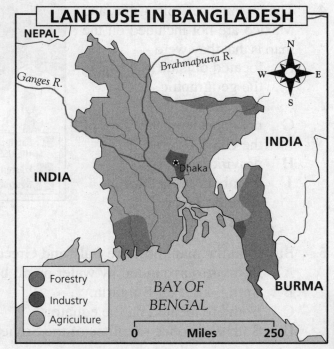

LAND USE IN BANGLADESH

11 To check the validity of this map, a geographer could best use —

    A the journals of `SSS 21(E)*`
ancient travelers to
see how land uses have changed

    B aerial photography to see if forest and farm areas correspond with those shown on the map

    C local newspapers for job advertisements in these occupations

    D a population density map to see where people are located

12 The land immediately surrounding Dhaka is most involved in —

    F farming

    G computer services

    H logging

    J manufacturing

`SSS 21(C)*`

Problem-Solving and Research Skills

This chapter corresponds to several pages of HMH's *World Geography*, indicated on the chart below.

❏ *Before Reading:* Think about a time when you had to solve a problem. What steps did you take? Was your method for solving the problem an effective one? Then think about a time when you had to write a research paper. What steps did you follow to choose your topic, find information, and write your report? In this chapter, you will learn the skills needed to conduct two important tasks: solving a problem and completing a research project. For each of these types of tasks, you will learn a series of steps to follow. You can begin your mastery of these skills by reading the TEKS, *Geographic Terminology*, *Important Ideas*, and *Essential Question* on page 46 of this book.

❏ *During Reading:* Then you should read the rest of this chapter, as well as pages 437 SK1–SK2, 537 SK1–SK2, 605 SK1–SK2, and 739 SK1–SK2 in HMH's *World Geography*. Check off each of the *Important Ideas* on page 46 of this book as you read about it.

❏ *After Reading:* You can reinforce your mastery of problem-solving by completing the *Acting as an Amateur Geographer* activity on page 49 below and the "Applying the Skill" on page 739 SK2 of HMH's *World Geography*. Then sharpen your research skills by completing the *Acting as an Amateur Geographer* on page 50, the *Applying What You Have Learned* activities on pages 53, 55 and 57, and the *Learning with Graphic Organizers* diagram on page 59 in this book and the "Applying the Skill" sections on pages 537 SK2 and 605 SK2 of HMH's *World Geography*.

Topics	*Mastering the TEKS*	HMH's *World Geography*
Problem-Solving	pp. 47–49	pp. 739 SK1–SK2
Identify the Problem	p. 47	pp. 739 SK1–SK2
Gather Information	p. 47	p. 739 SK2
List and Consider Options	p. 47	p. 739 SK2
Consider Advantages and Disadvantages	p. 48	p. 739 SK2
Choose and Implement a Solution	p. 48	p. 739 SK2
Judge its Effectiveness	pp. 48–49	p. 739 SK2
Completing a Research Project	pp. 50–58	pp. 97 SK1–SK2, 537 SK1–SK2, 605 SK1–SK2
Choosing a Well-Defined Geographic Question	p. 50	pp. 537 SK1, 605 SK1
Finding Information	pp. 51–53	p. 605 SK1
Taking Notes	pp. 53–54	
Analyzing Information	pp. 54–55	pp. 97 SK1, 605 SK1
Organizing Information	p. 55	pp. 537 SK, 605 SK1
Making an Outline/Graphic Organizer	p. 56	p. 605 SK1
Writing Your Report	p. 56	p. 537 SK1
Supporting a Position	p. 57	
Crediting Sources in a Bibliography	pp. 57–58	p. 537 SK1
Also see:		
Summarizing		pp. 331 SK1–SK2
Using standard grammar, spelling, sentence structure and punctuation		pp. 473 SK1–SK2

Using Multiple Sources of Information

• Look up the terms listed on page 46 in both books and make your own glossary or study cards.

• Use both books to create a poster or web page showing the steps one should follow to solve a problem or complete a research project.

Name _____ Date _____

PROBLEM-SOLVING AND RESEARCH SKILLS

CHAPTER 4

TEKS COVERED IN CHAPTER 4

- **Social Studies Skills 22(B)** Generate summaries, generalizations, and thesis statements supported by evidence.
- **Social Studies Skills 22(D)** Use standard grammar, spelling, sentence structure, and punctuation.
- **Social Studies Skills 23** The student uses problem-solving and decision-making skills, working independently and with others, in a variety of settings.
  - **Social Studies Skills 23(A)** Plan, organize, and complete a research project that involves asking geographic questions; acquiring, organizing, and analyzing information; answering questions; and communicating results.
  - **Social Studies Skills 23(C)** Use problem-solving and decision-making processes to identify a problem, gather information, list and consider options, consider advantages and disadvantages, choose and implement a solution, and evaluate the effectiveness of the solution.

In this chapter, you will learn how geographers approach problems and conduct research.

AN ESSENTIAL QUESTION

How do geographers approach problems and conduct research on geographic questions?

— IMPORTANT IDEAS —

A. To solve problems, geographers and other social scientists first identify a problem. Then they gather information, consider options, weigh the advantages and disadvantages of each option, try a solution, and evaluate how well it works.

B. To complete a research project, geographers first identify a well-defined geographic question. Then they find information from a variety of sources; take notes; compare and analyze facts and ideas; make an outline or graphic organizer; and communicate their results in a report or presentation.

GEOGRAPHIC TERMINOLOGY IN THIS CHAPTER

- Problem-Solving
- Options
- Brainstorming
- Solution
- Criteria
- Source of Information
- Gazetteer
- Atlas
- Internet
- Wikipedia
- Outline
- Thesis Statement

46

PROBLEM-SOLVING

How can countries deal with climate change? Where should new factories be located? How does migration affect a region? Geographers and other social scientists often have to make decisions and solve problems. In this chapter, you will learn how geographers go about solving problems and conducting research.

STEPS IN PROBLEM-SOLVING

In order to solve problems, geographers follow a logical six-step process:

Identify the Problem	Gather Information	List and Consider the Options
Consider Their Advantages and Disadvantages	**Choose and Implement a Solution**	**Develop Criteria and Judge Its Effectiveness**

STEP 1:
Identify a Problem

The first step is to identify a problem, such as the threat posed by climate change. Geographers often look at problems relating to such topics as the use of resources, migration, globalization, protecting the environment, or conflicts between groups.

STEP 2:
Gather Information

Next, you must gather information about the problem. You can often find information on the Internet or in your school or local library. Search for information on what causes the problem as well as suggestions by others for solving it.

STEP 3:
List and Consider Options

Now you need to explore all the ways or **options** you can think of to solve the problem. Look through the sources you found for helpful ideas and information. Then you can "brainstorm" ideas with others — listing as many possible solutions as you can. When **brainstorming**, people suggest as many ways of solving the problem as they can think of. The excitement of hearing other people's ideas often helps the members of a group think of new ideas on their own.

STEP 4:
Consider Advantages and Disadvantages

Next, you should consider the advantages and disadvantages of each option you have thought of. What would be the benefits of each option? Would it solve the problem? What would be the costs, risks, or other drawbacks of each option?

STEP 5:
Choose and Implement a Solution

Now you are ready to make a choice. Compare the proposed options to come up with your own solution. There is usually no simple or perfect answer to most major problems. For example, should all off-shore drilling of oil be banned after the 2010 oil leak in the Gulf of Mexico? Oil spills pose a serious threat to the environment. On the other hand, oil is a vital resource to our energy needs. Perhaps greater precautions can avoid future oil spills.

You must then decide which advantages are more important, based on your own values. Your solution often depends on what you value and think is "good." People value different things and frequently disagree about what should be done to deal with a problem.

Once you have chosen your solution, think about how you can **implement it** (*put it into effect*). Here are some actions you might take to implement a solution to a problem:

★ **Sign a Petition.** Get people who support your plan to sign a **petition** — a document signed by many people asking the government to take some action.

★ **Inform the Media.** Enlist the media in your cause. Write a letter to your local newspaper, television, or radio station explaining your plan.

★ **Speak to Community Leaders.** Invite one or two community leaders to your school to discuss the problem and your proposed solution.

★ **Contact Elected Representatives.** Write a letter to local public officials, your elected representatives in Austin, your U.S. Congressperson, or your U.S. Senator. You can even send a letter to the President of the United States in Washington, D.C.

STEP 6:
Develop Criteria and Judge Its Effectivness

Once a possible solution has been adopted, you need criteria to determine ways to judge its effectiveness. Criteria are standards for judging something. You need to develop specific criteria to measure how well your proposed solution actually works. For example:

Does it solve the problem?	What does it cost?	Have people agreed to carry it out?	Does it create new problems?

Now apply these criteria to evaluate the effectiveness of your adopted solution. The **solution** is effective if it solves the problem at minimal cost without creating other problems.

ACTING AS AN AMATEUR GEOGRAPHER

In a small group with three or four of your classmates, identify a geographical problem that you would like to investigate further.

_____

_____

_____

_____

PLANNING AND COMPLETING A RESEARCH PROJECT

Geographers and other social scientists often conduct research to find solutions to a problem or to learn more about a topic. In this section, you will learn how to plan your own research project based on a geographic question, find and analyze information, present a position supported by evidence, and give credit to your sources with a bibliography.

STEPS IN CONDUCTING RESEARCH

There are several steps to every research project:

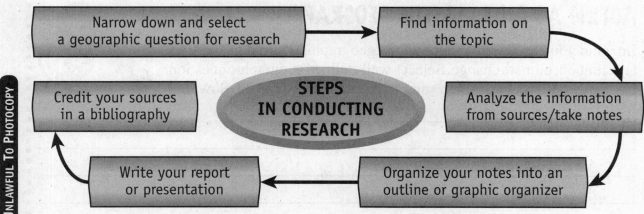

CHOOSING A
WELL-DEFINED GEOGRAPHIC QUESTION

The first and most important step in any research project is to choose a topic. You need to identify a well-defined geographic question that you can investigate.

Geographic questions are any questions that concern geography. They could involve the location of resources, distribution of populations, interactions between people and their environment, or anything else concerning the physical features of Earth's surface, or the location, movement and activities of people.

For example, you might be interested in writing a report about climate change. However, it would be too difficult to research and report on everything about climate change. This topic is just too broad and there is simply too much information to explore.

Instead, you need to narrow down the scope of your investigation. You need to select a specific aspect of climate change for your report. At the same time, your topic should not be so narrow that you cannot find enough information to write about it. For instance, you might want to research any one of the following well-defined geographic questions about climate change:

How has climate change affected the coast of Texas?	How has climate change affected the peoples of the African Sahel?	How has climate change affected recent hurricane patterns?

ACTING AS AN AMATEUR GEOGRAPHER

Imagine you have been assigned by a geographic journal to write an article about climate change. Select a well-defined geographic question that you think might be interesting to research and write it below:

_____

_____

_____

_____

FINDING INFORMATION

Once you have selected a well-defined geographic question to investigate, the next step is to find information. This process is called **research** because you are *searching* for information about your topic. A **source** is something that provides information. There are many different kinds of sources. These include the following:

ENCYCLOPEDIAS

An **encyclopedia**, like the *World Book* or *Encyclopedia Britannica*, has entries on a variety of topics. Often it is useful to first obtain an overview or background on the topic of your research.

ALMANACS

An **almanac** is a book that contains up-to-date information on a wide range of topics. A new edition is published every year to keep its information up-to date. Almanacs generally cover a variety of subjects, such as population statistics, descriptions of countries, and winners of Nobel Prizes and other awards.

BOOKS

A **trade book** is a book written for a general audience. These books often focus on a particular topic, like climate change or global trading patterns. More specialized books are often reviewed by experts, such as university professors, in the field.

GAZETTEERS AND ATLASES

A **gazetteer** is a geographical dictionary, or index of political and physical features of the Earth. It lists places — countries, cities, rivers, mountains — with descriptions of their geography and related statistical information. Gazetteers can be used to find the meanings of specific geographical terms. An **atlas** is a book of maps. An atlas presents the geographic features and political boundaries of places.

PERIODICALS

A **periodical** refers to a newspaper, magazine, or journal. These are called periodicals because they are published at periodic intervals. Articles in magazines and journals usually focus on a particular topic and report the latest news or research. Newspapers appear daily and report on current events.

VIDEOTAPES / DVDS

Videotapes and **DVDs** include newsreels, recorded interviews, and documentaries. Researchers often use these sources to discover views of actual events as they happened, to see interviews of leading figures, or to review documentary materials collected by the film-maker.

ELECTRONIC SOURCES

The **Internet**, the major electronic source of information today, has become the most widely used source of information. Almost any kind of information can be found on the Internet. Search engines like **AOL**, **Google**, or **Yahoo** are used to locate websites with information about a topic.

"Surfing" the Web. Each search engine has a box where you put the subject or keyword you wish to search. When you click the search button, your computer will search the web and create a list of sites for you to explore. Click on each site on the list to see if it provides information you can use. If your search provides many websites, use a narrower subject or keyword for your search. An advanced search feature often allows you to specify two or more keywords that the site you are searching for must have. This feature can help you narrow down your search.

Wikipedia is an Internet encyclopedia with entries often created or modified by users. It is a good place to get background information on a topic or to look for additional sources. However, you should not rely solely on Wikipedia for your research project. The same precaution should be exercised with other websites you may find. Remember that many websites are created by organizations or individuals committed to a particular viewpoint. As with all sources, information appearing on the Internet may be biased or may even be incorrect.

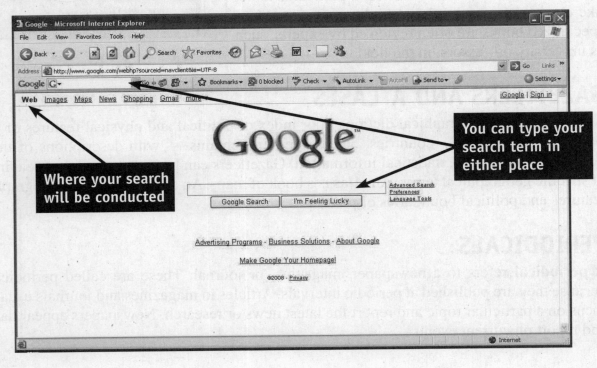

Where your search will be conducted

You can type your search term in either place

APPLYING WHAT YOU HAVE LEARNED

★ Suppose you are still completing a research project about the effects of global change on the African Sahel, a region just south of the Sahara Desert. This region has been severely impacted by a series of droughts. List two sources of information that you might consult to gather your information:

- ● _____

  _____

- ● _____

  _____

★ List two keywords you might use to search the Internet for information:

- ● _____
- ● _____

TAKING NOTES

After you locate your sources, you need to read them for information and to take notes. When taking notes for a research project, include only the information you need for your report. Do not take notes on information that does not relate to the topic of your report, even if this information seems interesting to you.

It is often helpful to use index cards when taking notes for a research project. Index cards are a convenient way to organize and sort your information. The following information is usually included on each note card:

★ **Subject.** Use a key word or phrase to identify the main subject of the note card. Later you will be able to organize the information you have collected by grouping your note cards together using these keywords.

★ **Notes.** Your notes should be brief. They should contain a short review of the main points you think you might use. You can always look back at your original source to find more details and factual information. To summarize information, write down the most important information without unnecessary details. A summary should always be much briefer than the source it is summarizing.

★ **Source.** Identify the source where you found the information. Provide the author and name of the book. You should also write down the publisher, place of publication and copyright date of the source on at least one card. You will need this information later for your bibliography.

Below is an example of information that might be included on a note card about climate change in the African-Sahel region.

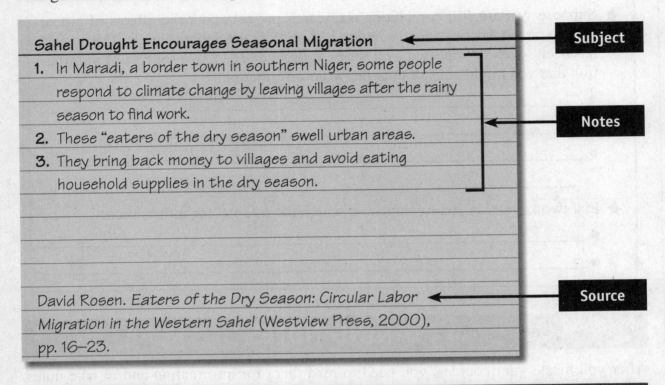

Sahel Drought Encourages Seasonal Migration ← Subject

1. In Maradi, a border town in southern Niger, some people respond to climate change by leaving villages after the rainy season to find work.
2. These "eaters of the dry season" swell urban areas. ← Notes
3. They bring back money to villages and avoid eating household supplies in the dry season.

David Rosen. *Eaters of the Dry Season: Circular Labor Migration in the Western Sahel* (Westview Press, 2000), pp. 16–23. ← Source

ANALYZING INFORMATION

When researching a topic, it is important to look at **multiple sources**. This helps the researcher to see the topic from more than one point of view. When reading a source, pay particular attention to the background and viewpoint of the author. Often, the author's background shapes his or her perspective — how the author views the problem or event.

For example, there are different views among experts on the effects of climate change on the Sahel. The scientific debate about the cause of these droughts has been a topic of intense discussion for decades.

Some scientists believe that because of climate change, droughts (*periods without rainfall*) in the Sahel will increase. This explains the extremely dry conditions of the soil in the Sahel.

Other scientists argue that higher temperatures will heat the Indian Ocean. These scientists say that rainfall in the Sahel region will eventually increase.

The Sahel has suffered from drought and famine in recent decades.

APPLYING WHAT YOU HAVE LEARNED

Why is it valuable to read several accounts with differing viewpoints to understand a geographic question?

_____

_____

_____

_____

_____

_____

As you can see, it is important to consider several points of view when researching a topic. By comparing these different points of view, you get a better understanding of what actually happened and why.

One way to compare sources and views is to use your note cards. You can group all cards on the same subject together to compare what your various sources say. You can summarize what these different sources say and make generalizations or draw your own conclusions based on the evidence you have found.

ORGANIZING INFORMATION

There are many ways to organize the geographical information you find.

★ **Chronological.** It often helps to organize events in the order in which they occurred. This helps us see how earlier events affected later ones. One way to organize events in this fashion is simply to describe them in order.

★ **Cause-and-Effect.** You can also arrange information based on cause-and-effect relationships. You may first describe several long-term causes of an event; then you can identify the short-term causes that triggered the event.

★ **Thematic Approach.** Sometimes you may organize information by various themes relating to your topic. Then you can describe or explain each theme.

★ **Problem-Solution Approach.** Many geographers deal with problems. You can organize your information by describing the problems and then identifying and describing one or more solutions to that problem.

MAKING AN OUTLINE OR GRAPHIC ORGANIZER

An **outline** is a brief plan in which each topic or major idea is divided into smaller units. An outline gives you a blueprint to follow for writing your report. The purpose of the outline is to show how the different parts of your report are related. It may help to think of your outline as the "road map" for your research paper.

Outlining your project before you write will help you to stay focused on your topic and to see connections that you otherwise might not have seen. You can also use your outline to decide the best order to present your points. A good outline will reveal if you have gathered enough information to write your report. Lastly, an outline helps you to see if some note cards are irrelevant to your report and should be discarded.

Your outline can be written in many different ways. The most common form of an outline begins with general topics and then provides additional details.

★ **Roman Numbers.** The major topics of an outline are usually identified by Roman numerals (*I*, *II*, *III*, etc.).

★ **Capital Letters.** If the topic listed by a Roman numeral needs to be divided, its sub-topics are identified by capital letters (*A*, *B*, *C*, etc.).

★ **Arabic Numbers.** If these sub-topics need to be divided even further, each smaller topic is given an Arabic numeral (*1*, *2*, *3*).

> **Effects of Climate Change on the Sahel Region**
>
> I. Characteristics of Climate Change
>   A. Global Warming
>   B. Higher Temperatures
>   C. Less Rainfall on Sahel
> II. Effects of Climate Change on Sahel
>   A. Famine and Migration
>   1. Droughts make growing food hard
>   2. Migration of livestock & people
>   B. Political Conflicts in Africa

Instead of an outline, you may decide to plan your report with a graphic organizer or concept map. These formats are simply another way to arrange your information.

WRITING YOUR REPORT

After you complete your outline or graphic organizer, you are ready to write your report or oral presentation in order to communicate your results to others. Turn each section of your outline into a separate paragraph or part of your presentation. Include facts and details from your note cards to support each of your main points.

As you write your report, be sure to re-read your work several times. You need to make sure that your report is logical and flows smoothly. Try to make use of transitions in your writing. Transitions, such as *moreover*, *in addition*, *because*, *in contrast*, or *furthermore*, indicate to your reader when you change times, locations, topics or ideas. Always use correct spelling and grammar.

SUPPORTING A POSITION

In your research project, you may present your own "**position**" — a special point of view, generalization or conclusion — based on the evidence. Some researchers present a general position on their topic in a **thesis statement** — a simple statement of the main point they are trying to make. Usually the thesis statement appears near the beginning of the report. For example, you might make the thesis that climate change is causing people to leave the Sahel region.

The Use of Evidence. You should try to persuade readers that any position or conclusion you present is correct by providing **evidence**. This evidence should consist of facts you have found in both primary and secondary sources. These facts should be clear, specific, and detailed. They should also be clearly related to what you are trying to show. The facts you present in your report should closely support the conclusions you have reached. If these facts are accurate and support your arguments clearly, your thesis becomes more persuasive and convincing.

APPLYING WHAT YOU HAVE LEARNED

What kind of evidence would you need to show your readers that this thesis — that climate change is causing people to leave the Sahel region — is correct?

_____

_____

_____

In order to show the reader that the information in a report is accurate, researchers also identify their sources.

CREDITING SOURCES IN A BIBLIOGRAPHY

When completing a report, it is important to give credit to your sources in a **bibliography** or a list of **works cited**. This allows readers to check your sources and your use of facts. Usually, the bibliography is found at the end of your report.

BOOKS

For each book, begin with the author's last name, followed by the first name and a period. Then write the title of the book, which is underlined and followed by a period. Next put the place of publication, a colon (:), the name of the publisher, a comma, the date of publication, and a period. Entries should be alphabetized by the author's last name.

The following example shows how this entry would appear:

> Low, Pak Sum. Climate Change and Africa. Cambridge:
> Cambridge University Press, 2006.

PERIODICALS

For a magazine or newspaper article, put the author's last name, then first name, followed by a period. Next, put the title or headline of the article in quotation marks, followed by a comma. Then the name of the periodical is underlined, followed by its date of publication, and the pages where the article can be found.

> Deweerdt, Sarah. "Climate Change Coming Home: Its Effect
> on Populations," World Watch, Vol. 20, May–June, 2007, pp. 33–49.

ENCYCLOPEDIAS

For an encyclopedia article that is not signed, put the title of the article in quotation marks, followed by a period. Then put the name of the encyclopedia, which is underlined. Next, put the copyright year, volume number, and pages. For an encyclopedia article that is signed, begin the entry with the name of the author of the article, followed by a period.

> "Sahel," New Illustrated Columbia Encyclopedia.
> 1998. Volume 19, pp. 5925–5926.

INTERNET SOURCES

The format for citing a website differs from the format for a printed source. Here, you begin with the name or title of the website underlined, followed by a period. Next is the name of the organization, editor or author (*if given*) followed by a period. The URL or electronic address of the website comes next, and then the date you accessed the site in parentheses.

> Africa, Explore the Region-Sahel. PBS.
> http://www.pbs.org/wnet/africa/explore/sahel/sahel_overview_lo.html
> (last visited June 1, 2010)

The reasons for including the date of your last visit to the website is that the Web is constantly changing or the entire website may have disappeared. Thus, you need to inform your reader of the date you last accessed that particular website.

Name _____ Date _____

LEARNING WITH GRAPHIC ORGANIZERS

Complete the graphic organizer below. Identify each step in planning and completing a research project. Then indicate why this is a necessary step in the process.

STEPS IN CONDUCTING A RESEARCH PROJECT

CHAPTER STUDY CARDS

Steps in Problem Solving

★ Identify the Problem
★ Gather Information
★ List and Consider the Options
  • **Brainstorming.** List all suggestions.
★ Consider Advantages and Disadvantages
★ Choose and Implement a solution
★ Develop Criteria and Judge its Effectiveness

Steps in Conducting Research

★ Select a geographic question.
★ Use sources to find information.
★ Analyze information from sources and notes.
★ Organize notes into an outline or graphic organizer. Ways of organizing information:
  • Chronological   • Thematic
  • Cause-and-Effect • Problem-Solution
★ Write your report or presentation.
★ Credit sources in a bibliography.

Types of Sources

★ Encyclopedia
★ Trade Books
★ Gazetteers and Atlases
★ Periodicals
★ Videotapes / DVDs
★ Internet Sources

When Doing Research You Should:

★ Research several different perspectives.
★ Accurately credit the sources used.

Crediting Sources in a Bibliography

★ It is important to credit sources to allow readers to check your sources and facts.
★ A **bibliography** is usually indicated at the end of the report.
★ List sources in alphabetical order.
★ Use the last name of the author first.
★ Underline or italicize books titles, periodicals, and encyclopedias.

CHECKING YOUR UNDERSTANDING

Directions: Put a circle around the letter that best answers the question.

1   Samantha is developing a thesis statement for her report on the causes of the Sahel in Africa. In her report, she intends to show that recent droughts in the Sahel have been caused by climate change. Which sentence states her thesis?

   A   Climate change has reduced annual rainfall in the Sahel region.   `SSS 22(B)*`
   B   Carbon dioxide emissions help cause global warming.
   C   Many people leave the Sahel for jobs in other parts of Africa.
   D   Scientists disagree about the impact of climate change.

_____

* In this chapter, we have identified some of the questions, indicated by an asterisk, solely by their skills.

EXAMINE **the question.** This question asks you to identify a thesis statement. RECALL **what you know.** You should recall that a thesis statement summarizes the main idea of the author of the report in a single sentence. APPLY **what you know. Choice B** is wrong, since it identifies an effect of climate change in the Sahel. **Choice C** is wrong. It presents specific background information. **Choice D** is also wrong. It concerns the effects of the droughts. Only **Choice A** states what Samantha intends to show in her report.

Now try answering some additional questions on your own:

2   Jane is writing a report on climate change. Which of the following practices should she avoid when conducting her research?
    F   finding multiple sources to get different points of view   `SSS 23(A)*`
    G   using both printed and online sources of information
    H   describing the recent views of several scientists
    J   relying on only one source for her report

3   Greg is completing a research paper. Where should he identify the various sources he has used to gather his information?
    A   before his table of contents   `SSS 23(A)*`
    B   in his introductory remarks
    C   on his title page
    D   in his bibliography

- EXAMINE The Question
- RECALL What You Know
- APPLY What You Know

4   Which heading best completes the partial outline below?

    I. _____
        A. Gazetteer
        B. Trade Books
        C. Encyclopedia
        D. Periodicals

    F   Sources of Geographic Information   **H**   Internet Sources   `SSS 23(A)*`
    G   Government Documents   **J**   Bibliography

5   Which source would be best to find information about the land area and current population of China?
    A   almanac   **C**   atlas   `SSS 23(A)*`
    B   novel   **D**   videotape

6   Why is it important for authors to cite their sources when writing a research paper?   SSS 23(A)*
   F   to show they did not copy word for word from a book
   G   to allow readers to check any facts and sources for themselves
   H   to show readers how hard they worked
   J   to help readers come up with their own ideas

7   Which topic would be best for a student research paper in world geography?   SSS 23(A)*
   A   What are the human and physical characteristics of regions?
   B   How does the elevation of the Andes Mountains influence its climate?
   C   What processes caused changes in settlement patterns throughout history?
   D   What has been the impact of global trading patterns on the world?

8   Which reference tool would provide the most information about Global Positioning Systems?   SSS 23(A)*
   F   the *American Heritage Dictionary*
   G   the "G" volume of the *Encyclopedia Britannica*
   H   a gazetteer in an atlas of the world
   J   the Internet

9   Which sequence of steps lists the order one should follow in solving a problem?   SSS 23(C)*
   A   identify the problem → implement a solution →
        judge its effectiveness → list the possible options
   B   consider the advantages and disadvantages → list the possible
        options → judge its effectiveness → implement a solution
   C   identify the problem → list the possible options → consider the
        advantages and disadvantages → implement a solution
   D   develop criteria → implement a solution → gather
        information → consider the advantages and disadvantages

10 What are the two main considerations in evaluating a solution to a problem?   SSS 23(C)*
   F   its relationship to other options and points of view
   G   its costs and effectiveness
   H   its timing and popularity
   J   its authors and their backgrounds

11 Which sequence of steps lists the correct order one should   SSS 23(A)*
        follow in planning and completing a research project?
   A   narrow down a geographic question to research → find information on the topic →
        write your report → analyze the information from sources
   B   credit your sources in a bibliography → find information on the topic → write
        your report → takes notes from your sources
   C   narrow down a geographic question to research → find information on the topic →
        write your report → credit your sources in a bibliography
   D   narrow down a geographic question to research → find information on the topic →
        credit your sources in a bibliography → organize your notes into an outline

UNIT 1 REVIEW
PULLING IT ALL TOGETHER

Write down *two* generalizations you learned about in Chapters 3 and 4.

1. _____

_____

2. _____

_____

Select *one* of the *Essential Questions* explored in this unit by checking the box. Then answer it below.

ESSENTIAL QUESTIONS REEXAMINED

☐ How do maps help us to represent geographic information?

☐ How do geographers approach problems and conduct research on geographic questions?

_____

_____

_____

_____

_____

_____

_____

_____

_____

_____

_____

_____

_____

_____

UNIT 1 CONCEPT MAP

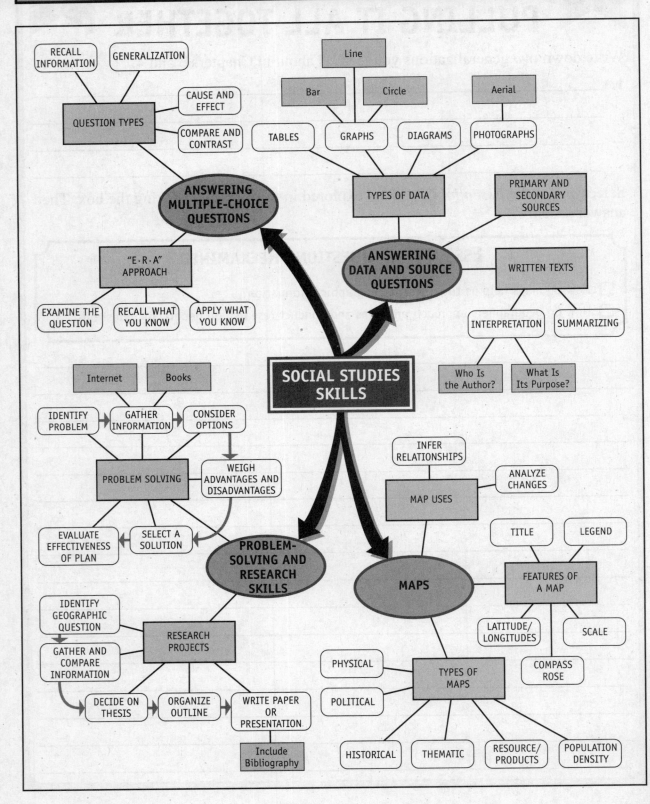

SOCIAL STUDIES SKILLS

ANSWERING MULTIPLE-CHOICE QUESTIONS

QUESTION TYPES
- RECALL INFORMATION
- GENERALIZATION
- CAUSE AND EFFECT
- COMPARE AND CONTRAST

"E·R·A" APPROACH
- EXAMINE THE QUESTION
- RECALL WHAT YOU KNOW
- APPLY WHAT YOU KNOW

ANSWERING DATA AND SOURCE QUESTIONS

TYPES OF DATA
- TABLES
- GRAPHS
  - Line
  - Bar
  - Circle
- DIAGRAMS
- PHOTOGRAPHS
  - Aerial

PRIMARY AND SECONDARY SOURCES

WRITTEN TEXTS
- INTERPRETATION
  - Who Is the Author?
  - What Is Its Purpose?
- SUMMARIZING

PROBLEM-SOLVING AND RESEARCH SKILLS

PROBLEM SOLVING
- IDENTIFY PROBLEM
- GATHER INFORMATION
  - Internet
  - Books
- CONSIDER OPTIONS
- WEIGH ADVANTAGES AND DISADVANTAGES
- SELECT A SOLUTION
- EVALUATE EFFECTIVENESS OF PLAN

RESEARCH PROJECTS
- IDENTIFY GEOGRAPHIC QUESTION
- GATHER AND COMPARE INFORMATION
- DECIDE ON THESIS
- ORGANIZE OUTLINE
- WRITE PAPER OR PRESENTATION
  - Include Bibliography

MAPS

MAP USES
- INFER RELATIONSHIPS
- ANALYZE CHANGES

FEATURES OF A MAP
- TITLE
- LEGEND
- LATITUDE/LONGITUDES
- SCALE
- COMPASS ROSE

TYPES OF MAPS
- PHYSICAL
- POLITICAL
- HISTORICAL
- THEMATIC
- RESOURCE/PRODUCTS
- POPULATION DENSITY

UNIT 2

PHYSICAL GEOGRAPHY

In this unit, you will learn about physical geography — the study of Earth's surface features. These features provide the setting for the human-environmental interactions and for the human geography that you will learn about later in this book.

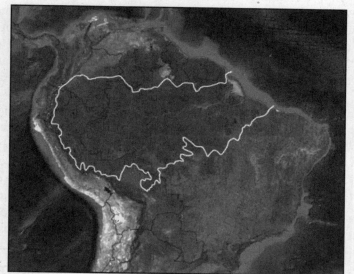

An aerial view of the Amazon Rainforest; the white line was added by the NASA.

Chapter 5. A World Gazetteer: A Look at the Seven Continents. A gazetteer is a reference book with geographical information. In this gazetteer, you will learn about the primary physical features of Earth's seven continents, including the world's most important mountains, deserts, lakes and rivers. You will also learn about physical regions.

Chapter 6: Processes Shaping Planet Earth. In this chapter, you will learn about Earth's lithosphere (*crust*), hydrosphere (*oceans*), and atmosphere. You will also learn about the physical processes shaping Earth's surface, including tectonic plate motion and erosion.

Chapter 7: People and Nature. In this chapter, you will learn about human-environmental interactions: how people adapt to their physical environment, and how they also modify and affect their physical environment.

A World Gazetteer: A Look at the Seven Continents

You cannot understand higher-level geographic concepts without a basic knowledge of the physical features of the seven continents. This chapter provides an overview of these features. It corresponds to the beginning sections of each regional unit of HMH's *World Geography*. For example, you can read an overview of the physical geography of North America on pages 68 to 69 of this book, and then learn more about its physical geography by reading pages 117 to 130 of HMH's *World Geography*.

❑ *Before Reading:* You might begin your study of the world's major physical features by reading the TEKS, *Geographic Terminology*, *Important Ideas* and the *Essential Question* on pages 67–68. You should also examine the physical maps at the beginning of each unit of HMH's *World Geography*. For example, for the physical geography and climate of the United States and Canada, study the maps on pages 103 and 107, and for Latin America, on pages 191 and 194.

❑ *During Reading:* Then you might turn to the text on pages 68 to 79 below to obtain a general overview of the world's physical geography. If your course is thematic — that is, concept-based — you might turn to sections of HMH's *World Geography* to learn about physical features of special interest to you, or if there is something you do not understand. For example, you might want to learn more about the Sahara Desert (pp. 420–421), the Amazon Rainforest (pp. 203, 207–208), or the physical geography of Europe (pp. 273–287). If your course is organized by region, then you might read this chapter first to get a general overview of all the regions, and then turn to HMH's *World Geography* to focus on the particular region your class is studying, such as North America. Check off each of the *Important Ideas* on page 67 of this book as you read about it.

❑ *After Reading:* Reinforce your learning by filling in the map exercises in this chapter and then by reviewing the study cards and answering the test questions at the end of the chapter.

Topics	Mastering the TEKS	HMH's *World Geography*
A Survey of Physical Geography:		
North America	pp. 68–69	pp. 117–130
South America	pp. 70–71	pp. 201–215
Africa	pp. 71–73	pp. 415–427
Europe	pp. 73–74	pp. 273–285
Asia		
Middle East (Southwest Asia)	pp. 75–76	pp. 487–499
North & Central Asia (Russia)	p. 76	pp. 345–356
East Asia (China, Korea, Japan)	pp. 77–78	pp. 619–631
South and Southeast Asia	pp. 78–79	pp. 689–691, 694–695, 698–699
Australia	p. 79	pp. 691–692, 695–697, 699–701
Antarctica	p. 79	p. 692
The Concept of Region	p. 81	p. 7
Physical Regions	p. 82	
Example: U.S. Sub-Regions		pp. 145–149
Formal Regions	p. 82	pp. 7–8

Using Multiple Sources of Information

- Use information from both books to write your own answers to the *Essential Questions* on page 67.
- Use information from both books to create your own illustrated atlas showing the main physical regions of the world.
- Your teacher should select members of your class to pretend to be citizens from different countries. Students should then describe the physical geography of the places where they live. Use information from both books to create your description.

Name _____ Date _____

CHAPTER 5

A WORLD GAZETTEER:
A Look at the
Seven Continents

TEKS
COVERED IN
CHAPTER 5

- **Geography 9** The student understands the concept of region as an area of Earth's surface with related geographic characteristics.
  - **Geography 9(A)** Identify physical and/or human factors such as climate, vegetation, language, trade networks, political units, river systems, and religion, that constitute a region.
  - **Geography 9(B)** Describe different types of regions, including formal ... regions.
- **Social Studies Skills 21(B)** Locate places of contemporary geopolitical significance on a map.
- **Social Studies Skills 22(C)** Use geographic terminology correctly.

Geographers are very interested in how the location and physical features of a place affect physical processes and human activities taking place there. In fact, each part of our planet has its own unique features not found anywhere else.

In this chapter, you will review some of the unique characteristics that make each location a distinct place. You will explore the main physical features of Earth's seven continents, including its major mountain ranges, deserts, and bodies of water.

AN ESSENTIAL QUESTION

What physical features would you find on a tour of the world's continents?

— IMPORTANT IDEAS —

A. Earth has five **oceans** — the Atlantic, Pacific, Indian, Arctic, and Southern.*

B. There are seven **continents** on Earth — Africa, Antarctica, Asia, Australia, Europe, North America, and South America. Each has its own unique blend of **physical features**, including mountains, deserts, plains, valleys, forests, and bodies of water.

D. Latitude, landforms, and nearness to bodies of water greatly affect climate.

E. **Landforms**, **soil**, and **climate** greatly affect the plants and animals that can be found in each place.

*Some geographers question whether the Southern Ocean should be considered a separate ocean.

GEOGRAPHIC TERMINOLOGY IN THIS CHAPTER

- Continents
- Sahara Desert
- Savanna
- Tropical Rainforest

- Tundra
- East Asia
- Subcontinent
- Peninsula

- Himalaya Mountains
- Regions
- Physical Region
- Formal Region

EARTH'S SEVEN CONTINENTS

Our planet has seven large landmasses that geographers call continents. Let's examine the main physical features of each one.

NORTH AMERICA

North America is the world's third largest continent in area. Located in the Western Hemisphere, it stretches from near the North Pole southwards almost to the equator. From east to west, it covers the territory between the Atlantic and Pacific Oceans.

Central America. North America is bordered by the Atlantic, Pacific, and Arctic Oceans. South of Mexico, the land narrows into Central America. **Central America** connects North America to South America. Although Central America contains far less than 1% of the Earth's surface, it has 7% of the world's biodiversity — various plants and animals.

West Indies. Northeast of Central America are the **West Indies**, made up of a large number of islands in the Caribbean Sea.

NORTH AMERICA

ARCTIC OCEAN

PACIFIC OCEAN

Canada

ROCKY MOUNTAINS

Great Lakes

St. Lawrence R.

Quebec

Montreal

Toronto

Boston

Chicago

New York

Cleveland

Philaelphia

United States

Mississippi R.

APPALACHIAN MOUNTAINS

ATLANTIC OCEAN

San Francisco

Los Angeles

Rio Grande

Miami

Scale of Miles

0   1000

Gulf of Mexico

Mexico

Cuba

Dom. Rep.

Mexico City

Jamaica

Haiti

Caribbean Sea

Belize

Honduras

Nicaragua

Guatemala

Panama

El Salvador

Costa Rica

Panama Canal

Countries

Oceans & Seas

Mountains

Physical Features

★ **Mountains.** Major mountain ranges found in North America include the **Rocky Mountains** to the west and the **Appalachian Mountains** to the east. The Rocky Mountains extend northward into Canada and southward into Mexico.

★ **Bodies of Water.** The **St. Lawrence River** separates parts of the United States from eastern Canada. The **Mississippi River** drains much of the United States. The **Great Lakes** — Lake Superior, Lake Michigan, Lake Huron, Lake Erie, and Lake Ontario — form the largest system of fresh water on Earth. The **Rio Grande** separates the United States from Mexico. The **Panama Canal**, located in Central America, connects the Atlantic and the Pacific Oceans.

★ **Plains.** West of the Mississippi River is a region known as the **Great Plains**, containing some of the world's most productive farmland.

★ **Rainforests.** Much of Central America and the islands of the West Indies have warm, humid climates and rainforests.

APPLYING WHAT YOU HAVE LEARNED

Use the outline map to label each of the following:

1. Canada

2. Great Lakes

3. Mexico

4. Mississippi River

5. Rio Grande

6. Rocky Mountains

7. Appalachian Mountains

8. West Indies

9. Atlantic Ocean

10. Pacific Ocean

11. Gulf of Mexico

12. Central America

SOUTH AMERICA

South America is located in the Western Hemisphere south of Central America. South America is the fourth largest continent in area. Stretching over 7,000 miles in length, it lies between the Atlantic and Pacific Oceans.

Physical Features

★ **Mountains.** The **Andes Mountains** are among the highest in the world. They extend over 4,500 miles in the western part of South America. The Andes were once the basis of the Inca Empire.

★ **Grasslands and Plains.** Mountains and poor soils make much of South America's land unproductive. One exception is the **pampas** of Argentina and Uruguay. The pampas provide large areas of fertile soil for growing crops and grazing cattle.

★ **Rainforests.** Rainforests are located on the east coast of Central America and the northern part of South America. They have warm, humid climates. The **Amazon Rainforest**, the

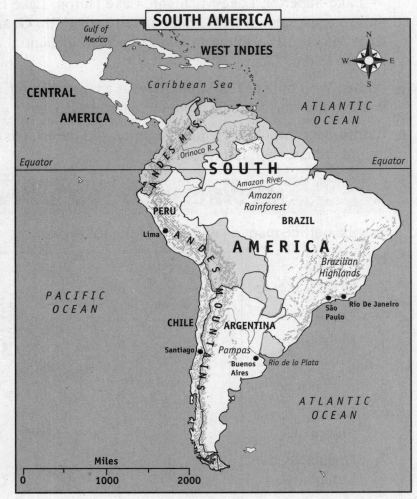

world's largest tropical rainforest, is in Brazil. Each year, part of the rainforest is being cut down (*deforestation*) to provide land for ranches and farms.

★ **Bodies of Water.** The **Amazon River** is the second longest river in the world. In addition, South America has the **Orinoco River** and the **Rio de la Plata**. A large percentage of South America's population lives on or near these river systems.

★ **Climate.** Much of South America is warm because it lies near the **equator**. However, because of its mountains and ocean winds, many places in South America have comfortable temperatures. Some of the greatest concentrations of people can be found in higher elevations where temperatures are cooler.

APPLYING WHAT YOU HAVE LEARNED

Using the outline map, locate and label the following:

1. Andes Mountains
2. Pampas
3. Amazon River
4. Equator
5. Chile
6. Peru
7. Brazil
8. Argentina
9. Amazon Rainforest
10. Rio de Janeiro

AFRICA

Africa is the second largest continent in area. It is almost three times the size of the United States. To the north, Africa is separated from Europe by the Mediterranean Sea. To the east lie the Red Sea and Indian Ocean. On the west, Africa is bordered by the Atlantic Ocean.

Physical Features

★ **Deserts.** The **Sahara Desert**, which takes up most of North Africa, is the world's largest desert. It separates Africans north and south of it because this dry, sandy region is difficult to cross. For centuries, the Sahara isolated sub-Saharan Africa (*Africa south of the Sahara*) from the rest of the world. Farther south, Africa also has the **Kalahari Desert**.

★ **Savannas.** Much of Africa is **savanna** — land where tall, wild grasses grow with some trees. Savannas are the best areas in Africa for growing crops and raising livestock. Most Africans live in the savanna region or along the coasts.

★ **Tropical Rainforests.** In Central and West Africa, hot and humid rainforests get 60 to 100 inches of rainfall a year. This climate produces thick forest and jungle areas, making travel difficult. Rainforests are the home to more plant and animal species than anywhere else on the globe.

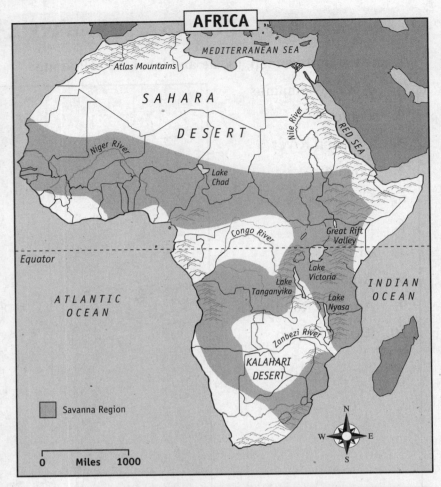

★ **Mountains and Valleys.** The **Atlas Mountains** are found on the northwest edge of Africa. The **Great Rift Valley** runs through the highlands of Ethiopia and Kenya, to the east.

★ **Bodies of Water.** Africa has several major rivers — the **Nile**, **Congo**, **Zambezi**, and **Niger**. The Nile, the world's longest river, flows 4,150 miles from Central Africa through Egypt into the Mediterranean. The banks of the Nile River

Africa's Great Rift Valley.

provide some of Africa's richest farmland. Important lakes include **Lake Victoria**, **Lake Tanganyika**, and **Lake Nyasa**.

★ **Climate.** Much of Africa is warm, with hot summers and mild winters. The amount of rainfall differs greatly; deserts receive too little water for farming, while some other areas receive too much rain.

APPLYING WHAT YOU HAVE LEARNED

Imagine you are a reporter for *National Geographic* magazine and you are writing an article about Africa's physical features.

★ Select one feature described on pages 67–69. Gather additional information about that feature and write a short paragraph describing it.

★ Then photocopy a picture from the Internet or library illustrating that feature. Paste it next to your one-paragraph description below.

_____

_____

_____

_____

_____

_____

_____

_____

EUROPE

Europe is the second smallest continent in land area. Europe and Asia actually both share the same land mass. This land mass is so large that geographers have divided it into two continents. Great Britain, Ireland and Iceland are island nations in the Atlantic Ocean that are considered part of Europe.

Geographers have called Europe a "peninsula of peninsulas." Its many peninsulas encouraged sea travel and trade.

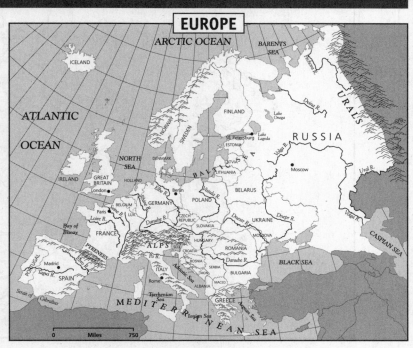

Physical Features

★ **Mountains.** There are many mountain ranges in Europe. They include the **Alps**, **Pyrenees**, **Apennines**, and **Balkans**. These mountains helped to create defensible borders between areas. They encouraged Europeans to develop many separate nationalities, each with its own language and customs.

★ **Bodies of Water.** Europe includes several major bodies of water. In the north are the **Baltic** and **North Seas**. In the south, there are the **Mediterranean Sea** and the **Black Sea**. Europe also has many major rivers, including the **Danube**, **Rhine**, **Loire**, **Rhone**, **Elbe**, **Vistula**, and **Volga**.

APPLYING WHAT YOU HAVE LEARNED

On the outline map of Europe, show the location of each of the physical features identified below.

★ **Seas:** Baltic, North Sea, Mediterranean, and Black Sea.

★ **Mountain Ranges:** Alps, Pyrenees, and Apennines.

★ **Rivers:** Danube, Rhine, Loire, Elbe, Vistula, and Volga.

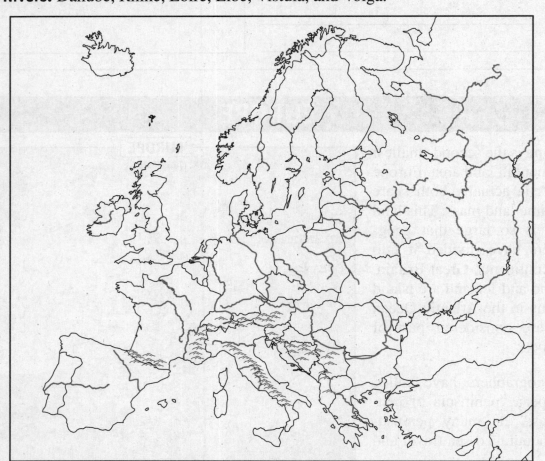

ASIA

Asia is the world's largest continent. Today, it is home to two-thirds of the world's population. Because of its immense size and the diversity of its cultures, geographers often think of Asia as being composed of several distinct regions.

THE MIDDLE EAST

The **Middle East** lies at the "crossroads" of three continents, connecting Africa, Asia and Europe. It contains one of the world's most important waterways, the **Suez Canal**, which shortens the traveling distance between Europe and Asia.

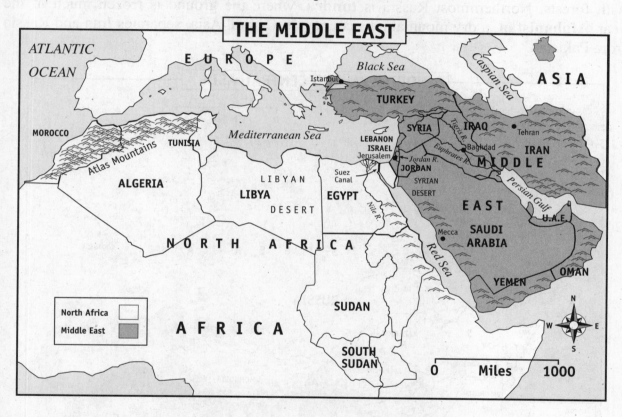

Physical Features

★ **Deserts.** Much of the Middle East is desert. For example, most of the Arabian Peninsula is occupied by 900,000 square miles of the Arabian Desert. The other major desert in the Middle East is the Syrian Desert.

★ **Bodies of Water.** There are several important rivers in the Middle East, including the **Jordan**, **Tigris**, and **Euphrates Rivers**. The mild climate and fertile soil found along these rivers made them centers of some of the world's earliest civilizations. Other major bodies of water bordering the Middle East include the **Mediterranean Sea**, **Black Sea**, **Red Sea**, and the **Persian Gulf**.

★ **Climate and Resources.** Most of the Middle East is located near the **equator**. The area has warm winters and hot, dry summers. While lacking adequate water supplies, the Middle East has about half of the world's known oil reserves.

NORTHERN AND CENTRAL ASIA

Northern Asia is occupied by **Russia**, which stretches from Eastern Europe to the Pacific. Russia is the world's largest country in area. Although the majority of its population is located in Europe, most of Russia's land area is in Asia. **Central Asia** consists of a vast corridor south of Russia, made up of mountains, deserts and **steppes** (*treeless grasslands*). The steppes provide good grazing land. **Siberia**, in northeastern Russia, is a cold region with forests. Northernmost Russia is **tundra**, where the ground is frozen much of the year. **Afghanistan**, a dry mountainous country in Central Asia, separates Iran and Russia from Pakistan.

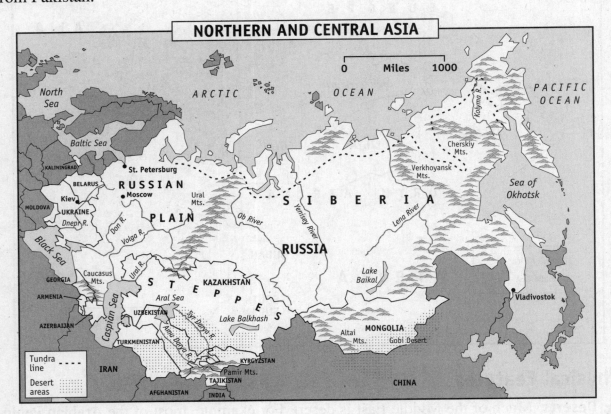

Physical Features

★ **Bodies of Water.** The **Arctic Ocean**, north of Russia, is frozen for most of the time. Major rivers in Asian Russia are the **Ob** and **Lena**.

★ **Mountains.** The **Ural Mountains** separate European and Asian Russia, while the **Pamir Mountains** separate Russia from China.

★ **Climate.** Most of Russia has long, cold winters and short mild summers.

EAST ASIA

East Asia includes three important countries: (1) China, (2) Korea, and (3) Japan.

★ **China** is the world's third largest country in area: only Russia and Canada are larger. It is also the world's most populous nation.

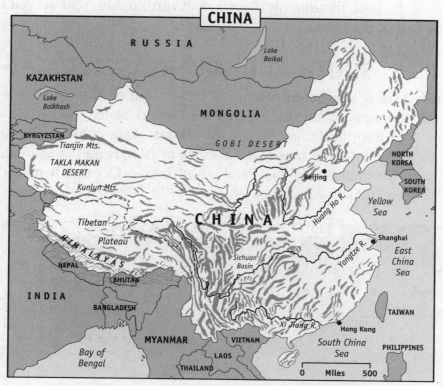

★ **Korea** is a peninsula extending from the northeastern coast of China.

★ **Japan** consists of four main islands and a number of smaller islands, separated from the Asian mainland by the Sea of Japan (known by the Koreans as the East Sea).

Physical Features

★ **Bodies of Water.** Important rivers include the **Hwang Ho** (*Yellow River*) and the **Yangtze** in China. These river valleys were the birthplace of early civilizations.

★ **Mountains.** China's southern and western borders are ringed by the **Himalayan**, **Kunlun**, and **Tianjin Mountains**. To the west is the mountainous plateau of **Tibet**.

Much of Japan and Korea are also mountainous. About 85% of Japan is covered by mountains and hills. **Mount Fuji**, an extinct volcano, is the highest and most famous mountain in Japan.

★ **Deserts.** The **Gobi Desert** is located to the north of China in Mongolia.

For much of the past, mountains, deserts, and surrounding seas served to separate East Asia from the rest of the world.

SOUTH AND SOUTHEAST ASIA

Most of **South Asia** is a **subcontinent** — a large piece of land smaller than a continent. The Indian subcontinent, about the size of the United States, looks like a large triangle jutting out of Asia into the Indian Ocean. **Southeast Asia** consists of a **peninsula** (*land surrounded by water on three sides*) and a series of islands on the southeast corner of the Asian mainland. Surrounded by the Pacific and Indian Oceans, it provides the shortest water route between these two oceans.

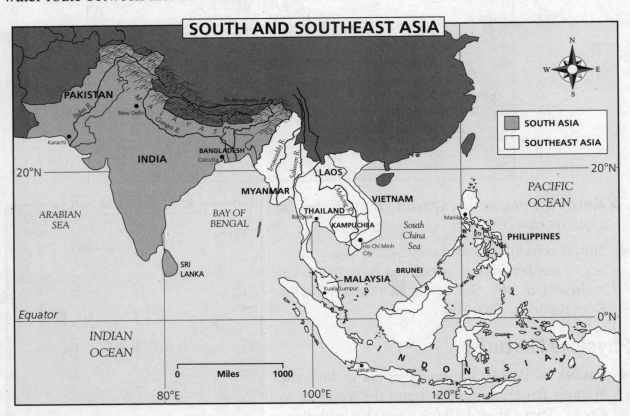

Physical Features

★ **Mountains.** The **Himalayas**, north of India, are the highest mountains in the world. They separate the Indian subcontinent from the rest of Asia. Mountains also cut off Southeast Asia from the rest of the continent. Divided by mountains, the peoples of Vietnam, Laos and Cambodia developed their own languages, customs and cultures.

★ **Bodies of Water.** The main rivers of the Indian subcontinent are the **Indus** and **Ganges**. Here, one of the world's earliest civilizations began. The **Mekong**, **Salween**, and **Irrawaddy Rivers** are major rivers in Southeast Asia.

★ **Climate.** Both South and Southeast Asia have warm winters and hot summers. The most important climatic feature is the **monsoons**. These violent winds blow over the region and bring heavy rains in the summer. Monsoon rains provide water for crops and support life, but also cause flooding, landslides, property damage, and even death. Entire villages have been swept away by strong monsoon rains.

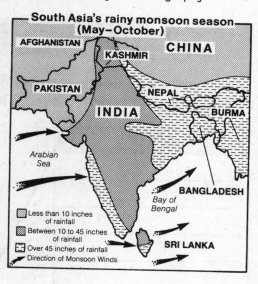

AUSTRALIA

Surrounded by the Indian and Pacific Oceans, Australia is cut off from Asia by the Arafura and Timor Seas. The central areas of Australia are mainly desert. The world's largest coral reef, the **Great Barrier Reef**, is found here. Australia is the only country that is an entire continent. It is home to many unique animals.

ANTARCTICA

Antarctica is the world's southernmost continent and covers the South Pole. It is surrounded by the Southern, Atlantic, Pacific, and Indian Oceans. Since 2000, most geographers call this the Southern Ocean. Antarctica is the coldest, driest, and windiest continent, and has the highest average elevation of all the continents. About 98% of this continent is covered by ice, averaging one mile in thickness. Only plants and animals that can adapt to the extreme cold can survive here.

ACTING AS AN AMATEUR GEOGRAPHER

Select one of the continents you studied in this chapter. Then create a bas relief, or three-dimensional map, of that continent. Your map should show the continent's major physical features. You can use paper maché, plaster or clay. Use a pencil to cut lines into the wet material to show rivers. Build up areas with extra paper maché, plaster or clay to indicate mountains, hills and plateaus. After your project dries, use blue paint to show rivers, lakes, and seas. Use yellow paint for deserts, and green to show forest areas.

◆◀≡ LEARNING WITH GRAPHIC ORGANIZERS

Complete the graphic organizer below. For each of the seven continents, indicate one characteristic about its size and location. Then identify one or more of its physical characteristics.

Africa

_____
_____
_____
_____
_____
_____

Asia

_____
_____
_____
_____
_____
_____

EARTH'S CONTINENTS

Antarctica

_____
_____
_____
_____
_____
_____

Australia

_____
_____
_____
_____
_____
_____

Europe

_____
_____
_____
_____
_____
_____

North America

_____
_____
_____
_____
_____
_____

South America

_____
_____
_____
_____
_____
_____

APPLYING WHAT YOU HAVE LEARNED

This chart lists some of the major physical features for each of the seven continents. Use an outline map of the world to complete the following task.

★ Select any *six physical features* from the chart below for each continent.

★ Locate and label each selected feature on your outline map.

Continent	Major Physical Features
Asia	Largest and most populous continent; Himalaya Mountains; Gobi Desert; Indian Subcontinent; Arabian Desert; Rivers: Tigris and Euphrates, Indus, Ganges, Mekong, Yangtze, Hwang Ho; Island nations include: Japan, Indonesia, Philippines, Malaysia.
Africa	Second largest continent; Atlas Mountains; Sahara Desert; Rivers: Nile, Congo, Niger; Great Rift Valley; Kalahari Desert; Tropical rainforests of Central and West Africa; Suez Canal.
North America	Third largest continent; Appalachian and Rocky Mountains; Great Lakes; Rivers: Mississippi, Rio Grande; West Indies; Central America; Panama Canal.
South America	Fourth largest continent; mostly in Southern Hemisphere; Andes Mountains; Amazon Rainforest; pampas; Amazon River and Rio de la Plata.
Europe	Shares its landmass with Asia; Mountains: Alps Balkans, and Pyrenees; Rivers: Danube, Rhine, Rhone, Loire, Elbe, Vistula, and Volga; Seas: Mediterranean, Baltic, North and Black Seas.
Australia	Great Barrier Reef; center of continent is desert.
Antarctica	Covers the South Pole; mainly frozen.

THE CONCEPT OF REGION

Just as historians divide the continuous thread of time into distinct time periods, geographers divide Earth's seamless surface into distinct **regions**. Each region has its own characteristics that set it apart from other regions. Regions can be based on either physical or human characteristics. The differences within in a region are fewer than the differences between the region and areas outside the region.

In this chapter, you will look at some of Earth's physical regions.

PHYSICAL REGION

A **physical region** can be defined by its common landforms, soils, climate, vegetation or animal life.

The **Amazon Rainforest** in South America is a good example of a physical region. Throughout the Amazon Rainforest region, the climate is hot all year, with frequent rain showers. A variety of tropical trees grow in the Amazon. Their interlocking tops form a dense canopy (*umbrella*) over the rainforest.

The Sahara Desert, the world's largest desert, is another example of a physical region with its own characteristics. The climate is extremely hot and dry. Much of the Sahara is sand without plant life. The northern and southern ends of the Sahara have some rainfall, grasslands, and desert shrubs.

Much of the Sahara is covered by sand dunes and sand seas.

Other examples of physical regions include the Himalayan Mountains and the Great Lakes. In Texas, people often divide their state into a number of different physical regions. According to the *Texas Almanac*, there are four main physical regions — the Gulf Coastal Plains, Interior Lowlands, Great Plains, and Basin and Range Province.

The same area may in fact belong to more than one region. For example, an area may belong to one region based on its landforms and another region based on its climate. Landforms and climate regions may also overlap. Finally, regions are constantly changing. Either their characteristics or their borders may change.

FORMAL REGION

Geographers define formal regions for purposes of study. A **formal region** has clear boundaries and is usually defined by having a common property, such as low rainfall. Any distinct area based on one characteristic (either physical or human) can be a formal region. A country or a climate region may be considered a formal region.

The Scottish Highlands provide an example of a physical region.

APPLYING WHAT YOU HAVE LEARNED

★ Select one of the continents you read about in this chapter. Then identify one physical region on that continent. Describe some of the characteristics that make this area a distinct region.

_____

_____

_____

_____

★ Make a chart or Venn diagram below comparing two continents you learned about in the chapter. Use the Internet or library to find information about their similarities and differences — locations, climates, soils, plants, and animal life.

CHAPTER STUDY CARDS

Earth's Seven Continents

★ **Africa.** Second largest continent in area.

★ **Antarctica.** Covers the South Pole.

★ **North America.** Consists of Canada, the United States, Mexico, Central America and the islands of the West Indies.

★ **South America.** Located between the Atlantic and the Pacific Oceans.

★ **Europe.** Second smallest continent in area; shares its landmass with Asia.

★ **Asia.** World's largest continent.

★ **Australia.** Surrounded by the Indian and Pacific Oceans.

Major Physical Features

★ **Oceans.** Atlantic, Pacific, Indian, Arctic, and and Southern.

★ **Seas.** Mediterranean Sea, Black Sea, Red Sea, Persian Gulf.

★ **Mountain Ranges.** Himalayas, Rockies, Appalachians, Andes, Alps, Pyrenees, Urals, Atlas.

★ **Rivers.** Mississippi, Rio Grande, St. Lawrence, Amazon, Nile, Rhine, Danube, Elbe, Vistula, Tigris, Euphrates, Volga, Ganges, Yangtze, Hwang Ho, Ganges.

★ **Deserts.** Sahara, Gobi, Kalahari, Arabian.

★ **Rainforests.** Amazon Rainforest.

CHECKING YOUR UNDERSTANDING

Directions: Put a circle around the letter that best answers the question.

Use the map of the world and your knowledge of social studies to answer questions 1 through 3.

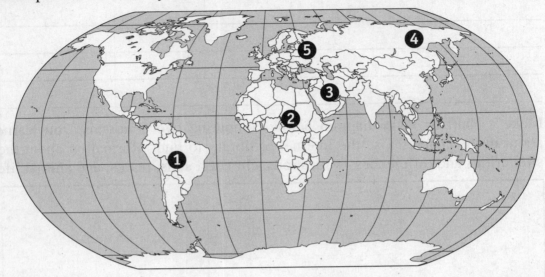

1   Which number on the map shows the location of the world's largest tropical rainforest with a vast degree of biodiversity, which now faces a threat from deforestation?

   A 1   **C** 3   `SSS 21(B)*`

   B 2   **D** 4

> **EXAMINE the question.** This question tests where one of the world's major physical features is located. **RECALL what you know.** You should recall that the world's largest tropical rainforest is the Amazon Rainforest, located in South America. **APPLY what you know.** On the map, **Choices B, C,** and **Choice D** are all located on continents other than South America. The best answer is **Choice A,** since it is the only one located in South America.

Now try answering some additional questions on your own.

2   Which number on the map shows the continent where the Sahara Desert is located?

   F 1   **H** 3   `SSS 21(B)*`

   G 2   **J** 4

3   On which continent would you find the Baltic Sea, the Pyrenees Mountains, and the Danube River?

   A 2   **C** 4   `SSS 21(B)*`

   B 3   **D** 5

---

* The test will assess various social studies skills along with the mastery of other objectives. In this chapter, we have identified some of the questions, indicated by an asterisk, solely by their skills.

4 One reason North Africa developed differently from the rest of Africa was that these areas were separated by the —

F Congo River Basin   H Nile River   `Geog 9(A)`
G Sahara Desert   J Arabian Sea

5 Which title best completes the chart?

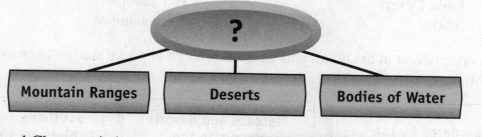

A Cultural Characteristics
B Absolute Locations
C Continents
D Features of Physical Geography

> • EXAMINE The Question
> • RECALL What You Know
> • APPLY What You Know

`SSS 21(B)*`

6 Which two features are part of the same distinct physical region on the continent of Africa?

F Sahara Desert and the Nile River   `SSS 21(B)*`
G Gobi Desert and the Himalayan Mountains
H Andes Mountains and the Amazon River
J Pyrenees Mountains and the Seine River

Use the map and your knowledge of social studies to answer questions 7 and 8.

7 Which continent is shown on the map to the right?

A South America   `SSS 21(B)*`
B Africa
C Asia
D Australia

8 Which mountains set apart the areas marked 1, 2, 3 and 4 on the map so that they constitute their own separate physical regions?

F Rocky Mountains   `Geog 9(A)`
G Pyrenees Mountains
H Himalayan Mountains
J Andes Mountains

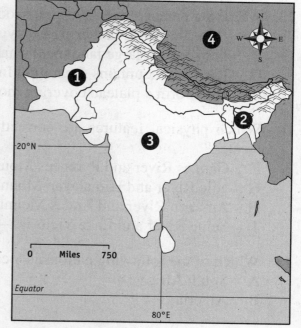

9 An important geographic similarity between Italy and India is that both countries are —

A	peninsulas	**C**	south of the equator
B	located between two oceans	**D**	affected by monsoons

SSS 21(B)*

10 Which feature should appear on a physical map of the continent of Africa?

F	Gobi Desert	**H**	pampas
G	tundra	**J**	savannas

Geog 9(A)

Use the information in the boxes and your knowledge of social studies to answer the following question.

Bordered by the Yellow Sea	Plateaus and deserts dominate the Western region	Southern and Western borders are ringed by the Himalayan Mountains

11 To which region do all of these geographic features belong?

A	Western Europe	**C**	India
B	China	**D**	Southeast Asia

Geog 9(A)

12 A ship traveling through the Panama Canal could be crossing from the —

F Pacific Ocean to the Atlantic Ocean
G Pacific Ocean to the Indian Ocean
H Atlantic Ocean to the Mediterranean Sea
J Red Sea to the Atlantic Ocean

Geog 9(A)

13 Which statement about Asia's monsoons is most accurate?

A They are winds that bring heavy rains to South Asia.
B They form a large land mass smaller than a continent.
C They are mountains separating India from the rest of Asia.
D They form a plateau covering most of the Indian peninsula.

SSS 22(C)*

14 Which physical features are correctly paired with the continent in which they are located?

F Ganges River and Pyrenees Mountains — Asia
G Nile River and Himalayan Mountains — Africa
H Amazon River and Andes Mountains — South America
J Seine River and Lake Victoria — Europe

Geog 9(A)

15 Which of the following nations is located in Sub-Sahara Africa?

A	South Africa	**C**	Egypt
B	Algeria	**D**	Libya

Geog 9(A)

Processes Shaping Planet Earth

This chapter corresponds to Chapter 2 of HMH's *World Geography* as well as to sections of later chapters.

❑ *Before Reading:* You might begin your study of this topic by reading the TEKS, *Geographic Terminology*, *Important Ideas* and *Essential Questions* on pages 89–90.

❑ *During Reading:* Next you might take each of Earth's four "spheres" in turn — the lithosphere, hydrosphere, atmosphere and biosphere. Read about each one in this book below, and then turn to the description of the same "sphere" in HMH's *World Geography*. For example, read about the lithosphere and the forces shaping it on pages 90-98 below, and then in HMH's *World Geography* on pages 28–29 and 33–47. After reading about the lithosphere, you might then look at some of the examples, found in the later pages of HMH's *World Geography*. For instance, if volcanoes interest you, you might look at pages 662 and 689–690 on volcanoes in Japan and Southeast Asia. There are many kinds of landforms, so you might look at some of the pages listed in the chart below to explore examples of these landforms from different regions of the world.

❑ *After Reading:* Reinforce your learning by reviewing the study cards and answering the test questions at the end of this chapter.

Topics	Mastering the TEKS	HMH's World Geography
Lithosphere	pp. 90–98	pp. 28
Plate Tectonic Motion	pp. 91–94	pp. 29, 37–39, 661
Causes	pp. 91–92	p. 37
Convection	pp. 91–92	
Gravity	p. 92	
Effects	pp. 93–94	
Mountain Building	p. 93	pp. 38, 551–552
Seafloor Spreading	p. 93	p. 36
Rift Valleys	p. 93	pp. 38, 416–417
Earthquakes	p. 93	pp. 39–40, 228–229, 520-521, 661–664
Tsunamis	p. 93	pp. 40, 662
Volcanoes	p. 94	pp. 40–41, 662, 689–690
Weathering	p. 94	pp. 42–43
Erosion	p. 95	pp. 43–44, 119
Deposition	p. 95	pp. 43, 44, 553–554
Soil	pp. 95–96	pp. 45, 65
Land Forms	p. 96	pp. 33–36, 119–121, 201–203, 273–275, 345–347, 415–417, 487–488, 551–553, 619–621, 689–692
Hydrosphere	pp. 99–100	pp. 28, 32–33
Water Cycle	p. 99	pp. 32–33
Lakes and Rivers		pp. 121, 202–203, 275, 347–348, 489, 552–553, 561–562, 621–622, 690
Tides	pp. 99–100	p. 32
Currents	p. 100	pp. 32, 35
Atmosphere	pp. 101–103	pp. 28, 49–53, 559
Vertical Climates	p. 101	p. 56
Monsoons	p. 101	pp. 557–558, 694–695
Hurricanes	p. 101	pp. 51, 627 (typhoons)
Seasons	pp. 101–102	p. 49
Climate Regions	pp. 102–103	pp. 54–58, 59–61, 207–209, 350–351, 421–422, 556–558, 625–627, 694–697

Biosphere	pp. 104–105	
Temperate Deciduous Forests	p. 104	pp. 66, 122, 349, 351
Tropical Rainforests	p. 104	pp. 66, 207–208, 245–248, 422–432, 554–555, 558
Grasslands	p. 104	pp. 66, 352, 422
Deserts	p. 104	pp. 66, 392, 420–421, 491–492, 620, 626–627, 697
Tundra	p. 105	pp. 66, 123–124, 280, 351, 625

Using Multiple Sources of Information

- Use information from both books to write your own answers to the *Essential Questions* on page 89.
- Create your own concept map around one of the *Important Ideas* on page 90. Use facts, examples and ideas from both books for your concept map.
- Use information from both books to create your own illustrated glossary, identifying the main types of landforms and bodies of water, and providing examples of each.
- Use information from both books to create a four-column chart comparing the Earth's lithosphere, hydrosphere, atmosphere, and biosphere.
- Use information from both books to create your own illustrated atlas showing the main physical regions of the world.
- Use information from both books to create your own video, slide show, Prezi or PowerPoint presentation on the forces shaping Earth's surface, including tectonic plate motion and erosion.
- Use information from both books to create a diagram or three-dimensional model showing how tectonic plates move, separate and collide.
- Use information from both books to create your own climate maps, showing the climates of different regions of the world.
- Use information from both books to create your own model, demonstrating how Earth moves around the Sun, creating the seasons.

CHAPTER 6

PROCESSES SHAPING PLANET EARTH

TEKS COVERED IN CHAPTER 6

- **Geography 3** The student understands how physical processes shape patterns in the physical environment.
  - **Geography 3(A)** Explain weather conditions and climate in relation to annual changes in Earth-Sun relationships.
  - **Geography 3(B)** Describe the physical processes that affect the environments of regions, including weather, tectonic forces, erosion, and soil-building processes.
  - **Geography 3(C)** Examine the physical processes that affect the lithosphere, atmosphere, hydrosphere, and biosphere.
- **Geography 4** The student understands the patterns and characteristics of major landforms, climates, and ecosystems of Earth and the interrelated processes that produce them.
  - **Geography 4(A)** Explain how elevation, latitude, wind systems, ocean currents, position on a continent, and mountain barriers influence temperature, precipitation, and distribution of climate regions.
  - **Geography 4(B)** Describe different landforms and the physical processes that cause their development.
  - **Geography 4(C)** Explain the influence of climate on the distribution of biomes in different regions.

In this chapter, you will learn about Earth's **lithosphere** (*Earth's crust and landforms*), **hydrosphere** (*oceans and other bodies of water*), **atmosphere** (*layers of gases surrounding Earth*), and **biosphere** (*plants and minerals*).

AN ESSENTIAL QUESTION

What forces have helped shape Earth's landforms, climate, and plant life?

GEOGRAPHIC TERMINOLOGY IN THIS CHAPTER

- Lithosphere
- Earth's Mantle
- Plate Tectonic Motion
- Convection
- Tsunami

- Weathering
- Erosion
- Deposition
- Water Cycle
- Tides and Currents

- Atmosphere
- Biomes
- Grasslands
- Steppes
- Tundra

— IMPORTANT IDEAS —

A. Lithosphere. The lithosphere is made up of the Earth's crust and solid upper mantle. It is broken up into **tectonic plates**. The movement of these plates shapes Earth's surface. New crust is made when plates spread apart. Crust folds into new mountain chains where continental plates collide. Earthquakes and volcanoes often occur at plate boundaries. **Weathering** and **erosion** tear down Earth's surface. Particles of rock and decayed plant and animal life form Earth's **soil**.

B. Hydrosphere. The world's oceans cover over 70% of our planet's surface area. Currents, caused by winds and differences in water density, move the ocean's waters around the planet. Water is also moved between the atmosphere, oceans, and land surfaces through the **water cycle**.

C. Atmosphere. The spinning of Earth, the unequal heating of air by the sun, the evaporation of water, and the effect of various landforms on the air result in **weather** — differences in temperature, wind, and precipitation. **Climate** is an area's average weather. Earth's tilt as it orbits the sun causes our seasons.

D. Biosphere. Differences in climate give rise to **biomes** — geographic regions that support different kinds of life — forests, grasslands, deserts and tundra.

LITHOSPHERE

Earth's crust forms a thick skin around the Earth, much like the crust of a loaf of bread. Below the crust is Earth's **mantle**, a region of hot, dense rock. The top of the mantle is solid.

As one travels deeper toward Earth's center, temperatures and pressure rise. About 100 km below Earth's surface, the rock is near its melting point and becomes semi-solid or plastic. Scientists are investigating how to use Earth's heat as a source of usable, clean, geothermal energy.

The **lithosphere** consists of Earth's crust and the top section of solid mantle. This brittle uppermost shell of the Earth is broken into a number of tectonic plates.

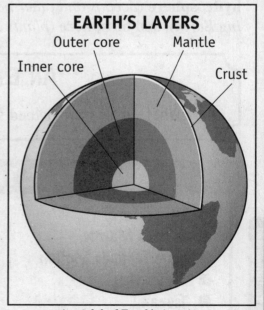

EARTH'S LAYERS

Outer core   Mantle
Inner core   Crust

A model of Earth's interior.

PLATE TECTONIC MOTION

If you look at a map of the world, you may notice that different continents seem to fit together like a giant puzzle. For example, eastern South America seems to fill the space below West Africa. Mountain ranges that end at one coastline seem to continue again on another coastline. Many scientists believe that several or even all of the present continents of the world once fit together into a single, giant continent. Gradually, this large land mass separated and its pieces drifted apart to their present locations.

Scientists refer to these ideas as **"plate tectonic" theory**. Earth's lithosphere is divided into large slabs of rock known as **tectonic plates**. Earth's continents are attached to these plates. Scientists believe that these plates move as solid chunks floating on top of the more "plastic" part of

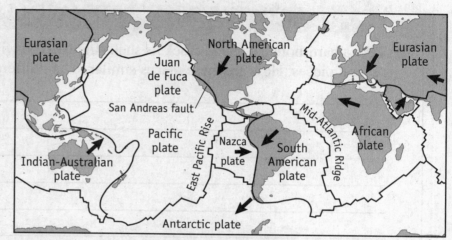

the mantle. The plates move only a few centimeters each year. Despite such slow movement, over hundreds of millions of years these plates can move thousands of kilometers.

WHAT CAUSES PLATE MOVEMENT?

Scientists believe heat and gravity may be responsible for the movement of tectonic plates.

CONVECTION

Convection is the spread of heat through the movement of a fluid substance. Inside the mantle, semi-solid rock is heated. As it is heated, it expands and becomes less dense. This lighter rock rises as gravity pulls down cooler, denser rock in its place.

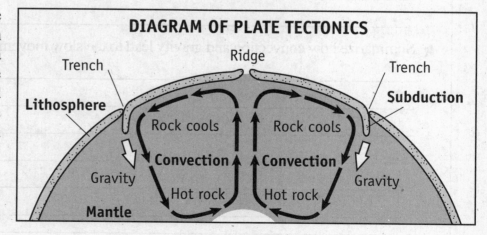

After the hotter rock rises, it begins to cool down. Once cooled, it sinks, creating a circular motion or current. This circular motion pushes the plates above.

GRAVITY

Gravity also contributes to plate movement. When oceanic and land plates collide, the dense oceanic plate is pulled by gravity under the lighter land plate. As one end of the oceanic plate sinks, it pulls on the rest of the plate as well.

APPLYING WHAT YOU HAVE LEARNED

★ Take a hard-boiled egg and crack its shell slightly. You will see the shell divide into several pieces. How are these pieces similar to and different from tectonic plates?

_____

_____

_____

_____

_____

_____

★ Look at a map of the world. Make your own hypothesis about which continents were once joined together. For example, some scientists believe the west coast of Africa fits next to the east coast of South America.

_____

_____

_____

_____

_____

★ Summarize how convection and gravity lead to the slow movement of tectonic plates.

_____

_____

_____

_____

_____

_____

_____

EFFECTS OF PLATE TECTONIC MOVEMENT

Tectonic plates push and pull against each other like bumper cars in an amusement park. These movements are responsible for some of the Earth's major land features.

MOUNTAIN BUILDING

When two land plates, known as **continental plates**, slowly push into one another, they often fold upwards, creating mountain chains. The Indian plate, for example, pushes northward against the Eurasian plate. The folding of these two plates has created the **Himalayan Mountains** — the world's highest mountain chain.

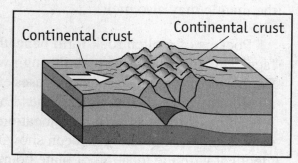

The Earth's crust under the oceans is thinner but denser than the continental crust. When oceanic crust collides into continental crust, the oceanic crust sinks downwards and slides under the continental crust, lifting it up. This can also build up mountains. For example, an oceanic plate has lifted up the continental plate of South America, creating the mountain range known as the **Andes Mountains**.

SEAFLOOR SPREADING AND RIFT VALLEYS

Some tectonic plates move apart. Scientists have discovered that in the middle of the Atlantic Ocean, the separation of plates is actually causing the seafloor to spread. As the plates move apart, magma rises up through the cracks in the ocean floor, creating a ridge of mountains.

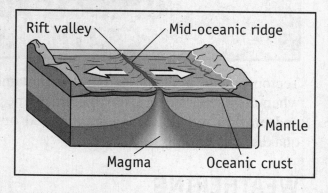

In other areas, the separation of tectonic plates has created **rift valleys** — long valleys between parallel ridges of mountains. This creation of new crust would increase the Earth's size, except that it is balanced by the folding and colliding of plates elsewhere.

EARTHQUAKES AND TSUNAMIS

Plate movements can cause a break in Earth's crust, known as a **fault**. Plate movements can also cause vibrations known as **earthquakes**. As plates move, they create tremendous stress at plate boundaries. Eventually, parts of the rocky crust will break, creating a fault and sending vibrations known as **seismic waves**. Scientists measure the waves sent by an earthquake with a **seismograph**. They can see that most waves originate at plate boundaries. When an earthquake occurs under or near the ocean, it creates immense ocean waves of destructive force known as **tsunamis**.

VOLCANOES

In places where tectonic plates diverge or where one plate dives under another, pressure in Earth's mantle is reduced and some of the hot, solid rock turns to liquid. Any part of the tectonic plate that sinks into the mantle may also melt.

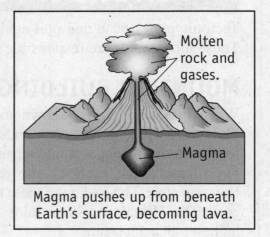

Molten rock and gases.

Magma

Magma pushes up from beneath Earth's surface, becoming lava.

Pockets of molten rock form beneath Earth's surface. This magma may break through weaknesses in Earth's crust. Magma, ashes and gases erupt and form a **volcano**. Once the magma reaches Earth's surface, it becomes known as **lava**. The location of most volcanoes and earthquakes has been shown to be almost identical with the location of plate boundaries.

For example, the "**Ring of Fire**" around the Pacific Ocean — a zone of volcanoes and frequent earthquakes — coincides with the boundaries of the Pacific tectonic plate. Many mountains and even islands have been formed by volcanoes. The Hawaiian islands are actually the tops of volcanoes in the Pacific Ocean.

OTHER FORCES AFFECTING EARTH'S LITHOSPHERE

Tectonic plate movements build mountains through folding. They also create new crust when they separate and new magma comes pouring through. The processes of weathering and erosion reduce the mountains and other land features created by volcanoes, earthquakes, and folding.

WEATHERING

The wearing down of rocks at the Earth's surface by the actions of wind, water, ice and living things is referred to as **weathering**. Water, for example, expands when it freezes. Water may seep into cracks or pores in rocks and expand these cracks if the temperature drops and the water freezes. Rain and running water will also break down rock into smaller particles. Some chemicals, like acids, will dissolve rocks. Microscopic organisms can also cause rocks to break down and disintegrate.

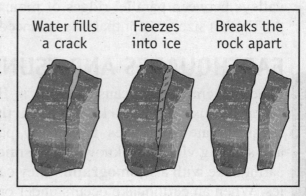

Water fills a crack   Freezes into ice   Breaks the rock apart

EROSION

The processes by which rock, sand, and soil are broken down and carried away are known as **erosion**. By erosion, a river can cut a canyon, like the **Grand Canyon**, through solid rock. An icy glacier can carve and wear away a region, leaving behind valleys and lakes, such as the **Great Lakes**.

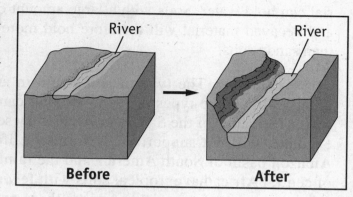

Before → After

DEPOSITION

The same forces that erode one place can deposit particles and sediment in another, building it up. Rivers carry sediment downstream and deposit this sediment where they meet the ocean. The action of ocean waves can bring sand to a beach.

APPLYING WHAT YOU HAVE LEARNED

Can you think of any examples of weathering, erosion or deposition that have affected your own community?

_____

_____

_____

_____

_____

_____

_____

_____

SOIL: BUILDING PROCESSES

Weathering breaks down rocks on Earth's surface. The material left from the rocks mixes with decaying plants and animals to make soil. Soil is therefore a mixture of several materials, including sand, clay, rocks, water, fungi, bacteria, and decayed plants and animal material (*humus*). A layer of soil covers much of Earth's land surface. There are many different types of soil, based on different mixtures of its basic ingredients. Each type of soil has its own texture, ability to hold water, and ability to support plant life.

For example, clay and dead plant and animal material can hold water. Soils with a large amount of clay and decayed material will therefore hold more water than sandy soils.

Soil Quality. The type of soil found in an area greatly affects the types of plant life that can grow there. The sands of the Sahara or Arabian Desert, for example, will not support many forms of life. The Amazon basin of South America and the rainforests of central Africa have tropical soils with few minerals or nutrients. Rain quickly washes these nutrients away. Plants take their nutrients instead from plants and animals that are still decomposing. Soils found in grassland areas — the Great Plains, pampas, and Russian steppes — have much organic matter and are among the best soils for farming.

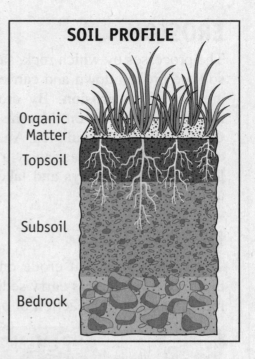

SOIL PROFILE

Organic Matter

Topsoil

Subsoil

Bedrock

EARTH'S MANY LAND FORMS

All these processes acting on Earth's lithosphere create typical landforms. These landforms include mountains, hills, plateaus, plains, valleys, canyons, deserts, and beaches.

★ **Mountains**, often formed by the collision of tectonic plates, can be thousands of feet high in elevation.

★ A **plateau** is a flat highland, whose sides drop suddenly because of erosion.

★ **Valleys** are long, low areas between ranges of mountains, hills or uplands. They are often created by erosion, and may have a river or stream running along the bottom.

★ A **canyon** is a deep gorge or ravine between cliffs, often carved from the landscape by a river.

A plateau.

Name ______________________________ Date ______________

APPLYING WHAT YOU HAVE LEARNED

★ Select one of the landforms identified on the previous pages that exists in your community. Take a photograph of it, find it on the Internet and print it out, or make a sketch of it. Place your image in the space below:

★ Now describe this landform in your own words. ______________________________

____

____

____

____

____

★ Finally, explain the forces that most likely created this landform. ______________

____

____

____

____

____

____

LEARNING WITH GRAPHIC ORGANIZERS

Complete the graphic organizer below.

Mountain Building

_____
_____
_____
_____
_____

Seafloor Spreading and Rift Valleys

_____
_____
_____
_____
_____

Earthquakes and Tsunamis

_____
_____
_____
_____
_____

Volcanoes

_____
_____
_____
_____
_____

FORCES AFFECTING EARTH'S LITHOSPHERE

Weathering

_____
_____
_____
_____
_____

Erosion

_____
_____
_____
_____
_____

Soil-Building

_____
_____
_____
_____
_____

THE HYDROSPHERE: Earth's Oceans

More than 70 percent of Earth's surface is covered by water. Scientists refer to this as the **hydrosphere**. About 97 percent of this water is in the ocean; most of the rest of it is frozen in the polar ice caps; less than one percent is found in the atmosphere, groundwater, or in freshwater lakes and rivers.

THE WATER CYCLE

Just as Earth's lithosphere undergoes various processes, so does its hydrosphere. One of the most important of these is the **water cycle**. Solar energy heats the surface of oceans, seas, and lakes. This causes some of the surface water to evaporate into the atmosphere. The water vapor rises until it becomes cooler. The water vapor then condenses into tiny droplets small enough to float in the atmosphere as clouds.

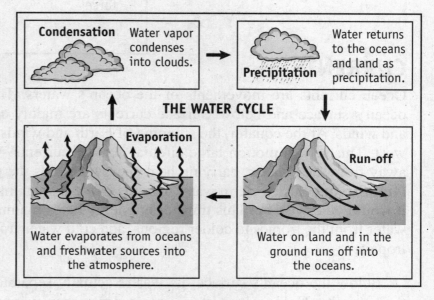

Condensation Water vapor condenses into clouds.

Water returns to the oceans and land as precipitation. **Precipitation**

THE WATER CYCLE

Evaporation

Run-off

Water evaporates from oceans and freshwater sources into the atmosphere.

Water on land and in the ground runs off into the oceans.

When the droplets grow larger and heavier, they fall back to Earth's surface as **precipitation** — rain, snow or hail. Some precipitation returns to the ocean, but some falls on land where it is absorbed by the ground or forms lakes, streams and rivers. Some of this precipitation evaporates, but the rivers and much of the groundwater eventually drains back into the oceans.

TIDES AND CURRENTS

Earth's ocean waters are in constant motion. This can be seen in the movement of their tides and currents.

TIDES

Each day, the surface level of the oceans rises and falls during *high* and *low tide*. Tides are caused by the gravitational pull of the moon on Earth's ocean waters. Ocean waters directly facing the moon bulge towards the moon, creating **high tide**, a time when sea levels are at their highest.

On the opposite side of Earth is another high tide, caused by the force of Earth's spin where the moon's pull is weakest.

Sea levels become highest when the moon and sun are both lined up on the same side of Earth, and lowest when they are on opposite sides.

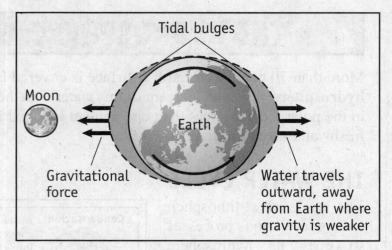

CURRENTS

Ocean currents are movements of the ocean's waters. These currents occur both at the ocean's surface and below. Surface currents are mainly caused by the spinning of Earth and winds. At the equator, the spinning of Earth and winds push surface water towards the west. This sets in motion large circular surface currents. Water heated by the sun moves away from the equator, carrying heat energy towards the polar regions. For example, the **Gulf Stream** carries warm water towards Great Britain, making that country warmer than it would otherwise be. This transfer of energy helps maintain a balance — carrying warm water from the tropics to colder regions, and cold water from the polar regions towards the tropics.

Below the ocean's surface, its waters actually separate into different layers based on their density. Cold, salty water is more dense than warm, less salty water. At the poles, cold, salty water sinks. It then slowly moves towards the equator, pushing warmer water away. During this process, this cold water gradually warms up as it absorbs heat from the layers of water above it. This slow but steady circulation of the ocean's deep waters takes hundreds of years.

APPLYING WHAT YOU HAVE LEARNED

Use the Internet, library, or other resources to find out more about Earth's ocean currents. Identify one ocean current and one effect from that current.

_____

_____

_____

_____

THE ATMOSPHERE AND CLIMATE

Around Earth is an envelope of gases known as the **atmosphere**. It consists mainly of nitrogen (78%) and oxygen (21%). The atmosphere absorbs solar radiation, moderates temperatures, and distributes water. **Weather** refers to conditions in the atmosphere closest to Earth, including humidity, winds, and precipitation (*rain, snow,* or *hail*). Different processes in the atmosphere lead to differences in **climate**, the average weather conditions of a place over a long period of time.

THE GEOGRAPHY OF WEATHER

Weather is affected by latitude, elevation (*height above sea level*), wind patterns, ocean currents, and mountain barriers. For example, temperatures are generally warmer the closer an area is to the equator. Temperatures tend to decrease as you move away from the equator to higher latitudes. Temperatures are also cooler at higher **elevations**, such as on mountains or high plateaus. Geographers refer to different climates at different altitudes in the same area as **vertical climates**.

Winds are influenced by Earth's spin. Depending on the location of a place, winds may bring moist air and rain, such as the **monsoons**; or they may leave an area dry. Distance from major bodies of water also affects climate. Because air cools as it rises over a mountain barrier, the ocean side of a mountain often has heavy rainfall. The air loses moisture and is drier when it reaches the other side of the mountain.

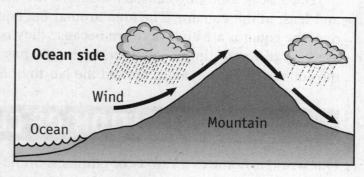

For example, **tropical hurricanes** occur in tropical regions in late summer and early fall when the ocean water is very warm. The warm ocean water evaporates so quickly that it creates an area of low pressure. Air around a rising air column begins to spiral at high speeds. The hot air rises until it cools and condenses — releasing energy and causing heavy rains, strong winds, and dangerous lightning strikes.

EARTH'S SEASONS

The Earth tilts on its axis as it revolves around the sun. Because of this tilt, the sun's rays hit the Northern Hemisphere longer and more directly in summer than in winter. The sun appears to rise higher in the sky, temperatures are warmer, and the days are longer.

When it is summer in the Northern Hemisphere, it is winter in the Southern Hemisphere. This is because the Southern Hemisphere is tilting away from the sun and receives less direct solar rays.

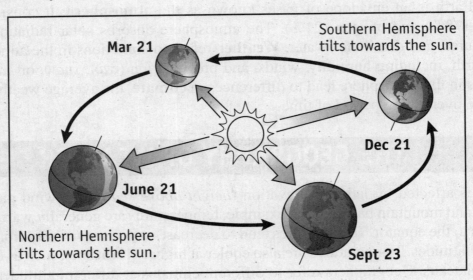

Because seasons are caused by Earth's tilt, seasonal differences are greatest at the poles and least at the equator. The area around the equator is not affected by Earth's tilt. Areas near the equator are always warm because they receive the sun's direct rays. The two poles are very different. In the summer, each pole has 24 hours of sunlight, while in the winter, the sun never rises in areas around the North or South Pole.

DISTRIBUTION OF CLIMATE REGIONS

Our world is home to a variety of climates. Some geographers divide the world into regions based on similarities in climate, including average temperatures and rainfall. Climate zones are most affected by latitude and elevation.

★ **High-Latitude Climates.** The North and South Poles have similar "polar climates" with very cold winter temperatures.

★ **Mid-Latitude Climates.** Places in the middle latitudes with low elevations generally have warm summers and cool winters. These are also known as "moist mid-latitude climates," with either mild or cold winters, or as "**temperate** climates."

★ **Low-Latitude Climates.** Central Africa, Central America, Northern South America, South Asia and Southeast Asia have warm and humid climates. These are sometimes called "**tropical** moist climates." North Africa, the Middle East, Western Australia, and Asia have warm and dry climates. In these areas, the evaporation of water can be greater than precipitation.

Name _____ Date _____

The map below shows some of the main climate regions around the world:

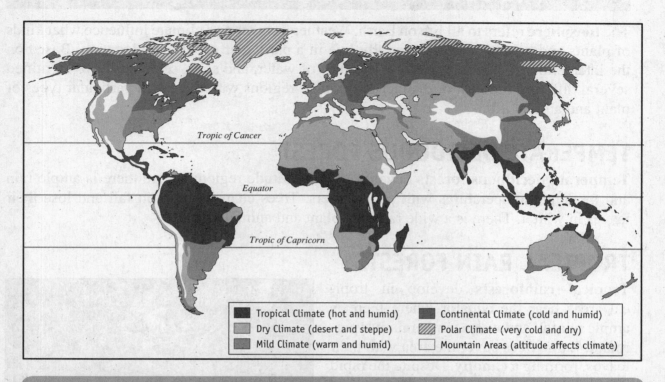

Tropic of Cancer

Equator

Tropic of Capricorn

■ Tropical Climate (hot and humid)	■ Continental Climate (cold and humid)
▨ Dry Climate (desert and steppe)	▨ Polar Climate (very cold and dry)
▨ Mild Climate (warm and humid)	□ Mountain Areas (altitude affects climate)

APPLYING WHAT YOU HAVE LEARNED

Select one continent and compare its climate regions with the description of its major physical characteristics described in **Chapter 5:** *A World Gazetteer.*

★ What factors — such as latitude, elevation, and mountain barriers — affect the climate of that continent?

_____

_____

_____

★ How does this continent's climate affect its physical features? State your answer in outline form or in a flow chart.

THE BIOSPHERE: Climate and Biomes

The **biosphere** refers to all life on Earth. Weather patterns and climate influence what kinds of plants and animals can successfully live in a particular geographic location. Based on the interaction of climate, landforms, bodies of water, and soils, scientists have identified several different **biomes**, or distinct geographic regions with their own particular types of plant and animal life.

TEMPERATE DECIDUOUS FOREST

Temperate deciduous forests develop in mid-latitude regions where there is ample rain and moderate temperatures with cool winters. Trees change colors in fall and lose their leaves in winter. There is a wide range of plant and animal life.

TROPICAL RAIN FORESTS

Tropical rainforests develop in tropical areas near the equator where there is ample rainfall and warm temperatures year-round. Large trees cover the area with their leaves, forming a **canopy**. Despite the rapid growth of trees, the topsoil is actually very thin. Tropical rainforests are marked by a great abundance of animal and plant life, displaying greater biological diversity than any other biome.

GRASSLANDS AND SAVANNA OR STEPPES

Grassland areas exist where the climate is drier and there is not enough rainfall to support large amounts of trees. Instead, grasses dominate these areas with large grazing animals, like cattle, antelope or bison. **Savannas** are grasslands with some trees.

DESERTS

Deserts are regions that receive less than 10 inches of rainfall annually. Deserts in the tropical latitudes, such as the Sahara Desert, have their own special forms of plant and animal life, which have adapted to the lack of water and extremes of temperature. Cacti, for example, store water in their stems.

TUNDRA

Tundra is found closer to the polar regions. The soil of the tundra is so cold that trees cannot grow. Much of the ground is frozen part of the year. Tundras constitute a distinct biome, with their own plant and animal life, including grasses, small shrubs, large mammals and birds that migrate to these regions in the warmer spring and summer months.

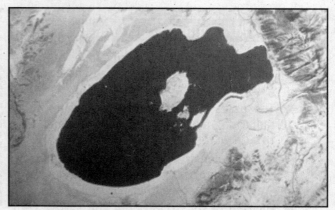
In a tundra, much of the ground is frozen.

APPLYING WHAT YOU HAVE LEARNED

★ Choose one of the biomes described on the previous page. Use the Internet, library or other resource to find a specific place where that biome is found. Then write a brief description of the landforms and climate distinguishing that place, and the plants and animals found there.

★ In what way are climate regions and biomes related?

_____

_____

_____

CHAPTER STUDY CARDS

Tectonic Plate Movement

★ **Lithosphere.**
  • Crust and top layer of mantle
  • It is divided into shifting tectonic plates.
★ **Effects:**
  • Earthquakes   • Mountains
  • Volcanoes   • Rift valleys
  • Seafloor spreading
★ **Other Forces affecting Earth's Surface:**
  • **Weathering.** Rocks broken apart by wind, water, ice, and organisms.
  • **Erosion.** Rocks and particles are broken down and carried to a new location.

Hydrosphere

★ The hydrosphere is made up of all water on Earth's surface.
★ Seventy percent of Earth's surface is covered by oceans.
★ The gravitational pull of the moon causes **tides** — a cyclic rise and fall of the oceans.
★ Ocean water is moved by surface and deep-sea currents.
★ **The Water Cycle.** Water circulates through evaporation, condensation, precipitation, and run-off.

Atmosphere and Weather	Climate
★ The atmosphere is an envelope of gases around Earth. It is mainly made up of nitrogen and oxygen.	★ **Average Weather Conditions.** Weather conditions of a place are affected by its:
★ The gases of the atmosphere absorb solar radiation, moderate temperatures and distribute water.	• Latitude • Ocean currents • Elevation • Mountain barriers • Winds
★ Weather consists of temperature, humidity, precipitation, and wind. The atmosphere creates distinct weather patterns.	★ **Climate Regions.** Regions based on similarities in climate. Examples include: • Polar Climates • Tropical Climates
★ Heating of the atmosphere and Earth's spin create wind patterns. Surface features like mountains also affect weather.	★ **Biomes.** Variations in climate lead to distinct regions based on similarities of plant and animal life: temperate forests, tropical rainforests, grasslands, deserts, and tundras.

CHECKING YOUR UNDERSTANDING

Directions: Put a circle around the letter that best answers the question.

1 The diagram to the right illustrates an important scientific theory. What does this theory claim?

    Geog 3(B)

A Earth moves around the sun.

B Earth's continents are slowly moving together.

C There is little difference in the climatic patterns found on most continents.

D Millions of years ago, Earth's continents formed one giant continent.

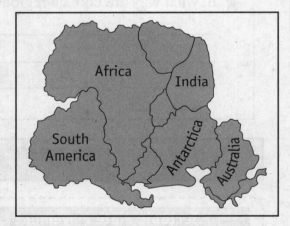

EXAMINE **the question.** This question requires you to read a map and recall information about Earth's structure and processes. RECALL **what you know.** You should recall that tectonic plate theory suggests that continents are attached to giant tectonic plates, which move over time. Some scientists believe our present continents were once joined in a single land mass. The map shows how several continents may have once been connected. APPLY **what you know. Choice A** and **Choice C** are unrelated to the map. **Choice B** is also wrong, since the way continents now fit together is evidence they broke apart, not that they are moving together. Therefore, the best answer is **Choice D.**

Now try answering some additional questions on your own:

2   A farmer sees an area he believes will be good for farming because of its rich topsoil.
Which process contributed most to forming this rich topsoil?

F   sand storms

G   ocean currents

H   decaying plant life

J   folding of Earth's crust

> • **EXAMINE The Question**
> • **RECALL What You Know**
> • **APPLY What You Know**

`Geog 3(B)`

3   Which is the best example of weathering?

A   the cracking of rocks caused by the freezing and melting of water   `Geog 3(B)`

B   the transportation of sediment in a stream

C   the condensation of water vapor into droplets in clouds

D   the formation of a sandbar along the side of a stream

4   Which best explains why we experience four seasons on Earth?

F   the gravitational pull of the moon

G   the distance between Earth and the sun   `Geog 3(B)`

H   the tilt of the Earth on its axis as it revolves around the sun

J   the effect of tectonic plate movement on Earth's oceans

Use the information in the map and line graph and your knowledge of social studies to answer the following question.

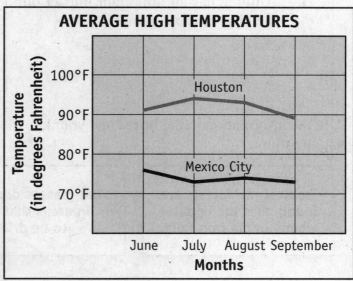

AVERAGE HIGH TEMPERATURES

5   Mexico City in central Mexico is closer to the equator than Houston, Texas. Its average summer temperatures are cooler than Houston's. What best explains this?

A   Mexico City has a higher elevation than Houston.   `Geog 4(A)`

B   The use of air conditioners has raised temperatures in Houston.

C   Mexico City is subject to periodic storms, lowering temperatures.

D   Mexico City is farther from the Gulf of Mexico than Houston.

6   Which of the following is caused by the very rapid evaporation of warm ocean water in late summer months?

   F   the erosion of a sandy beach
   G   a tropical hurricane
   H   a catastrophic forest fire
   J   a tornado

Geog 3(C)

• **E**XAMINE The Question
• **R**ECALL What You Know
• **A**PPLY What You Know

7   The most frequent cause of major earthquakes is the —

   A   pressure from tectonic plate movement
   B   occurrence of landslides
   C   gravitational pull of the moon as it orbits Earth
   D   change in underwater currents

Geog 3(B)

8   Which of the following generalizations can be made from this diagram?

   F   Vertical climates have   Geog 4(A)
         no effect where
         people live.
   G   Altitude has little effect on the grow-
         ing season of crops.
   H   Most crops cannot be grown above
         sea level.
   J   Altitude has an important impact on
         the kind of crops grown.

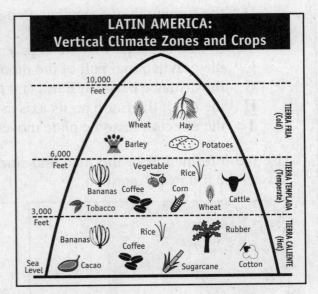

LATIN AMERICA:
Vertical Climate Zones and Crops

Use the information in the boxes and your knowledge of social studies to answer the following question.

| Tropical rainforests are found near the equator where ample rain falls. | Tall grasses dominate in areas that tend to be drier. | Plants that store water exist in areas with temperature extremes and little rainfall. |

9   Which conclusion can best be drawn from these three examples?

   A   Tall grasses grow well in the Great Plains.
   B   Climate greatly influences the types of biomes found in different regions.
   C   Cacti are usually found in desert areas where it tends to be dry.
   D   Rainfall is one cause for the rapid growth of tropical rainforests.

Geog 4(C)

People and Nature

This chapter describes how people interact with their physical environment. It corresponds with special sections found in every regional unit of HMH's *World Geography*. The last section of the first chapter for each region in that book always concerns "Human-Environment Interaction."

❑ *Before Reading:* You might begin your study of this topic by reading the TEKS, *Geographical Terminology*, *Important Ideas* and *Essential Question* on pages 111–112.

❑ *During Reading:* Next you might read the text of this chapter to learn how people are affected by their environment and how, in turn, people modify their environment — such as through agriculture, urban growth and building dams. You will also learn about GIS (Geographic Information Systems), extreme weather conditions and the environmental challenges facing humanity in the future, including climate change. You can then learn more about each of these topics by reading corresponding sections of HMH's *World Geography*, as shown on the chart below. For example, to learn more about the effects of volcanoes and other seismic events, you might read about the eruption of Krakatoa in the Pacific Ocean, both on page 116 of this book and on pages 710–711 of HMH's *World Geography*.

❑ *After Reading:* Reinforce your learning by reviewing the study cards and answering the test questions at the end of the chapter.

Topics	*Mastering the TEKS*	HMH's *World Geography*
How the Environment Affects People	pp. 112–113	pp. 8
Bodies of Water	p. 112	pp. 54, 121, 438–439, 560–563
Landforms	pp. 112–113	pp. 117–121, 201–202, 352, 420–421, 491–493
Climate	p. 113	
Plant and Animal Life	p. 113	pp. 53, 354–355, 597–599
Seismic Activity	p. 113	pp. 494, 558, 614
		pp. 228–229, 520–521, 662–663, 689–690
How People Modify the Environment	pp. 114–115	
Agriculture	p. 114	pp. 127, 210–211, 353–354, 695
Irrigation	p. 114	pp. 127, 149, 427, 438, 492–439, 495–496
Urban Growth	p. 115	pp. 128, 176–179, 211–212, 293
Dams	p. 115	pp. 67, 426–427, 562–563, 628–630
Energy (Fossil Fuels)	p. 115	pp. 425–426, 439–440, 497–499, 529–530
Canals/Inland Water		pp. 129, 487
Extreme Weather/Natural Disasters	pp. 116–118	pp. 39–41, 51–53, 107, 126, 150–151, 578–579, 661–663
Vesuvius	p. 116	
Krakatoa	p. 116	pp. 710–711
San Francisco Earthquake	p. 116	
Indonesian Tsunami	p. 117	
Icelandic Volcano	p. 117	
Hurricane Katrina	p. 117	
El Niño	p. 117	p. 57
Earthquake in Turkey		pp. 520–521
Earthquakes in Haiti and Chile, 2010		pp. 228–229
Cyclone of 1970		pp. 578–579
Yangtze River Flood of 1931		pp. 640–641
Famine in Somalia		pp. 436–437

Using Multiple Sources of Information

- Use information from both books to write your own answer to the *Essential Question* on page 111.
- Create your own concept map around one of the *Important Ideas* on page 111. Use facts, examples, and ideas from both books for your concept map.
- Use information from both books to create your own illustrated glossary, defining each of the phrases listed as *Geographic Terminology* on page 112.
- Use information from both books to create an expanded chart, showing how people modify their environment, based on *Applying What You Have Learned*, page 114. Be sure to include photographs from the Internet and other sources.
- Use information from both books to create your own video, slide show, Prezi or PowerPoint presentation reporting on an example of extreme weather or another natural disaster, and how people responded to it.
- Use information from both books to design a questionnaire about emergency plans in the event that some extreme weather or other natural disaster occurs in your community. Then ask these questions to your parents and other adults you know, or to local public officials in your local police department, fire department and hospital.
- Use information from both books to prepare a written or oral report on pollution, the ozone layer, acid rain or any other environmental challenge facing us in the future.
- Use information from both books to create your own poster, promoting sustainable development.

Name _____ Date _____

PEOPLE AND NATURE

From its origins, humankind has had to deal with the challenges posed by nature. From nature, humans have always obtained their food, shelter and clothing. When nature acts harshly, bringing storms, droughts, or fires, people have to respond.

In this chapter, you will learn how people are connected to their environment. You will study how humans interact with and modify their physical setting. You will also learn about the challenges that people sometimes face because of extreme weather, natural disasters, and limited natural resources.

AN ESSENTIAL QUESTION

○— How do people adapt to or modify their physical environment?

— IMPORTANT IDEAS —

A. Humans depend on, **adapt** to, and **modify** their physical environment.

B. Humans sometimes must respond to conditions of extreme weather or natural disasters, such as floods, tsunamis, and volcanoes. GIS can help people respond to such extremes of weather or natural disasters.

C. People now seek to use **renewable resources**, to conserve non-renewable resources, and to pursue **sustainable development** to protect our environment.

111

GEOGRAPHIC TERMINOLOGY IN THIS CHAPTER

- Seismic Activity
- Tsunami
- El Niño / La Niña
- Climate Change
- Renewable Resources
- Non-renewable Resource
- Biodiversity
- GIS
- Sustainable Development

HUMAN-ENVIRONMENTAL INTERACTION

Like all animals, people must adapt to the climate, landforms, vegetation, and natural resources they find in the place where they live. However, unlike most animals, humans also have the ability to **modify**, or change, their environment greatly.

HOW PEOPLE ARE AFFECTED BY THE ENVIRONMENT

There are many ways in which people are affected by their physical environment. The environment affects their choice of foods, shelter, clothing, and general way of life. Certain aspects of the physical environment are especially important:

BODIES OF WATER

Fresh water is essential to human life. Indeed, the earliest civilizations arose in river valleys. Ancient Egyptians, for example, developed their civilization along the Nile River. Even today, most cities are located near a major body of water.

LANDFORMS

People are also affected by landforms. People generally settle in flat, fertile valleys and plains, where they can build homes and grow crops easily. Fewer people live in mountains, swamps or desert areas. However, even in these harsher environments, different groups often develop their own way of life. For example, the Berbers live in desert areas of North Africa, between the Sahara and the Mediterranean Sea. Their lifestyle is closely based on a close connection to their natural surroundings.

A Berber village in the desert.

Few crops are able to be grown in frigid, barren areas above 10,000 feet. However, the ancient Incas flourished high in the Andes Mountains where they were able to develop root crops, such as the potato.

CLIMATE

Climate has a profound effect on how people live. For example, the Vikings of Norway wore heavy clothing made of wool, animal hides, and fur to protect them from the cold. In contrast, people who live in warm areas, like Egypt, wear light clothes to keep cool. Climate also affects what can grow in a region, and what livestock can live there. In the moist, warm areas of Southeast and East Asia, people developed the culture of growing rice as their main food. Growing

Rice farmers at work in a rice paddy.

rice in flooded fields generally requires cooperation, strengthening social bonds among people. They make use of water brought by monsoon rains.

PLANT AND ANIMAL LIFE

The types of vegetation and animals in an area also greatly affect human lifestyles. People often make use of local plants and animals as sources of food, clothing, and building materials. For example, the steppes of Central Asia are made up of dry, grassy hills and plains. These steppes receive enough rainfall to support the grasses and other plant life on which grazing animals feed, but not enough rain for farming crops. As a result, on these lands animal domestication and herding became the dominant way of life. For this reason, the peoples of Central Asia have generally been herders who were skilled at horsemanship. On the grasslands of North America, Native American Indians were hunters who lived on the meat and hides of the large numbers of wild buffalo. Peoples on the steppes of Asia and the Great Plains of North America both lived in tents made of animal skins, which they could move easily to follow animal herds.

SEISMIC ACTIVITY

Seismic activity refers to earthquakes and volcanoes. Because of seismic activity in the Pacific region, people in Japan have usually built their homes out of lightweight materials. These materials are less harmful if a building collapses during an earthquake. Often wood houses do not use nails. Instead, wood beams are grooved to fit together, so that the house will shift with an earthquake rather than crumble.

APPLYING WHAT YOU HAVE LEARNED

★ What are some of the ways in which the physical environment affects people's lifestyles? _____

_____

_____

_____

★ Give one example of how your activities are influenced by your environment.

_____

_____

_____

_____

HOW PEOPLE MODIFY THEIR ENVIRONMENT

Just as people are affected by their environment, they also affect their environment. Culture and technology often influence how people modify nature. Here are some of the chief ways that humans have modified the environment:

AGRICULTURE

Agriculture (*farming*) is the growing of food. Ten thousand years ago, people in the Middle East found that if they planted seeds and watered plants, they could grow fruits, grains and vegetables. They selected certain seeds to replant in order to grow the most nourishing plants.

Crop cultivation brought about modification and manipulation of the environment to increase food production — it altered the landscape by clearing existing vegetation, and cutting the soil by tilling it. People also learned to irrigate their fields to increase their productivity. Since humans first learned to plant seeds, civilizations around the world have generally turned forests, grasslands, and marshes into productive farmland.

Ancient peoples learned to plant seeds to grow food.

URBAN GROWTH

People also modify nature by building towns and cities. The first cities arose in the Middle East. By 7,000 B.C., the city of Jericho had 3,000 residents. Sumer, the world's earliest known civilization, began on the plains of Mesopotamia in 3500 B.C. Later, ancient cities like Rome had as many as a million inhabitants.

The remains of ancient Sumerian streets and markets.

In the Middle Ages, urban centers were generally smaller. Agricultural improvements in the 1700s, increased overseas trade, and the rise of manufacturing during the Industrial Revolution led to the rapid growth of cities. Today, most people in industrialized countries live in cities. Urbanization changes the environment by concentrating thousands, even millions, of people in small, treeless areas. Cities replace open fields and forests with paved, concrete roads and tall buildings of steel, concrete, and glass. Public parks preserve some open areas.

THE BUILDING OF DAMS

Another way that people modify nature is by constructing dams to drain swamps, prevent floods, and to store water for drinking and irrigation. Dams also serve to generate electric power.

ENERGY

Humans further modify the environment to provide energy for their needs. Thousands of years ago, humans discovered the power of fire to warm themselves, to cook food and to heat water. This allowed humans to spread to new places where the climate was colder. Later, humans discovered they could also burn coal, whale oil, and forms of petroleum for light, heat, and power. Modern society continues to depend on burning fossil fuels like coal and oil. We dig mines in the ground for coal and drill holes for oil. However, the demand for oil can have destructive effects on the environment, such as the massive leak of crude oil when an oil rig exploded in the Gulf of Mexico in 2010. Its use also causes air pollution.

Early humans discovered the power of fire to protect and warm.

APPLYING WHAT YOU HAVE LEARNED

Complete the chart below. Indicate at least one of the positive and one of the negative effects of each of these human modifications to the environment:

Human Changes to the Environment	Positive Effects	Negative Effects
Agriculture		
Urban Growth		
Building Dams		
Energy		

EXTREME WEATHER AND OTHER NATURAL DISASTERS

Extreme weather and other natural disasters pose special problems. These are not the typical conditions that people usually expect. Tornadoes, hurricanes, fires, earthquakes, tsunamis, and volcanoes, although infrequent, are events that can kill thousands of people and destroy buildings, bridges, and roads. Although unusual, people have always had to deal with extreme conditions and natural disasters, from ancient times to the present.

★ **Vesuvius Volcano.** In 79 A.D., the volcano at Mount Vesuvius erupted. Thousands of Romans were buried under volcanic ash in the city of Pompeii. The eruption also changed the course of the Sarno River and raised the sea.

★ **Krakatoa Volcano.** The island of Krakatoa was located in the Pacific Ocean. Its volcano exploded in 1873 with a force thousands of times more powerful than the atomic bombs used in World War II. It blew the island apart in one of the most violent eruptions in recorded history.

★ **San Francisco Earthquake.** In 1906, most of San Francisco was destroyed by a great earthquake, killing over 3,000 people. Scientists predict future earthquakes in this region.

★ **Indonesian Tsunami.** In 2004, an undersea earthquake in the Indian Ocean led to a giant tidal wave or **tsunami**. More than two hundred thousand people were killed in Indonesia and Thailand. Waves raced across the Pacific Ocean at hundreds of miles per hour, and waves as high as 100 feet struck coastal communities.

★ **Icelandic Volcano.** In 2010, a volcanic eruption in Iceland halted air travel throughout Europe for several days.

Volcanoes, earthquakes and tsunamis are often caused by tectonic plate movement. The location of many of these disasters, such as the "Pacific Rim of Fire," can often be foreseen. Because these events are infrequent, people continue to return and rebuild in these otherwise inviting areas.

EXTREME WEATHER

Weather also sometimes brings dangerous conditions — including **hurricanes**, **tornadoes**, **floods**, **droughts**, and **extreme heat** or **cold**. For example, some scientists believe that rising temperatures from global climate change may be responsible for the increasing number of droughts. Lack of rainfall has brought **desertification** (*changing into a desert*) to areas like Africa's Sahel region, south of the Sahara Desert. Rising global temperatures may also be responsible for the greater severity of tropical hurricanes. In 2005, **Hurricane Katrina** devastated the Gulf Coast and became one of the costliest natural disasters in United States history.

Hurricane Katrina flooded 80% of New Orleans, with some areas under 15 feet of water.

El Niño and La Niña. Rising global temperatures may also be contributing to the periodic warming of the surface of the Pacific Ocean, leading to **El Niño** (*the little boy*). This creates increased rain in the eastern Pacific Ocean and along the west coasts of the United States and South America. At other times, known as **La Niña**, the surface of the Pacific is cooler, with opposite effects. La Niña brings heavier than usual rains to Southeast Asia.

HUMAN RESPONSES

There is no way to prevent extreme weather or periodic natural disasters. The challenge for humans is to predict them, prepare for them, and to reduce their devastating effects. For example in 1989, an earthquake in San Francisco led to far fewer deaths and less property damage than less severe recent earthquakes in India, Iran, China, or Haiti. Fewer deaths and less devastation occurred in San Francisco because buildings were specially designed to move with earthquakes rather than collapse.

The global community now cooperates when natural disasters strike. In 2004, many nations contributed to help those injured or displaced by the tsunami. In 2010, Haiti was hit by a devastating earthquake, killing 300,000 Haitians and leaving a million people homeless. People from nations around the world contributed food, medical supplies and help in the wake of this natural disaster.

Part of the devastation caused by the earthquake in Port-au-Prince, Haiti.

GIS AND GLOBAL DISASTERS

Geographic Information Systems (*GIS*) are spatial information systems that merge information from satellites and land-based sources. These systems use global data from satellite photography, land-based maps, statistics, and other sources. Computers store this in digital form at each location on a map.

For example, a system was established in 1985 as an environmental database covering members of what is now the European Union. This system collected information on soil, landforms, climate, water resources, and pollution, as well as economic data. The United Nation's Environment GRID (*Global Resources Information Database*), based in Kenya, collects similar information for the entire world. Officials are able to use this data base to check information, to visualize issues, and to make accurate models and predictions. The environment GRID is now being used for a global deforestation project to study the decline of the world's forests.

GIS is especially useful for handling natural disasters. In the event of an earthquake, fire, or flood, officials can quickly obtain detailed information about landforms, water bodies, pipelines, power lines, sewer systems, buildings, roads, flood zones, and weather predictions for each location. Officials can quickly pinpoint potential hazards and can rapidly notify people and even evacuate areas.

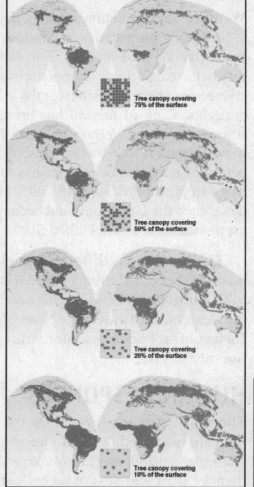

Tree canopy covering 75% of the surface

Tree canopy covering 50% of the surface

Tree canopy covering 20% of the surface

Tree canopy covering 10% of the surface

Maps created by the U.N. Environment Grid.

Name _____ Date _____

APPLYING WHAT YOU HAVE LEARNED

Select a recent natural disaster. Prepare a three-minute oral presentation about that disaster. Describe what happened during the disaster and what efforts people made to cope with the disaster. Include a map and a photograph as part of your presentation. Use the space below to outline your presentation.

CHALLENGES FOR THE FUTURE

Today, human activities threaten many of Earth's natural processes.

POLLUTION

The rise of industry and the growth of world population in the past 200 years have led to a decline in air and water quality. Exhaust from cars and factories, together with liquid and solid wastes from manufacturing and urban centers, cloud the air and clog water supplies. Oil spills cover spots of the ocean and shoreline. Since almost all living organisms depend upon clean air and water, pollution poses a severe threat to the survival of life on Earth.

★ **Climate Change.** The burning of fossil fuels like coal and oil (*gasoline*) has significantly increased amounts of carbon dioxide in the atmosphere. Carbon dioxide and water act together to wrap the planet in a blanket, holding in heat. With increased amounts of carbon dioxide, less heat is able to escape, leading to the "**greenhouse effect.**" If temperatures continue to rise, part of the polar ice caps could melt and sea levels would rise.

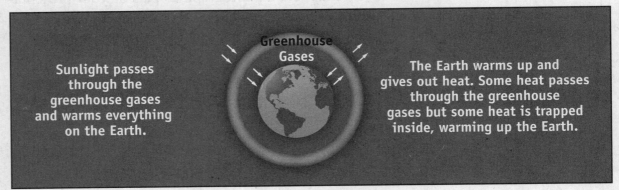

Sunlight passes through the greenhouse gases and warms everything on the Earth.

Greenhouse Gases

The Earth warms up and gives out heat. Some heat passes through the greenhouse gases but some heat is trapped inside, warming up the Earth.

★ **The Ozone Layer.** Free oxygen combines with oxygen molecules to create ozone in the Earth's upper atmosphere. This ozone absorbs much of the sun's ultraviolet radiation. Without an ozone layer, ultraviolet radiation would cause mutations in most living cells. The use of chlorofluorocarbons as coolants in refrigerators and air conditioners threatens the ozone layer. Each CFC molecule can break down thousands of ozone molecules. As a result, an ozone "hole" has appeared in the Earth's atmosphere, leading to increased incidents of skin cancer. Countries have agreed to ban CFCs, although some still use them.

★ **Pesticides.** Poisonous chemicals are used to control insects that threaten crops, but pesticides then become part of the water and soil, endangering other organisms, such as birds. Some pesticides may also be absorbed by the crops we grow for food. On the other hand, banning pesticides would make it difficult to grow enough food for everyone.

★ **Acid Rain.** When coal and oil are burned, they dump pollutants into the atmosphere. Many pollutants like sulfur dioxide turn into acids. These acids get washed out of the air when it rains. When these pollutants return, they are highly toxic, killing fish, destroying forests, eroding soil and further endangering the environment. The United States established the **Acid Rain Program** in 1990 to reduce pollutants causing acid rain. Acid rain is now two-thirds less than in 1976.

Acid rain damages forests, especially those at higher elevations.

DEPLETION OF NATURAL RESOURCES

Some resources, like trees, can renew themselves after a period of time. These are **renewable resources**. Other resources, like oil and coal, are **non-renewable**, and can only be used once. Many human activities, like the burning of fossil fuels, are using up Earth's non-renewable resources, while other activities are using renewable resources, like trees, at a faster rate than they can renew themselves.

DESTRUCTION OF NATURAL HABITATS

One of the greatest threats to the environment is the destruction of many natural habitats. As the human population expands, more and more forests, wetlands, and grasslands are destroyed to build farms, factories, and cities. The destruction of tropical rainforests is one of the most dramatic examples of the loss of natural habitats. Tropical rainforests have the greatest **biodiversity** (*diversity of species*) and the greatest concentration of plant life on Earth.

The destruction of areas like the Amazon Rainforest reduces the amount of oxygen in the atmosphere and leads to the extinction of many species. More plant and animal species now become extinct each year than at any other time since the extinction of dinosaurs. This is especially important, since genetic material in some of the species facing extinction may contain cures to many diseases.

THE QUEST FOR SUSTAINABLE DEVELOPMENT

In order to solve these problems and challenges, many countries now seek **sustainable development**. This means using resources in a way that can meet future as well as present human needs. If we continue to rely on non-renewable resources and to pollute the Earth's atmosphere, land, and water at current rates, there will not be sufficient resources available for use by future generations. To achieve sustainable development means using renewable resources at a slower rate, so that nature is able to replenish itself.

This requires that both industrialized and developing nations must find ways to achieve economic growth without the reckless, wasteful and harmful use of natural resources. Ultimately, sustainable development is the realization that, since humans depend on their physical environment, they must also act to protect that physical environment.

Polluting Earth's resources threatens future generations.

LEARNING WITH GRAPHIC ORGANIZERS

Complete the graphic organizers below. Describe how people are affected by the environment. Then describe how people modify their environment.

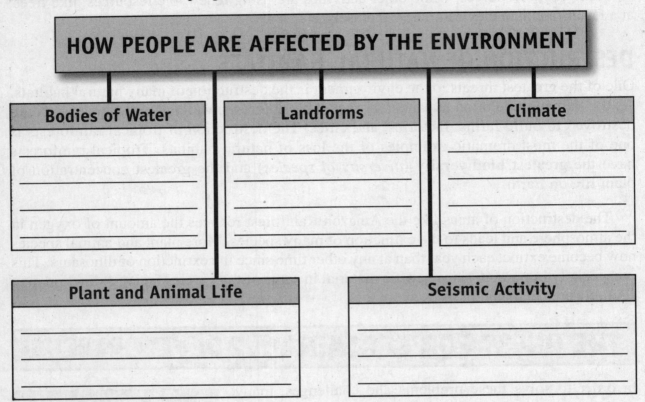

HOW PEOPLE ARE AFFECTED BY THE ENVIRONMENT

Bodies of Water

Landforms

Climate

Plant and Animal Life

Seismic Activity

HOW PEOPLE MODIFY THE ENVIRONMENT

Agriculture

Urban Growth

Building Dams

Energy

CHAPTER STUDY CARDS

Effects of Environment on People

★ **Bodies of Water.** People tend to settle close to water.

★ **Landforms.** People settle in flat, fertile valleys where farming is easier.

★ **Climate.** Average temperatures and precipitation have large impact on shelter, agriculture, and clothing.

★ **Plant and Animal Life.** The crops and livestock in an area greatly affect people's foods, clothing and homes.

★ **Seismic Activity.** Earthquakes and volcanoes may influence how homes are built.

How People Modify Their Environment

Just as people are affected by their environment, people can modify their environment in a number of ways:

★ **Agriculture.** People cut down forests and plow grassy plains to create farms.

★ **Urban Growth.** People build towns and cities.

★ **Building of Dams.** People seek to prevent floods and store water for drinking and irrigation.

★ **Energy.** People cut down trees, mine for coal, and drill for oil to meet their energy needs.

Natural Disasters

★ Natural disasters pose special problems to people's lives and property.

★ Earthquakes, tsunamis, and volcanoes caused by tectonic plate movement.
  • **Earthquakes.** e.g. Haiti in 2010.
  • **Tsunamis.** Indian Ocean tsunami (2004).
  • **Volcanoes.** e.g. eruption at Krakatoa in 1873 and in Iceland in 2010.

Extremes in Weather

★ Changes in weather patterns can bring devastating conditions to some areas.
  • **Hurricanes**   • **El Niño**
  • **Tornadoes**   • **La Niña**

Earth's Resources

★ **Renewable Resources** include animals and plants, which can replenish themselves.

★ **Non-renewable Resources** include resources like fossil fuels that do not replenish themselves: oil, coal, natural gas.

Sustainable Development

★ Reducing pollution and using Earth's resources at a slower rate so that they can be replenished.

★ Using resources to satisfy future as well as present needs.

CHECKING YOUR UNDERSTANDING

Directions: Put a circle around the letter that best answers the question.

1 The current destruction of rainforests around the world is primarily due to the —

`Geog 8(A)`

   A diseases carried by insects

   B wildfires occurring during dry seasons

   C devastation caused by high winds from tropical storms

   D human demand for timber and farmland

EXAMINE **the question.** This question asks for the cause of a current phenomena — the destruction of rainforests. RECALL **what you know.** You should recall that some countries, such as Brazil, are cutting down some of their rainforests to sell lumber and to create new ranches and farms. APPLY **what you know. Choice A** is wrong. Although diseases bourne by insects may attack some trees, that is not the main threat to rainforests. **Choice B** is wrong. Because of humidity, forest fires are not the main threat to most rainforests. **Choice C** is also wrong. Storms do not threaten most rainforests. **Choice D** is the best answer. The human demand for timber and farmland represents the greatest current threat to rainforests.

Now try answering some additional questions on your own:

2   The term El Niño is best defined as —

F   a massive earthquake

G   a warming of the surface of the Pacific Ocean

H   added amounts of carbon dioxide in the atmosphere

J   the melting of parts of the polar ice caps

`Geog 8(B)`

3   Which phrase best completes the partial outline below?

- EXAMINE The Question
- RECALL What You Know
- APPLY What You Know

> **I.** How People are Affected by their Environment
>
>   **A.** _____
>
>   **B.** Most people settle near bodies of water
>
>   **C.** Crops help determine what people eat and how they dress

A   Rise in greenhouse gases

B   The eruption at Krakatoa

C   Tsunamis are caused by tectonic plate movement

D   People often settle in flat, fertile areas

`Geog 8(A)`

4   Government officials are able to pinpoint detailed information about a precise location in order to prepare for an impending natural disaster. What kind of system does this refer to?

F   GPS

G   GIS

H   aerial photography

J   desalinization

`Geog 8(B)`

5   Sustainable development can best be characterized as —
   A   enacting laws to prevent water pollution
   B   using resources in order to meet current and future needs
   C   greater dependence on Earth's non-renewable resources
   D   eliminating industrial development in developing nations

Geog 8(C)

6   Which human activity would be most likely to have a negative impact on the environment?
   F   using reforestation to control soil erosion
   G   burning non-renewable resources to generate electric power
   H   preserving endangered species
   J   investigating the use of biological controls for pests

Geog 8(C)

7   What will most likely happen in the future if people continue to use fossil fuels at the same rate as today?
   A   People will have even more fossil fuels in the future.
   B   Countries will reach a state of sustainable development.
   C   Fossil fuels will gradually disappear while air pollution will increase.
   D   Scientists will discover how to renew fossil fuels.

Geog 8(C)

Use the information in the boxes and your knowledge of social studies to answer the following question.

Steel reinforcements are embedded in a home's joints to make them stronger.	**Skyscrapers use special lightweight materials that sway when stressed but do not break.**	**Several buildings are rigidly tied together to allow them to behave as a single mass.**

8   All of the measures indicated above are steps taken by builders in earthquake zones. These measures show that —
   F   people have the ability to prevent earthquakes
   G   humans can adapt to different challenges in the physical environment
   H   little can be done to minimize the effects of earthquakes
   J   structural engineering has been unable to respond to natural threats

Geog 8(A)

9   What lesson can be learned from the flooding of New Orleans after Hurricane Katrina in 2005?
   A   A hurricane is unlikely to reach New Orleans again.
   B   International cooperation can prevent hurricanes.
   C   The human response to a natural disaster can influence its destructiveness.
   D   Hurricanes are a major contributor to pollution in the Gulf of Mexico.

Geog 8(B)

UNIT 2 REVIEW
PULLING IT ALL TOGETHER

Write down *two* generalizations you learned about physical geography in this unit.

1. _____

_____

2. _____

_____

Select *one* of the *Essential Questions* explored in this unit by checking the box. Then answer it below.

ESSENTIAL QUESTIONS REEXAMINED

☐ What physical features would you find on a tour of the world's continents?

☐ What forces have helped shape Earth's landforms, climate, and plant life?

☐ How do people adapt to or modify their physical environment?

_____

_____

_____

_____

_____

_____

_____

_____

_____

_____

_____

_____

_____

_____

_____

Name _____ Date _____

UNIT 2 CONCEPT MAP

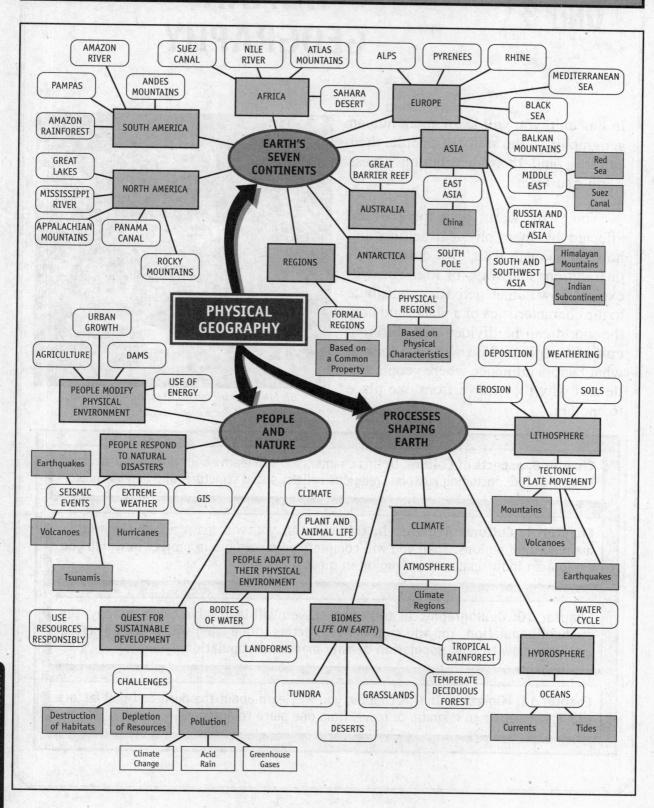

AMAZON RIVER — SUEZ CANAL — NILE RIVER — ATLAS MOUNTAINS — ALPS — PYRENEES — RHINE

PAMPAS
ANDES MOUNTAINS
AFRICA — SAHARA DESERT — EUROPE
MEDITERRANEAN SEA
AMAZON RAINFOREST
SOUTH AMERICA
BLACK SEA
GREAT LAKES
ASIA
BALKAN MOUNTAINS
Red Sea
MISSISSIPPI RIVER
NORTH AMERICA
EARTH'S SEVEN CONTINENTS
GREAT BARRIER REEF
EAST ASIA
MIDDLE EAST
Suez Canal
China
APPALACHIAN MOUNTAINS
PANAMA CANAL
AUSTRALIA
RUSSIA AND CENTRAL ASIA
ROCKY MOUNTAINS
REGIONS
ANTARCTICA
SOUTH POLE
SOUTH AND SOUTHWEST ASIA
Himalayan Mountains
Indian Subcontinent

PHYSICAL GEOGRAPHY

FORMAL REGIONS
PHYSICAL REGIONS
URBAN GROWTH
Based on a Common Property
Based on Physical Characteristics
AGRICULTURE — DAMS
DEPOSITION — WEATHERING
EROSION — SOILS
USE OF ENERGY
PEOPLE MODIFY PHYSICAL ENVIRONMENT
LITHOSPHERE
PEOPLE AND NATURE
PROCESSES SHAPING EARTH
PEOPLE RESPOND TO NATURAL DISASTERS
TECTONIC PLATE MOVEMENT
Earthquakes
SEISMIC EVENTS
EXTREME WEATHER
GIS
CLIMATE
Mountains
Volcanoes
PLANT AND ANIMAL LIFE
CLIMATE
Volcanoes
Hurricanes
ATMOSPHERE
Earthquakes
Tsunamis
PEOPLE ADAPT TO THEIR PHYSICAL ENVIRONMENT
Climate Regions
WATER CYCLE
USE RESOURCES RESPONSIBLY
QUEST FOR SUSTAINABLE DEVELOPMENT
BODIES OF WATER
BIOMES (LIFE ON EARTH)
HYDROSPHERE
LANDFORMS
TROPICAL RAINFOREST
CHALLENGES
TEMPERATE DECIDUOUS FOREST
OCEANS
TUNDRA
GRASSLANDS
Destruction of Habitats
Depletion of Resources
Pollution
Currents
Tides
DESERTS
Climate Change
Acid Rain
Greenhouse Gases

UNIT 3

HUMAN GEOGRAPHY

In this unit, you will learn about human geography — the study of people, their cultures, and their distribution across Earth's surface.

You will learn how people are affected by their physical setting and how they create their own **cultures** — or traditions and ways of life. You will explore how human activities contribute to the characteristics of a place, and how the world can be divided into different **cultural regions**. You will also look at what factors influence where people settle and why they move from one place to another.

Buddhism, with over 350 million followers, is one of the world's major religions.

Chapter 8. Aspects of Culture. In this chapter, you will learn about different aspects of human culture, including customs, religious beliefs, social structure, and gender roles.

Chapter 9. Cultural Regions. In this chapter, you will learn about the world's main cultural regions. Then you will complete your own group project in which you explore an individual cultural region in greater depth.

Chapter 10: Demography. In this chapter, you will learn about demography, the study of population. You will consider the factors influencing where people settle, and learn how to read population density maps and population pyramids.

Chapter 11: Migration. In this chapter, you will learn about the push-and-pull factors that cause people to migrate, or move, from one place to another.

Aspects of Culture

This chapter corresponds to Chapter 4 of HMH's *World Geography* and with special features found throughout the rest of that book, as indicated on the chart below.

❑ *Before Reading:* You might begin your study of culture by reading the TEKS, *Geographic Terminology*, *Important Ideas* and *Essential Questions* on pages 130–131.

❑ *During Reading:* Next read the text below, pages 131–132. Consider what culture is and the many aspects of culture, including roles, customs and institutions. Then turn to Chapter 4 of HMH's *World Geography*, pages 71–74, to learn even more about different elements of culture, including language. Also look at some of the case studies, such as "Feasts" (pp. 446–447) or "Masks" (pp. 656–657). Next return to this book and read pages 133–137 for an overview of the world's major religions. You can then read about the same religions on pages 75–77 of HMH's *World Geography*. You can also look at each of these religions in greater depth in the later sections of HMH's *World Geography*, as noted on the chart below. For example, you can learn more about Islam by reading pages 370–371 and 503–507. Finish your focus on religion by completing the graph and map exercise in *Applying What You Have Learned* on pages 137–138 below. Read about rural and urban settings, social classes, social mobility and gender roles on pages 140–142 of this book. You can look for specific examples of these on the pages of HMH's *World Geography* in the chart below. Finally, complete your study of culture by considering ethnic groups, heterogeneous societies, and the problems faced by minorities, including genocide, on page 143 below and on the pages of HMH's *World Geography* shown on the chart.

❑ *After Reading:* Reinforce your learning by reviewing the study cards and answering the test questions at the end of the chapter.

Topics	*Mastering the TEKS*	HMH's *World Geography*
Culture	pp. 131–132	pp. 71–77, 151 TX1–5 (Texas Culture)
Customs	p. 131	pp. 71, 240–241, 446–447, 656–657
Roles	pp. 131–132	
Institutions/Cultural Perceptions	p. 132	
Language	pp. 123, 143–144	pp. 73–74
Religion	pp. 132–139	pp. 75–76, 508–509
Animism	p. 133	p. 75
Hinduism	pp. 133–134	pp. 76, 560, 568–574, 583, 585, 708
Buddhism	p. 134	pp. 76–77, 572, 582, 584, 638, 648, 709
Judaism	p. 135	pp. 75, 315, 365, 510, 512, 532
Christianity	pp. 135–136	pp. 75, 370–371, 510, 532, 572, 585
Islam	pp. 136–137	pp. 75–76, 370–371, 503–507, 511, 517, 519, 576, 585–586
Sikhism	p. 137	pp. 569, 572
Rural Settings	p. 140	pp. 433, 565, 637, 644–645, 707
Urban Settings	p. 140	pp. 87–90, 176–179, 293, 301, 464, 506, 630–631, 637–638, 677
Social Classes	p. 141	p. 572
Social Mobility	p. 141	
Gender Roles	p. 142	pp. 135, 306, 441, 506–507, 531
Ethnic Group	p. 143	pp. 71, 311, 322, 386, 434–435
Homogeneous/Heterogeneous	p. 143	pp. 180–183, 224–225, 314, 454–455, 585
Minority	p. 143	pp. 293, 298, 301, 314–315, 718–720
Genocide or "Ethnic Cleansing"	p. 143	pp. 231, 298, 314–315, 319–322, 386–387

Using Multiple Sources of Information

• Use information from both books to write your own answers to the *Essential Questions* on page 130.

ASPECTS OF CULTURE

Chapter 8

TEKS COVERED IN CHAPTER 8

■ **Culture 16** The student understands how the components of culture affect the way people live and shape the characteristics of regions.
- **Culture 16(B)** Describe elements of culture, including, language, religion, beliefs and customs, institutions, and technologies.
- **Culture 16(C)** Explain ways various groups of people perceive the characteristics of their own and other cultures, places, and regions differently.
- **Culture 16(D)** Compare life in a variety of urban and rural areas in the world to evaluate political, economic, social, and environmental changes.

■ **Culture 17** The student understands the distribution, patterns, and characteristics of different cultures.
- **Culture 17(A)** Describe and compare patterns of culture such as language, religion, land use, education, and customs that make specific regions of the world distinctive.
- **Culture 17(B)** Describe major world religions, including animism, Buddhism, Christianity, Hinduism, Islam, Judaism, and Sikhism, and their spatial distribution.
- **Culture 17(C)** Compare economic, political, or social opportunities in different cultures for women, ethnic and religious minorities, and other underrepresented populations.
- **Culture 17(D)** Evaluate the experiences and contributions of diverse groups to multicultural societies.

■ **Culture 18(C)** Identify examples of cultures that maintain traditional ways....

ESSENTIAL QUESTIONS

◯— How is each of us a product of our culture?

◯— What beliefs and traditions are held by the world's great religions?

— IMPORTANT IDEAS —

A. **Culture** refers to a people's way of life — including how they meet their needs, and their language, religion, beliefs, customs, institutions, and technology.

B. Different major **religions** exist around the world, including animism, Buddhism, Christianity, Hinduism, Islam, Judaism, and Sikhism. Each religion has its own beliefs, moral code, and traditions.

C. Lifestyles differ between urban and rural areas.

D. Different cultures have different social structures and distributions of wealth.

E. Family structures and gender roles differ between cultures.

F. Ethnic and religious minorities enjoy different opportunities in various cultures.

GEOGRAPHIC TERMINOLOGY IN THIS CHAPTER

- **Culture**
- **Customs**
- **Animism**
- **Hinduism**
- **Buddhism**

- **Judaism**
- **Christianity**
- **Islam**
- **Sikhism**
- **Gender Roles**

- **Urban**
- **Rural**
- **Multicultural**
- **Social Class**
- **Social Mobility**

In this chapter you will learn about culture and examine these aspects:

Language and Customs	**Religious Beliefs**	**Social Structure**
Urban or Rural Setting	**Family Structures and Gender Roles**	**Treatment of Ethnic Groups**

WHAT IS CULTURE?

People develop complex ways to meet their needs, which they are able to hand down to their children. This gives rise to human cultures. **Culture** refers to a people's way of life. It includes how people meet their basic needs for food and shelter. Culture includes a people's language, literature, music, and art. It also includes their beliefs about the world and religion. Culture even includes a people's technology and their material objects.

CUSTOMS

Culture includes **customs** — things people usually do, such as how they dress, the foods they eat, and how they celebrate holidays and the great turning points in life — birth, coming-of-age, marriage, parenthood, and death.

How people dress is a key part of their culture.

ROLES

Roles are based on rules for the proper behavior of individuals in particular positions and situations. A mother, for instance, may be expected to behave in a certain way toward her children.

Once a role in society is learned, people know how they are supposed to act. These roles also form part of a society's culture.

INSTITUTIONS

Culture also includes **institutions** — organizations developed by each society to make social roles clear and to take care of social needs. Such institutions include:

FAMILIES	**SCHOOLS**	**GOVERNMENTS**
Families arrange for reproduction, the care of family members, and the upbringing of the young.	Schools teach the young the values of society and prepare them for the responsibilities of adulthood.	Governments protect us from outsiders, promote social cooperation, and regulate individual behavior.

Other institutions include the army, hospitals, and churches.

CULTURAL PERCEPTIONS

In fact, culture is everything that makes a people who and what they are. Culture not only affects lifestyles in a society, but also how people **perceive** those from other cultures. For example, a person from a very traditional culture might have difficulty understanding a person from a more modern culture. Sometimes differing cultural perceptions can even lead to misunderstandings or conflicts. During the Cold War (1945–1990), people from Communist and democratic, free enterprise cultures were suspicious and distrustful of each other. Each suspected the other of trying to spread its beliefs and practices throughout the world.

APPLYING WHAT YOU HAVE LEARNED

What are some of the cultural traits you share with members of your family, including your parents, brothers and sisters, cousins and other relatives?

_____

_____

_____

_____

_____

MAJOR WORLD RELIGIONS

One of the most important aspects of culture is religion. There are several characteristics that define a religion.

WHAT IS RELIGION?

A set of beliefs about the meaning of life, the nature of the universe, and the existence of the supernatural (including God or a Supreme Being).

A set of customs and practices that relate to the worship of God (or several gods) and a set of rules for the conduct of a good life.

An organization, such as a church or other place of worship, which oversees the conduct of religious practices.

Most religions designate some special places as sacred or holy.

Today, seven major religions have the greatest number of followers around the world: animism, Hinduism, Buddhism, Judaism, Christianity, Islam and Sikhism.

ANIMISM

Animism is the belief that many things in nature have their own spirit. Animism is one of the earliest forms of religion. Many different people have held animistic beliefs. In sub-Saharan Africa, tribes believed that animals, plants, and even places had their own spirits. Medicine men attempted to make contact with the spirit world, and young men had experiences with the spirits during ceremonies marking their passage from childhood to adulthood.

In Native American societies, people similarly believed that animals and objects in nature had their own spirits. Each group of families, known as a **clan**, identified with a particular animal and never harmed or ate that animal. In ancient Japan, people also believed that many spirits, known as **kami**, existed in nature. These animistic beliefs gave rise to the Japanese religion of **Shintoism**.

HINDUISM

Like animism, **Hinduism** is a very ancient religion. It teaches its disciples that the principles of life can be discovered through meditation. Hinduism has no single holy book, but Hindu writings like the **Upanishads** and the **Bhagavad-Gita** provide guidance and inspiration.

Many Hindus believe that God is revealed through the ancient laws and principles contained in Hindu scriptures, which speak of a struggle between order and chaos. Hinduism is the third largest religion in the world, and the most popular religion in modern India and Nepal. There are about one billion Hindus in the world today.

Gods. Hindus believe that there are many gods and goddesses. Each of these gods, however, is a manifestation (*form*) of one Supreme Being.

Reincarnation. Hindus believe that at death, a person's soul is reborn as another living thing. This creates an endless cycle of rebirth for each soul.

MAJOR BELIEFS OF HINDUISM

Karma. *Karma* refers to a person's behavior in life, which Hindus believe determines that person's form in the next life. People who live a good life will be reborn in a higher caste. Those who do not are reborn in a lower caste.

Sacred Objects. Hindus believe the Ganges River is sacred and has the power to wash away sin and evil. The cow is also considered sacred. As a result, religious Hindus do not eat beef.

BUDDHISM

Buddhism began in Nepal around 500 B.C. Prince **Siddhartha Gautama** lived a life of great luxury. One day, he looked out beyond his palace walls and was shocked by the human suffering he saw all around him. This prompted him to leave his family and to set out in search of truth. After six years of searching, he came to believe suffering was caused by human desire. Gautama became known as "Buddha." He taught that to end suffering, a person must come to accept the world as it is and to block out selfish desires. Buddhist missionaries carried his ideas throughout India and to China, Korea and Japan. Today, Buddhism remains popular in East and Southeast Asia.

Basic Philosophy. Buddhism is based on a philosophy of self-denial and meditation. Buddhists also believe in reincarnation.

Gods and Holy Books. Buddhists do not believe in a single Supreme Being (*God*). They also do not have a primary holy book. Their basic beliefs are found in books called **Sutras.**

MAJOR BELIEFS OF BUDDHISM

Four Noble Truths. These truths explain life's meaning. They explain that pain and suffering is caused by human desires, such as the desire for material wealth and selfish pleasures. Only by giving up wrongful desires can a person find peace and harmony.

Eightfold Path. To give up selfish human desires, Buddhists believe one should follow this path: give up wealth, act in a worthy manner, speak truthfully, live righteously, respect all living things, and meditate.

Nirvana. By following the Eightfold Path, an individual can escape the soul's endless reincarnations and achieve **nirvana** — a state of eternal peace and bliss.

JUDAISM

In the Middle East, three religions arose, linked by their belief in a single God, known as **monotheism**. From the Middle East, these monotheistic religions later spread to Europe, Africa, Asia, and the Americas.

The oldest of these, **Judaism**, was the first religion known to assert the existence of one God. The Jewish religion emerged 4,000 years ago in the area along the Mediterranean occupied by present-day Israel, Lebanon, and Jordan. According to Jewish tradition, the ancient Hebrews migrated from Israel to Egypt to escape food shortages from drought. They remained in Egypt for hundreds of years, where they became enslaved by the Egyptians. **Moses** later led the Jews out of Egypt and back to Israel. According to the Bible, as the Jewish people were leaving Egypt, Moses presented the Jewish people with the **Ten Commandments**, which he said came directly from God.

KEY FEATURES OF JUDAISM

Monotheism. Other ancient peoples were **animists** (*believing each object had its own spirit*), or **polytheists** (*believing in many gods*). In contrast, the Hebrews were **monotheists** (*believing in only one God*).	**Ten Commandments**. The Jewish religion emphasizes the importance of living justly and following God's commandments. These ten simple laws forbade believing in false gods, stealing, murder, adultery, and other forms of immoral behavior.	**Old Testament**. The history of the ancient Hebrews and their relationship with God is told in the first books of the **Bible**, known as the **Old Testament**. Jews refer to the first five books of the Old Testament as the **Torah**.

Of the world's 17 million Jews today, 40% live in Israel, and another 40% reside in the United States.

CHRISTIANITY

Christianity began about 2,000 years ago. It is based on the teachings of **Jesus**, a Jew born in Bethlehem. Jesus preached forgiveness, mercy, and sympathy for the poor and helpless. The Romans crucified Jesus for claiming he was the **Messiah** or Savior. After his death, a band of his followers, known as the **Apostles**, believed Jesus had risen from the dead to redeem mankind. This prompted his followers to spread the new Christian religion. Followers were attracted to the belief in an afterlife in which all believers, including the poor and humble, would be rewarded.

Eventually, Christianity became the major religion of the Roman Empire. Later, Christians divided into Orthodox Christians, Catholics and Protestants. The Pope is the head of the Catholic Church; Catholics believe he is God's deputy on Earth. Orthodox Christians are mainly found in Greece and Russia.

Protestants reject the Pope's authority and believe that people should interpret the Bible for themselves. Today, Christianity is the principal religion in Europe and the Americas. Many Christians also live in Africa and Asia. With two billion followers, Christianity is the world's most popular religion.

MAJOR BELIEFS OF CHRISTIANITY

Role of Jesus. Christians believe Jesus was the son of God, and sacrificed himself to save humankind from punishment for their sins. Christians believe that after his death, Jesus was resurrected and rose to Heaven.

Christian Conduct. Christians believe they will be saved and will go to Heaven after death if they have faith in Christ as their savior and treat others with love and respect. Christians believe in the Golden Rule — "do unto others as you would have them do onto you."

The Christian Bible. The sacred book of Christianity consists of the **Old Testament** (*the Jewish Bible*) and the **New Testament**, which describes the life of Christ and the works of the Apostles.

ISLAM

"**Islam**" means "submission" (to Allah) in Arabic. A follower of Islam is called a **Muslim**, or "one who submits (to God)." Islam was founded by **Mohammed**, around 600 A.D. Mohammed had a vision that commanded him to convert Arab tribes to the belief in a single God, known as "**Allah**" — the same God worshipped by Jews and Christians. Merchants grew jealous of Mohammed's growing influence in Mecca, where he lived. Mohammed fled to Medina in 622, where he emerged as a major religious leader. His followers believed that Mohammed was God's last and greatest prophet. His teachings are contained in the **Qu'ran** (*Koran*), Islam's holiest book. **The Five Pillars of Faith** are the basic religious duties that all followers of Islam must fulfill:

FIVE PILLARS OF FAITH

Confession of Faith Muslims must affirm: "There is no God but Allah and Mohammed is his prophet."

Prayer Muslims must pray five times a day, while facing east towards the city of Mecca.

Charity Muslims must give money to the poor and pay taxes to the mosque.

Fasting During the month of Ramadan, Muslims cannot eat or drink during daylight hours.

Pilgrimage If physically able, a Muslim must make a pilgrimage (*religious trip*) to Mecca.

Over one billion people follow the Islamic faith today. About one-fifth of them live in Arabic-speaking countries. Pakistan, Bangladesh, and Indonesia are also Muslim nations.

SIKHISM

Sikhs live mainly in Northern India. Sikhism combines both Hindu and Muslim beliefs. Like Hindus, Sikhs believe in reincarnation. Like Muslims, Sikhs believe in one God. Sikhs believe that God can be known through **meditation** (*a form of deep contemplation*). The goal of every Sikh is to build a close and loving relationship with God. Sikhs believe that everyone has equal status in the eyes of God. Therefore, unlike Hindus, Sikhs do not have **castes** — hereditary social classes. Sikh men do not cut their hair, which is often worn under a **turban**.

A Sikh prays at the Golden Temple in India, the holiest of Sikh shrines.

APPLYING WHAT YOU HAVE LEARNED

Using the information provided in the table, create a bar graph in the space below to show membership in the world's major religions. Be sure to create a title, and a horizontal and vertical axis for your bar graph.

Religion	Members	Religion	Members
Christianity	2 billion	Buddhism	350 million
Islam	1.2 billion	Judaism	17 million
Hinduism	1 billion	Sikhism	16 million

APPLYING WHAT YOU HAVE LEARNED

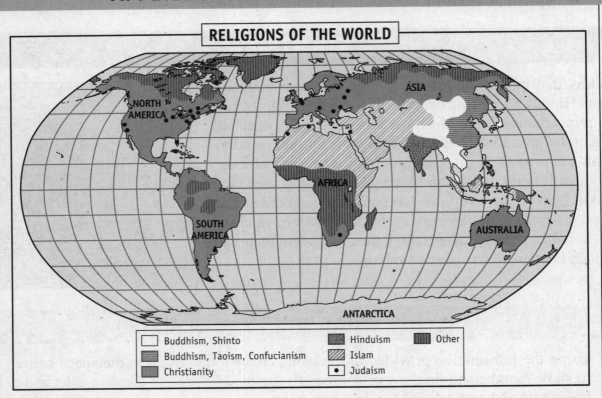

RELIGIONS OF THE WORLD

Buddhism, Shinto	Hinduism	Other
Buddhism, Taoism, Confucianism	Islam	
Christianity	Judaism	

Examine the map at the top of this page showing the distribution of major world religions. In a small group, pick one of these religions. Then discuss those physical and human factors that explain its distribution. Think about the place where the religion first started and then how it spread. Also consider that some religions attempt to appeal to all peoples, while others restrict their appeal to a single ethnic group. Write down your conclusions below.

_____

_____

_____

_____

_____

_____

_____

_____

_____

◆ **LEARNING WITH GRAPHIC ORGANIZERS**

Complete the graphic organizer below. For each religion, identify one or two of its beliefs. Then note where most of its followers are spatially distributed (*located*).

Hinduism
_____
_____
_____
_____
_____
_____

Buddhism
_____
_____
_____
_____
_____
_____

Animism
_____
_____
_____
_____
_____
_____

Sikhism
_____
_____
_____
_____
_____
_____

MAJOR RELIGIONS

Christianity
_____
_____
_____
_____
_____
_____

Judaism
_____
_____
_____
_____
_____
_____

RURAL OR URBAN SETTING

Another aspect of culture is how people live together. In some cultures, people live mainly in the countryside. Their homes are small huts of mud and thatch, or simple cottages. In these rural areas, people often work as farmers, livestock herders, or village craftsmen. They spend their entire lives communicating only with those in the immediate area, and maintain **traditional** ways. Many cannot read or write.

In other cultures, most people live in large cities with advanced levels of technology. They have roads, bridges, and buildings constructed of steel, concrete, and glass. They enjoy running hot and cold water, sewage systems, electricity, telephones and the Internet. People read newspapers, watch television, attend schools, and travel widely. They generally have more opportunities than those in rural villages do.

A rural farmer tills with traditional methods.

The skyline of Shanghai, China, today.

ACTING AS AN AMATEUR GEOGRAPHER

Examine the two pictures above. One shows a **rural** (*countryside*) setting and the other shows a modern **urban** (*city*) setting. Describe how these settings differ in how people generally make their livings, govern themselves, and influence their physical environment.

_____

_____

_____

_____

_____

_____

SOCIAL STRUCTURE

Another aspect of every culture is its **social structure**. In every known society, some members enjoy greater wealth and wider opportunities than others. People who share similar wealth, power, and prestige are said to belong to the same **social class**. The following social classes exist in most societies:

★ **Upper Class.** This group earns or inherits wealth and owns a large share of the property in that society. They lead a luxurious lifestyle and often serve in various leadership roles in the society.

★ **Middle Class.** This is an intermediate group of educated and mostly successful people — managers, professionals, shopkeepers, and small business owners.

★ **Working Class.** This group is composed of manual workers who work in factories, mining, or transportation, or who work as independent craftsmen.

★ **Peasants.** These are farm workers or owners of small farms mainly engaged in **subsistence agriculture** — farming to meet their immediate needs. They have little education and limited experience of the world outside their own villages.

★ **Lower Class.** These people are often uneducated and unskilled. They take the least desirable and worst-paying jobs. Often, members of lower classes face prejudice and other social handicaps from members of the higher social classes.

The differences between social classes vary from culture to culture. Before the Industrial Revolution, most cultures had an upper class and peasantry with a very small middle class. Industrial societies generally have an upper class, a substantial middle class, a large working class, and a lower class.

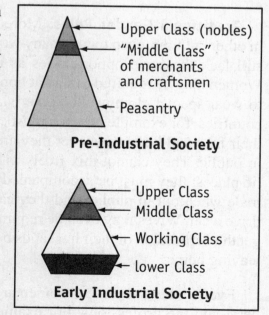

Pre-Industrial Society

- Upper Class (nobles)
- "Middle Class" of merchants and craftsmen
- Peasantry

Early Industrial Society

- Upper Class
- Middle Class
- Working Class
- lower Class

Social Mobility. In some societies, an immense gulf separates the different social classes. Traditional Hindu society, for example, was divided into castes. There was no movement from one caste to another. One's caste, inherited from one's parents, determined what work one could do and who one's friends were. "Untouchables" were treated as social outcasts. In other societies, it is easier to move from one class to another. **Social mobility** refers to how easy it is to change one's social class. A worker might save and eventually start a business, or send his children to college.

FAMILY STRUCTURE AND GENDER ROLES

Yet another aspect of culture is **family structure**. In some societies, parents live with just their young children. After the children finish high school, they live on their own. In other cultures, children, parents, and even grandparents remain in extended families under the same roof for their entire lives. Related families stay close together.

Gender roles are roles specifically assigned to men and women. In most societies, past gender roles were very restrictive. These societies gave greater opportunities to men than to women. Men worked and appeared in public, while women were expected to take care of the family and to perform household chores.

In most societies in the world, women traditionally took care of the children and home.

Changing Gender Roles. That situation began to change in the early 20th century, when women in America and several European nations gained the right to vote. In most modern societies today, men and women enjoy equal rights. They earn the same pay for the same work, while women can become doctors, lawyers, and teachers just like men. Even in these advanced societies, however, women often still remain under-represented in top jobs in government and business.

Traditional Gender Roles. Moreover, in other cultures, even today, many women still lack the same opportunities as men. Women may be required to stay at home or to wear special clothing. In some Islamic countries, for example, women must cover their face and body whenever they are out in public. They cannot mix freely in public places; they must be accompanied by a male when out in public; and they cannot drive a car. Wives may even be required to get the permission of their husbands before leaving home.

Women in public wearing a burqa.

Even in these societies, women are now striving for a greater role in government, business, and the professions. For example, several countries in which Muslims comprise a majority have recently been led by women. Almost one-third of Egypt's parliament are now made up of women. Indeed, throughout the world, women are making steady progress in achieving full equality with men.

MULTICULTURAL SOCIETIES

In looking at cultures, it is important to consider how a culture treats its ethnic and religious minorities. An **ethnic group** refers to a group of people with a common ancestry and a common culture, most often based on religion and language. Around the world, there are two basic types of societies:

★ In **homogeneous societies**, like Saudi Arabia, almost everyone belongs to the same ethnic group and shares the same language and traditions. Japan is another example of a highly homogeneous society. Non-Japanese, mostly Koreans and Chinese, make up only about one percent of Japan's population. The rest of Japan's population has the same common ancestry.

★ Other societies are **multicultural**, or **heterogeneous**, containing a mix of peoples and cultures. Ethnic groups are often mixed throughout the country, as in the United States and Brazil. Sometimes an ethnic group is connected to a particular region, like the Kurds in northern Iraq.

Some countries, such as those in Western Europe, were once largely homogeneous but are now becoming increasingly multicultural.

Even in multicultural societies, there is usually one dominant ethnic group and several minorities. A **minority** is any ethnic or religious group other than the dominant group. Some societies, like the United States, have strong safeguards in place to protect the rights of ethnic and religious minorities. In other societies, minorities are not protected, and may even be persecuted.

SPECIAL PROBLEMS FACED BY SOME MINORITIES

Ethnic Prejudice. The dominant group may treat minority group members as inferior. Minority members may be denied political power. Often the dominant group uses force to keep minority groups under control.

Discrimination and Exclusion. In many societies, ethnic and religious minorities are denied civil and political rights. Minority members may not be allowed to own property or to use public facilities like parks or public transportation. Intermarriage between groups may be illegal. In South Africa, under apartheid, the majority were actually treated as a minority.

Expulsion and Genocide. Sometimes actions against minority groups become extreme. This is may result in the expulsion of the minority group or their extermination. The most famous example was the Nazi attempt to eliminate the Jews of Europe by murdering more than 6 million. More recent examples include ethnic massacres and "**ethnic cleansing**" by Serbians in Bosnia of its Muslim population.

Despite the problems often faced by ethnic minorities, members of minority groups have made important contributions to every multicultural society.

ACTING AS AN AMATEUR GEOGRAPHER

Choose one ethnic or religious minority in any part of the world. Using the Internet or your library, describe the economic, political or social opportunities open to members of this minority.

Economic Opportunities (ways of making a living)	Social Opportunities (ways of relating to others)	Political Opportunities (ways to partake in government)

CHAPTER STUDY CARDS

What is Culture?

Culture. A people's way of life, which includes:

★ Language, literature, art, and music.

★ Beliefs, including religion.

★ Customs, including clothes, foods, forms of shelter, holidays, and traditions.

★ Institutions (social organizations), including family, schools and government.

★ Technology and material goods.

Aspects of Culture

★ **Family Structure.** How many generations live together; how family decisions are made.

★ **Social Structure.** How society is organized into different social groups or classes.

★ **Multicultural (*heterogeneous*) Society.** A society made of various ethnic or cultural groups. Some societies give minority ethnic and religious groups more rights and opportunities than others.

★ **Gender Roles.** Roles assigned to men and women. In a traditional society, women are expected to care for children and do household chores.

Hinduism

Most popular religion in modern India.

★ Believe in many gods, each of which is a form of one Supreme Being.

★ **Reincarnation.** A person's soul is reborn as another living thing.

★ **Karma.** People who lead a good life will be reborn into a higher caste, while those who do not are reborn into a lower caste.

★ **Castes.** Hereditary social classes.

★ **Sacred Object.** Believe the cow is sacred; Hindus will not eat beef.

Buddhism

★ A leading religion in Tibet, Japan, Thailand, and China.

★ Buddhists follow the teachings of **Buddha**, who taught that selfish desires were the source of all human suffering.

★ **Eightfold Path.** Tells Buddhists to give up wealth, act worthily, live righteously, and respect all living things.

★ **Nirvana.** A person can achieve final reincarnation and eternal bliss by following the Eightfold Path.

Judaism

★ First religion to teach **monotheism** — belief in one God.

★ **Old Testament.** History of Jewish people told in the first books of the Bible.

★ **Ten Commandments.** Established a moral code of conduct. Judaism emphasizes living justly:
- Believe in one God.
- Honor one's parents.
- Do not kill.
- Do not steal.
- Do not commit adultery.

Christianity

Begun by **Jesus**, a Jew born in Bethlehem.

★ Christians believe Jesus was the son of God, sent to save humankind.

★ Christians believe Jesus rose from the dead to go to Heaven.

★ Christians believe they will be saved and go to Heaven if they have faith and treat others with love and respect.

★ Includes Catholics, Protestants, and Eastern Orthodox Christians; main region in Europe and the Americas; also found in Africa and Asia.

★ It is the world's most popular religion.

Islam

Founded by Mohammed around 600 A.D.

★ Muslims believe in one God, **Allah**.

★ **Qu'ran** (or **Koran**). Holy book which contains God's message as given to Mohammed.

★ **Five Pillars of Faith.** Basic religious duties that Muslims must fulfill:
- There is no other God but Allah.
- Pray five times a day facing Mecca.
- Must give money to the poor.
- Fast during the holy month of Ramadan.
- Must make a pilgrimage (*trip*) to Mecca.

★ Popular in the Middle East, South and Southeast Asia.

Sikhism

Found mostly in Northern India.

★ Sikhism combines beliefs from Hinduism and Islam.

★ Like Hindus, Sikhs believe in reincarnation, but do not have castes.

★ Following Islam, Sikhs believe in one God. Everyone has equal status in the eyes of God.

★ Men do not cut their hair and often wear turbans over their hair.

CHECKING YOUR UNDERSTANDING

Directions: Put a circle around the letter that best answers the question.

1   Culture is sometimes referred to as "a blueprint for living" because it —

    Cult 16(B)

    A   thrives best in traditional societies

    B   is determined by heredity

    C   provides plans for the exploration of new territories

    D   includes all aspects of how people behave in society

This question asks you to identify how the phrase "a blueprint for living" applies to the term "culture." You should recall that culture is a people's way of life. **Choice A** is wrong. Culture is an essential aspect of every society — traditional or modern. **Choice B** is wrong. Culture is learned, not inherited. **Choice C** is also wrong. Although it is blueprint, culture is not restricted to plans for exploration. **Choice D** is therefore the best answer. Culture is all-encompassing and includes all aspects of how people behave in a society.

Now try answering some additional questions on your own:

2   Which is a valid generalization about customs?

    Cult 16(B)

    F   They cannot be changed.

    G   They usually lead to political reforms.

    H   They have little influence on the development of the economy.

    J   They include both how people dress and the foods they eat.

Use the information in the passage and your knowledge of social studies to answer the following question.

"East Africa is changing…. When my children go … with us to visit my parents [in their village] they feel out of place. They see a bare floor, the different food, and they cannot understand it as we can…. They will never scorn [reject] their origins, but it is just no longer their way of life. They have something better to look forward to."

— A Kenyan mother speaking about her children, 2010

3   Which development most likely contributed to the changes discussed in this quotation?

    Cult 16(D)

    A   boundaries drawn by Europeans in colonial Africa

    B   climate change in Africa

    C   the movement of Africans from rural to urban areas

    D   political control by European governments

4 One similarity between Buddhism in India and animism in Africa is that both —
   F   use the Ten Commandments to establish law codes   `Cult 17(B)`
   G   stress the importance of the Eightfold Path
   H   have no basic religious text
   J   base social rank on a caste system

5 Which practice is associated with the Islamic faith?
   A   refusing to eat meat on Fridays
   B   praying five times a day
   C   following the Eightfold Path
   D   worshipping many gods

> • EXAMINE The Question
> • RECALL What You Know
> • APPLY What You Know

`Cult 17(B)`

6 The religions of Judaism and Christianity share a common belief in —
   F   the New Testament   **H**   reincarnation   `Cult 17(B)`
   G   the existence of one God   **J**   the role of Jesus

7 Buddhism teaches that salvation can be achieved by —
   A   following the Ten Commandments   `Cult 17(B)`
   C   learning to give up selfish desires
   B   worshipping only one God
   D   making a pilgrimage to Mecca

Use the information and your knowledge of social studies to answer the following question.

> "In the name of Allah, Most Gracious, Most Merciful.
> Praise be to Allah, The Cherisher and Sustainer of the Worlds;
> Most Gracious, Most Merciful; Master of the Day of Judgment.
> Thee do we worship, And Thine aid we seek.
> Show us the straight way, the way of those on whom Thou hast bestowed
> Thy Grace, those whose [portion] Is not wrath, And who go not astray."
>
> — *Qur'an* (Koran)

8 Which concept is best reflected in this passage from the Koran?
   F   reincarnation   **H**   monotheism   `Cult 17(B)`
   G   karma   **J**   animism

9 Which is an important difference in outlook between people living in rural and urban communities?
   A   People in rural communities more often follow traditional beliefs.   `Cult 16(D)`
   B   People in urban communities are more likely to work at home.
   C   People in rural communities enjoy a greater variety of products.
   D   People in urban communities are generally more religious.

Use the information and your knowledge of social studies to answer the following question.

> **In 2006, Iran's Parliament passed a law discouraging women from wearing Western clothing, and funded a campaign to promote the wearing of Islamic-style garments.**

> **In 2010, French lawmakers passed a ban on veils that cover the face — including the burqa, the full-body covering worn by some Muslim women in public schools and hospitals**

10 Which reason best explains both of the events described above?

    F Lawmakers seek to limit religious freedom in France. `Cult 16(C)`

    G Iran's government is opposed to Western culture in their country.

    H Different cultures perceive their own and other cultures differently.

    J There is a global effort to have people dress in a similar fashion.

11 In some parts of India today, the caste system is still followed; in the social hierarchy of colonial Latin America, the status of a person was determined by birth. What do these two examples demonstrate?

    A Diversity is welcomed in most multicultural societies. `Cult 18(C)`

    B In a multicultural society, all groups may face intolerance.

    C Traditional practices in many societies reinforce social differences.

    D Minority groups face similar experiences in all multicultural societies.

12 Which of the following examples describes an institution at work?

    F People in the Middle East enjoy eating pita bread. `Cult 16(B)`

    G Religious Roman Catholics attend church each Sunday.

    H Teenagers in Western Europe often text message their friends.

    J Many herders in Africa's Sahel region have moved away to avoid drought.

Use the information and your knowledge of social studies to answer the following question.

> "We, the governments in the Fourth World Conference on Women recognize that the status of women has advanced in some important respects in the past decade, but that progress has been uneven, inequalities between women and men persist and obstacles remain, with serious consequences for the well-being of people …"
>
> — *The Beijing Declaration and Platform for Action, September 1995*

13 The "Beijing Platform for Action" was necessary because —

    A progress in women's rights has almost ended gender discrimination `Cult 17(C)`

    B some cultures still maintain traditions that limit women's opportunities

    C women have made modest progress in achieving economic and social equality

    D scientists have found that women and men often look at problems differently

Cultural Regions

This chapter identifies different types of regions and provides an overview of the main cultural regions found around the world today. In this sense, it is similar to Chapter 5 above. That chapter described the world's physical regions, while this one describes the world's cultural regions. This chapter corresponds to the second chapter found in each regional unit of HMH's *World Geography*. This deals with the human geography of each region. Sections look at smaller areas in each region, such as individual countries.

❑ *Before Reading:* You might begin your study of the world's chief cultural regions and their characteristics by reading the TEKS, *Geographical Terminology*, *Important Ideas* and *Essential Questions* on pages 150–151. Pay special attention to the types of regions.

❑ *During Reading:* Then read the text below, pp. 151–153, to learn about the different types of regions. You can look at HMH's *World Geography*, pp. 7–8, to reinforce your understanding of these different types. Then read pages 154–162 in this book for an overview of the world's cultural regions. If your course is thematic or concept-based, turn to sections of HMH's *World Geography* for additional information about cultural regions of special interest to you. For example, you might want to learn more about the culture of the Middle East, including its traditions, politics, and economics (pp. 503–519), or about the culture of China (pp. 635–639). If your course is organized by region, then you should read this chapter for a general overview of the world's main cultural regions, and then turn to HMH's *World Geography* to focus on the specific region your class is studying. Finish your study of human regions by completing the *Acting as an Amateur Geographer* activity on pages 163–164 below.

❑ *After Reading:* Reinforce your learning by reviewing the study cards and answering the test questions at the end of the chapter.

Topics	Mastering the TEKS	HMH's World Geography
Cultural Regions	pp. 150–153	p. 7
Texas	p. 152	pp. 151, TX1–5
Middle East	pp. 152–153	pp. 503–507, 510–519
Types of Regions		
Formal Regions	pp. 153	p. 7
Functional Region	pp. 153	p. 8
Perceptual Region	pp. 153	p. 8
Survey of World Cultural Regions	pp. 154–162	
North America	pp. 154–155	pp. 161, 135–169
Latin America	pp. 155–156	pp. 217–239
Europe	pp. 156–157	pp. 289–315
Russia and the Commonwealth of Independent States	pp. 157–158	pp. 361–379
North Africa	pp. 158–159	p. 438
Sub-Sahara Africa	p. 159	pp. 431–437, 442–457
Middle East/Southwest Asia	p. 159	pp. 503–507, 503–519
East Asia: China	p. 159	pp. 635–639
East Asia: Japan	p. 160	pp. 651–655
South Asia	p. 161	pp. 567–587
Southeast Asia	p. 162	pp. 705–715
Australia and Oceania	p. 162	pp. 712–715, 718–732

Using Multiple Sources of Information

• Use information from both books to write your own answers to the *Essential Questions* on page 150.
• Use information from both books to create your own illustrated atlas showing the main cultural regions of the world, or to make a poster attracting tourists to one cultural region.

 CHAPTER 9 # CULTURAL REGIONS

- ■ **History 1(A)** Analyze the effects of physical and human geographic patterns ... including significant physical features and environmental conditions that influenced migration patterns and shaped the distribution of culture groups today.
- ■ **Geography 5** The student understands how political, economic, and social processes shape cultural patterns and characteristics in various places and regions.
  - • **Geography 5(A)** Analyze how the character of a place is related to its political, economic, social, and cultural elements.
- ■ **Geography 9** The student understands the concept of region as an area of Earth's surface with related geographic characteristics.
  - • **Geography 9(A)** Identify physical and/or human factors such as climate, vegetation, language, trade networks, political units, river systems, and religion that constitute a region.
  - • **Geography 9(B)** Describe different types of regions, including formal, functional, and perceptual regions.
- ■ **Government 13(A)** Interpret maps to explain the division of land, including man-made and natural borders, into separate political units such as cities, states, or countries.
- ■ **Culture 16** The student understands how the components of culture affect the way people live and shape the characteristics of regions.
  - • **Culture 16(A)** Describe distinctive cultural patterns and landscapes associated with different places in Texas, the United States, and other regions of the world, and how these patterns influenced the processes of innovation and diffusion.
  - • **Culture 16(B)** Describe elements of culture, including language, religion, beliefs and customs, institutions, and technologies.
- ■ **Culture 17** The student understands the distribution, patterns, and characteristics of different cultures.
  - • **Culture 17(A)** Describe and compare patterns of culture such as language, religion, land use, education, and customs that make specific regions of the world distinctive.
  - • **Culture 17(D)** Evaluate the experiences and contributions of diverse groups to multicultural societies.
- ■ **Social Studies Skills 21(B)** Locate places of contemporary geopolitical significance on a map.
- ■ **Social Studies Skills 23(A)** Plan, organize, and complete a research project that involves asking geographic questions; acquiring, organizing, and analyzing information; answering questions; and communicating results.

In this chapter, you will learn about cultural regions and take a look at the various continents concerning their language, religion, and institutions.

ESSENTIAL QUESTIONS

- ◯— How do different cultural regions around the world compare to one another?
- ◯— Where can you find the main countries and major cities of the world?

— IMPORTANT IDEAS —

A. The characteristics of a place include its cultural, political, economic, and social elements.

B. A **cultural region** is a region with people who share common cultural characteristics. Such characteristics include language, political system, religion, foods, customs, and participation in trading networks.

C. A **functional region** is an area with a common function, often organized around a key focal point. People may perceive the characteristics of their own and other cultures and regions differently. A **perceptual region** is a region based on commonly held human attitudes and feelings about an area.

D. Language, religion, government, land use, education and customs make each cultural region distinctive. Geographers recognize several major cultural regions in the world today, including the Middle East, Latin America, North America, Europe, Russia, Sub-Saharan Africa, China, Japan, South Asia, and Southeast Asia.

GEOGRAPHIC TERMINOLOGY IN THIS CHAPTER

- ■ Cultural Region
- ■ Functional Region
- ■ Perceptual Region
- ■ Middle East
- ■ Suez Canal
- ■ Latin America
- ■ Panama Canal
- ■ Sub-Saharan Africa
- ■ Oceania

CULTURAL REGIONS

Physical geography and the level of technology greatly influence a people's culture. Landforms, nearness to bodies of water, climate and natural resources interact with a people's beliefs, traditions and history to create distinct ways of life.

A **region** is an area that has common characteristics that distinguish it from neighboring areas. A **cultural region** is defined by the common characteristics of the people living there.

The Amish people of Pennsylvania comprise a cultural region.

The people in a cultural region may speak the same language, practice the same religion, share the same customs, or live under the same government. They generally have more contacts with each other than with people outside the region.

The **State of Texas**, for example, could be considered as a distinct cultural region. Once home to several groups of Native American Indians, it later became the northernmost part of Mexico. There were so few Spanish settlers that Americans were invited to settle in Texas in the 1820s. Soon, the number of American settlers in Texas grew so large that in 1836 they declared their independence. Today, Texas is part of the United States. Texans are united by shared historical experiences, by their common state and national gov-

Texans sign their Declaration of Independence from Mexico.

ernment, by their educational system, and by common ways of life. Texans are especially proud of their multicultural heritage, which adds to the diversity and richness of the state.

The Middle East: A Cultural Region. Often cultural regions correspond to physical regions. For example, the Middle East might be viewed as a physical region. This region has a warm, dry climate with many deserts and mountain areas. The Middle East also has several fertile river valleys and mild coastal areas. Besides being a physical region, the Middle East is also cultural region. It is the crossroads of three continents — Africa, Asia and Europe. In fact, it is where human civilization first developed.

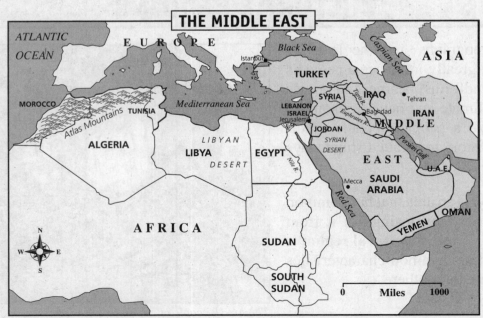

A large number of people in the Middle East today have a common history and heritage. The vast majority of these people are Muslims. Most speak Arabic. At one time, almost all of this region was ruled by the Ottoman Empire. Finally, the peoples of the Middle East communicate and trade more with each other than with peoples outside the region.

TYPES OF REGIONS

Geographers define regions in different ways, depending on the type of criteria used to set their boundaries.

FORMAL REGION

A **formal region** is one with clear boundaries. It is defined by at least one common human or physical characteristic. This may be a common government, such as a political unit. To learn more about formal regions, see page 82.

FUNCTIONAL REGION

A **functional region** is an area defined by one function that may cross political boundaries. This might be a drainage basin of a great river, connecting several states. Often a functional region is organized around a focal point, such as a city and its metropolitan area. People in the region are linked by commuting patterns, television and radio broadcasts, shopping, and entertainment.

PERCEPTUAL REGION

A **perceptual region** is based on people's attitudes and emotions about a place, such as the "Deep South," "Dixie," or "The Big Apple" (New York City). Unlike formal or functional regions, a perceptual region may not be based on real facts or conditions. In fact, if you asked people to draw a line around the "Deep South" or the "Midwest" on a map of the United States, their boundaries might differ.

APPLYING WHAT YOU HAVE LEARNED

How do **formal**, **functional**, and **perceptual regions** differ from one another? Select and describe an example for each one. _____

_____

_____

_____

_____

SURVEY OF WORLD CULTURAL REGIONS

Cultural regions can be grouped according to a variety of characteristics. The map below shows one way geographers have grouped the world's main cultural regions. One of these, the Middle East, has already been described on pages 143–144.

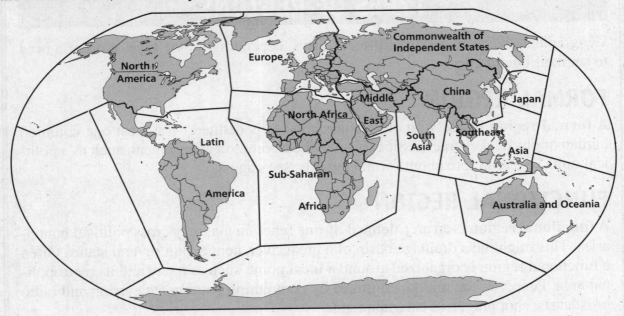

NORTH AMERICA

Canada and the **United States** are often considered as belonging to the same cultural region. The majority language in both countries is English. Both countries were once British colonies. The majority of people in both countries follow the Christian religion. Both were once home to Native American Indians and had sparsely settled spaces in the West, which were gradually settled by pioneers. Both countries have democratically elected governments. Citizens in both countries follow similar occupations and enjoy similar ways of life.

Canada is the world's second largest country in area. Its population is concentrated along its southern border. Canada plays a key role in the world's economy and is a major trading partner of the United States. Canada has a long history of conflict between its English and French-speaking citizens, a division that continues today. In Quebec, the official language is French. The majority of the rest of Canada speaks English. At the federal (*national*) level, the country is officially bilingual.

Within the **United States**, geographers often identify several distinct cultural regions, such as New England, the Middle Atlantic States, the Midwest, the South, Texas, the Southwest, and the Far West. Each of these regions has its own distinct cultural patterns, including regional accents, favorite foods and fashions, and typical occupations.

Regions of Texas. Even within Texas itself, geographers can identify several regions: the Gulf Coast, South Texas Plains, Piney Woods, Prairies and Lakes, Hill Country, Big Bend Country, and the Panhandle Plains. Each of these regions has its own landscapes and traditions. For example, the Big Bend Country in the southwest is dry, while the Gulf Coast is warm, humid, and densely populated.

Major Cities. In Canada, major cities include Montreal, Toronto, Quebec, and Vancouver. Major cities in the United States include New York City, Los Angeles, Dallas, Philadelphia, Chicago, Miami, and Washington, D.C. Major cities of Texas include Houston, Dallas, Fort Worth, Austin, San Antonio, and El Paso.

LATIN AMERICA

The name "**Latin America**" is applied to all of the Americas south of the United States. This large cultural region consists of four main areas — Mexico, Central America, the West Indies (*Caribbean*), and South America.

This region is called "Latin America" because it was once colonized by Spain and Portugal, whose languages come from Latin. European conquerors failed to recognize Native American ownership of their land, since they saw "Indians" as non-Christian and uncivilized.

Many Latin Americans today are of mixed Native American Indian and European descent. Most speak Spanish or Portuguese and follow the Catholic religion. People in this region share a common history and many traditions.

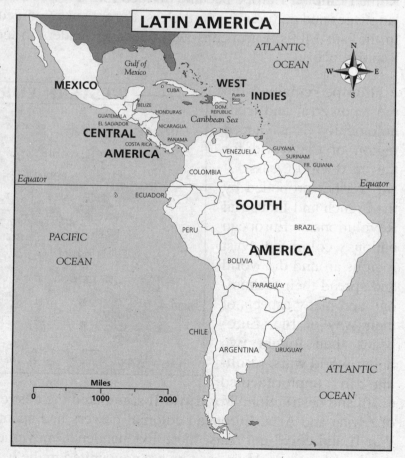

Major Features. A **country** is a human-made political unit, with its own government and boundaries. Major countries in Latin America include Mexico, Brazil, Argentina, Chile, Peru, Venezuela and Cuba. Major cities in the region include Mexico City, Rio de Janeiro (*Brazil*), Buenos Aries (*Argentina*), Lima (*Peru*), and Santiago (*Chile*). The **Panama Canal** is another important human-made feature in this region. This 48-mile canal through Panama joins the Atlantic and Pacific Oceans and serves as a major route for international trade.

EUROPE

Europe and Asia share the same land mass, which is so large that geographers have divided it into two continents. Europe's location, close to Africa and the Middle East, enabled Europeans to borrow heavily from the cultures of both of these regions.

The Greeks were the first Europeans to develop their own civilization. Their culture has had a lasting impact on Western civilization. It set standards against which later peoples measured themselves. Much of Europe was later united by the Romans. After the fall of the Roman Empire, Europe became divided into a series of warring kingdoms with their own languages and cultures. Nevertheless, Europeans remained united by the Christian religion. In the late 1400s, Europeans again became leaders in technology and culture during the Renaissance.

Europe remained the most powerful and technologically advanced region of the world for the next 500 years. It was further propelled by the French and Industrial Revolutions. European nations colonized vast regions around the world and spread their technology and many aspects of their way of life. Europeans then fought two major world wars, resulting in unprecedented

death and destruction. World War II stimulated the desire for independence in the colonies of Africa and Asia. European colonial powers had spent their energies fighting in World War II and could not resist these independence movements. Today, Europe consists of a number of nations. Most of them are now united in the **European Union**. In general, Europeans have democratic governments, high standards of living, strong educational systems, and small families. Many Europeans follow the Christian religion.

Major Features. Europe's countries include Britain, France, Germany, Belguim, Austria, Spain, Portugal, Italy, Ireland, Norway, Denmark, Sweden, and Poland. Major cities include London, Madrid, Paris, Copenhagen, Rome, and Berlin.

APPLYING WHAT YOU HAVE LEARNED

Use an atlas or the Internet to find information, to complete the outline map below:

★ Write in the name of each of the countries mentioned above;

★ Place the name of each city mentioned above in its proper location.

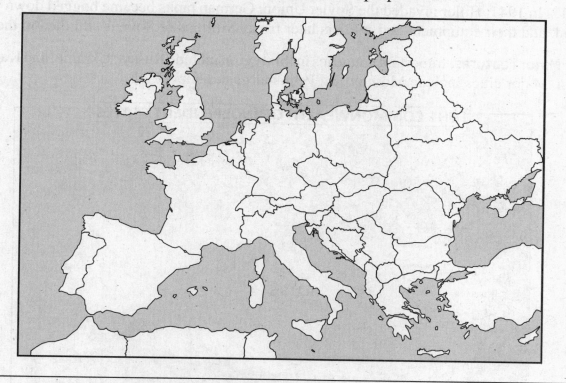

RUSSIA AND THE COMMONWEALTH OF INDEPENDENT STATES (CIS)

Extending from Northern Europe eastward into Asia, Russia was separated from the rest of Europe for much of its history. Russia's rulers adopted Eastern Orthodox Christianity from Constantinople. Russia was later conquered by the Mongols of Asia.

A new ruler, known as the **Tsar**, later emerged with absolute power. Originally, Russia was a small state centered in Moscow. In the 18th century, Russia's tsars introduced Western European ways. Russia then set about conquering neighboring territories, greatly expanding its size. Meanwhile, the bulk of Russia's vast peasant population continued to live in great poverty.

During World War I, the Tsar's government collapsed. Soon after, Russia became the world's first Communist country — known as the **Soviet Union**. The Soviet Union and other nearby Communist states developed their own distinct culture based on state-ownership, Communist ideals, and totalitarian government. In 1991, after nearly 80 years as a Communist dictatorship, the Soviet Union dissolved into Russia and several smaller states. These remain loosely associated as the **Commonwealth of Independent States**. These states share a common history, often speak several related languages, and have common ethnic minorities.

Foreign invaders have sometimes failed to conquer Russia because of its vast interior and cold winters. Napoleon lost half a million soldiers to the bitter cold temperatures in 1812. In 1941, Hitler invaded the Soviet Union. German tanks became bogged down in the mud, and their equipment and soldiers later froze. Millions of Soviets still died in the war.

Major Features. Important countries in this region include Russia, Ukraine, and Kazakhstan. Major cities include Moscow, St. Petersburg, and Kiev.

THE COMMONWEALTH OF INDEPENDENT STATES

NORTH AFRICA

The region of **North Africa** is found north of the Sahara Desert. In this region, ancient Egypt once gave rise to one of the world's first civilizations. Because contacts between African peoples were limited by geographical barriers, each people or tribe developed its own culture, language, and traditions. North Africa was then colonized by Britain, France, and Italy. Today, the peoples of North Africa are mainly of Arab descent and the dominant religion is Islam. Because of these factors, this region is often considered to be closely tied to the Middle East.

Major Features. Countries in North Africa include Algeria, Egypt, Libya, Morocco, and Ethiopia. Major cities include Cairo, Alexandria, and Addis Abba. Completed in 1869, the 120-mile **Suez Canal** connects the Mediterranean Sea with the Indian Ocean.

SUB-SAHARAN AFRICA

The area of Africa south of the Sahara Desert, with its different climate, topography, and non-Arab populations, is seen as forming a separate and distinct cultural region. Most of this region has a warm climate. Many people in this region were once subject to the slave trade or European colonial rule. People remain divided into a large number of separate ethnic groups, or tribes, each with its own language and culture. They often share similar religious beliefs. Africans have been influenced by both Islam and Christianity, as well as by local animist traditions.

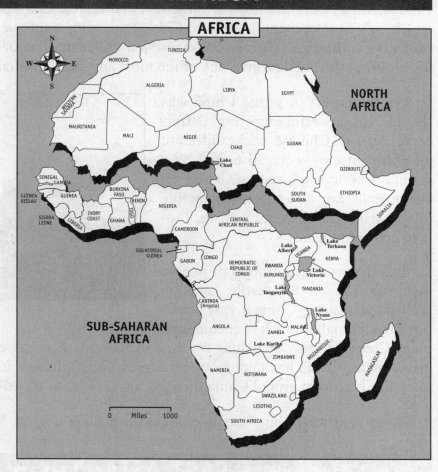

Major Features. Countries in Sub-Saharan Africa include Nigeria, Kenya, Uganda, and South Africa. Major cities include Nairobi (*Kenya*), Lagos (*Nigeria*), and Cape Town (*South Africa*).

THE MIDDLE EAST

You already learned about the Middle East (or *Southwest Asia*) as a cultural region on pages 143 and 144. Once ruled by the Ottoman Empire, most people in the Middle East today are Muslims, with a minority of Arab Christians and Jews. The major language spoken is Arabic.

Major Features. Important countries in the Middle East include Turkey, Iran, Iraq, Saudi Arabia, Israel, and Syria. Major cities include Jerusalem (*Israel*), Baghdad (*Iraq*), and Tehran (*Iran*).

EAST ASIA: China

China has been the world's most populous country for most of its history. Today, one of every five people in the world is Chinese. Mountains, deserts, and seas once helped isolate China from the rest of the world. Eastern China consists of a vast plain with fertile river valleys. Most of China's population settled in this area. China's isolation had a great impact on China's development. It allowed China to develop a unique culture separate from other centers of civilization. This isolation also led to a centralization of power and concentration of resources that made China one of the most advanced civilizations for many centuries.

For thousands of years, China was ruled by all-powerful emperors. Different groups of Chinese spoke different dialects, but they were all united by a common system of writing, based on characters. They also shared distinctive religious beliefs — Confucianism, Taoism, and Buddhism.

The largest concentration of people in China live on the fertile lands in the east and along China's vast coastline. Traditionally, this has encouraged

Beijing, China's skyline.

many Chinese to rely on fishing for their livelihoods. Since opening its economy to foreign investments, China has undergone an economic revolution. Its educated, low-wage labor force has helped to propel China forward, making it the world's fastest-growing economy.

Major Features. China's main cities today include Beijing, Shanghai, and Hong Kong.

EAST ASIA: Japan

Japan consists of four main islands and thousands of smaller ones. Although ancient Japan was greatly influenced by China, it developed its own language, system of writing, religious beliefs, and customs. It was the first Asian nation to borrow Western ways and to industrialize.

Although 85% of Japan's land is covered by mountains, it has a relatively large population. Its high population density has led to a social closeness and promoted the ability of its people to work together. Japan lacks many natural resources necessary for modern industry and must import much of what it needs. Japan's major cities include Tokyo, Osaka, Kyoto, and Hiroshima.

Traditional Japanese dress.

ACTING AS AN AMATEUR GEOGRAPHER

★ Why do geographers divide Africa into two separate major cultural regions?

_____

_____

★ Using the Internet or your school or local library, look up a city listed for China or Japan. Then answer the questions below:

• What is the city's current population? _____

• How old is the city? _____   • What are some of the city's key features?

_____

_____

SOUTH ASIA

The **Himalaya Mountains** are the highest in the world. They separate the Indian subcontinent from the rest of Asia. This has allowed peoples on both sides of the mountains to develop their own separate languages, customs, and cultures. The main rivers of the Indian subcontinent, the **Indus** and **Ganges**, were the sites of some of the world's earliest civilizations. In ancient times, Aryan invaders conquered the subcontinent and introduced the Hindu religion and caste system.

The subcontinent's nearness to the Middle East next led to the spread of Islam into the region. In the 1700s, much of India fell under British rule. When India later became independent in 1947, it separated into Hindu India and Muslim Pakistan. Former East Pakistan later became **Bangladesh**. Today, India is the world's second most populous country. Most Indians are Hindus. Indians speak English as well as Hindi and other local languages. To the north, mountainous **Afghanistan** separates this region from the Middle East.

Major Features. India's main cities include Mumbai (*Bombay*), Delhi, Calcutta, and Madras. Pakistan's major cities include Islamabad and Lahore.

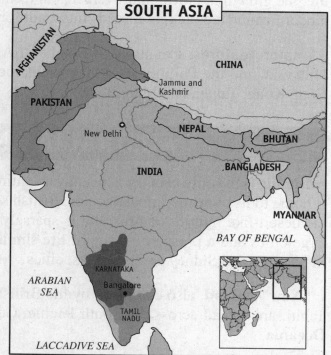

SOUTH ASIA

AFGHANISTAN
PAKISTAN
CHINA
Jammu and Kashmir
New Delhi
NEPAL
BHUTAN
INDIA
BANGLADESH
MYANMAR
BAY OF BENGAL
KARNATAKA
Bangalore
ARABIAN SEA
TAMIL NADU
LACCADIVE SEA

SOUTHEAST ASIA

Southeast Asia pro-vides the shortest route between the Pacific and Indian Oceans. As a result, Southeast Asia has been heavily affected by the large mix of peoples coming into this region, especially Chinese, Indi-ans, Arabs, and European colonial powers. The islands of Southeast Asia, once known as the East Indies, export important spices such as pepper, cin-namon, and nutmeg, used in cooking all over the world. In earlier times, these spices were highly

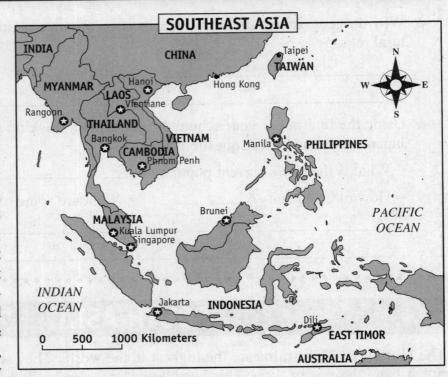

prized in Europe and the Middle East because they provided a way of preserving food that was more flavorful than using only salt. Arab traders brought Islam to the region, where it spread rapidly. Although much of the region continues to follow traditional ways of life, the growth of cities, improvements in technology, and government programs aimed at modernization are making inroads into traditional village life.

Major Features. Countries of Southeast Asia include Indonesia, Thailand, Vietnam, Malaysia, and the Philippines. Major cities include Bangkok, Jakarta, Singapore, Hanoi, Hong Kong, Taipei, and Manila.

AUSTRALIA AND OCEANIA

Australia is the only country to occupy an entire continent. Located in the Pacific Ocean, it is home to its own aboriginal peoples. British settlers established a colony in 1788. Today, the desert-like interior of Australia is sparsely populated. Its south and east coasts boast large cities and a prosperous way of life similar to that of Europe and the United States. Melbourne and Sidney are the largest cities.

New Zealand, also colonized by the British, and other smaller island nations, such as Tahiti, are spread across the South Pacific. Geographers refer to these Pacific islands as **Oceania**.

ACTING AS AN AMATEUR GEOGRAPHER

You have just learned about eleven major world cultural regions. Now you should look at these regions in more depth. Your teacher will divide your class into groups. Each group will be assigned one cultural region from this chapter. Your goal is find additional information about your assigned region. Investigate the following questions about your region:

Languages	• What are the major languages spoken in the region? _____ _____
Government	• What forms of government do they have? _____ _____ • What rights do people in the region enjoy? _____ _____ _____
Religions / Belief Systems	• What are the main religions or belief systems? _____ _____ • What beliefs do members of those religions share? _____ _____ _____
Urban / Rural	• Do most people live in towns, cities or in the countryside? _____ _____ • What are people's homes like in the region? _____ _____ _____
Family Relationships	• Do people have large or small families? _____ • How are their families organized? _____ _____ _____

CONTINUED

Social Structure / Wealth	• What social groups (*classes*) exist in the region? _____ _____ • Is wealth concentrated or more evenly spread out? _____ _____
Fashion, Literature, Art, and Music	• What are their fashions, literature, music and art like? _____ _____ • Who are some of the important artists in the region? _____ _____
Education	• How do people educate their young? _____ _____ • What do children learn at home or at school? _____ _____
Land Use	• How is land owned and shared? _____ _____ • Is land used for farming, livestock or manufacturing? _____ _____
Trading Networks	• What kinds of goods and services do people exchange? _____ _____ • What items do they trade with those outside the region? _____ _____
Diversity	• What are the main minority groups in the region? _____ _____ • How equally are men and women treated? _____ _____

After searching the Internet or your school or public library for this information, you should prepare a short PowerPoint presentation. Create a handout for your assigned region. Your PowerPoint presentation and handout should provide information for one of the areas listed on the previous pages.

CHAPTER STUDY CARDS

Types of Regions

★ **Cultural Regions** are based on common cultural characteristics, such as language, religious beliefs, customs, and art forms.

★ **Formal Regions.** Have a common human or physical characteristic and clear boundaries.

★ **Functional Regions.** Based on a function they serve, such as an area of connected rivers that serves as a drainage basin.

★ **Perceptual Regions.** Based on people's feelings about an area.
  - Big Apple
  - Dixie
  - Deep South
  - Midwest

World Cultural Regions (1 of 3)

★ **Middle East.** This is both a physical and cultural region; mostly Islamic and Arabic.

★ **Latin America.** Mexico, Central America, West Indies, and South America; most people speak Spanish or Portuguese; mainly follow the Catholic religion.

★ **Sub-Saharan Africa.** Many different ethnic groups with animistic, Christian, and Islamic religions; many affected by the slave trade or European colonization.

★ **North America.** Consists of Canada and the United States; strongly influenced by Europe.

World Cultural Regions (2 of 3)

★ **Europe.** Superior technology from 1500 to 1900; high standards of living; mainly Christian; many ethnic groups.

★ **China.** Most populous country; isolated from other cultures by physical barriers; united by written language (characters) and an all-powerful emperor; today, ruled by Communist Party. Becoming an economic power.

★ **Russia.** Separated from rest of Europe by vast distances; influenced by Orthodox Christianity, Mongol conquests from Central Asia, absolute power of Tsars, and experiences under Communist rule.

World Cultural Regions (3 of 3)

★ **South Asia.** India, because of the Himalayan Mountains, developed its own separate language, customs, and culture. India is the world's second most populous country; the area was once colonized by Britain; independence was granted in 1947: Today, India is Hindu and Pakistan and Bangladesh are Muslim.

★ **Southeast Asia.** Peninsular and island nations subject to many influences — China, India, Arabia, and Europe.

★ **Australia.** Small, dry continent colonized by the British; life-styles similar to those of the United States and Europe.

CHECKING YOUR UNDERSTANDING

Directions: Put a circle around the letter that best answers the question.

1   Which identifies one cultural factor that unites the people of Latin America?

    A   They are citizens of the same country.

    B   Most are Roman Catholics.

    C   Most speak English or Arabic.

    D   They were once ruled by the same powerful Emperor.

`Cult 17(A)`

If you examine the question, you see that it asks you to identify the one cultural factor that unites Latin Americans. **Choice A** is wrong. Latin Americans belong to a number of different countries, not just one country. **Choice C** is wrong because most Latin Americans speak Spanish or Portuguese, not English or Arabic. **Choice D** is also wrong, because Latin America was never united under a single powerful emperor. **Choice B** is the best answer. Most people in Latin America follow the Roman Catholic religion, which was introduced to the region by the Spanish.

Now try answering some additional questions on your own:

2 Which feature might appear on a map showing cultural differences?
  F   religious groups
  G   climatic zones
  H   major river systems
  J   mountain ranges

> • EXAMINE The Question
> • RECALL What You Know
> • APPLY What You Know

Cult 16(B)

3 Which statement about culture is the most accurate?
  A   Most members of a culture has the same social status.
  B   Culture is characterized by democratic government.
  C   The people in a culture always practice the same form of religion.
  D   Culture includes a people's language, religion, land uses and customs.

Cult 16(B)

4 The Middle East is considered a single cultural region by most geographers because —
  F   it has a warm, dry climate
  G   fertile river valleys
  H   it has many deserts and mount areas
  J   its people share a common history and heritage

Geog 9(A)

5 The American Midwest, the British Empire, and the Confederate States of America (1860–1865) are all examples of —
  A   cultural regions   C   physical regions
  B   functional regions   D   perceptual regions

Geog 9(B)

6 A functional region is often organized around a specific focal point. Which of the following is most clearly a functional region?
  F   Middle East
  G   Sub-Saharan Africa
  H   Dallas / Ft. Worth Metroplex
  J   Asia

Geog 9(B)

Name _____ Date _____

Use the map and your knowledge of social studies to answer questions 7 and 8.

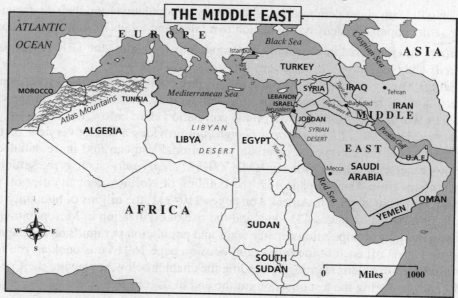

7 Which two regions on the map are most often linked because of their common language, religion, and cultural traditions?

A   The Sahara Desert and Europe
B   Europe and North Africa
C   North Africa and the Middle East
D   Europe and the Middle East

> • **EXAMINE** The Question
> • **RECALL** What You Know
> • **APPLY** What You Know

Geog 9(A)

8 Which two bodies of water on the map are connected by the Suez Canal?

F   Atlantic Ocean and the Mediterranean Sea
G   Black Sea and the Red Sea
H   Caspian Sea and the Black Sea
J   Red Sea and the Mediterranean Sea

Geog 6(A)

Use the information in the boxes and your knowledge of social studies to answer the following question.

| Its people are mainly of Arab descent | The dominant religion is Islam | Most people speak the Arabic language |

9 To which cultural region do all of these statements most likely apply?

A   North Africa   C   Latin America
B   Sub-Saharan Africa   D   European Union

Cult 17(A)

10 In which cultural region would you find the cities of Bangkok, Hanoi, Manila, and Singapore?

A   Middle East   C   South Asia
B   North Africa   D   Southeast Asia

Cult 16(A)

Demography

In this chapter, you will learn about demography — the study of populations and their characteristics, including where people settle, population density, population pyramids, and trends in world population growth.

❏ **Before Reading:** You might begin your study of demography by reading the TEKS, *Essential Questions*, *Important Ideas* and *Geographic Terminology* on pages 169–170.

❏ **During Reading:** Then you might turn to the text of this book, pages 170–178, to learn more about these subjects. As you read about each aspect of demography, you might look at the corresponding pages of HMH's *World Geography*, shown on the correlation chart below, to learn more. For example, page 170 of *Mastering the TEKS in World Geography* provides a brief overview of the history of human settlements and the emergence of urban populations. You can find more detailed information about these processes in specific regions in HMH's *World Geography*, such as the settlement of North America by nomads from Asia on page 127, the building of North American cities on page 128, the settlement and rise of cities in Latin America on pages 210–211, the origins of humanity and the rise of civilization in East Africa on pages 431–432, and the rise of civilization in Mesopotamia on page 516. There are also examples of population density maps and population pyramids on the pages indicated in the chart below. Check off each of the *Important Ideas* on page 169 of this book as you read about it.

❏ **After Reading:** Reinforce your learning by reading the chapter below, reviewing the Concept Map and Study Cards, and answering the test questions at the end of the chapter.

Topics	*Mastering the TEKS*	HMH's *World Geography*
History of Human Settlements	p. 170	pp. 127, 210–211, 431–432, 438–439, 516, 573
Emergence of Urban Populations	p. 170	pp. 87, 128, 211–212, 431, 544, 573
Factors Influencing Where People Settle	p. 171	pp. 80–82
Physical Factors	p. 171	pp. 80–82
Human Factors	p. 172	pp. 80–82
Changes in Settlement Patterns	p. 172	p. 81
		Examples: Bantu Migrations, p. 448; Middle East, pp. 476, 525–528; Southeast Asia, pp. 730–732
Population Density Maps	pp. 172–174	pp. 81–82, 107, 264, 528, 547, 594, 615
Patterns in Size and Distribution of Cities	pp. 174–175	pp. 725, 87–90, 195
Population Pyramids	pp. 175–177	pp. 79, 596, 616
Trends in World Population Growth	pp. 178–179	pp. 78–82, 593–595, 639, 668–669

Using Multiple Sources of Information

• Use information from both books to write your own answers to the *Essential Questions* on page 169.
• Use facts and examples from both books to create your own concept map around one of the *Important Ideas* on page 169.
• Use information from both books to create your own slide show, PowerPoint presentation or video on trends in world population growth.

CHAPTER 10 — DEMOGRAPHY

TEKS COVERED IN CHAPTER 10

■ **Geography 6** The student understands the types, patterns, and processes of settlement.
- **Geography 6(A)** Locate and describe human and physical features that influence the size and distribution of settlements.
- **Geography 6(B)** Explain the processes that have caused changes in settlement patterns, including urbanization, transportation, access to and availability of resources, and economic activities.

■ **Geography 7** The student understands the growth, distribution, movement, and characteristics of world population.
- **Geography 7(A)** Construct and analyze population pyramids and use other data, graphics, and maps to describe the population characteristics of different societies and to predict future population trends.

Demography is the study of population. In this chapter, you will study the factors that influence where people settle and the processes that lead to changes in settlement patterns. You will also examine population density maps and population pyramids, and investigate recent trends in world population growth and distribution.

ESSENTIAL QUESTIONS

○— What factors influence where people settle?

○— Is the world's population growing too fast?

— IMPORTANT IDEAS —

A. Many human and physical factors influence the size and distribution of human settlements. These factors include landforms, climate, nearness to bodies of water, natural resources, economic activities, the level of technology, and relationships with neighboring peoples.

B. Many processes lead to changes in settlement patterns, including urbanization, transportation, access to resources, and economic activities.

C. Demographers use **population density maps**, **population pyramids**, and other geographic data to describe population characteristics and trends. A **population density map** shows where population is distributed in an area. A **population pyramid** shows the distribution of population in a country by age and sex.

D. The world's population is now growing at an accelerating rate. More people are alive now than at any other time in history.

GEOGRAPHIC TERMINOLOGY IN THIS CHAPTER

- Demography
- Urbanization
- Settlement Patterns
- Population Density
- Population Pyramid
- Shanty Towns

A BRIEF HISTORY OF HUMAN SETTLEMENT

THE FIRST HUMAN SETTLEMENTS

Most anthropologists believe that humans first appeared in the Great Rift Valley in East Africa many hundreds of thousands of years ago. From there, humans spread to the Middle East, Asia, Europe, the Americas and Oceania.

Around 10,000 years ago, people in the Middle East discovered they could plant seeds to grow their own food. Wherever agriculture was introduced, people no longer needed to follow a **nomadic** way of life — wandering in constant search of food. Instead, populations settled in one location and grew. Although agriculture was first discovered in the Middle East, it was later discovered independently in China, India, Africa and the Americas.

THE EMERGENCE OF URBAN POPULATIONS

In some areas, agriculture became especially successful. This was true in the river valleys of Egypt, Mesopotamia, India, and China, which had fertile soil from annual flooding. This led to abundant harvests. In these locations, the first cities arose. People were able to grow a surplus of food to feed a non-farming, urban population. Urban dwellers included new specialized groups — priests, soldiers, traders, scribes, and craftspeople. As urban populations increased in size, a need for government developed.

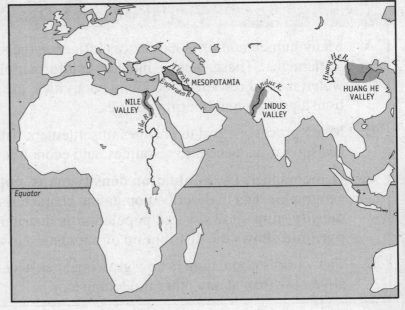

INDUSTRIALIZATION AND URBANIZATION

Starting in the 1700s, the **Industrial Revolution** greatly increased the speed of **urbanization** — the movement of greater numbers of people into cities. People began to leave the rural countryside to find jobs in the new factories. Towns and cities started to grow up around these factories. Cities also grew up at points where goods were exchanged or transferred — such as seacoast ports where rivers met, and later, where different railroad lines crossed.

FACTORS INFLUENCING WHERE PEOPLE SETTLE

What explains the distribution of people around the world? Both physical and human factors affect where people settle, even today. Three-quarters of the world's population now live on less than 5% of Earth's surface. Most of the world's population is concentrated in five areas, with more than half in the first two:

(1) East Asia, including China, Korea, Japan, and Taiwan
(2) South Asia, with India, Pakistan, Bangladesh and Sri Lanka
(3) Southeast Asia
(4) Europe
(5) North America

PHYSICAL FACTORS

Physical factors play a very large role in where people live. Population tends to cluster around seaports and fresh water sources. Most people live near the ocean or near a river with access to the ocean. In fact, two-thirds of the world's population today live within 500 miles of the ocean.

Major cities in China have some the highest population densities in the world.

Much of the Earth's land surface is unfriendly to human habitation. In fact, eight of the 10 most populous cities in the world are on or near earthquake faults. Population is typically sparse in extremely dry, wet, cold, or mountainous areas. These areas usually have a low population density. Instead, people tend to settle in low-lying areas with fertile soil and a temperate or mild climate.

HUMAN FACTORS

Human factors also affect where people settle. The need to establish a capital city at a central location or to establish new transportation routes may lead people to settle in a particular area. As technology improves, people are able to explore and settle in new areas, despite physical barriers. Economic activities also bring people to new areas. The discovery of valuable resources, such as gold, diamonds or oil, may attract settlers to an otherwise unfavorable area.

CHANGES IN SETTLEMENT PATTERNS

Settlement patterns sometimes change over time. As areas urbanize, surrounding areas attract new settlers. The discovery of new resources or the construction of new transportation routes can also encourage new settlement. The Far West of the United States, for example, was sparsely populated until the discovery of gold in California and the construction of the transcontinental railroad.

POPULATION DENSITY MAPS

Geographers measure patterns of settlement by looking at **population density** — how many people live within a given area. They often measure the average number of people in a square mile. Geographers also use special maps to show the distribution of population density.

A **dot population map** uses dots to indicate where major towns and cities are located. Each dot represents a certain number of residents. The key to the map tells how many people each dot represents. Other symbols, like diamonds or circles, may be used to indicate larger cities. In this map, each dot represents 300,00 people. The map shows a concentration of people along the Nile, the coast of the eastern Mediterranean, the north side of Turkey, the rivers of Iraq, and the central plateau of Iran. Notice also that in the desert areas of Saudi Arabia and Egypt, there is an absence of dots. This indicates fewer people live in those areas.

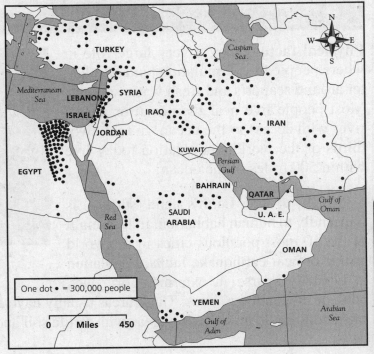

One dot ● = 300,000 people

0   Miles   450

APPLYING WHAT YOU HAVE LEARNED

What conclusions can you draw about where people in the Middle East prefer to settle?

_____

_____

_____

_____

_____

_____

A **population density map** can also use patterns or colors to show how many people live in a given area. Regions of different population density are separately indicated. The key explains what each pattern or color represents. For example, in this map of Africa, light gray horizontal lines indicate a population of 0 to 10 people per square mile. In other words, on average 10 or fewer people live on each square mile of any areas shown with gray horizontal lines.

The map shows this very sparse population across North Africa, where the Sahara Desert is located. Along the Nile River at the northeast tip of Africa, and along several coastal locations, the population density is greater than 150 people per square mile. These densely populated areas include the cities of Cairo, Alexandria, Lagos, and Capetown.

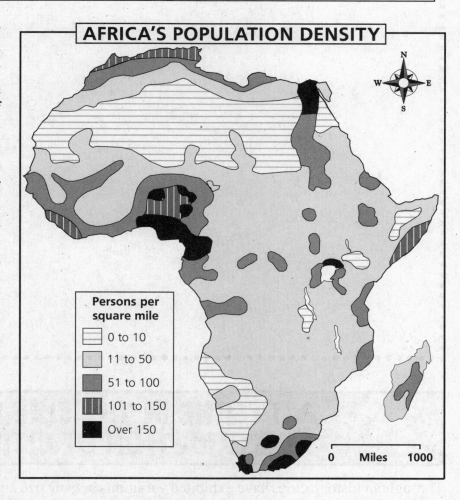

AFRICA'S POPULATION DENSITY

Persons per square mile

- 0 to 10
- 11 to 50
- 51 to 100
- 101 to 150
- Over 150

0   Miles   1000

ACTING AS AN AMATEUR GEOGRAPHER

Five small countries with high population densities are Macau, Monaco, Hong Kong, Singapore, and Gibraltar.

★ Use an almanac or the Internet to find the square mileage for each country and the size of its population. Also locate each one on a map.

★ Use a calculator to divide the population by the total square miles of land for each country. This will give you the number of people living there per square mile.

★ Create a bar graph below, showing this information. Remember to create a title for the graph and to label both the horizontal and vertical axes.

PATTERNS IN THE SIZE AND DISTRIBUTION OF CITIES

Throughout history, cities have exhibited variations in their size and distribution. Cities began undergoing changes as they matured. Often the business district was located in the city's center, surrounded by residential neighborhoods. As newcomers from the countryside moved to the center of the city, wealthier residents often began to move to the city's outskirts.

In more recent times, **suburbs** have developed outside cities. Often, these suburbs come to form satellite cities around the older city center. As the population increases further, these cities may merge into a single **metropolitan region**.

In less developed countries, people often arrive from the countryside without education or resources. These newcomers may settle in **squatter settlements** or shanty towns, usually found outside of the city. A **shanty town** is a slum settlement where poor people live in dwellings made from scrap materials — such as plywood, corrugated metal, and plastic sheets.

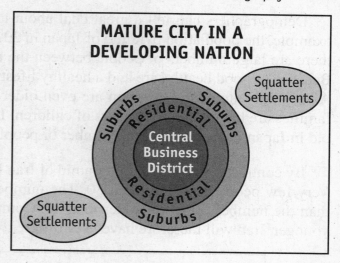

POPULATION PYRAMIDS

Demographers study the characteristics of human populations as well as where people settle. For example, they compare the numbers of males and females in a society. They also look at the average ages of its members.

To display this information, demographers use a **population pyramid**. The pyramid typically shows the number of males on the left side and the number of females on the right. A vertical line runs through the middle. Each age group is represented by a different bar. In a sense, a population pyramid is actually a type of bar graph. The different bars are stacked up to create the pyramid.

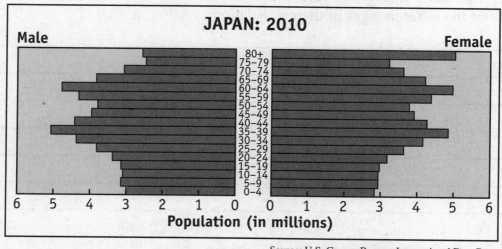

Source: U.S. Census Bureau, International Data Base.

Demographers can tell a great deal about a culture by examining its population. For example, the population pyramid of Japan in 2010 (see page 165) shows a society in which there are large numbers of people between the ages of 35 and 40 and between 60 and 65. Because of good health care and a healthy lifestyle, many Japanese are living into old age. A very large number of women are even older than 80. However, not so many Japanese families are having large numbers of children. In fact, the number of people over 60 years old in Japan is greater than the number of people under 20 years old.

By contrast, the population pyramid of Iran in 2010 shows a much younger population. Very few people are older than 80. The number of people under age 20 is much greater than the number of people older than 60. Compared to Japan, Iran's population is much younger. Iran will therefore have very different social needs than Japan has.

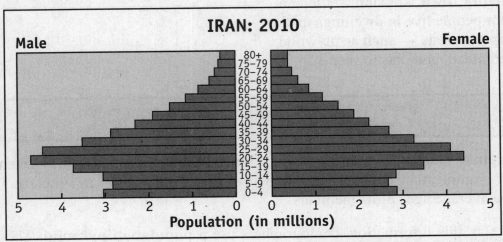

Source: U.S. Census Bureau, International Data Base.

APPLYING WHAT YOU HAVE LEARNED

Identify two ways that you would expect Japan and Iran to have different needs because of the different ages of their populations:

 _____

_____

_____

 _____

_____

_____

_____

Name _____ Date _____

ACTING AS AN AMATEUR GEOGRAPHER

★ Listed below are the population figures for the nation of Sudan in Africa for the year 2000. Each number represents a thousand people. Use the information to construct your own population pyramid below for the nation of Sudan.

Ages	Males	Females	Ages	Males	Females
Birth to 4	2,600	2,550	50 to 54	450	400
10 to 14	1,900	1,700	60 to 64	300	200
20 to 24	1,300	1,200	0 to 74	100	90
30 to 34	900	800	Age 80+	20	10
40 to 34	600	600			

★ What conclusions can you draw about Sudanese society from this population pyramid?

_____

_____

_____

TRENDS IN WORLD POPULATION GROWTH

Patterns of settlement and the distribution of the world's population have changed greatly over time. World population growth was uneven until agriculture was first introduced. World population then grew gradually. Famines, plagues, and wars kept population growth in check. During the Industrial Revolution, Europe and North America became the first places to use new farming techniques and to apply modern science to decrease death rates. As a result, population growth accelerated by almost ten times in Great Britain.

At the same time, average birth rates in these regions gradually decreased from the 1700s onwards. This kept the pace of population growth somewhat in check.

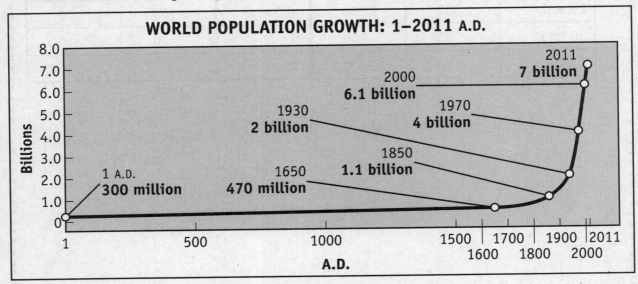

As Europeans colonized new areas, they spread their medical advances and new farming methods to these regions. This enabled local peoples to live longer. These peoples did not always decrease their birth rates. There has now been a population explosion in Asia, Africa, and Latin America, especially in the years since World War II (1939–1945).

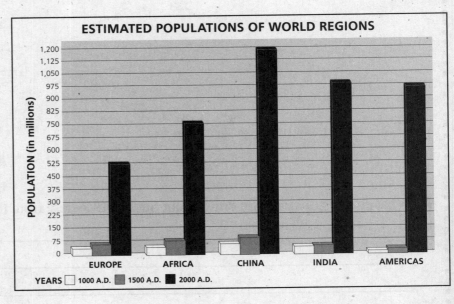

Many countries in Asia, Africa, and Latin America are now struggling to reduce their birth rates to bring population growth under control. For example, China encourages families in cities and towns to have only one child.

ACTING AS AN AMATEUR GEOGRAPHER

★ Based on the bar graph on page 168, in which region of the world did the population grow the most between 1500 and 2000?

_____

★ What will the distribution of world population become in 2100 if current trends continue?

_____

_____

★ What environmental challenges does the world's growing population create?

_____

_____

_____

_____

_____

★ Working with classmates in a group, brainstorm various ways to deal with the problems created by world population growth.

_____

_____

_____

_____

★ Briefly describe how the pace of world population growth might be slowed down.

_____

_____

_____

_____

◆ LEARNING WITH GRAPHIC ORGANIZERS

Complete the graphic organizer below. Indicate how each of these physical and human factors affects where people live.

Natural Resources

_____
_____
_____

Bodies of Water

_____
_____
_____

Climate

_____
_____
_____

Landforms

_____
_____
_____

PHYSICAL FACTORS

FACTORS INFLUENCING WHERE PEOPLE SETTLE

HUMAN FACTORS

Level of Technology

_____
_____
_____

Economic Activities

_____
_____
_____

Transportation Routes

_____
_____
_____

Urbanization

_____
_____
_____

CHAPTER STUDY CARDS

Physical Factors Influencing Where People Live

★ People tend to settle in temperate, fertile, non-mountainous areas, such as valleys and plains.

★ People settle near sources of fresh water.

★ People settle not too far from oceans.

★ Fewer people settle in dry, wet, cold or mountainous areas.

Human Factors Affecting Settlement

★ **Political and Economic Centers.** People move to areas of political or economic importance, such as capital cities.

★ **Transportation Routes.** People often settle along transportation routes, such as coastlines, rivers, canals, railroad lines, or roads.

★ **Technology.** Improvements in technology can expand areas of settlement.

★ **Urbanization.** Since the start of the Industrial Revolution, urbanization (people moving from the countryside to cities) has increased greatly.

Population Density Maps

★ **Population Density Map.** A map showing how many people live per square mile in a given area. It shows the distribution of population in that area.

★ **Dot Population Map.** A map using dots to indicate the location of major towns and cities. Dots are also used to show the concentration of where people live.

Population Pyramids

★ These compare the numbers of males and females in a particular country.

★ Stacked bars indicate the number of people for each age group.

★ They are used by demographers to show the age distribution in a society.

Trends in World Population Growth

The world's population has steadily increased over time.

★ **Pre-Industrial.** The world's population grew slowly.

★ **After the Industrial Revolution.** The world's population grew rapidly. Europe and North America grew fastest due to new farming methods and industrialization.

★ **European Colonization.** As Europeans colonized new areas, they spread new farming methods and modern medicine.

★ **Current Trends.**
   • Population growth has greatly accelerated.
   • China, India and Africa are struggling to reduce birth rates to bring population growth under control.

CHECKING YOUR UNDERSTANDING

Directions: Put a circle around the letter that best answers the question.

Use the map and your knowledge of social studies to answer questions 1 and 2.

1   According to the map, which statement is most accurate?

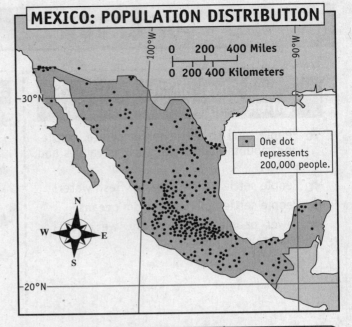

MEXICO: POPULATION DISTRIBUTION

One dot represents 200,000 people.

A   Most people live in northern Mexico.

B   The population density is greatest near the border with the United States

C   Most Mexicans live in the cooler central highlands.

D   Mexico's population is concentrated along its coasts.

Geog 7(A)

This question asks you to interpret a population density map. **Choice A** is wrong, because there are few dots in the north. You can therefore conclude that most people do not live in the north. **Choice B** is wrong because there are few dots along the border with the United States. **Choice D** is also wrong, because most of the dots do not lie along the coastline of Mexico. The best answer is **Choice C**. The most dots are found inland, in the highlands of Mexico. This is because its temperatures are cooler in these higher elevations.

Now try answering some additional questions on your own:

2   What does each dot on the map represent?

F   100,000 people

G   200,000 people

H   a million people

J   a town or city

Geog 6(A)

Use the information in the boxes and your knowledge of social studies to answer the following question.

| Siberian Plains | Sahara Desert | Amazon Rainforest | Russian Steppes |

3   Which characteristic is common to all four of these areas?

A   They are all sparsely populated.

B   They are all found on the continent of Asia.

C   They are all located near the equator.

D   They are all in mountainous areas.

Geog 6(A)

Use the map and your knowledge of social studies to answer the following question.

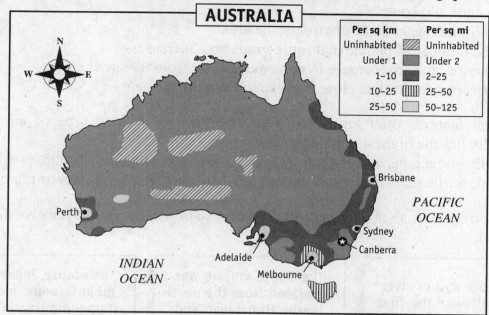

4   What conclusion can be drawn from the map?

F   Most Australians live along its coastline.

G   The heaviest population centers are found along the northern coastline.

H   Australia's population is spread evenly throughout the country.

J   Canberra is Australia's largest city in population.

`Geog 7(A)`

Use the population pyramid and your knowledge of social studies to answer the following question.

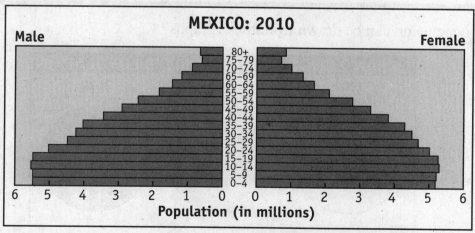

Source: U.S. Census Bureau, International Data Base.

5   Based on the population pyramid, which statement about Mexico is most accurate?

A   Most Mexican women live much longer than men.

B   More Mexicans are over age 60 than under age 20.

C   Most Mexicans live to be more than 80 years old.

D   The four largest age groups range from birth to 19 years old.

`Geog 7(A)`

6 Which of the following is the most likely effect of building a railroad to reach an area rich in natural resources?

    F Railroad owners take control of the area.   `Geog 6(A)`

    G The number of people that settle in the area increases.

    H There is a sharp increase in movement away from the area.

    J Government leaders close the area to future settlement.

7 Physical features often influence where people live. Which type of environment typically has the highest population density?

    A hills, mountains and plateaus   **C** wet bogs and swamps   `Geog 6(A)`

    B flat, fertile plains and river valleys   **D** dry and barren desert regions

Use the information in the boxes and your knowledge of social studies to answer the following question.

The fertile soil of river valleys allowed the first civilizations to develop.	**The Gupta Empire was separated from the north by the Himalayan and Hindu Kush Mountains.**	**Because Japan is mountainous, most of its people live in areas near the coast.**

8 Which conclusion is best supported by these examples?

    F Major urban centers are found only along rivers.   `Geog 6(A)`

    G Without mountains and rivers, people cannot become civilized.

    H The physical geography of a region influences its human development.

    J The spread of new ideas is often limited by political conflict.

9 Which conclusion can be drawn from these graphs?

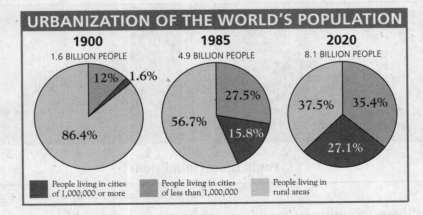

URBANIZATION OF THE WORLD'S POPULATION

1900 — 1.6 BILLION PEOPLE — 12%, 1.6%, 86.4%

1985 — 4.9 BILLION PEOPLE — 27.5%, 15.8%, 56.7%

2020 — 8.1 BILLION PEOPLE — 37.5%, 35.4%, 27.1%

People living in cities of 1,000,000 or more   People living in cities of less than 1,000,000   People living in rural areas

    A The average size of cities has remained unchanged since 1900.   `Geog 7(A)`

    B Cities of less than one million are growing faster than larger cities.

    C Since 1985, the world's population has almost tripled.

    D The proportion of people in rural areas has declined over the last century.

Migration

This chapter looks at the causes and effects of migration — the movement of people from one place to another. It corresponds to various case studies of migration found in HMH's *World Geography*.

❏ *Before Reading:* You can begin your study of migration by reading the TEKS, *Geographic Terminology*, *Important Ideas* and *Essential Questions* on page 186.

❏ *During Reading:* Next, you might read pages 186–192 of this book, identifying the reasons why people migrate. Then turn to HMH's *World Geography* to learn more about individual case studies of migration. For example, you might be interested in learning how the drought in the Sahel is causing many people to migrate (pp. 424–425, 436–437), or how people sometimes migrate to escape ethnic persecution (pp. 517, 526–527). You might want to learn more about how people migrated to escape ethnic persecution in Rwanda (pp. 81, 433, 469). Afterwards, learn how physical geography can affect the flow of migration — the routes that migrants take when they move. People tend to avoid natural barriers, such as mountains, and to move through valleys and over water routes (this book, pp. 192–193). Lastly, think about how all these different factors have resulted in the current distribution of world cultures today (p. 193). Be sure to examine the distribution of human cultures on the maps in HMH's *World Geography* on the pages in the chart below. For example, page 74 shows world languages, page 76 shows world religions, page 142 shows ethnic minorities in the United States, and page 267 shows the languages of Europe.

❏ *After Reading:* Reinforce your learning by reviewing the study cards and answering the test questions.

Topics	Mastering the TEKS	HMH's World Geography
Why People Migrate	pp. 186–192	pp. 81, 135–136, 138, 238, 370–371, 448
Push-Pull Factors	p. 187	pp. 81, 730–731
Social: Religious Factors	p. 187	
Jewish Migration	p. 187 (Middle Ages)	pp. 315, 515 (modern)
Hindus/Muslims in India (1947)		pp. 568, 574
Political Factors	p. 188	
Cubans	p. 188	
Afghans	p. 188	pp. 517, 517–519
Palestinians	(see Chapter 16)	pp. 512–513, 527
Social: Ethnic Persecution	p. 189	pp. 517, 526–527
Burundi & Rwanda	p. 189	pp. 81, 433, 469
Economic Motives	p. 189	pp. 88, 221, 238, 448
"Guest Workers" in Germany	p. 189	p. 301
Environmental Factors	pp. 190–191	pp. 81, 150–151 (Dust Bowl)
Potato Famine in Ireland	p. 190	p. 305
Drought in the Sahel	p. 191	pp. 424–425, 436–437 (Somalia)
Economic/Social: Forced Migration	pp. 191–192	
Slave Trade	p. 191	pp. 136, 224–225, 236, 449
How Physical Geography Affects Migration Flows	pp. 192–193	
Physical Barriers	pp. 192–193	pp. 420–421, 491–492, 551–553, 619
Distribution of Human Cultures Today	p. 193	pp. 73–74, 76, 80, 142–143, 181, 267, 341, 370, 406–407, 454, 469, 482–483, 516, 546, 568, 571, 591, 615, 683, 713 (includes regional maps showing ethnic groups, languages and religions).

Using Multiple Sources of Information

• Use information from both books to write your own answers to the *Essential Questions* on page 186.

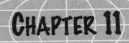

CHAPTER 11

MIGRATION

TEKS COVERED IN CHAPTER 11

- **History 1(A)** Analyze the effects of physical and human geographic patterns ... including significant physical features and environmental conditions that influenced migration patterns and shaped the distribution of culture groups today.
- **Geography 7(B)** Explain how political, economic, social, and environmental push and pull factors and physical geography affect the routes and flows of human migration.

Physical and human factors influence where people settle. However, people do not always stay in one location. **Migration** refers to the movement of people from one area to another. Generally, migration refers to a permanent move by people to a new location.

AN ESS ENT IAL QUESTION

 What reasons cause people to migrate to different areas?

— IMPORTANT IDEAS —

A. Political, economic, social, and environmental push-and-pull factors cause people to **migrate**, or move, from one place to another.

B. Physical geography often affects the routes that human migrations take.

GEOGRAPHIC TERMINOLOGY IN THIS CHAPTER

- Migration
- Push-and-Pull Factors
- Social Factors
- Ethnic Persecution
- Religious Persecution
- Environmental Factors
- Forced Migration
- Physical Barriers
- Land Bridge

WHY PEOPLE MIGRATE

Geographers generally divide the reasons for migration into "push" and "pull" factors. **Push factors** are those events that *push* people out of their old location, while **pull factors** are the attractions that lure migrants to a new location.

PUSH FACTORS	PULL FACTORS
◆ Oppression ◆ Poverty ◆ Political Conflicts ◆ Environmental Factors	◆ Freedom ◆ Economic Opportunity ◆ Cultural Ties

Often, people migrate because of a combination of both "push" and "pull" factors. Let's look at some of the most important factors that cause people to migrate.

FACTORS LEADING TO MIGRATION

SOCIAL FACTORS: Religious Persecution

Social factors concern how people organize into groups, such as religious groups. Throughout history, many societies have persecuted people because of their religious beliefs. Religious minorities will often leave a place if they face such persecution.

CASE STUDY: Jewish Migrations

Under the Roman Empire, Jewish people were driven from Israel after they rebelled against Roman rule. In the Middle Ages, Jews in Europe often faced prejudice and discrimination from their Christian neighbors.

In 1290, England expelled its Jewish community. France followed in 1394. In 1492, Ferdinand and Isabella of Spain ordered all Jews to convert to Christianity or leave Spain. Some Jews converted, but the vast majority chose to leave. From these countries, Jews migrated to Holland, Hungary, Poland and Italy, where they were welcomed. Many Jews also migrated to the Ottoman Empire, where they settled in Istanbul or Palestine.

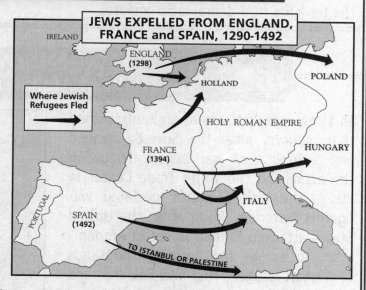

POLITICAL FACTORS

Political factors can also lead people to migrate. **Politics** concerns governments, government policies, wars, and citizens' rights. People often flee their homes when they become scenes of armed conflict arising out of political differences. Such fighting might occur because of an invasion by another country or because of a civil war caused by conflicts between rival groups. People also migrate to escape political persecution or to enjoy greater political freedoms and rights in a new place.

CASE STUDY:
Cubans Flee Communism

In 1959, Fidel Castro came to power in Cuba. He promised to create a democracy in Cuba. However, once in power, Castro set about establishing a Communist dictatorship. Cubans who spoke out against Castro's policies were imprisoned. All newspapers, radio and television stations opposed to Castro's regime were either shut down or put under government control. Thousands of Cubans, disillusioned by his policies and opposed to Communism, fled Cuba for the safety of the United States. Once there, they could enjoy the benefits of a democratic society.

Many Cubans fled on homemade boats in an attempt to reach the United States.

CASE STUDY:
The Flight of Afghan Refugees

In 1979, some citizens of Afghanistan fled their country after the Soviets invaded and a long civil war began. Following the attack on the World Trade Center in 2001, the United States declared war against terrorism. Soon after, the United States attacked Taliban forces in Afghanistan. To escape the fighting, thousands of Afghan refugees fled into Pakistan and other neighboring countries. By the end of 2001, there were 5 million Afghan refugees living in Pakistan.

SOCIAL FACTORS: Ethnic Persecution

People also migrate when they are persecuted for being members of a particular ethnic group.

CASE STUDY:
Burundi and Rwanda

In 1994, bitter fighting began in Central Africa between the Hutu and the Tutsi tribes of Burundi and Rwanda. The Tutsi tribal people are generally taller than the Hutus and have other distinguishing characteristics that make their physical appearance distinct. In Rwanda, the majority Hutu-dominated army massacred almost half a million of the Tutsi people. Millions of Rwandans, fearing for their lives, fled to neighboring Tanzania and Zaire, where they lived in refugee camps. Thousands died in these refugee camps from epidemics of diseases common to the camps, such as cholera and dysentery.

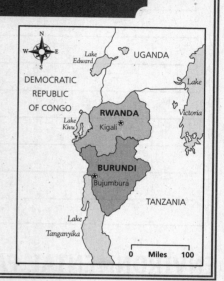

ECONOMIC MOTIVES

When people in a society suffer from extreme poverty, this "pushes" some of them to attempt to leave. The motivation is greater if people have heard that conditions elsewhere are better. For example, in the early 20th century, many people left impoverished conditions in Eastern and Southern Europe to come to the United States, where they sought new economic opportunities. Economic motives may be strengthened by social ones when other relatives have already migrated to a place.

CASE STUDY:
Guest Workers in Germany

After World War II, many Turks, attracted by higher wages, left Turkey to work as "guest workers" rebuilding West Germany. Many of these workers later returned to Turkey, but a large number continued to remain in Germany. Many of these guest workers live in "ghettos," where they do not speak German. Their housing and education are below average. Most of them are still not German citizens, even after living for decades in the country.

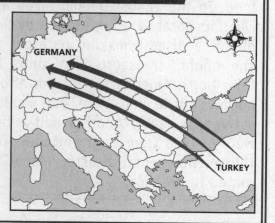

APPLYING WHAT YOU HAVE LEARNED

Using two of the case studies on the previous page, explain the importance of both "push" and "pull" factors to migration.

_____

_____

_____

_____

_____

_____

_____

ENVIRONMENTAL FACTORS

People sometimes migrate because of the environment. Some groups traditionally migrate with the seasons. For example, the Fulani of Africa move south with their herds in the dry season, and return north in the wet season. Changes in the environment, such as cooling or rising temperatures, or a series of droughts, may lead people to migrate. Sudden environmental catastrophes, such as crop failures, floods, fires, and earthquakes, can also force people to migrate.

CASE STUDY:
Irish Potato Famine

In the early nineteenth century, many Irish people depended on potatoes as their main food. In the 1840s, Ireland faced a disaster when its potato crop was struck by the potato blight, a disease making potatoes inedible. The blight, transported in ships traveling from North America to Ireland, affected the nation's entire crop. More than a million Irish starved to death. Another half-million Irish were evicted from their cottages. Driven by this environmental disaster, many Irish emigrated to America.

Food riots in Ireland.

CASE STUDY:
Drought in the Sahel

The Sahel region of Africa has undergone a series of severe droughts. Some scientists believe that these droughts have been caused by world climatic changes and the overgrazing of cattle. A majority of the people in the Sahel region are involved in nomadic herding. The impact of drought has been devastating to the Sahel. It has led to the erosion of the soil and to the deaths of large numbers of livestock. During the 1970s, multi-year droughts led to the deaths of more than 300,000 people. Thousands of Africans have now migrated from the Sahel region to neighboring areas. Subsistence farmers must relocate because they do not have food. Extended periods of drought can also lead to dust storms, making herding and farming almost impossible.

The Sahel region in Africa.

ECONOMIC AND SOCIAL FACTORS: Forced Migration

Sometimes migration is not voluntary but forced. Forced migration has accompanied war and the persecution of people, throughout most of history.

CASE STUDY:
The Atlantic Slave Trade

Between 1500 and the mid-1800s, millions of Africans were forcibly taken from their homelands and shipped to the West Indies, Brazil, or the United States, where they were treated as slaves. Those who survived the voyage were sold at slave auctions and lived in captivity. The slave trade had a strongly disruptive effect on African cultures, encouraging tribes to go to war

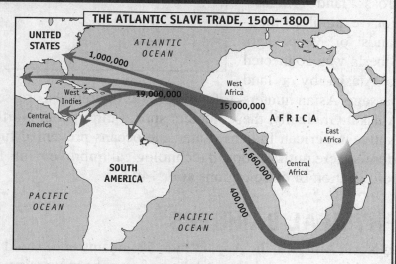

with one another and draining talent and labor. It led to the migration of millions of Africans to the Americas.

Another example of forced migration occurred in North America. British and American settlers uprooted millions of Native American Indians. These Native American Indians were forcibly relocated to distant and often inhospitable reservation lands. Native tribes were similarly removed from their lands in South Africa and Australia so that they could be replaced by white farmers and settlers.

HOW PHYSICAL GEOGRAPHY AFFECTS THE FLOW OF MIGRATION

Factors of physical geography will often determine the particular path that migration takes. Some factors — mountains, deserts, or dense forests — may pose natural barriers to migration or shape its course. People usually migrate through valleys and along water routes.

They may also cross "land bridges." For example, thousands of years ago, Siberia was connected to Alaska by a land

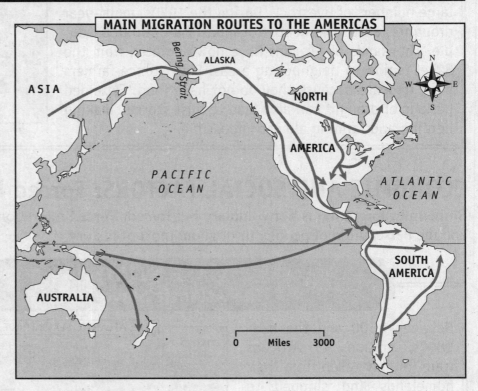

passage. Asian hunters, following herds of animals, crossed this land passage to migrate to Alaska. Gradually, these hunters spread throughout North and South America, becoming Native American Indians. Later, the oceans prevented further migration into the Western Hemisphere until European technological improvements led to the European conquest and colonization of these regions after 1492.

PHYSICAL BARRIERS

In North America, the Appalachian Mountains once stood as a barrier to migration from the East. Migration only occurred through specific mountain passes. Later, the Rocky Mountains and deserts of the Southwest remained natural barriers to migration. To reach California quickly, people sailed to Panama (*8 weeks*) or around South America (*3 months*); overland travel took even longer, until the first transcontinental railroad was completed in 1869.

In Africa, the Sahara Desert acted as a physical barrier limiting the amount of migration between North and Sub-Saharan Africa. Instead, these regions developed separately, with different groups of people migrating within each region. Physical barriers also once limited migration to China. To prevent Central Asian tribes from crossing the Asian steppes and mountains into China, China's emperors built the Great Wall. This human structure reinforced these natural barriers to migration.

THE DISTRIBUTION OF HUMAN CULTURES TODAY

Most scientists believe that human beings first originated in East Africa. From there, people spread throughout the world. The result of all these migrations is the distribution of cultural groups we find around the world today, which you studied in Chapter 9 (Cultural Regions), earlier in this unit.

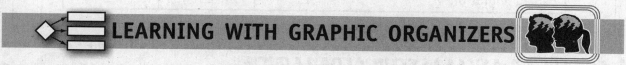

LEARNING WITH GRAPHIC ORGANIZERS

Complete the graphic organizer below. Identify each factor that sometimes causes people to migrate. Then provide one or more examples of each.

Religious Persecution

_____
_____
_____

Ethnic Persecution

_____
_____
_____

Environmental Factors

_____
_____
_____

WHY PEOPLE MIGRATE

Economic Motives

_____
_____
_____

Political Factors

_____
_____
_____

Forced Migration

_____
_____
_____

APPLYING WHAT YOU HAVE LEARNED

Classify these as "push" or "pull" factors causing groups to migrate.

	Push	Pull	Both
Religious Persecution	☐	☐	☐
Political Factors	☐	☐	☐
Economic Motives	☐	☐	☐
Ethnic Persecution	☐	☐	☐
Environmental Factors	☐	☐	☐
Forced Migration	☐	☐	☐

ACTING AS AN AMATEUR GEOGRAPHER

Select a person to interview, with the approval of your parents, who has migrated to the United States. Briefly summarize his/her responses:

★ Why did you decide to come to the United States? _____

_____

★ What route did you take to get here? _____

_____

★ Were conditions in America what you expected them to be? _____

_____

CHAPTER STUDY CARDS

Factors that Lead to Migration

★ **Push Factors.** These are factors pushing people to leave a place: to escape religious persecution, oppression, poverty, political conflicts, and environmental disasters.

★ **Pull Factors.** Factors attracting people to a place: to search for greater political or religious freedom, the search for economic opportunity, and to reinforce cultural ties.

Physical Factors Affecting Migration Routes

★ People often migrate through valleys, across grasslands, and along water routes.

★ Groups of migrating people generally avoid natural barriers like mountains, deserts, and dense forests.

★ Some physical factors can change, i.e. the land-bridge from Siberia to Alaska.

CHECKING YOUR UNDERSTANDING

Directions: Put a circle around the letter that best answers the question.

Use the diagram and your knowledge of social studies to answer the following question.

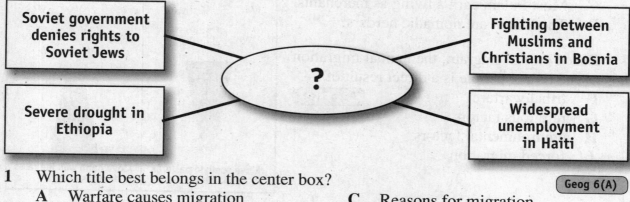

1   Which title best belongs in the center box?   Geog 6(A)
    A   Warfare causes migration   **C**   Reasons for migration
    B   Increased ethnic violence   **D**   World environmental disasters

This question seeks to test your understanding of the factors that cause people to migrate from one place to another. Remember in answering this type of question, that the title found in the center box should identify a theme common to all four boxes surrounding it. Only **Choice C** was a common effect of all four examples.

Now try answering some additional questions on your own:

Use the information and your knowledge of social studies to answer the following question.

"In 2007, the Intergovernmental Panel on Climate Change (IPCC) predicted that rising sea levels, caused by glacial and ice cap melting, will contribute to greater erosion and the gradual disappearance of some island nations in the South Pacific and Caribbean. Approximately 44% of the world's population live within 93 miles of a coastline. The report found a 3.3 feet rise in sea levels could affect nearly 24 million people alone in the densely populated Ganges, Mekong, and Nile river deltas, and greatly reduce the land available for agriculture."

— *Fourth Assessment by the Intergovernmental Panel on Climate Change (2007)*

2   Which is the best conclusion from this information?
    F   Sea levels will drop in Asia due to ice cap melting.   Geog 7(A)
    G   People should live close to a coastline.
    H   Climate changes may result in massive world-wide migration.
    J   Migration has led to global environmental change.

Use the diagram and your knowledge of social studies to answer questions 3 and 4.

3   What conclusion can best be drawn from this diagram?

Movement of the Fulani People

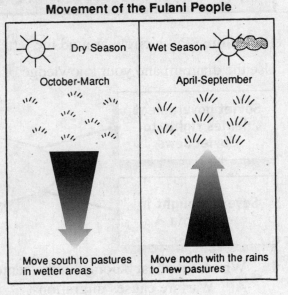

    A   The Fulani are hunters.   `Geog 7(A)`
    B   The Fulani are farmers.
    C   Most Fulani earn a living as merchants.
    D   The Fulani are nomadic herders.

4   Based on the diagram, the annual migration of the Fulani people is a direct result of —
    F   tribal warfare   `Geog 7(A)`
    G   religious factors
    H   environmental factors
    J   forced migration

Use the information and your knowledge of social studies to answer the following question.

- **Somalia and Ethiopia.** In the 1990s, many people in Somalia and Ethiopia moved to avoid civil war, drought, and famine.
- **Iraq.** Hundreds of thousands of Kurds moved to Turkey and Iran after the civil war that followed the Persian Gulf War in 1991.
- **Yugoslavia.** The disintegration of this country in the 1990s caused the displacement of many people, especially Bosnians, Croats, and Serbs.
- **Rwanda.** In the mid-1990s, millions of Hutus fled to avoid retaliation after earlier massacres of Tutsis.

5   What conclusion can be drawn from all *four* of these examples?
    A   Wars in Africa are particularly violent.   `Geog 7(A)`
    B   Political, economic and social factors can lead to human migration.
    C   Ethnic wars no longer trouble the world.
    D   Internal migration of people is important in shifting populations.

6   Increasing numbers of people from Latin America have migrated to the United States over the last three decades. What has been the primary reason for this increased migration?
    F   to escape from the threat of Communism   `Geog 7(A)`
    G   to obtain religious freedom
    H   to avoid natural disasters
    J   to find new economic opportunities

Use the photographs and your knowledge of social studies to answer the following question.

The division of India in 1947 into two nations forced Hindus from Muslim Pakistan.

Sudanese refugees fled war and famine in the mid-1980s.

An economic recession in China forced workers to move out of cities to the rural countryside.

7 Which conclusion can best be drawn from these three photographs?

   A Few people in the world still live in poverty.   `Geog 7(A)`

   B Many people in China now live in urban areas.

   C A variety of push-and-pull factors may cause people to migrate.

   D Religion is the principal reason why most people migrate.

---

8 Which of the following is an example of human migration caused by an economic "pull" factor?

   F Puritans migrated to Massachusetts to freely practice their religion.   `Geog 7(A)`

   G Afghan refugees fled to Pakistan to escape war involving Taliban and U.S. forces.

   H Turkish workers migrated to Germany after 1945 to fill jobs in that nation.

   J East Berliners crossed into West Berlin in the 1960s to escape Communist rule.

9 Muslim peoples from the Middle East crossed into India, where they spread the Islamic religion. How was their migration route most affected by physical geography?

   A They avoided streams and rivers along their migration route.   `Geog 7(A)`

   B They were unable to migrate because of unfavorable weather conditions.

   C They migrated along the route that took them through the densest forests.

   D They migrated through the Kyber Pass to avoid going over mountains.

Use the information and your knowledge of social studies to answer the following question.

> Each year some 3,000 Tibetans escape from threats and persecution posed by China's invasion of Tibet. Tibetans journey across the Himalayas through the Nangpa La Mountain Pass, at a height of 18,880 feet, to reach Nepal and India. Their trip takes months since they travel on foot and at night to avoid Chinese patrols. Tibetans risk hypothermia, snow blindness, falling down crevasses, dying of cold or hunger, or being shot by Chinese border guards.
>
> — *The Free Tibet Association*

10 What conclusion can be drawn from this passage?

   F People are afraid to migrate across routes that are unsafe.   `Geog 7(B)`

   G The flow of human migration is affected by a variety of factors.

   H Tibet poses a serious threat to China.

   J The Nanga La Mountain pass is a safe route for most Tibetan exiles.

UNIT 3 REVIEW
PULLING IT ALL TOGETHER

Based on what you learned in this unit, list *two* possible topics for a research project on human geography that you would like to investigate further.

1. _____

_____

2. _____

_____

Select *one* of the *Essential Questions* explored in this unit by checking the box. Then answer it below.

ESSENTIAL QUESTIONS REEXAMINED

☐ How is each of us a product of our culture?

☐ What beliefs and traditions are held by the world's great religions?

☐ How do different cultural regions around the world compare to one another?

☐ Where can you find the main countries and major cities of the world?

☐ What factors influence where people settle?

☐ Is the world's population growing too fast?

☐ What reasons cause people to migrate to different areas?

_____

_____

_____

_____

_____

_____

_____

_____

_____

_____

UNIT 3 CONCEPT MAP

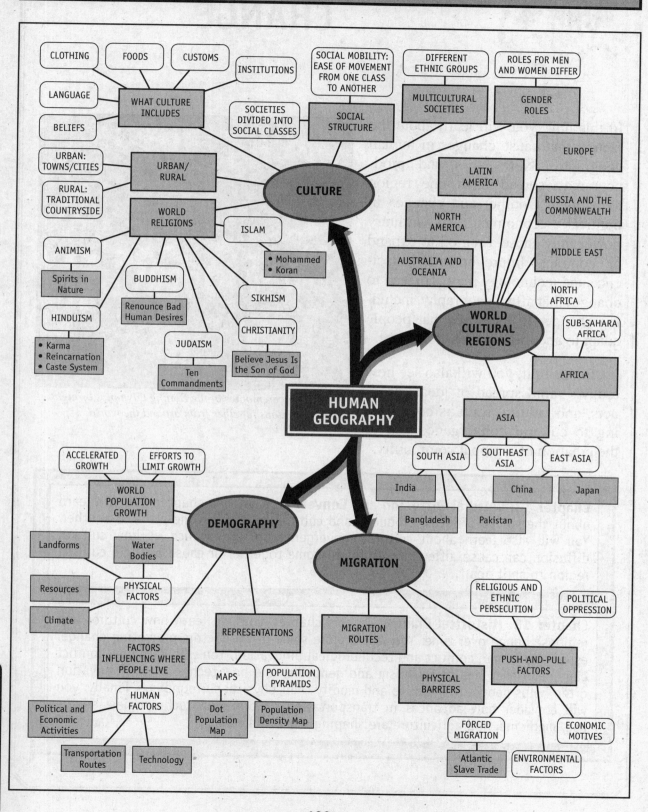

CLOTHING

FOODS

CUSTOMS

INSTITUTIONS

WHAT CULTURE INCLUDES

LANGUAGE

BELIEFS

SOCIAL MOBILITY: EASE OF MOVEMENT FROM ONE CLASS TO ANOTHER

SOCIETIES DIVIDED INTO SOCIAL CLASSES

SOCIAL STRUCTURE

DIFFERENT ETHNIC GROUPS

MULTICULTURAL SOCIETIES

ROLES FOR MEN AND WOMEN DIFFER

GENDER ROLES

URBAN: TOWNS/CITIES

URBAN/ RURAL

RURAL: TRADITIONAL COUNTRYSIDE

WORLD RELIGIONS

ISLAM

• Mohammed
• Koran

ANIMISM

Spirits in Nature

BUDDHISM

Renounce Bad Human Desires

SIKHISM

CHRISTIANITY

HINDUISM

JUDAISM

Believe Jesus Is the Son of God

• Karma
• Reincarnation
• Caste System

Ten Commandments

CULTURE

EUROPE

LATIN AMERICA

RUSSIA AND THE COMMONWEALTH

NORTH AMERICA

MIDDLE EAST

AUSTRALIA AND OCEANIA

WORLD CULTURAL REGIONS

NORTH AFRICA

SUB-SAHARA AFRICA

AFRICA

HUMAN GEOGRAPHY

ASIA

SOUTH ASIA

SOUTHEAST ASIA

EAST ASIA

India

China

Japan

Bangladesh

Pakistan

ACCELERATED GROWTH

EFFORTS TO LIMIT GROWTH

WORLD POPULATION GROWTH

Landforms

Water Bodies

DEMOGRAPHY

Resources

PHYSICAL FACTORS

Climate

FACTORS INFLUENCING WHERE PEOPLE LIVE

REPRESENTATIONS

MIGRATION ROUTES

MIGRATION

RELIGIOUS AND ETHNIC PERSECUTION

POLITICAL OPPRESSION

HUMAN FACTORS

MAPS

POPULATION PYRAMIDS

PHYSICAL BARRIERS

PUSH-AND-PULL FACTORS

Political and Economic Activities

Dot Population Map

Population Density Map

Transportation Routes

Technology

FORCED MIGRATION

ECONOMIC MOTIVES

Atlantic Slave Trade

ENVIRONMENTAL FACTORS

Name _____ Date _____

UNIT 4

CHANGE

In this unit, you will learn about the factors that cause changes in human geography. New ideas and products may spread from one region to another. Conflict and changes in political, economic, and military power may cause a region to expand or contract. Improvements in science and technology may also lead to changes that affect geography, including changes in the ways that people adapt to and modify their landscape.

In this unit, you will also see how today's rapid spread of ideas, products, and cultural traits is contributing to cultural convergence and to the creation of a global community.

Opening ceremonies at the Beijing Olympics brought nations together from around the world.

Chapter 12. Cultural Diffusion and Convergence. In this chapter, you will learn about the spread of ideas, products, and cultural traits from one place to another. You will also learn about cultural convergence and divergence — how cultural diffusion can cause different cultures to come together or cause a single cultural region to split apart.

Chapter 13. Historical Change. In this chapter, you will learn how cultures and regions change over time. You will explore some of the factors promoting change, especially human conflict and technological innovation. You will learn how conflict can sometimes lead to terrorism and genocide, and how technological innovation often helps people to adapt to and modify their physical surroundings. Finally, you will consider how advances in transportation, information technologies, energy use, medicine, and agriculture are shaping our world today.

Cultural Diffusion and Convergence

This chapter corresponds to pages 72–77 of HMH's *World Geography*.

❑ **Before Reading:** You might begin your study of cultural diffusion by reading the TEKS, *Geographic Terminology*, *Important Ideas* and *Essential Question* on pages 202–203.

❑ **During Reading:** Next read about cultural diffusion on pages 203–209 below. You might then turn to HMH's *World Geography* for more information about the Silk Road (pp. 375–376), Chinese inventions (p. 638), the Columbian Exchange (pp. 136, 222–223), pandemics, including AIDS (pp. 435, 452, 465–467), the spread of modern technologies (pp. 569–570) and American popular culture (pp. 143, 646, 654). You can return to this book and read pages 209–210 to learn about cultural divergence and how this process sometimes leads societies to break apart. You might examine specific examples found in HMH's *World Geography*, such as the Roman Empire (pp. 291), the division of Charlemagne's empire (pp. 296–297), the separation of the Balkans into smaller states (p. 311), and the division of British India into India and Pakistan (p. 568). Finally, you should read pages 211–214 in this book to learn about cultural convergence and how globalization is speeding up that process. Complete your study of convergence by reading sections of HMH's *World Geography* for more about the spread of democracy (pp. 249–251, 253, 315, 454–455, 568–569), global sports (pp. 308–309) and the convergence of Aztec and Spanish cultures in Mexico (pp. 217–219).

❑ **After Reading:** Reinforce your learning by filling in the graphic organizers, reviewing the study cards, and answering the test questions at the end of the chapter.

Topics	Mastering the TEKS	HMH's World Geography
Patterns of Diffusion	pp. 203–206	p. 72
Spread of New Products	pp. 203–205	
Silk Road	p. 203	pp. 375–376
Chinese Inventions	p. 204	p. 638
Columbian Exchange	p. 204	pp. 136, 222–223
Modern Technologies	p. 205	pp. 569–570 ("Green Revolution" in India)
Spread of New Ideas	pp. 205–206	pp. 504 (Islam); 638 (Buddhism)
Spread of Chinese Culture to Japan	p. 206	pp. 651, 654
Spread of Cultural Traits	pp. 206–207	p. 72, 506
American Popular Culture	p. 207	pp. 143, 519 (modern vs. traditional life-styles); 646 (Taiwan); 649 (South Korea); 654–665 (Japan)
Pandemics: Spread of Disease	pp. 207–209	pp. 435, 452, 465–467 (AIDS)
Bubonic Plague	p. 208	pp. 294–295
"Old World" Diseases to the Americas	p. 208	pp. 223, 231, 236
Cultural Divergence and Convergence	pp. 209–210	pp. 180–183
Cultural Divergence	pp. 209–210	
Roman Empire	p. 210	pp. 290–291, 296, 311
India	p. 210	pp. 567–568
Aztecs & Yaquis	p. 210	pp. 218–219 (Aztecs)
Cultural Convergence and Globalization	p. 211	pp. 72, 212–213, 219, 224–225, 665–667
Recent Examples of Convergence	pp. 211–213	
Spread of Democracy	pp. 211–212	pp. 249, 253, 315, 454–455, 568–569
English Language	p. 212	pp. 143, 571
New Technologies	p. 213	p. 299
Global Sports	p. 213	pp. 307–309

Using Multiple Sources of Information

• Use information from both books to write your own answer to the *Essential Question* on page 202.

Name _____ Date _____

CULTURAL DIFFUSION AND CONVERGENCE

CHAPTER 12

■ **History 1** The student understands how geography and processes of spatial exchange influenced past events and helped shape the present.
  • **History 1(B)** Trace the spatial diffusion of phenomena such as the Columbian Exchange or the diffusion of American popular culture and describe the effects on regions of contact.
■ **Geography 7(D)** Examine benefits and challenges of globalization, including ... pandemics.
■ **Culture 18** The student understands the ways in which cultures change and maintain continuity.
  • **Culture 18(A)** Analyze cultural changes in specific regions caused by ... diffusion.
  • **Culture 18(D)** Evaluate the spread of cultural traits to find examples of cultural convergence and divergence such as the spread of democratic ideas, U.S.-based fast-food franchises, the English language, technology, or global sports.

TEKS
COVERED IN
CHAPTER 12

In this chapter, you will look at how ideas, products, and even cultural traits can spread from one culture to another. Geographers and other social scientists refer to this process of spatial exchange as **cultural diffusion**.

AN ESSENTIAL QUESTION

How does the spatial diffusion of ideas, products, and traits lead to change, including cultural divergence and convergence?

— IMPORTANT IDEAS —

A. Processes of spatial exchange, or **diffusion**, have influenced events in the past and continue to shape the present.

B. During the **Columbian Exchange**, new plants, animals, ideas and even diseases were exchanged between the peoples of the Americas and those of Europe, Asia and Africa. More recently, aspects of American popular culture have spread throughout the world. Such spatial diffusions have affected regions of contact.

C. **Cultural divergence** occurs when different cultural influences cause an area to divide into separate parts. **Cultural convergence** occurs when different cultures exchange ideas and become more similar.

D. **Cultural diffusion** today is leading to **cultural convergence** on a global scale, creating a common global culture. This can be seen in the spread of democratic ideas, the English language, technology, and global sports.

GEOGRAPHIC TERMINOLOGY IN THIS CHAPTER

- ■ **Diffusion**
- ■ **Spatial Exchange**
- ■ **Columbian Exchange**
- ■ **Cultural Convergence**
- ■ **Cultural Divergence**
- ■ **Pandemics**

A thousand years ago, separate cultural regions thrived in the Americas, the Middle East, Europe, India, China and Sub-Saharan Africa. These independent regions often had very little contact or communication with one another, or none at all.

Various elements of culture — including food, clothing, shelter, religious beliefs, and technology — were then quite different in each part of the world. Today, developments in one region often spread quickly to other areas of the world, creating more similarities.

PATTERNS OF DIFFUSION

Diffusion refers to how something *diffuses* or spreads. A drop of ink, for example, will spread through a glass of water until the ink and water blend into a single mixture. Plants, animals, goods and ideas are all capable of diffusing in new regions or cultures.

Geographers and historians are especially concerned with the patterns that such diffusion takes. They look at the spread of a phenomenon, the speed of its diffusion, the path it takes, and the effects it has on various regions of contact. As with migration, features of physical geography may pose natural barriers preventing or slowing down diffusion.

Let's examine some of the ways in which cultural diffusion takes place:

THE SPREAD OF NEW PRODUCTS

Sometimes contact between two different cultures leads to an exchange of products. Travelers and merchants bring the new products back to their homelands. Use of these new products quickly spreads, stimulating trade. People demand more of the product, and merchants compete to obtain it. Other people will try to produce the good locally to meet the rising demand.

Trade Along the Silk Road. For example, Middle Eastern and Roman merchants established overland trade with ancient China along the Silk Road. Over this route, Chinese silk was introduced to Europe. Romans had never encountered a material as fine and smooth as Chinese silk. Previously, Romans had only worn wool, linen or cotton. Silk quickly became a symbol of wealth and high status in elite Roman society. The Silk Road also saw the exchange of chariots, languages, and metallurgy. In particular, the Chinese traded silks for horses and camels for use by their armies to prevent foreign invasions.

CASE STUDY:
Chinese Inventions Foster European Exploration

At the time of the Middle Ages in Europe, China developed gunpowder, the compass, and printing. European merchants like Marco Polo brought news of these inventions back to Europe. Borrowing from the Chinese, Europeans copied these products. They used gunpowder to construct cannons and adapted the compass to improve their seafaring skills. These Chinese inventions later allowed the rulers of Spain and Portugal to launch voyages of exploration across the Atlantic Ocean.

Marco Polo was 17 when he left Venice with his father and uncle for China. This illustration shows their arrival in China.

CASE STUDY:
The Columbian Exchange

European and Native American cultures encountered each other for the first time in 1492. This encounter, referred to as the Columbian Exchange, led to the introduction of new products to both cultures. Europeans brought horses, goats, cattle, pigs, chickens, wheat, and goods like cannons, crossbows and steel

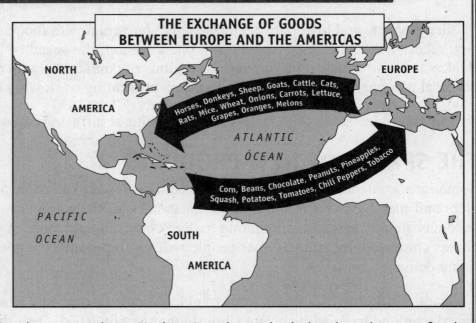

THE EXCHANGE OF GOODS BETWEEN EUROPE AND THE AMERICAS

NORTH AMERICA

EUROPE

Horses, Donkeys, Sheep, Goats, Cattle, Cats, Rats, Mice, Wheat, Onions, Carrots, Lettuce, Grapes, Oranges, Melons

ATLANTIC OCEAN

Corn, Beans, Chocolate, Peanuts, Pineapples, Squash, Potatoes, Tomatoes, Chili Peppers, Tobacco

PACIFIC OCEAN

SOUTH AMERICA

to the Americas. At the same time, Native Americans had developed many foods unknown to Europeans. An important result of the encounter was that the European diet was greatly improved by the introduction of new foods such as tomatoes, chocolate, potatoes, beans, peppers, pumpkins, squash, sweet potatoes, peanuts, and corn. Europeans also learned how to smoke tobacco.

APPLYING WHAT YOU HAVE LEARNED

How might history have been different if the cultures of Europe and the Americas had never come into contact?

_____

_____

_____

_____

The Spread of New Technologies. Today, the spread of new products is especially rapid. People learn of new products through travel, newspapers, television, and telephone conversations. For example, personal computers did not exist before the 1980s. They were first developed in the United States, but they quickly spread throughout the world.

Even more recently, scientists and engineers developed cellular (*mobile*) phones. These have spread rapidly even to less developed nations, which lack enough telephone cables for landline telephones. In just a few years, cellular phones have spread from America, Japan, and Europe to every region of the world.

APPLYING WHAT YOU HAVE LEARNED

"Smart phones," like Apple's iPhone, allow people to have access to the Internet from their cell phone. Use the Internet to research which smart phones are now available in other countries. What does this tell you about the speed at which new products spread around the world today?

_____

_____

_____

_____

_____

THE SPREAD OF NEW IDEAS

Contacts between different cultures can also lead to important exchanges of ideas. Religious beliefs, political ideas (*like democracy*) and other ideas often spread from one culture to another. The great world religions all spread from their places of origin to neighboring areas. Islam, for example, arose on the Arabian Peninsula. Arab peoples then brought Islam to the rest of the Middle East, North Africa, and Spain. Later, Islam spread to parts of South and Southeast Asia.

CASE STUDY:
The Spread of Chinese Culture

Japan's location close to China brought many aspects of Chinese culture to Japan. For example, Japan's rulers claimed to be absolute emperors, like those of China. Buddhism and Confucianism also came from China and interacted with Japanese beliefs to create new values and beliefs. Confucianism taught loyalty to the ruler, while Buddhism taught the Japanese to reject selfish desires. Japan also adapted Chinese characters to create their own written language. Chinese music, art, pottery, weaving, and cooking further influenced Japanese styles and tastes.

China greatly influenced Japan's writing and other aspects of Japanese culture.

APPLYING WHAT YOU HAVE LEARNED

Japan's location close to China had a great influence on its culture. Briefly describe another example in which ideas from one culture spread to another.

_____

_____

_____

_____

_____

_____

_____

THE SPREAD OF CULTURAL TRAITS

Even such elements of culture as clothing fashions, art styles, ways of cooking food, and music can spread from one region to another. Walk down the streets of any American city and you might find Italian and Chinese restaurants or women wearing shoes based on styles from Europe.

CASE STUDY:
The Global Reach of American Popular Culture

American culture is a product of many influences, including those from Native American, English, French, Spanish, African, Asian, and other cultures. In the early 20th century, a vibrant American culture emerged with new technologies, like the radio, record player, moving picture, and television. After World War II, American popular music and movies became popular in Europe and later spread to every continent. Today, people throughout the world see American movies and television programs, dance to American "pop" music, and use English as an international second language. Many wear American casual dress styles, such as tee shirts with logos, and large numbers even eat at American fast-food franchises, like McDonald's and Taco Bell. American artists like Michael Jackson and Lady Gaga are international icons, known in almost every corner of the world.

A McDonald's restaurant in the heart of Beijing, China.

APPLYING WHAT YOU HAVE LEARNED

What factors do you think have most helped American popular culture to spread throughout the world over the past 50 years?

_____

_____

_____

PANDEMICS: The Spread of Disease

We often think of the diffusion of a new phenomenon as beneficial, but it can sometimes have negative effects. One example of this is the spread of new diseases from one culture to another. The disease diffuses as the microorganisms that cause the disease are spread.

CASE STUDY:
The Bubonic Plague

Bubonic Plague was a highly contagious disease that first emerged in China and Central Asia. The bacteria causing the disease were carried by fleas that lived on rats. European merchant ships unknowingly carried these rats to Italy in the 1340s. The disease spread quickly to Italy, Spain, and France. It soon reached England, Germany and the Netherlands. In less than ten years, almost one-third of Europe's population was killed by the spread of this disease.

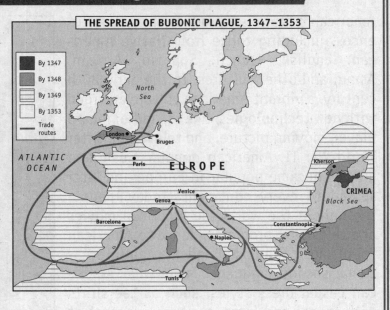

THE SPREAD OF BUBONIC PLAGUE, 1347–1353

By 1347
By 1348
By 1349
By 1353
Trade routes

North Sea
London
Bruges
ATLANTIC OCEAN
Paris
EUROPE
Kherson
Venice
Genoa
Black Sea
CRIMEA
Barcelona
Constantinople
Naples
Tunis

CASE STUDY:
Spread of "Old World" Diseases to the Americas

The Spanish conquest of the Americas brought important changes to the Americas. One change had devastating effects on the Native American population. Unknown to the European explorers of the 1500s, they brought new diseases to the Americas — including smallpox, typhus and measles. Native American Indians had never been exposed to these diseases and lacked immunity to them. Scientists believe that since Native American Indians did not live among domesticated herd animals, a rich breeding ground for diseases, they never developed natural immunities to such diseases. A large portion of the Native American Indian population died from these illnesses after their encounter with Europeans.

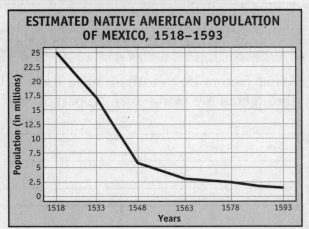

ESTIMATED NATIVE AMERICAN POPULATION OF MEXICO, 1518–1593

Population (in millions)
25
22.5
20
17.5
15
12.5
10
7.5
5
2.5
0
1518   1533   1548   1563   1578   1593
Years

Native American populations declined rapidly because they lacked immunity to diseases brought by the conquerors like measles and smallpox.

Today, we live in an increasingly interconnected world. People travel more than ever on airlines that reach every corner of the globe. In addition, our global food supply plays a role in the spread of disease. Mass production and the global distribution of foods make it easier for some illnesses to spread.

New diseases are therefore emerging at an unprecedented rate. Often they have an ability to cross borders rapidly and spread from one country to another. Some scientists fear a **pandemic flu**, a new strain of influenza that might lead to a global **pandemic** (*an epidemic over a wide geographic area*).

CASE STUDY:
The Avian Flu Threat

In 2004, a serious threat of pandemic occurred. An **avian flu** virus was detected in birds in Vietnam. The virus that causes this infection in birds can mutate (*change*) to infect humans, who have no immunity against it. It was feared that this virus in birds might combine with a human flu virus, leading to a highly contagious and deadly outbreak. At first, it appeared that this would indeed occur. In 2005, cases of avian flu (*H5N1*) were identified in Turkey, Russia, Mongolia and China. Cases were also later identified in Romania, Greece, Croatia, Bularia and the United Kingdom. Fortunately, fears of a global pandemic, which might have killed millions of people, were not realized.

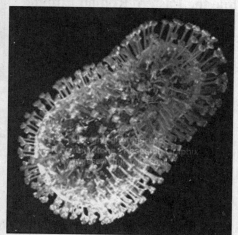
The H5N1 Avian flu virus under high magnification.

CULTURAL DIVERGENCE AND CONVERGENCE

Cultural diffusion can play an important role in both **cultural divergence** and **cultural convergence**. To *diverge* is to separate, or to go in different directions. To *converge* is to come together.

CULTURAL DIVERGENCE

Cultural divergence is the tendency of societies, or even groups within a society, to become increasingly dissimilar with the passage of time. Often this happens from exposure to new ideas through cultural diffusion. Physical barriers, like mountains, might also separate people in different regions. Isolated from one another, they gradually develop completely different cultures.

The Roman Empire. For example, cultural divergence occurred in the later Roman Empire. At one time, this giant empire covered most of Europe, the Middle East, and North Africa. However, waves of Germanic tribes from Northern Europe later attacked the Western part of the empire. These invaders introduced new cultural elements to the Western Roman Empire, while the Eastern Roman Empire, with its capital at Constantinople, fell under the influence of Greek culture. This cultural divergence eventually led the Roman Empire to break apart.

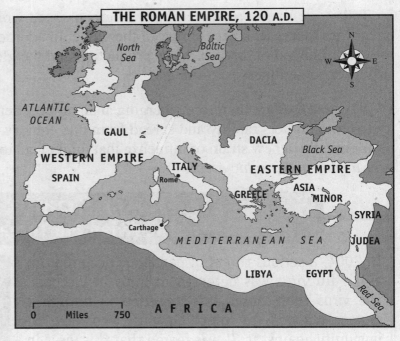

THE ROMAN EMPIRE, 120 A.D.

India. In another example, Aryan India was once unified by a common Hindu culture. But the arrival of Islamic influences from the northwest led India to become divided into Hindu and Muslim areas.

Aztecs and Yaquis. Yet another example of cultural divergence can be seen between the Aztecs and the Yaquis of Mexico. Many scholars believe that several thousand years ago, they once spoke the same language and shared a common culture. However, the Yaquis and Aztecs later became separate cultural groups. The Aztecs then migrated southwards to Central Mexico. Aztecs and Yaquis came to speak different languages and to hold different religious beliefs.

APPLYING WHAT YOU HAVE LEARNED

Identify another example of cultural divergence — a region or people that became divided because of different cultural influences. Use the Internet, your library, your own notes, or other outside sources to research an example. Then explain how your example illustrates cultural divergence.

_____

_____

_____

_____

_____

CULTURAL CONVERGENCE AND GLOBALIZATION

Cultural diffusion can also lead to **cultural convergence**, in which different cultures become similar or even come together.

For example, at the end of the fifteenth century, European and Native American Indian cultures were completely separate. The Columbian Exchange brought about cultural convergence. European ideas and customs (such as Catholicism, landholding, the Spanish language, and royal government) merged with Native American traditions (such as using tobacco and eating corn, tomatoes, chocolate, and squash) to create a new "Latin American" culture.

*A street in Tokyo —
notice how many signs are in English.*

Globalization. Today, the rapid pace of cultural diffusion is contributing greatly to cultural convergence. Every society quickly learns, through air travel, newspapers, television, telecommunications, and the Internet — what is happening in other societies. Global transportation and trade make it easier to exchange products with other cultures. Each society borrows or adapts what it finds best in other societies. This cultural convergence has led to the phenomenon known as **globalization** — the creation of a common global culture. We realize that we are all citizens, not only of our own countries, but of a common global community.

RECENT EXAMPLES OF CONVERGENCE

Cultural convergence today can be seen in the global spread of democratic ideas, the English language, new technologies, and even global sports.

DEMOCRATIC IDEAS

In 1980, many countries did not enjoy democratic government. Much of the world was still ruled by communist regimes and military dictatorships. However, in the late 1980s and 1990s, democracy was on the march.

Democracy spread to many new regions of the world, including the Philippines, Chile, Nicaragua, Argentina, Panama, and Haiti. News of events in one area quickly spread to other areas. In Africa, dictators fell from power in Somalia, Liberia, and Ethiopia.

The movement for democracy led to the destruction of the Berlin Wall and the re-unification of Germany.

The Communist Party lost its monopoly of power in the Soviet Union. Poland, Hungary, Bulgaria, Czechoslovakia, and East Germany all toppled their communist dictatorships in favor of democratic governments. In 1991, the Soviet Union itself split apart into Russia and other states, all of which chose popularly elected governments. Despite some pessimism about democracy's future in Russia and countries of the former Soviet Union, there is strong support for democracy as the best form of government among most of its citizens.

THE ENGLISH LANGUAGE

In a business conference today, participants from Saudi Arabia, India, China, Russia, Ghana, Holland, and Israel would almost certainly speak English to one another. There is an increasing trend to use English as an international second language. This is another example of global cultural convergence.

Israeli signs in Hebrew, Arabic, and English.

Today almost a half billion people speak English as their primary language. In addition, in most countries, people usually learn English as their second language. More than a billion people now understand English.

The use of English in British colonies like Egypt and India, the spread of American popular culture since World War II, the location of many multinational businesses in the United States and Britain, and the recent increase in the use of computers and the Internet have all contributed to this adoption of English as a global language. Educated people understand that there are well-paid careers and global opportunities for those who speak English.

NEW TECHNOLOGIES

The spread of new technologies is also contributing to cultural convergence and globalization. At one time in history, different parts of the world did not even know about each other's existence. It took months to reach some places by ship. There were no other means of communication. Today, people in every culture are familiar with telephones, televisions, computers, cell phones, and the Internet. These new technologies link us closer together than at any other time in history.

Even a small home business with access to the Internet can now market its products to people around the globe. Not only can people communiciate all around the world, but they also share the common experience of using these tehnologies. This shared experience and enhanced ability to communicate is helping to build a common global culture.

An Arabic woman talks on her cell phone.

GLOBAL SPORTS

Even competitive team sports have gone global. With cable television, space satellites and the Internet, people can follow sports taking place in every part of the world. Global cultural convergence is further advanced when teams from different countries come together to compete periodically in international sporting events — such as the Olympics or the World Cup in soccer.

A U.S. player scores a goal against Algeria in the 2010 FIFA World Cup held in South Africa.

These sporting events appeal to a wide global audience. They bring people together as citizens of a new global community. The rules of the game rise above differences. Sports contribute to social unity, tolerance and integration. Sports provide a universal language that can bridge cultural gaps, resolve conflicts, and bring about greater understanding among people of different backgrounds and nationalities.

APPLYING WHAT YOU HAVE LEARNED

Choose one of the examples of cultural convergence discussed above. Look up this development on the Internet or in the library. Find out more information and write a brief newspaper article reporting about it. Include a headline for your article.

_____

_____

_____

_____

_____

_____

_____

_____

_____

_____

_____

LEARNING WITH GRAPHIC ORGANIZERS

Complete the graphic organizer below. Define cultural divergence and convergence.

CULTURAL DIVERGENCE AND CONVERGENCE

Cultural Divergence	Cultural Convergence
_____	_____
_____	_____
_____	_____
_____	_____
_____	_____

LEARNING WITH GRAPHIC ORGANIZERS

Complete the graphic organizer below. For each type of diffusion, identify one example and describe it.

Spread of New Products	**Spread of New Ideas and Technologies**
_____ _____ _____ _____ _____ _____ _____ _____ _____	_____ _____ _____ _____ _____ _____ _____ _____ _____

CULTURAL DIFFUSION

Spread of Cultural Traits	**Spread of Diseases**
_____ _____ _____ _____ _____ _____ _____ _____	_____ _____ _____ _____ _____ _____ _____ _____

CHAPTER STUDY CARDS

Cultural Diffusion

★ **Cultural diffusion** is a process of spatial exchange in which ideas, products, cultural traits and even diseases spread from one place to another.

★ Examples of cultural diffusion include —

- **The Columbian Exchange.** Europeans learned new ideas and products. Native Americans obtained new animals and faced deadly diseases.

- **Spread of American Popular Culture.** American movies, "pop" music, TV programs, "fast foods," and casual dress styles have all spread around the world.

Types of Cultural Diffusion

★ The exchange of products.

★ The spread of technology.
  - Europeans adopted gunpowder, the compass, and printing from China.

★ The spread of ideas.
  - Religions often spread their beliefs from one place to another.
  - Buddhism, Christianity, Islam.

★ The spread of cultural traits.

★ **Pandemics.** Spread of diseases:
  - **Bubonic Plague**
  - Spread of smallpox in the Americas to Native American Indians.

Cultural Convergence and Globalization

★ **Democratic Ideas.** In the 1980s and 1990s, democratic government spread to many new areas of the world, replacing military dictatorships and communist states.

★ **English Language.** English has become quite widespread as the international second language throughout the world.

★ **New Technologies.** Satellite television.

★ **Global Sports Competitions.**
  - Winter and Summer Olympics.
  - World Cup in soccer.

Cultural Convergence and Divergence

★ **Cultural Convergence.** Different cultures acquire common ideas, products, and traits, becoming more similar.

★ **Cultural Divergence.** Different parts of a cultural region are exposed to different influences and become dissimilar.

For example:
- Roman Empire divided into Western and Eastern Empires.
- Islamic influences in India divided the region into Hindu and Muslim.
- Aztecs and Yaquis.

CHECKING YOUR UNDERSTANDING

Directions: Put a circle around the letter that best answers the question.

1   Which activity provides an example of cultural diffusion from the Middle East to Africa?

    A   weaving traditional kente cloth in Ghana   (Cult 18(A))

    B   using masks in traditional African ceremonies

    C   making bronze sculptures in ancient Benin

    D   practicing Islam in Nigeria

Choice **A** is wrong. Weaving kente cloth is a traditional activity that was not introduced from the Middle East. **Choice B** is wrong. The use of masks are part of traditional ceremonies developed in Africa. **Choice C** is also wrong. Benin was known for its bronze sculptures. Although knowledge of bronze may have come to Benin through cultural diffusion, this knowledge would have come from Egypt not the Middle East. **Choice D** is the best answer. Islam did not originate in Nigeria: it first arose in Saudi Arabia in the Middle East. Cultural diffusion eventually brought it to Nigeria in Africa.

Now try answering some additional questions on your own:

Use the map and your knowledge of social studies to answer questions 2 and 3.

2   Which process is illustrated by the map?
   F   the Columbian Exchange
   G   the movement of goods
   H   cultural diffusion
   J   cultural divergence
   [Hist 1(B)]

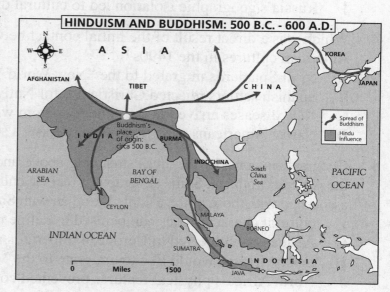

HINDUISM AND BUDDHISM: 500 B.C. - 600 A.D.

3   What conclusion can best be drawn from the information in the map?
   A   Buddhism failed to have any influence on Japan.
   B   Buddhism was unable to spread to islands in the Pacific.   [Hist 1(B)]
   C   Buddhism began in northern India and spread throughout much of Asia.
   D   Buddhism moved from Indonesia to India and then into Afghanistan.

4   Hindu scholars contributed to mathematics by developing the decimal system and the concept of zero. Arab mathematicians transmitted these ideas to Western Europe. Which conclusion is best drawn from these facts?
   F   Hindus and Arabs developed the first civilizations.
   G   The study of mathematics first began in Europe.   [Cult 18(A)]
   H   New ideas are often spread through contacts between cultures.
   J   Europeans had no ideas to share with Hindus and Arabs.

5   Which of the following is the best example of cultural convergence?

   A   Different countries in Europe today have similar standards   `Cult 18(D)`
           of living and systems of government.
   B   Some Turkish "guest workers" in Germany cannot read or write in German.
   C   People in the Sahel region of Africa are moving to nearby regions to escape dry
           conditions from drought.
   D   Some universities do not require students to study a foreign language.

6   The Eastern Orthodox Church and the Cyrillic alphabet originated in the Byzantine
       Empire. What does the practice of this religion and the use of this alphabet in nearby
       Russia indicate?

   F   Russia was conquered by the Byzantine Empire.   `Hist 1(B)`
   G   Russia's leaders eliminated the influence of the Mongols.
   H   Russia was affected by the spatial diffusion of phenomena.
   J   Russia's geographic isolation led to cultural diversity.

7   Which was a direct result of the initial contact between European cultures and Native
       American cultures in the 1490s?

   A   Most Spaniards migrated to the "New World."   `Hist 1(B)`
   B   Spanish settlers rejected Christianity for Native American religious beliefs.
   C   New diseases arrived in the Americas from which natives lacked immunity.
   D   Native Americans used Spanish settlers as a source of cheap labor.

8   Geographers consider the areas stretching above and below the Sahara Desert as part of
       the African continent. Some geographers feel the cultures of North Africa are more closely
       associated with those of the Middle East than with Sub-Saharan Africa. This shows that —

   F   cultural characteristics can be used to define regions.   `Geog 9(A)`
   G   Africa was subjected to European imperialism.
   H   most Africans would like to emigrate to the Middle East.
   J   North Africa's physical features prevented contact with the Middle East.

Use the information and your knowledge of social studies to answer the following question.

> "The Mongols made no technological breakthroughs, founded no new religions, wrote
> few books, and gave the world no new crops or methods of agriculture. Their own crafts-
> men could not weave cloth, cast metal, make pottery, or bake bread. They manufactured
> no porcelain or pottery, painted no pictures, and built no buildings. Yet, as their army
> conquered culture after culture, they collected and passed all of these skills from one
> civilization to the next …"
> — *Jack Weatherford*

9   What conclusion can be drawn from this paragraph about the Mongols ?

   A   The Mongols rejected technology.   `Cult 18(A)`
   B   The Mongols were urbanized.
   C   The Mongols were a peaceful people.
   D   The Mongols contributed to cultural diffusion.

Historical Change

This chapter examines the theme of change. It explores how physical geography changes over time and especially how human geography changes over time as the result of migration, cultural diffusion, trade, armed conflict, and technological innovation.

❏ *Before Reading:* You might begin your study of this period by reading the TEKS, *Geographical Terminology, Important Ideas* and *Essential Questions* on pages 221–222.

❏ *During Reading:* Then read the chapter below on pages 222–223, to see how physical geography itself can change over time. Chapter 6 of this book also discussed the processes causing physical geography to change, such as tectonic plate motion and erosion. You can learn more about Beringia, the land bridge that once connected Siberia and Alaska, on page 127 of HMH's *World Geography*, and you can read about recent changes to the Aral Sea on pages 353–354 of that book. You will then be ready to learn about changes in human geography, which is the main focus of this chapter. Begin by reading pages 223 to 234 in this book. For each cause of change or example, explore further by reading the corresponding sections of HMH's *World Geography*, as indicated on the correlation chart below. For example, if you are learning how trade fostered change, first read p. 226 below and then read p. 310 in HMH's *World Geography* to learn how Eastern Europe was a crossroads of trade; pp. 431–432, to learn how trade affected East Africa; pp. 442–443, to learn how trade changed West Africa; pp. 505–506 to learn how trade, especially in petroleum, has changed life on the Arabian Peninsula; p. 568 to learn how the arrival of European traders affected India; p. 636 to learn how European trade influenced China; and pp. 665–667 to learn how trade affected Japan and continues to affect the nations of East Asia today. You can similarly find additional information about each of the roots of change by using the correlation chart below.

❏ *After Reading:* Reinforce your learning by completing the graphic organizers, reviewing the study cards and answering the test questions at the end of the chapter.

Topics	Mastering the TEKS	HMH's *World Geography*
How Geography Changes Over Time	pp. 224	
Changes in Physical Geography	pp. 222–223	
Sahara Desert	p. 222	pp. 420–421 (Sahara today)
Siberian-Alaskan Land Bridge	p. 223	p. 127
Changes to Aral Sea		pp. 353–354
Changes in Human Geography	pp. 223–224	pp. 304, 312, 362, 404, 480–481, 574, 612–613, 643, 653, 706
The Americas	p. 223	pp. 104–105, 135–137, 157, 192–193, 222
The Roman Empire	p. 224	pp. 290–291
The Roots of Change	pp. 225–229	
Migration	p. 225	pp. 73, 81, 180–181
Cultural Diffusion	p. 226	pp. 72, 151 TX3, 468, 648–649, 654, 706–706
Trade	p. 226	pp. 310, 431–432, 442–443, 505–506, 568, 636, 665–667
Conflict	pp. 227–229	
Civil Wars & Genocide	pp. 227–228	pp. 319–321, 371–372, 469, 512–513, 568
International Conflict	pp. 228–229	pp. 138, 298, 311–312, 363, 516–517, 600–601, 707
Impact of Conflict	p. 229	pp. 219 (Spanish conquest of Aztecs); 230–231 (Spanish conquest of Inca); 449 (colonization of Africa); 505, 511 (colonization of Middle East); 568 (colonization of India); 642–644 (Mongol Empire); 706–707 (colonization of Southeast Asia)
The Crusades	p. 229	pp. 291, 510

Using Multiple Sources of Information

- Use information from both books to write your own answers to the *Essential Questions* on page 221.
- Create your own concept map around one of the *Important Ideas* on page 222. Use facts, examples, and ideas from both books for your concept map.
- Use information from both books to create your own series of maps of the same area at different points of time, revealing how that area's physical geography has changed.
- Use information from both books to make an illustrated chart identifying the different forces that lead societies to change, such as migration, cultural diffusion, trade, innovation and war.
- Use information from both books to create your own video, slide show, Prezi or PowerPoint presentation about how societies change.
- Use information from both books and other outside sources to prepare an oral or written report on an incident of genocide. Consider what happened, why it happened, and the consequences. Then give your opinion on what steps should be taken to prevent similar acts of genocide in the future.
- Use information from both books to hold a panel discussion in your classroom on the causes of international conflict and how conflict can be avoided.
- Use information from both books to create an illustrated timeline of leading technological innovations and their social impact.

HISTORICAL CHANGE

CHAPTER 13

TEKS
COVERED IN
CHAPTER 13

- **History 2** The student understands how people, places, and environments have changed over time and the effects of these changes.
  - **History 2(A)** Describe the human and physical characteristics of the same regions at different periods of time to evaluate relationships between past events and current conditions.
  - **History 2(B)** Explain how changes in societies have led to diverse uses of physical features.
- **Culture 18** The student understands the ways in which cultures change and maintain continuity.
  - **Culture 18(A)** Analyze cultural changes in specific regions caused by migration, war, trade, innovations, and diffusion.
  - **Culture 18(B)** Assess causes, effects, and perceptions of conflicts between groups of people, including modern genocides and terrorism.
  - **Culture 18(C)** Identify examples of cultures that maintain traditional ways....
- **Technology 19** The student understands the impact of technology and human modifications on the physical environment.
  - **Technology 19(A)** Evaluate the significance of major technological innovations in the areas of transportation and energy that have been used to modify the physical environment.
  - **Technology 19(B)** Analyze ways technological innovations have allowed humans to adapt to places, such as air conditioning and desalinization.
  - **Technology 19(C)** Examine the environmental, economic, and social impacts of advances in technology on agriculture and natural resources.
- **Technology 20** The student understands how current technology affects human interaction.
  - **Technology 20(A)** Describe the impact of new information technologies such as the Internet, Global Positioning System (GPS), or Geography Information Systems (GIS).
  - **Technology 20(B)** Examine the economic, environmental, and social effects of technology such as medical advancements or changing trade patterns on societies at different levels of development.

In this chapter, you will study how culture and places change over time and the effects of those changes. You will see that even entire physical and cultural regions may change. You will further examine how human conflict, technological innovation and other factors bring about change.

ESSENTIAL QUESTIONS

- How does the physical and human geography of the world change over time?
- What are the main causes of historical change?

— IMPORTANT IDEAS —

A. Some societies maintain **traditional** ways.
B. Cultures, places and environments change over time.
C. The same region may have different physical and human characteristics at different time periods.
D. Migration, war, trade, cultural diffusion and technological innovation can lead to change.
E. Change can lead to new and different uses of physical features.
F. **Human conflict** is often a major cause of change. Conflicts can lead to **genocide** and **terrorism**.
G. **Technological innovation** is another major cause of change. Technological innovations in transportation and energy have led to human modifications of the physical environment. They have also allowed people to move to new places.
H. Technological developments such as medical advances, improvements in agriculture and the introduction of new information technologies have had profound effects on economies, societies, and the environment.

GEOGRAPHIC TERMINOLOGY IN THIS CHAPTER

- ■ **Traditional Ways**
- ■ **Cultural Diffusion**
- ■ **Genocide**
- ■ **Terrorism**
- ■ **Technology**
- ■ **Technological Innovation**
- ■ **GPS**
- ■ **GIS**
- ■ **Desalinization**

HOW GEOGRAPHY CHANGES OVER TIME

Earlier chapters in this book dealt with the geography of the world as it is today. These chapters looked at many of the world's current physical and human features. Now think about how the world came to be what it is today, and how it will be tomorrow. In fact, the geography of the world is in a process of constant change.

CHANGES IN PHYSICAL GEOGRAPHY

As you may recall, forces like tectonic plate movement and erosion gradually change the shape of Earth's surface. These processes cause Earth's physical geography to change. Such changes can often take thousands of years.

The Sahara Desert. The Sahara Desert in North Africa provides an example of physical geography changing. Scientists believe it was once a fertile and flourishing land, covered in forests and flowing rivers. As Earth's climate grew warmer, the Sahara grew drier. Gradually, over a span of thousands of years, the Sahara became a desert.

Name _____ Date _____

The Siberian-Alaskan Land Bridge. A land bridge once connected Siberia and Alaska during the last Ice Age, about 11,500 years ago. Siberia and Alaska were then parts of the same physical region. When the Earth became warmer, glaciers melted, causing sea levels to rise and burying the land bridge. Alaska and Siberia became separated by the sea and were no longer connected. This represents another example of geographic change.

APPLYING WHAT YOU HAVE LEARNED

Why do physical regions sometimes change over time? _____

_____

_____

_____

_____

CHANGES IN HUMAN GEOGRAPHY

Human geography often changes more quickly than physical geography. A cultural region or political unit can expand, contract, or even disappear over time. The characteristics of a culture — its ways of doing things – can also change.

CASE STUDY:
The Americas

North and South America, for example, once consisted of many Native American Indian cultural groups. These groups divided the Americas into different regions — such as the Inca and Aztec empires, the tribal lands of the Iroquois, and the Great Plains, inhabited by such tribes as the Sioux. The arrival of Europeans greatly disrupted these Native American Indian tribes. The Americas changed into new cultural regions based on European exploration and colonization. Former Native American Indian lands came under the rule of European powers — New Spain, New France, and the thirteen English colonies.

AREAS CLAIMED BY ENGLAND, FRANCE, SPAIN, NETHERLANDS

CASE STUDY:
The Roman Empire

The ancient Roman Empire once formed a vast cultural region. It changed over time and eventually disappeared. Ancient Rome began as a city-state near the west coast of central Italy. After conquering the rest of Italy, Rome defeated Carthage, its main rival in the Mediterranean. Next Rome conquered Spain, Gaul (*present-day France*), Greece, Egypt and Britain. This allowed Rome to extend its control throughout much of Europe and the Mediterranean world. As it

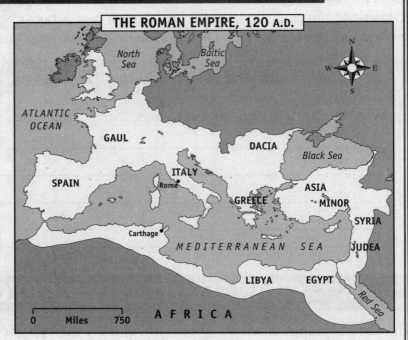

THE ROMAN EMPIRE, 120 A.D.

expanded, Rome also changed its system of government. The Roman Republic, ruled by leading noble families in the Senate, was replaced by an all-powerful emperor. Ways of earning a living changed, too. Foods from all over the empire flooded into Rome. People in the capital city relied more on slave labor. After several centuries, Rome began to shrink under the impact of attacks by hostile barbarian tribes. Eventually, this region divided into two separate empires and finally collapsed.

APPLYING WHAT YOU HAVE LEARNED

Why do cultural regions often change faster than physical regions? _____

_____

_____

Some societies resist change. Members of these **traditional societies** prefer to do things much as their ancestors have done. In the modern world, however, most societies are now changing more rapidly than ever before. Some traditional societies, such as the Amish in the United States and the Bedouin tribes in the deserts of North Africa and the Middle East, deliberately resist modernization. Traditional societies may even shun all contact with the modern world. In 2007, the U.N. confirmed the existence of 67 traditional, "uncontacted" peoples living in Brazil. Brazil now surpasses New Guinea as the country with the largest number of "uncontacted" peoples.

THE ROOTS OF CHANGE

What factors cause human cultures and regions to change? You have looked at examples of change but you have not yet explored the causes of change. Geographers and historians have identified several important processes that often contribute to change. You may already be familiar with some of them:

| **Migration** | **Cultural Diffusion** | **Trade** |

| **Conflict / War** | **Technological Innovation** |

MIGRATION

Migration is the movement of people from one place to another. When new people arrive, they often bring new beliefs, technologies and ways of doing things with them. Their arrival may also lead to conflict or conquest.

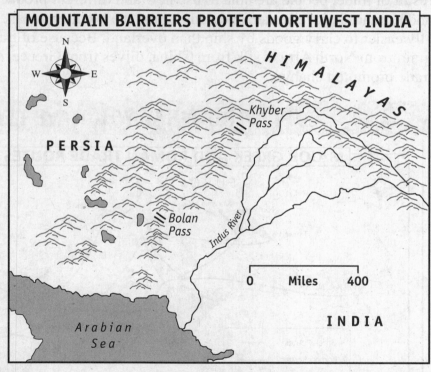

MOUNTAIN BARRIERS PROTECT NORTHWEST INDIA

For example, in ancient times, Arayan tribes entered India and transformed Indian society by introducing Hinduism and the caste system. In the 900s, invading Muslim peoples brought the Islamic religion through the 33-mile Khyber Pass to India. As a result, parts of India were again totally transformed. They came under the control of Muslim rulers and adopted Islam. Many books in Sanskrit were translated into Arabic.

In another example, European immigrants in the 19th century brought new ideas, foods, customs and traditions to Texas and the rest of the United States.

CULTURAL DIFFUSION

As you know, **Cultural diffusion** is the spread of ideas, goods, technologies, and cultural traits from one society to another. Cultural diffusion is often a major cause of change. The arrival of Chinese ideas and cultural traits, for example, played a large role in transforming Japanese society. Contact with Europe similarly changed the Native American Indian cultures in Mexico and Peru. More recently, cultural diffusion led to political changes in North Africa and the Middle East during the "**Arab Spring**" or "Arab Awakening." A successful popular protest in Tunisia led to further public demonstrations in Egypt, Algeria, Jordan, Yemen, Syria and Libya. In Tunisia, Egypt, and Libya, existing dictatorial governments were overthrown.

TRADE

Trade is any exchange of goods and services. Trade can occur within a country or between people in different countries. Trade encourages the spread of people, ideas, and goods. As a result of trade, people are able to use new and different products. For example, the Greeks and Romans enjoyed extensive trade across the Mediterranean. In those times, it was generally easier to carry goods by ship than overland. Because of trade, Romans obtained cheap grain from North Africa, silk from China, olives from Greece, and many other goods. Such trade promoted change.

APPLYING WHAT YOU HAVE LEARNED

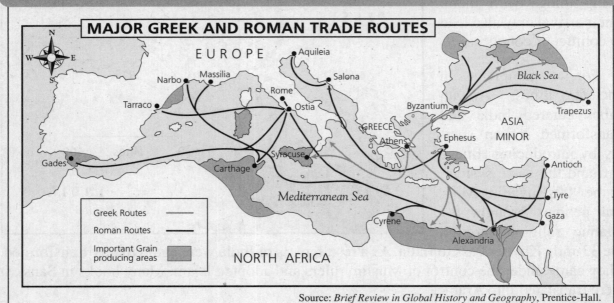

Source: *Brief Review in Global History and Geography*, Prentice-Hall.

CONTINUED

★ Based on the map on page 212, which cities in the Mediterranean did Rome trade with? _____

_____

★ How did trade between Greeks and Romans promote change? _____

_____

_____

_____

★ Using the Internet or your school or local library, identify one current trading partner of the United States. Then identify one way that trade has brought about change in that country.

_____

_____

_____

CONFLICT

Human conflict is another important cause of change. Armed conflicts occur either within a society or between different societies. There are many reasons for conflicts:

CIVIL WARS AND GENOCIDE

Different groups in the same society may compete for scarce resources or for political power. Different ethnic groups or religious groups in the same society may also fight with one another. One ethnic group may want to eliminate another. Or believers of one religion may want to convert, remove, or even exterminate those holding different religious beliefs.

Genocide. If a dominant group tries to completely eliminate a religious or ethnic group, this is known as **genocide** — the mass murder of a people.

As many as a million Tutsi were killed in the genocide carried out against them in Rwanda.

For example, during World War II, Nazi German leaders tried to murder all the Jews of Europe in the **Holocaust**. Six million Jews were shipped in railroad cars to Nazi concentration camps, where they were brutally murdered in gas chambers.

Attempts at genocide continue in more recent times. In the 1990s, Hutus killed Tutsis in Rwanda, while Serbs attacked Bosnian Muslims.

Jewish prisoners on the way to Birkenau for mass extermination.

INTERNATIONAL CONFLICTS

Countries also sometimes enter into armed conflict with one another. They may disagree over their borders or have other disputes. The leaders of one country may simply feel they can defeat and conquer another country. They might go to war to take away some of its land or resources.

Competition for Wealth and Resources. For example, in the 18th and 19th centuries, European powers fought against one another to establish colonies in the Americas, Asia, and Africa. They also fought against native peoples who resisted colonization. Wars between colonial powers and native inhabitants continued throughout the nineteenth century.

★ **Sepoy Mutiny.** British troops put down rebels in India during the Sepoy Mutiny of 1857.

★ **Zulu British Wars.** British soldiers also fought against the Zulus in South Africa and local tribes in the Sudan.

★ **Opium War.** In the 1850s, the British fought against the Imperial government of China in the Opium War to obtain exclusive trading rights.

★ **Mexican Cession.** The United States invaded Mexico to resolve a border dispute over Texas. It used this victory to seize the Mexican Cession — lands that included present-day California, New Mexico, and Arizona.

The British fought the Zulus in South Africa.

★ **Spanish-American War.** The United States went to war with Spain in 1898 over issues that arose in Cuba. An American victory allowed the United States to obtain its first colonies — Puerto Rico, Hawaii, and the Philippines.

★ **World War II.** In the 1930s, Nazi Germany and Imperial Japan sought to expand. They went to war against their neighbors in order to conquer them. Britain and France entered the war in order to stop German and Japanese expansion.

Conflicts over Ideals. Countries also sometimes go to war against each other over ideas. In the 16th century, Catholics and Protestant rulers fought against each other in wars of religion. In the late 18th century, countries fought over the French Revolution. After World War II, democratic and communist countries were suspicious of each other. They competed throughout the world to spread their ideologies (*belief systems*) and ways of life. This led to the Cold War. In some nations, such as Korea and Vietnam, the Cold War erupted into actual fighting.

Terrorism. Sometimes a group does not feel strong enough to challenge a government openly. Instead, its members commit acts of violence like a suicide bombing in order to attract attention and create a sense of terror among the citizens of its enemy. Terrorist groups then demand certain concessions in order to halt their acts of terror.

THE IMPACT OF CONFLICT

All of these different conflicts can lead to cultural change. War can disrupt a society, breaking it apart. It can lead to the conquest of one society by another or cause a government to collapse. The need for better ways of fighting can promote new weapons and other technological innovations, which can have peacetime uses.

CASE STUDY:
The Crusades

Wars can even promote cultural diffusion and the spread of new ideas. For example, for hundreds of years Christians traveled to Jerusalem to visit where Jesus was born. When Muslims gained control of Jerusalem, the Pope called on all Christians to retake the Holy Land. In the ensuing Crusades, thousands of European warriors were exposed

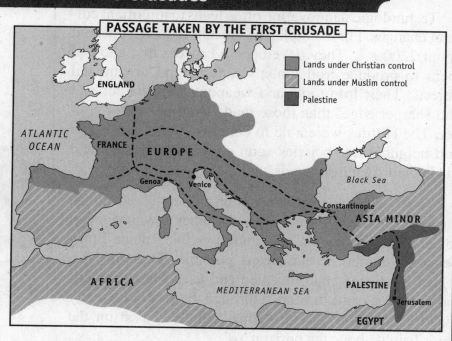

PASSAGE TAKEN BY THE FIRST CRUSADE

Lands under Christian control
Lands under Muslim control
Palestine

ENGLAND
ATLANTIC OCEAN
FRANCE
EUROPE
Genoa   Venice
Black Sea
Constantinople
ASIA MINOR
AFRICA
MEDITERRANEAN SEA
PALESTINE
Jerusalem
EGYPT

to Muslim technological achievements, such as the use of zero in mathematics. The interaction of European and Muslim cultures stimulated a new demand for Muslim and Asian goods in Europe, such as silks, rice, spices, coffee and glass mirrors. This demand led to increased trade with other parts of the world.

ACTING AS AN AMATEUR GEOGRAPHER

Using the Internet, your library, or your notes and other resources, select one conflict in world history. Then describe the conflict and explain how the conflict caused change.

_____

_____

_____

_____

_____

_____

TECHNOLOGICAL INNOVATIONS

Technology is the use of materials, tools, and skills to meet human needs. **Technological innovation** is the development of new technologies.

Technological innovation often leads to important cultural changes. For example, the ancient Hittites appeared about 2200 B.C. They developed a process that allowed them to produce iron tools, weapons, and ornamental objects. Their iron tools and weapons were harder and had sharper edges than those made from bronze or copper. The Hittites were able to conquer Egypt, but Egypt and neighboring societies soon copied the Hittites and made their own iron goods.

The Hittites used iron to build a three-man chariot, a technological innovation in warfare.

Some technological innovations directly encourage change. The use of the compass and other new navigation tools, borrowed from China and elsewhere, made European exploration of the oceans possible. The astrolabe, which the Greeks had invented and used for astronomical purposes, came to Europe through the Arabs. It greatly aided exploration by calculating latitudes based on the sun's height above the horizon.

In 1450, **Johann Gutenberg** invented moveable type. This allowed books and pamphlets to be printed cheaply. News and ideas could then spread much more quickly. Gutenberg's printing press helped launch the Protestant Reformation by spreading criticism of the Catholic Church.

CHANGES IN TRANSPORTATION AND ENERGY

Technological innovations in transportation and energy have even led to significant modifications of the physical environment. For most of human history, people relied on their own legs, sailboats, or animal power to travel from one place to another. In order to speed communications and the movement of armies, some rulers built paved roads and set up posts with fresh horses. Others dug canals to connect natural waterways.

Steam Engine. Things changed dramatically in the 1700s with the invention of the **steam engine**. The steam engine provided a new source of power that could be used in factories. It also provided power for transportation. The steam engine was quickly applied to power steamboats to travel long distances on the water, even against the current, and to power railroad trains on land.

Automobiles and Airplanes. At the end of the 19th century, transportation was further improved with the invention of the internal combustion engine. This was used to power the automobile, and shortly afterwards, the airplane. Each of these improvements in transportation increased the range of places people that could travel to, or from which people could ship goods easily.

EFFECTS OF CHANGES IN TRANSPORTATION

Advances in transportation brought about dramatic changes. The steamboat made it possible for European explorers to move upstream deep into the interior sections of Africa, where they now established far-flung colonial empires. The railroad likewise made it possible for Americans to settle the Far West.

Construction of the transcontinental railroad allowed Americans to cross the Great Plains.

Wherever steamboats and trains went, people transformed their physical environment by establishing ranches, farms, plantations and mines, and by building towns and cities. Later, countries around the world began laying down roads and highways for automobiles and trucks. Earth's surface has been gradually transformed by a network of roads, railroads, bridges and tunnels that connect farms, factories, towns and cities.

Meanwhile, the demand for energy has led people to dig mines for coal and to drill holes for oil and natural gas. The burning of these fossil fuels by factories, homes, cars, and trucks has released large amounts of pollution into the atmosphere.

OTHER RECENT TECHNOLOGICAL DEVELOPMENTS

It is not only in transportation that important technological innovations have occurred. In the last fifty years, the pace of technological change has become more rapid than at any other time in human history.

New Information Technologies. New information technologies, based on computers and the Internet, are bringing more information to greater numbers of people than ever before. The Internet connects millions of computers together and makes vast amounts of information easily available. People from the United States and other countries with access to the Internet can now tap into this vast storehouse of information.

Global Positioning Systems (GPS). Satellites, powered by solar energy, circle the Earth in outer space. These satellites send signals to Earth that are used by GPS devices. Users can now locate their exact position on Earth at any time. Navigation devices in cars, which can find addresses and map routes, make use of GPS to assist drivers. Originally developed for military use, GPS devices can

A space satellite makes possible the use of GPS devices.

also be used to search for and rescue airplanes, to guide hi-tech weapons, and to eavesdrop on potential enemies.

Geographic Information Systems (GIS). Computers also make **Geographic Information Systems** possible. In GIS, mapmaking and database technology are merged. Computers capture, store, manage, and analyze information and store this digital information at each location on a map. With GIS, we can better understand, interpret, and visualize data in a variety of ways to show relationships, patterns, and trends in the form of maps, reports, and charts.

Air Conditioning. Other technological innovations allow people to move to places where they could not previously live as comfortably. In the United States, the population was once concentrated in the Northeast. Many Americans found the South and West to be too hot in the summer. The invention of air conditioning made it possible to cool the insides of buildings even in extremely hot and humid weather. As a result, there has been a major shift in the population of the United States to the warmer South and West. Since the 1960s, when air conditioning began to come into wider use, the Northeast and the Midwest have increased in population just 27%, while the South and West have grown more than four times as much.

Desalinization. In many places of the world, there is a lack of fresh drinking water. Scientists are experimenting with ways of heating and cooling salt water in order to separate the salt and make fresh water. This process is known as **desalinization**. Israel is a dry desert country on the edge of the Mediterranean Sea. Israeli scientists have built several desalination plants to provide fresh water. One of the world's largest desalinization plants is also in El Paso, Texas. Like air conditioning, this

The Ashkelon desalinization plant in Israel sits next to the Mediterranean Sea.

technological advance allows people to adapt to new environments. More efficient desalinization will make it possible for people to live and farm in new areas.

Agriculture. Technology also assists farmers in agriculture. The introduction of the **tractor** in the early 20th century transformed agriculture. Today, scientists have developed better seeds, improved fertilizers, and stronger pesticides to kill harmful insects. Farmers grow more plants with less water, land, and labor. Computers help plan, harvest and sell crops more efficiently. Satellites help farmers obtain more accurate reports of weather conditions. Due to these

The modern farm tractor is capable of plowing, tilling, planting, and many other tasks.

technological changes, American agricultural production has doubled in the past fifty years. This makes more food available for our growing population or for export to other countries.

Trade. Technological innovations have also led to changes in trading patterns. In ancient times, people mainly traded with nearby communities. They obtained a few highly prized goods by trading with distant communities across the sea. Later, ships grew larger and societies carried on more active trade across the world. The development of modern large ships with containerized cargo, combined with the use of trucks and freight trains, has made possible global trade to an extent unimaginable in earlier times. If you look around your house, you will probably find goods made in China, Mexico, Japan, Chile, Italy and many other countries.

Medicine. Technological innovations, many based on new information technologies, are also leading to improvements in medicine. Scientists now understand DNA, the genetic basis for human life. They are able to design and test new medicines to fight specific diseases. Scientists also have new tools like CAT-scans (*Computerized Axial Tomography*) and MRI (*Magnetic Resonance Imaging*). These use computers to put together three-dimensional images based on thousands of pictures of the patient. Scientists are better able to understand why we sometimes become ill and can now develop new cures.

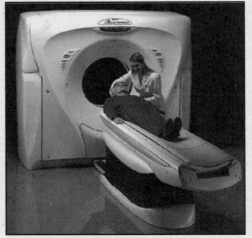

A patient about to undergo a CAT-scan.

ACTING AS AN AMATEUR GEOGRAPHER

Using the Internet, your school or public library, your notes, and other sources, select *one* recent technological innovation. Briefly describe the innovation. Then explain how that innovation has led to change, especially in the ways people use their resources, how they interact with others, or where they are able to live.

★ Technological innovation: _____

_____

★ How this innovation has promoted change: _____

_____

_____

_____

_____

_____

_____

_____

_____

_____

_____

_____

LEARNING WITH GRAPHIC ORGANIZERS

Complete the graphic organizer below. Explain how each of these factors can cause change. Then provide one example for each.

Migration

_____

_____

_____

_____

Example: _____

Cultural Diffusion

_____

_____

_____

_____

Example: _____

CAUSES OF CHANGE

Trade

_____

_____

_____

_____

Example: _____

Conflict / War

_____

_____

_____

_____

Example: _____

Technological Innovation

_____

_____

_____

_____

Example: _____

CHAPTER STUDY CARDS

How Regions Change

Physical Regions

★ Physical regions change gradually as processes slowly change Earth's surface.
- The **Sahara Desert** was once a jungle.
- A **land bridge** once connected Siberia (*in Russia*) to Alaska.

Human Regions

★ Human regions expand and contract as one culture gains or loses power.
- Europeans conquer Native Americans and colonized the "New World."
- The Roman Empire changed as Rome expanded and then declined.

Roots of Historical Change

There are several factors that can cause a region or culture to change.

★ **Migration.** The arrival of a new group of people.

★ **Cultural Diffusion.** The arrival of new ideas, products, technologies, or cultural traits.

★ **Trade.** Exchange of goods with others.
- Rome obtained goods from Egypt, China and Greece.

★ **Conflict.** (*See Conflict Study Card below*).

★ **Technological Innovation.** (*See Technological Innovation Study Card below*).

Roots of Change: Conflict

Conflict is another reason that causes a region or culture to change. Armed conflict is the use of force by opposing groups.

★ One group may conquer another group.

★ A country may collapse.

★ **International Conflict.** Conflicts between nations for territory, wealth, or resources.

★ **Genocide.** Attempt to kill an entire group of people. For example:
- Nazi genocide of Jews in Europe.
- Hutu genocide of Tutsis in Rawanda.

★ **Terrorism.** The use of threats of terror against innocent civilians to gain attention and achieve a group's aims.

Roots of Change: Technological Innovation

A major cause of change is **technological innovation**:

★ **Technology** is the use of tools, materials, skills to meet human needs.

★ Changes in transportation and energy:
- Steam engine: factory, steamboat, train.
- Automobiles and airplanes.

★ New Information Technologies.
- Computers, Internet, GPS, GIS.

★ Other Recent Developments:
- Air conditioning
- Desalinization
- Agriculture
- Trade

CHECKING YOUR UNDERSTANDING

Directions: Put a circle around the letter that best answers the question.

Use the information and your knowledge of social studies to answer the following question.

> "The speed with which computers have spread is so well known it hardly needs elaboration. Costs have dropped so sharply and capacity has risen so spectacularly that according to one authority, 'If the automobile industry had done what the computer industry has done in the last 30 years, a Rolls-Royce would cost $2.50 and would get 2,000,000 miles to the gallon.'"
>
> — Alvin Toffler, *The Third Wave*

1   Which sentence best summarizes the main idea of the passage?
     A   Technology has replaced skilled workers.   `SST 20(A)`
     B   Computers can perform ever more complicated tasks more quickly.
     C   Technological innovation has led to rapid changes to society.
     D   Computers are becoming more expensive and more efficient.

This question asks you to read a passage and determine what it is primarily about. **Choice A** is wrong. Although the types of skills needed may have changed, technology has not replaced skilled workers. Also, this is not what Toffler discusses. **Choice C** is wrong. Although technological innovation has led to change, this is not the topic of this passage. **Choice D** is also wrong. Toffler says computers are becoming cheaper, not more expensive. **Choice B** is the best answer. Toffler says computers are becoming faster, cheaper and better.

Now try answering some additional questions on your own:

2   The establishment of a democracy in India and the establishment of Portuguese as the official language of Brazil indicates that European colonizers —
     A   influenced the cultures of the regions under their control   `Hist 2(A)`
     B   respected the governments of the native peoples
     C   promoted the Christian religion over native religions
     D   favored local traditions over their own policies

3   Which advancement in technology revolutionized the way ideas were spread throughout Western Europe at the end of the 15th century?
     A   development of the astrolabe   `Cult 18(A)`
     B   introduction of the telegraph
     C   improvements to the printing press
     D   creation of the telescope

4   For years, the Sahara Desert was an obstacle for Europeans while some Africans used the desert as a highway. Which conclusion is supported by this statement?
     A   Trade between Africa and Europe decreased.   `SST 19(A)`
     B   Empires in Africa avoided contact with Europeans.
     C   Desertification reduced the fertile land available to Africans and Europeans.
     D   Initially, Europeans lacked the technology needed to travel in the desert.

5   What was an important result of the Crusades?
     A   Arabs and Christians divided Jerusalem between them.   `Cult 18(A)`
     B   Islamic kingdoms expanded into Europe.
     C   The exchange of goods increased between Europe and the Middle East.
     D   The Catholic Pope sought to block Crusaders from going to the Holy Land.

Name _____ Date _____

Use the maps and your knowledge of social studies to answer the following question.

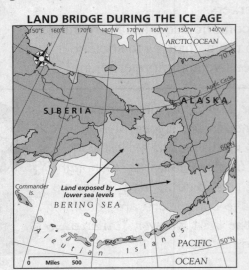 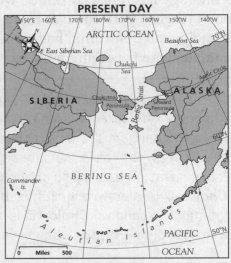

6   According to the maps above, how has this physical region changed?

   A   Alaska and Siberia are no longer connected by land.   Hist 2(A)

   B   Alaska and Siberia are colder now than during the Ice Age.

   C   Alaska and Siberia are now covered by water.

   D   The Bering Sea is smaller than during the Ice Age.

Use the maps and your knowledge of social studies to answer the following question.

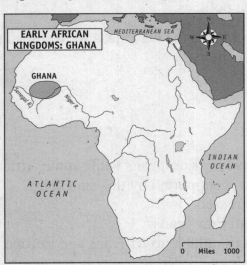 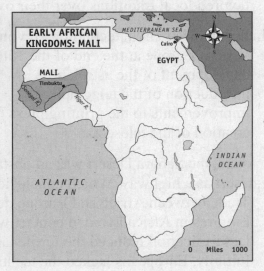

7   Based on these maps, which statement best describes the changes to West Africa along the Niger River between 1200 and 1240?

   A   The climate of this region significantly changed.   Hist 2(A)

   B   A new political and cultural region replaced an earlier region.

   C   There was a change in the region's plants and animals.

   D   European colonial powers introduced new technologies to the region.

UNIT 4 REVIEW
PULLING IT ALL TOGETHER

Select a development or event from this unit. Identify *two* types of change that led to that development.

1. _____

   _____

2. _____

   _____

Select *one* of the *Essential Questions* explored in this unit by checking the box. Then answer it below.

ESSENTIAL QUESTIONS REEXAMINED

☐ How does the spatial diffusion of ideas, products, and traits lead to change, including cultural divergence and convergence?

☐ How does the physical and human geography of the world change over time?

☐ What are the main causes of historical change?

_____

_____

_____

_____

_____

_____

_____

_____

_____

_____

_____

_____

_____

_____

_____

UNIT 4 CONCEPT MAP

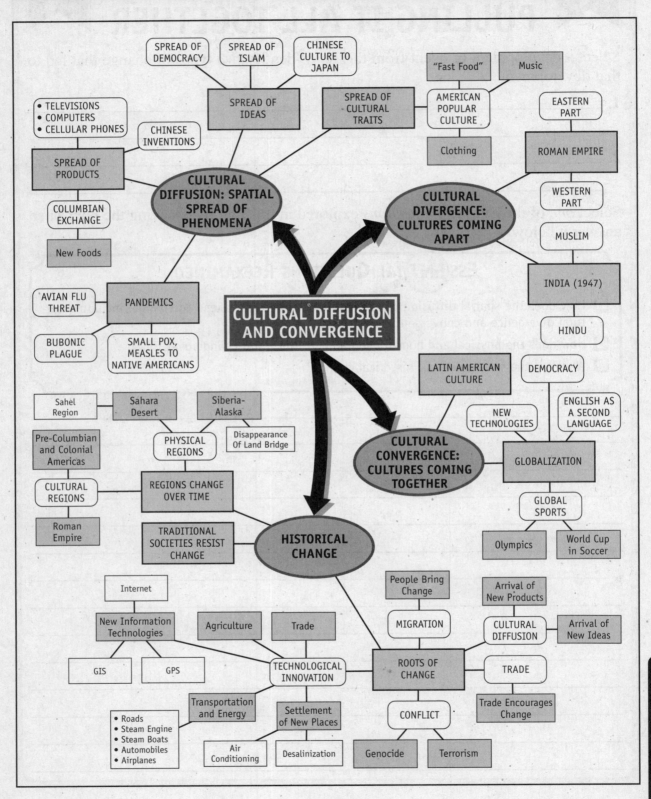

SPREAD OF DEMOCRACY

SPREAD OF ISLAM

CHINESE CULTURE TO JAPAN

"Fast Food"

Music

SPREAD OF IDEAS

SPREAD OF CULTURAL TRAITS

AMERICAN POPULAR CULTURE

EASTERN PART

- TELEVISIONS
- COMPUTERS
- CELLULAR PHONES

CHINESE INVENTIONS

Clothing

ROMAN EMPIRE

SPREAD OF PRODUCTS

WESTERN PART

COLUMBIAN EXCHANGE

CULTURAL DIFFUSION: SPATIAL SPREAD OF PHENOMENA

CULTURAL DIVERGENCE: CULTURES COMING APART

MUSLIM

New Foods

INDIA (1947)

AVIAN FLU THREAT

PANDEMICS

HINDU

BUBONIC PLAGUE

SMALL POX, MEASLES TO NATIVE AMERICANS

CULTURAL DIFFUSION AND CONVERGENCE

LATIN AMERICAN CULTURE

DEMOCRACY

NEW TECHNOLOGIES

ENGLISH AS A SECOND LANGUAGE

Sahel Region

Sahara Desert

Siberia-Alaska

Pre-Columbian and Colonial Americas

PHYSICAL REGIONS

Disappearance Of Land Bridge

CULTURAL CONVERGENCE: CULTURES COMING TOGETHER

GLOBALIZATION

CULTURAL REGIONS

REGIONS CHANGE OVER TIME

Roman Empire

TRADITIONAL SOCIETIES RESIST CHANGE

HISTORICAL CHANGE

GLOBAL SPORTS

Olympics

World Cup in Soccer

Internet

People Bring Change

Arrival of New Products

New Information Technologies

Agriculture

Trade

MIGRATION

CULTURAL DIFFUSION

Arrival of New Ideas

GIS

GPS

TECHNOLOGICAL INNOVATION

ROOTS OF CHANGE

TRADE

- Roads
- Steam Engine
- Steam Boats
- Automobiles
- Airplanes

Transportation and Energy

Settlement of New Places

CONFLICT

Trade Encourages Change

Air Conditioning

Desalinization

Genocide

Terrorism

UNIT 5

POLITICAL GEOGRAPHY

In this unit, you will learn about governments and their impact on geography. You will learn about different types and levels of governments, and how these political units create borders between one another.

You will also explore how political power is distributed spatially, and how this distribution can be displayed on maps. Finally, you will consider how concepts of citizenship differ from place to place.

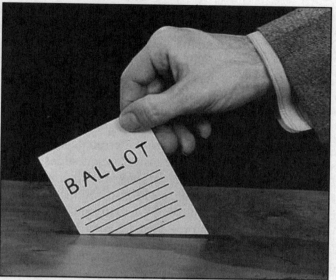

Voting in elections is a major characteristic of a democratic government.

Chapter 14. Types of Government. In this chapter, you will learn about different types of government, including a monarchy, republic, democracy, dictatorship, totalitarian system and theocracy.

Chapter 15. Nations: Borders and Powers. In this chapter, you will explore how governments establish boundaries and use their power. Finally, you will look at how independent sovereign states interact with each other.

Chapter 16. Political Processes and Citizenship. In this chapter, you will learn how different points of view influence public policies and decision-making at the local, state, national and international levels. You will also look at several political "hot spots" in the world today.

Types of Government

In this chapter, you will learn about the basic types of government — monarchy, republic, democracy, dictatorship, theocracy and totalitarian regime. This chapter corresponds with the basic overview found on page 83 of HMH's *World Geography*, and with later sections found throughout that book.

❑ *Before Reading:* You might begin your study of government types by reading the TEKS, *Geographical Terminology*, *Important Ideas* and *Essential Question* on page 243.

❑ *During Reading:* Then read pages 244–247 to learn how to identify each of these types of government. If your course is organized around principal themes and concepts, you might read this entire chapter and then look at specific examples of each of these types of governments in HMH's *World Geography*. Use the pages indicated on the correlation chart below. If your course is organized around regions, then you might read about each of the different types of governments in this book whenever you come across that type in connection with countries studied in each region. For example, when you study the constitutional monarchy of Great Britain or the absolute monarchy of Saudi Arabia, you might look at page 244 below to learn about the essential characteristics of monarchy. When you study Iran, you might look at page 247 on theocracy. When you have finished learning about monarchy, democracy and dictatorship, read the imaginary dialogue between Thomas Jefferson, King Louis XIV of France, and the dictator Joseph Stalin, on pages 248–249 below. Then answer the questions at the bottom of page 249. Use evidence from both this book and HMH's *World Geography* to support your choices. Finally, complete the *Acting as an Amateur Geographer* activity on page 250. Use information from Unit 6 (Africa) of HMH's *World Geography* and from the Internet to conduct the activity and fill in the map.

❑ *After Reading:* Reinforce your learning by completing the graphic organizers, reviewing the study cards, and answering the test questions at the end of the chapter.

Topics	*Mastering the TEKS*	HMH's *World Geography*
Types of Government	pp. 244–249	p. 83
Monarchy	p. 244	pp. 83, 297–298, 303, 443, 505, 635–636, 648, 651–652
Divine Right	p. 244	pp. 298, 362
Constitutional Monarchy	p. 244	pp. 158, 303, 720
Republic	p. 244	p. 290 (see also Representative Democracy)
Democracy	p. 245	pp. 83, 139, 218, 249–251, 253, 289, 303–304, 469; 568-569
Direct Democracy	p. 245	p. 289
Representative Democracy	p. 245	pp. 139, 139 CF1–4, 249–251, 253, 290, 303–304, 444, 455, 469, 471, 568–569
Dictatorship	pp. 245–246	pp. 83, 232, 249–250, 298, 468, 574
Totalitarian	p. 246	pp. 298, 363, 517, 519, 636–637, 649
Theocracy	p. 247	pp. 517, 519
Which is the Best Form of Government?	pp. 248–249	
Political System of Africa (Student Project)	p. 250	pp. 433, 443–444
See also: "Stateless Societies" of Africa		pp. 443, 449

Using Multiple Sources of Information

• Use information from both books to write your own answers to the *Essential Questions* on page 243.
• Select a foreign nation and pretend that you live there. Use information from both books to give an oral presentation about your type of government.

CHAPTER 14

TYPES OF GOVERNMENT

■ **Government 14(B)** Compare how democracy, dictatorship, monarchy, republic, theocracy, and totalitarian systems operate in specific countries.

In this chapter, you will examine several different types of government — monarchy, republic, democracy, dictatorship, totalitarian regime, and theocracy.

AN ESSENTIAL QUESTION

◯— What is the best form of government?

— IMPORTANT IDEAS —

A.   There are several different types of government:
   • In a **monarchy**, a hereditary ruler controls the government and decides what it should do.
   • In a **republic**, people govern themselves without a monarch.
   • In a **democracy**, ordinary citizens hold supreme power because all government decisions ultimately comes from the people.
   • In a **dictatorship**, power rests in the hands of an individual or a small group that tells everyone else what to do.
   • In a **totalitarian system**, a dictatorial government closely controls every aspect of a citizen's life.
   • In a **theocracy**, religious leaders control government.

GEOGRAPHIC TERMINOLOGY IN THIS CHAPTER

■ **Monarchy**
■ **Constitutional Monarch**
■ **Republic**

■ **Democracy**
■ **Direct Democracy**
■ **Representative Democracy**

■ **Dictatorship**
■ **Totalitarianism**
■ **Theocracy**

Human beings need the help of one another to survive and prosper. They therefore live in communities. The organization that people set up to protect their community and to enforce its rules is called **government**.

The role of government is to protect the lives, liberties and property of members of the community and to provide those services that individuals cannot otherwise provide on their own. To exercise authority, governments are given **power** — the authority to use force.

TYPES OF GOVERNMENT

There are many different types of governments:

MONARCHY

Monarchy is probably the oldest form of government. The main characteristic of a monarchy is that the ruler *inherits* power. When the ruler dies, power automatically passes to one of the monarch's children or close relatives. Monarchs — kings, emperors, or sultans — fulfill their role as supreme ruler by surrounding themselves with followers and advisors who help them govern.

RULE BY DIVINE RIGHT

In older forms of monarchy, the king or queen claimed absolute power. Rulers often claimed to hold this power by "**divine right**," or the will of God. Ordinary people had no rights or freedoms, except those that the monarch allowed.

King Henry VIII of England was a monarch.

CONSTITUTIONAL MONARCHY

In more recent times, monarchs have shared power with an elected legislature. Subjects of the monarch enjoy many traditional, protected rights. This system is known as a **constitutional monarchy**. Great Britain provides an example of a constitutional monarchy. Britain has a hereditary monarch and an elected House of Commons. The monarch serves as the symbolic head of state while elected members of Parliament govern the country.

REPUBLIC

When a society overturns its monarchy, it becomes a republic. A **republic** is simply a government without a king or queen. Often, the people in a republic choose representatives to make decisions. The United States, for example, is a republic. A republic might also be governed by a group of hereditary nobles, such as the Republics of Venice and Genoa once were.

DEMOCRACY

In a **democracy**, government authority is based on the will of the people. People either vote on issues directly, or they elect representatives who make government decisions for them. In a democracy, people also enjoy certain basic rights. This gives them the confidence to criticize the government freely.

DIRECT DEMOCRACY

The first known democracy arose in ancient Athens in the fifth century B.C. In fact, the very word **democracy** is Greek for "people-power." Citizens of ancient Athens assembled to make important decisions facing their city-state. They voted on these issues directly. This system is sometimes referred to as **direct democracy**.

REPRESENTATIVE DEMOCRACY

The Romans developed the first **representative democracy**. Different social groups elected their own representatives, who met in assemblies. The nobles were represented in the **Senate**. Governmental power was divided between these two branches and they voted on various issues.

LATER DEMOCRACIES

Later in history, various countries developed their own national assemblies. In England, land owners elected representatives to the House of Commons, one of the two chambers in the English Parliament. When the English set up colonies in North America, each colony had its own colonial legislature. After the United States became independent, it created an elected national law-making body, known as Congress. In the nineteenth century, several Latin American countries became democracies after achieving inde-

Ghanaians celebrating 50 years of independence. In 1957, Ghana became the first sub-Saharan African country to gain independence from colonial rule.

pendence. Many countries in Europe became democratic after World War I. After World War II, many countries in Africa and Asia established democracies when they attained their independence. More recently, several countries in North Africa and the Middle East became new democracies after the "Arab Spring."

DICTATORSHIP

A **dictatorship** is a system of government in which a single person or small group exercises complete power over others. A dictator does not inherit power like a king.

The dictator either seizes control by force, or is placed into a position of authority by others. In some countries, especially in Latin America and Africa, the military sometimes seized power and established a dictatorship. After achieving their independence, some African nations became one-party states in which some leaders became dictators. For example, **Idi Amin Dada** became a brutal military dictator while serving as President of Uganda from 1971 to 1979. In Zimbabwe, **Robert Mugabe** was elected to power. He quickly became a dictator who used police to block opponents from voting. Mugabe even arrested and tortured opponents.

Dictators are free to do as they please, while other citizens in a dictatorship have few rights. Ordinary citizens in a dictatorship have very little influence over government policies. The main advantage of a dictatorship is that decisions can be made quickly. In ancient times, the Romans appointed a dictator when they were at war and needed strong leadership. When the war was over, the dictator was supposed to give up his power. In more recent times, dictators tend to hold on to power until they are overthrown.

Dictators sometimes hold elections to obtain legitimacy for their government. An election victory may appear to justify the rule of the dictator, but in reality these elections are not truly free. People are afraid to criticize or oppose the dictator, and opposition parties are not permitted.

TOTALITARIAN SYSTEMS

Modern dictators, like Adolf Hitler in Germany, Joseph Stalin in the Soviet Union, and Saddam Hussein in Iraq, established **totalitarian systems** in which the government controlled all aspects of individual life.

Under totalitarianism, people can only belong to organizations controlled by the government. No separate political parties, labor unions, or other organizations are allowed. The government either controls or prohibits all churches and religious groups. One leader or political party maintains total control over all aspects of society. This control extends to the police, military, communications, economy and the educational system.

Adolf Hitler and Joseph Stalin

The government also controls all television, radio, and newspapers. Government censorship prohibits all books or articles criticizing the government. All dissent is suppressed and citizens are terrorized by secret police. People who oppose the government are arrested and sent to labor camps or killed.

THEOCRACY

A **theocracy** is a government run by religious leaders. Like monarchy, theocracy is an old form of government. In a theocracy, the government claims to be directed by God, or divinely blessed. There is no legal separation between church and state, and citizens of other faiths are often excluded or expelled.

In ancient times, rulers were often priests. The Pharaohs of ancient Egypt, for example, were believed to be gods. The Byzantine Empire was ruled by an emperor who was also head of the church. In the Middle Ages, the head of the Catholic Church, the Pope, ruled extensive territories in Italy. In early colonial times, Puritan ministers helped govern Massachusetts.

Iran's Theocracy. More recently, Muslim religious leaders seized power in Iran in 1979. The Iranian Constitution emphasizes the importance of religion and Islamic law (*Sharia*). Today, Iran has both a theocratic and democratic government. Voters elect the President and representatives to the legislature. However, these officials remain subject to the control of Iran's religious leader — the head of state or **Supreme Leader** — an Islamic cleric who is appointed for life. As the name indicates, the Supreme Leader is the head of government, even above the

The Supreme Leader of Iran, Ayatollah Ali Khamenei, rules Iran as a theocracy.

elected President. The Supreme Leader interprets religious law, can dismiss the President, and can declare war.

APPLYING WHAT YOU HAVE LEARNED

Choose one type of government discussed above. Look up this type of government on the Internet or in the library. Find a country where this type exists or once existed. Then briefly describe how it operates (or operated).

_____

_____

_____

_____

_____

_____

_____

WHICH IS THE BEST FORM OF GOVERNMENT?

It would be interesting if you could listen to a discussion by leaders who actually once directed these different governments. Imagine what it would be like to overhear:

★ **Thomas Jefferson**, the principal author of the Declaration of Independence and third U.S. President, who is recognized as a leading supporter of **democracy**;

★ **Joseph Stalin**, a former leader of the Soviet Union, who was a feared **dictator**;

★ **Louis XIV**, King of France in the late 17th century, who built up the power and authority of the French **monarchy**.

If you listen very carefully, you might be able to hear these three men discussing which is the best type of government:

Jefferson: Gentlemen, a dictatorship and monarchy may have advantages, but democracy is surely the best government. Only a democracy protects its citizens' rights. In a dictatorship or monarchy, people who express dissatisfaction with the government are often arrested. Except for the king or dictator, no one else has any real say in how the government is run. People live in fear. Dictatorship and monarchy are based on the ruler's will. This is not so in a democracy.

Stalin: Comrade Jefferson, I agree that the purpose of government is to help the people. This was always my goal as ruler. The problem is that people don't always know what is best. A good ruler can do more than a bunch of arguing politicians unable to make up their minds. I was able to improve our economy in a shorter period than any democracy could have done.

Louis XIV: Messieurs, I agree with Stalin. Democracy is unable to truly protect people's rights. In a democracy, the people have to protect their own rights. What kind of government is that? It's a government of chaos, fighting, and disorder. Nobody benefits. In a monarchy, the king is the true representative of the interests of the people before God. A king has only his people's welfare at heart. God tells the king what is best for his people, and the king carries out God's will.

Stalin: Comrades, a dictator is not chosen by birth, like a king. A dictator is chosen on the basis of talent. A dictator fights to get to the top. Only the best individual will succeed. Once in power, the dictator can bring together all the interests of society to achieve a single goal. A dictator's aim is always to improve the welfare of the people. The dictator has the advantage of absolute power to achieve this end. A dictator can do more in two years than a democracy can in twenty. In a democracy, listening to everybody's opinion takes far too much time and forces people to make poor compromises. For centuries, Russia was ruled by monarchs and fell far behind the West. I changed all that. We built factories, produced cement and steel, and manufactured tractors.

CONTINUED

Some people who disagreed with me died along the way, but that is not so important. In the long run, we were all be better off.

Louis XIV: I agree with you, Monsieur Stalin. The will of one person can achieve wonderful things when given complete control over a society. Everyone bends to that person's rule. Society moves towards one goal — whether it is building the economy or defeating an enemy. In contrast, citizens in a democracy are always disagreeing. As soon as the government starts to accomplish something, a new group is voted into power and changes direction. Dictatorships have one weakness, however: the dictator does not rule by inheritance, like a king. For this reason, the dictator is always insecure, always out to win public support through great deeds or by terrorizing opponents. The dictator never knows when someone might try to overthrow him. Your own career is proof of this, Monsieur Stalin. You murdered millions to keep control. You were never sure of yourself. No king would ever act this way by waging war on his own people.

Jefferson: Gentlemen, both of you pretend that the ruler has the interests of the people at heart, but is this true? Your own records are not very convincing. Mr. Stalin, you killed millions in your desire for power. Your Majesty was little better. You dragged your country into senseless wars to increase your glory and power.

Stalin: Comrade Jefferson, you oversimplify. You say democracy protects the people from over-active governments, but what about poor harvests, floods, or attacks from enemies? By the time a democracy agrees to act, it is often too late. If I did not have total power, my nation could not have responded quickly to threats.

Jefferson: Gentlemen, no system of government is perfect. At times there may have been a good dictator or king, but most dictators and kings have proven to be short-sighted, vain, and selfish. The people can only rely on themselves to create a government that looks after their interests. Only democracy recognizes the dignity of each person. I prefer putting my trust in the people.

APPLYING WHAT YOU HAVE LEARNED

★ Which government do you think is best? _____ Explain your answer.

_____

_____

_____

★ What would the ruler of a theocracy add to this debate? _____

_____

_____

_____

ACTING AS AN AMATEUR GEOGRAPHER

★ Using the Internet, an encyclopedia, or a recent almanac, select ten countries in Africa and identify the type of government each country has today. Using the map below, make your own map showing those ten governments. Create a legend in the lower left corner with symbols or colors identifying each type of government.

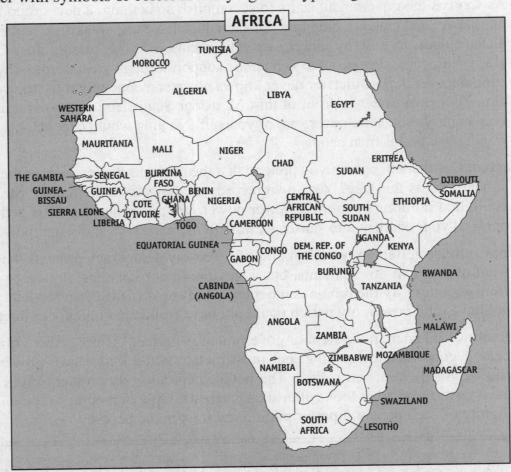

AFRICA

★ What patterns in government do you see on your map? Can you draw any conclusions from this map?

_____

_____

★ Which of these countries were affected by the "Arab Spring"? Why were these particular countries the ones affected?

_____

_____

LEARNING WITH GRAPHIC ORGANIZERS

Complete the graphic organizer below. Describe each type of government and provide one example.

Monarchy
_____
_____
_____
_____
_____
_____

Theocracy
_____
_____
_____
_____
_____
_____

Dictatorship
_____
_____
_____
_____
_____
_____

GOVERNMENT TYPES

Republic
_____
_____
_____
_____
_____
_____

Totalitarian System
_____
_____
_____
_____
_____
_____

Democracy
_____
_____
_____
_____
_____
_____

CHAPTER STUDY CARDS

Types of Governments

★ **Monarchy.** Ruler inherits power.
- **Rule by Divine Right.** Monarch claims to rule by the will of God. Ordinary people have no rights or freedoms.
- **Constitutional Monarch.** Power is shared with a legislature. Monarch serves as symbolic head of state.

★ **Democracy.** Government authority is based on the consent of the governed.
- **Direct democracy.** Citizens decide issues directly by voting.
- **Representative Democracy.** People elect representatives to decide issues.

Types of Governments

★ **Republic.** A government without a monarch. Representatives in government are chosen by the people.

★ **Dictatorship.** System of government in which one person or party has total power.
- Citizens have no individual rights; only participate in support of the government.
- Force used against opponents.
- Rule over government by one party.

★ **Totalitarian System.** A dictatorship with complete control over all aspects of life.

★ **Theocracy.** A system of government controlled by a religious leader.

CHECKING YOUR UNDERSTANDING

Directions: Put a circle around the letter that best answers the question.

Use the information in the boxes and your knowledge of social studies to answer the following question.

Usually has a single ruler	Ruler is not bound by law	People have no rights

1   Which types of government are most closely linked with these characteristics?

- **A**   theocracy / republic
- **C**   monarchy / democracy
- **B**   democracy / dictatorship
- **D**   monarchy / dictatorship

Govt 14(B)

- **EXAMINE** The Question
- **RECALL** What You Know
- **APPLY** What You Know

Begin by carefully **examining** the question. This question tests your understanding of the three main types of government. You should **recall** what a monarchy, democracy, theocracy, republic, and dictatorship are. Both a monarchy and a dictatorship often have a strong ruler who is not bound by any laws. **Apply** this information to the answer choices, you should select **Choice D** as the best answer since the information in the boxes are characteristics of both a monarchy and a dictatorship.

Now try answering some additional questions on your own:

2   Which citizenship practice best characterizes a dictatorship?
   F   voting to elect those opposed to the dictator
   G   attending demonstrations to show support of the government
   H   writing letters to newspapers attacking government policies
   J   joining a political party opposed to the government

`Govt 14(B)`

3   A theocratic government is often characterized by —
   A   the existence of multiple political parties
   B   censorship, religious laws, and repression
   C   a written constitution
   D   direct elections for governmental decisions

`Govt 14(B)`

Use the information and your knowledge of social studies to answer the following question.

In this passage, revolutionary leader Simón Bolívar discusses what form of government Venezuela should adopt after it achieves independence from Spain.

> "Give Venezuela an executive power in the person of a president chosen by the people, and you will have taken a great step toward national happiness. No matter what citizen occupies this office, he will be aided by the Constitution, and being authorized to do good, he can do no harm, because his ministers will cooperate with him only insofar as he abides by the law. If he attempts to infringe upon the law, his ministers will desert him, isolating him from the Republic, and they will bring charges against him in the Senate...."
>
> — *Simón Bolívar, 1819*

4   In this passage, which type of government does Simón Bolívar propose for Venezuela?
   F   theocracy
   G   democracy
   H   monarchy
   J   dictatorship

`Govt 14(B)`

- **EXAMINE** The Question
- **RECALL** What You Know
- **APPLY** What You Know

5   Which characteristics are shared by the political cultures of the United States, Great Britain and Mexico?
   A   a union of political and religious authority
   B   a hereditary monarch
   C   a totalitarian government
   D   a democratically elected national legislature

`Govt 14(B)`

6   Which was a characteristic of many African nations after their independence?
   F   one-party systems
   G   theocratic government
   H   constitutional monarchy
   J   direct democracy

`Govt 14(B)`

Nations: Borders and Power

This chapter describes nations — territories with their own governments and fixed borders. The information in this chapter corresponds with various sections found throughout HMH's *World Geography*, as indicated in the correlations chart below.

❑ *Before Reading:* You might begin your study of this topic by reading the TEKS, *Geographical Terminology, Important Ideas* and *Essential Questions* on page 255.

❑ *During Reading:* Next you should read the beginning of this chapter, pages 256–261, to learn about political regions, how these regions sometimes overlap, and about the supremacy of national governments. You will also learn how national borders are established and sometimes change over time. Turn to HMH's *World Geography*, pp. 86–87, to learn about natural and artificial boundaries, regional political systems and levels of government. Then look at the pages indicated on the chart below to learn more about each example of changing borders found in this book: for example, read pages 259–260 in this book to learn about Poland's shifting borders, and then read pages 264–265 and 311–312 in HMH's *World Geography*. Next read pages 262–264 in this book to learn about political maps, and examine the political maps in HMH's *World Geography* listed on the chart below to see where national borders are located at this moment in time. A political map is included in the special atlas at the front of each regional unit of HMH's *World Geography*. Finally, read about international relations, the "balance of power," the world's major powers, and international organizations on pages 264–267 below. Finish your study of this unit by reading the corresponding sections of HMH's *World Geography* for each of the world's major superpowers, the United Nations and the European Union.

❑ *After Reading:* Reinforce your learning by completing the graphic organizer, reviewing the study cards and answering the test questions at the end of the chapter.

Topics	*Mastering the TEKS*	HMH's *World Geography*
Political Regions	p. 256	p. 86
Houston's Government	p. 256	
Supremacy of National Government	p. 256	p. 86
Borders	pp. 257–261	pp. 85–86
Expansion of United States	pp. 257–258	pp. 105, 136–137
Mexico	pp. 258–259	pp. 192–193, 217, 220
Poland	pp. 259–260	pp. 264–265, 311–312
France	p. 260	pp. 264–265, 299
Israel and Palestine	pp. 260–261	pp. 480–481, 512–513
Political Maps	pp. 261–266	pp. 84, 105, 193, 265, 312, 481, 545, 613, 681
International Relations	pp. 264–265	
"Balance of Power"	p. 264	
World's Major Powers	p. 265	
United States	p. 265	pp. 138–144, 174–175
China	p. 265	pp. 622–623, 635–639
Russia	p. 265	pp. 363–367, 385–395
Japan	p. 265	pp. 622–623, 651–655
United Nations	p. 266	pp. 86
European Union	p. 266	pp. 292, 305, 326–329

Using Multiple Sources of Information

• Use information from both books to write your own answers to the *Essential Questions* on page 255.

• Your teacher should divide members of your class into groups representing the "great powers" on page 265. Use information from both books to prepare an oral report on the foreign policy of your assigned "great power" and present it to the class.

NATIONS:
Borders and Power

■ **Government 13** The student understands the spatial characteristics of a variety of global political units.
  • **Government 13(B)** Compare maps of voting patterns or political boundaries to make inferences about the distribution of political power.
■ **Government 14** The student understands the processes that influence political divisions, relationships, and policies.
  • **Government 14(A)** Analyze current events to infer the physical and human processes that lead to the formation of boundaries and other political divisions.
  • **Government 14(C)** Analyze the human and physical factors that influence the power to control territory and resources, create conflict/war, and impact international political relations of sovereign nations such as China, the United States, Japan, and Russia and organized nation groups such as the United Nations, the European Union....

In this chapter, you will learn about **political power** — the power to control or force behavior. You will also look at how nations set their borders and interact through international relations.

Essential Questions

◯— What factors determine where boundaries between countries are established?

◯— How do different countries relate to one another?

— IMPORTANT IDEAS —

A. Governments generally set up clear **boundaries** and exercise their power within these **boundaries**, creating **political units**.

B. **Political maps** show political units, such as countries, and their borders.

C. **Political power** is distributed spatially within a political region or unit.

D. A nation's power affects its international role.

GEOGRAPHIC TERMINOLOGY IN THIS CHAPTER

■ **Political Power**
■ **Political Region**
■ **Political Unit**

■ **Borders**
■ **Sovereign Government**
■ **International Relations**

■ **Balance of Power**
■ **United Nations**
■ **European Union**

POLITICAL REGIONS

Each government usually establishes clear **boundaries**, over which it asserts its authority. The area that a government controls creates a **political region** or **political unit**. Boundaries between countries are known as **borders**.

Each country usually has several **levels of government** — such as cities, counties, or states (*provinces*). This creates several overlapping units with authority over the same area. Just as each place may belong to more than one physical or cultural region, it can belong to more than one political region.

Houston's Overlapping Governments. For example, the citizens of Houston, belong to several political units. First, they have their own **city government**. Houston has a Mayor-Council form of government, with elected officials serving concurrent two-year terms. The City Charter provides the constitutional framework within which its government operates. Houstonians also belong to Harris County. This **county government** provides services to the entire

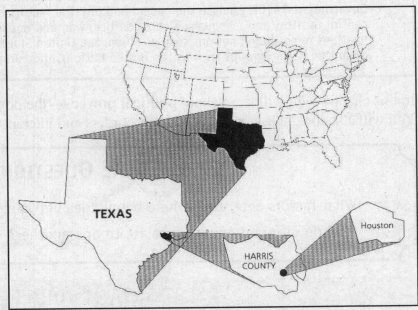

TEXAS

HARRIS COUNTY

Houston

Each level of government has its own boundaries.

county. The residents of Houston are also citizens of the State of Texas. Texas passes its own state laws, regulates schools and businesses, issues licenses to drivers, defines crimes and their punishments, maintains state highways, and provides many other services to its citizens.

Finally, the citizens of Houston also belong to the United States. Our **national** (*or federal*) government deals with issues that affect the entire country, such as national defense. Houstonians pay federal taxes, vote in federal elections, and obey federal laws. Some work for the federal government or serve in its armed forces.

Supremacy of the National Government. Our national government is our highest level of government. If there is a clash between a local or state government with our national government, the national government is supreme. According to the U.S. Constitution, federal laws always preempt state law. Our national government is **sovereign** — it is not subject to any higher governmental authority.

APPLYING WHAT YOU HAVE LEARNED

Create a Venn diagram, based on your own community, showing the functions of your national (*federal*), state, county, and local governments.

THE QUESTION OF BORDERS

The world today is divided into many separate independent, national states. Each such nation has its own **sovereign government**, like our federal government. Each sovereign government has final control over what happens within its borders. It is not subject to any higher authority on its own territory.

Every nation has both a sovereign government and fixed borders. Who decides where those borders are? Physical features often provide the first step. Rivers, mountains, lakes, seas, and oceans frequently serve as borders between countries. But the boundaries between states are also often the product of historical circumstances or political agreements.

EXPANSION OF THE UNITED STATES

Take, for example, the United States. Its eastern border, the Atlantic coast, was set by geography, but its western border continually shifted in its early history. At the time of its independence in 1783, the country's western border was the Mississippi River. Americans were interested in expanding westwards, but they were surrounded by areas claimed by other powers. To the north, Canada belonged to Britain. To the south and west were lands ruled by Spain.

The United States was able to acquire some of these lands through negotiation and purchase. In 1804, the United States purchased the Louisiana Territory from France. In 1819, they bought Florida from Spain.

GROWTH OF U.S. TERRITORY, 1783-1853

CANADA

CEDED BY GREAT BRITAIN
Convention of 1818

Added by
Webster-Ashburn Treaty
with Great Britain, 1842

OREGON TERRITORY
Ceded by
Great Britain, 1846

LOUISIANA PURCHASE
From France, 1803

THE UNITED STATES, 1783
Treaty of Paris with
Great Britain, 1783

ORIGINAL 13 STATES

MEXICAN CESSION
Treaty of Guadeloupe-Hidalgo, 1848

ATLANTIC OCEAN

PACIFIC OCEAN

ANNEXATION OF TEXAS
By congressional
resolution, 1845

GADSDEN PURCHASE
From Mexico, 1853

FLORIDA CESSION
Adams-Onis Treaty
with Spain, 1819

GULF OF MEXICO

MEXICO

0   Miles   700

In 1836, settlers in Texas won their independence from Mexico. In 1845, Texas was admitted to the United States. The United States then expanded to the Pacific Ocean by dividing the Oregon Territory with Great Britain. The United States also obtained territories (*Mexican Cession*) from western Texas to California by defeating Mexico in the Mexican-American War (1846–1848). America's borders were thus set by purchase and conquest, as well as by geography.

MEXICO

Mexico is another nation that has seen its borders change. Between 1,800 and 300 B.C.E., before the first contact with Europeans, Mexico was home to several Mesoamerican civilizations — the Olmecs, Teotihuacans, Mayas, Toltecs, and Aztecs. In the early 1500s, the Spanish exploror Hernan Cortés led a small army of conquistadors to conquer the ruling Aztec civilization. The territory, which Cortés named New Spain, was then colonized and became a part of the Spanish Empire.

PRE-COLUMBIAN MEXICO

PACIFIC OCEAN

GULF OF CALIFORNIA

Tenochtitlan-Tlatelolco

Tarascan State

Tlaxcalla

GULF OF MEXICO

Xicalanco

0 200 Mi
0 200 Km

AZTECS (Mexica) Xoconochco

NEW SPAIN IN 1786–1821

PACIFIC OCEAN

GULF OF CALIFORNIA

Mexico City

GULF OF MEXICO

0 200 Mi
0 200 Km

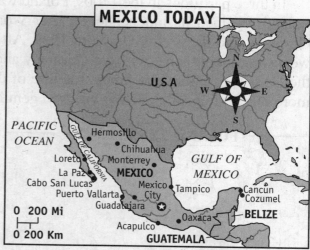

In 1821, Mexico received its independence from Spain. A province of Mexico, known as Texas, broke from Mexico and achieved independence in 1836. In 1846, a border dispute between the United States and Mexico, led to war. Mexico surrendered nearly half its land to the United States, including California and New Mexico. In 1854, the U.S. purchased parts of Arizona and New Mexico — known as the Gadsden Purchase. This settled the borders Mexico still enjoys today.

POLAND AND ITS SHIFTING BORDERS

Some countries lack good natural borders. For example, Poland sits on a flat plain near Europe's center. It is bounded by the Baltic Sea to the north and the Carpathian Mountains to the south. However, Poland has no natural defensible borders to the east and west. For this reason, its borders have shifted throughout its history. During its "Golden Age" in the early 17th century, Poland included Lithuania and the Ukraine, and extended from the Baltic Sea almost to the Black Sea.

In three partitions in the 1700s, Poland was then completely carved up by its neighbors. Poland regained its independence after World War I, but it was invaded again by Nazi Germany and the Soviet Union in 1939. After World War II, Poland's border was shifted westward, taking territory from Germany and giving territory to the Soviet Union. During the Cold War, Poland became a satellite of the Soviet Union and fell under its control. In more recent times, Poland has enjoyed genuine independence.

FRANCE

France is another country that once sought to expand its borders. It was prevented by conflict and by international political relations. Louis XIV fought a number of wars to expand France's borders eastwards. Napoleon expanded France even further, but these gains were lost when Napoleon was defeated in 1814–1815. Belgium and the Rhineland, each part of France's "natural frontiers" based on physical geography, were deliberately kept out of French hands by the other "Great Powers." The French kept the city of Strasbourg, but it was taken by Germany after the Franco-Prussian War (1870). When Germany was defeated in World War I, Strasbourg was returned to France. The Nazis got Strasbourg back when they conquered France in 1940. The city was returned to France in 1945, when Germany lost the war. This example again demonstrates how historical as well as geographic factors determine a country's borders.

ISRAEL AND PALESTINE

In 1947, the United Nations voted in favor of creating of a Jewish state, but this proposal was rejected by Arab leaders. When Israel declared its independence in 1948, neighboring Arab states immediately declared war on Israel. Today, after several wars and shifting borders, Israelis and Palestinians are now debating the future borders of Israel and Palestine. One major issue is whether a new Palestinian state should include some part of the city of Jerusalem. Look at the map on the next page to predict what might happen.

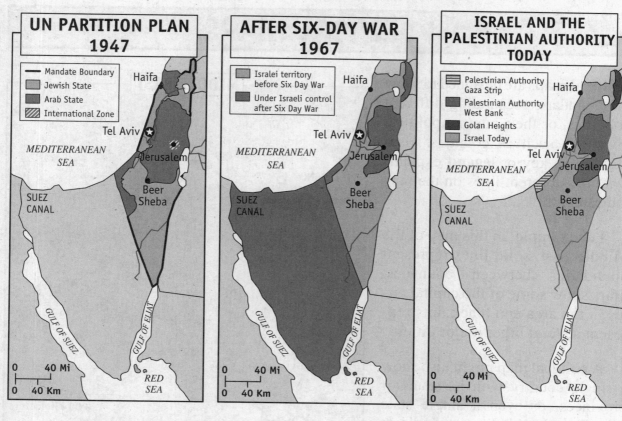

As all of these examples show, the creation of national boundaries is guided by physical geography but is also shaped by history — especially by the outcome of conflicts between neighboring states for the control of territory. Both physical and human factors shape countries' borders as well as their internal political divisions.

ACTING AS AN AMATEUR GEOGRAPHER

★ Imagine you are creating a new local government for your community. Where would you place its new borders?

_____

_____

_____

_____

★ Why would you place them there? _____

_____

_____

_____

POLITICAL MAPS

Political maps are designed to show the boundaries separating different countries, or their internal political divisions, such as counties. Usually a map key or **legend** explains what the different lines on the map indicate.

For example, in this map of the Middle East, solid lines represent boundaries between countries. Stars show some of the capital cities in the area and black dots represent several other major cities.

A political map might also show a single country with its states or provinces, or even a single state (like Texas) with lines to indicate the borders between counties.

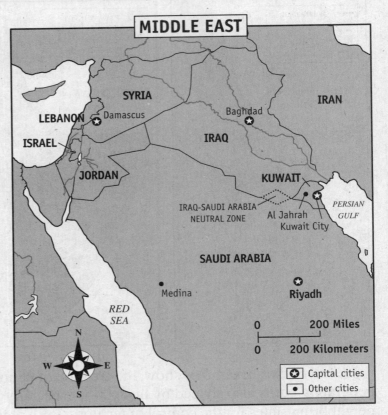

APPLYING WHAT YOU HAVE LEARNED

Based on the map of the Middle East above:

★ What is the capital of Syria? _____

★ In which country is the city of Al Jahrah located? _____

★ Identify one physical feature of Saudi Arabia that helps explain the location of

   its borders. _____

   _____

   _____

Perhaps you remember that maps have been called the "language of geography." Maps can even be used to indicate the distribution of political power or voting patterns. For example, the map of the world on the next page identifies those countries with the largest armed forces, an important indicator of military power.

TEN COUNTRIES WITH THE LARGEST ARMIES

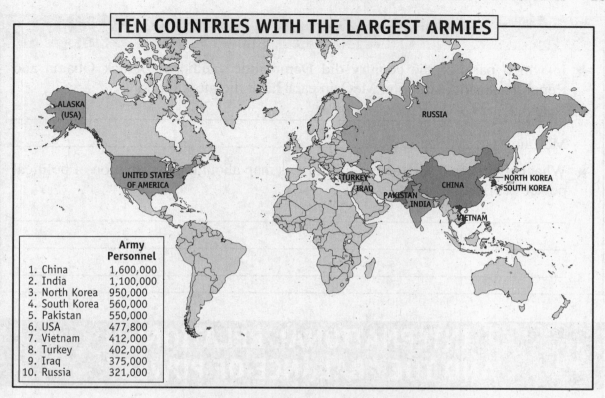

	Army Personnel
1. China	1,600,000
2. India	1,100,000
3. North Korea	950,000
4. South Korea	560,000
5. Pakistan	550,000
6. USA	477,800
7. Vietnam	412,000
8. Turkey	402,000
9. Iraq	375,000
10. Russia	321,000

Election Maps. Maps can also be used to show how people voted in an election or to see voting trends. They help us to understand the spatial distribution of political power. For example, the map below shows the results of the 2008 U.S. Presidential election:

U.S. PRESIDENTIAL ELECTION FOR 2008

McCain
Obama

APPLYING WHAT YOU HAVE LEARNED

★ In which parts of the country did Democratic candidate Barack Obama and Republican candidate John McCain each have the most support?

Obama: _____

McCain: _____

★ What conclusions can you draw from this map about the distribution of political power in 2008?

_____

_____

_____

INTERNATIONAL RELATIONS AND THE "BALANCE OF POWER"

Within each country, a national government holds sovereign power. However, there is no world government with sovereign power over nations. For this reason, nations often compete and even conflict in order to protect themselves. They are seeking greater security.

Balance of Power. Geographers and historians sometimes speak of a "**balance of power**" between sovereign nations. This is the idea that if one country becomes too strong, other countries will band together against it. It is also the idea that the amount of power that the largest states enjoy should not become too unequal. The purpose of this "balance" is to prevent any single nation from becoming so powerful that it is tempted to force its will upon other nations. The main aim of the "balance of power" is to manage and limit conflict among the most powerful sovereign nations. Some experts argue that with the threat of nuclear weapons, a new "balance of terror" has replaced the traditional "balance of power" in the world.

Many physical and human factors influence how much power an individual nation actually possesses:

What is the size of the country's area?	**What is the population of the country?**	**How well educated and united is its population?**
How large and well-equipped are its armed forces?	**What are the country's physical features?**	**How productive is the country's economy?**

The amount of power a country enjoys greatly affects its control of territory and resources, its ability to defend itself or wage war, and its influence on the course of international relations generally.

THE WORLD'S MAJOR POWERS

Countries like the United States, China, Russia, and Japan exercise a large influence on international relations today because they either have powerful armed forces, a large population, or a dynamic economy. Many of these countries have all three of these characteristics.

★ **United States.** Americans have the benefit of a large land area, rich natural resources, high standards of living, and an educated population. It also possesses a highly skilled, experienced army with superior weapons. After the World War II, the U.S. emerged as a Superpower, with the world's first nuclear weapons. From 1946 to 1990, America had the world's largest economy, while it engaged in the **Cold War** with the Soviet Union. The United States also pioneered the development of new information technologies, like the computer and Internet. After the attacks on the World Trade Center in 2001, America became engaged in costly wars in Iraq and Afghanistan. At the same time, Americans are being challenged by rising economic competition from overseas. America remains the world's foremost power with the largest economy and most nuclear weapons.

★ **China.** Mao Zedong established a Communist totalitarian dictatorship in China in 1949. Although China had the world's largest population and army, it had low standards of living and inferior technology. China's economy was then dominated by government activity. In 1978, more than 90% of its economy was controlled by state-run enterprises. After Mao's death, China allowed greater freedom of choice in its economy. Starting in the 1990s, China also began welcoming foreign investors and technology into China. By 2009, only 30% of its production was still created by state-run enterprises. Since then, China has developed into the world's fastest growing economy. It also continues to have the world's largest military force, with more than 1.6 million troops as well as its own nuclear weapons. Some experts predict that China will soon become the world's greatest power.

★ **Russia.** Russia was the leading part of the Soviet Union, one of the two major Superpowers after World War II. Following its defeat in the Cold War with the United States, Russia has faced great economic challenges in its transition from a Communist to a free-style economy. It continues to have a large and advanced military and possesses the world's second largest arsenal of nuclear weapons.

★ **Japan.** Japan has a much smaller population than China, the United States, or Russia. As the target of the world's only nuclear attack at the end of World War II, Japan has also renounced the use of nuclear weapons. Because of the high education standards and inventiveness of its people, Japan is still a major world power based on its economic strength.

THE UNITED NATIONS

Some associations of countries are also very influential in international relations. The **United Nations** is an organization of all the sovereign nation states in the world. Founded after World War II, the aim of the United Nations is to promote peace, prevent war, and encourage development in all nations. All member states belong to the **General Assembly**. A group of especially powerful states, including the

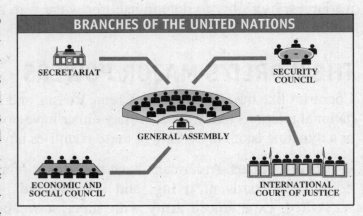

BRANCHES OF THE UNITED NATIONS

SECRETARIAT

SECURITY COUNCIL

GENERAL ASSEMBLY

ECONOMIC AND SOCIAL COUNCIL

INTERNATIONAL COURT OF JUSTICE

United States, China, Russia, Britain and France, belong to the **UN Security Council**. The Security Council has the power to send UN peace-keeping forces to areas of conflict around the world.

EUROPEAN UNION

The **European Union** is another association of countries with influence on international relations. The EU is an economic and political union of member states. Now composed of a large number of European states, the EU forms a large area in which people and goods can pass freely. EU members also cooperate on many matters and follow EU directives and regulations. Most use the Euro, a common currency. Citizens in member states even elect representatives to a European Parliament in Strasbourg, France.

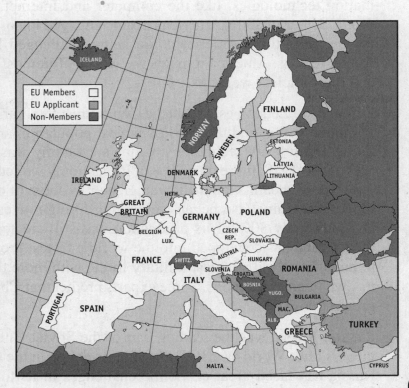

EU Members
EU Applicant
Non-Members

ICELAND
NORWAY
SWEDEN
FINLAND
ESTONIA
LATVIA
LITHUANIA
DENMARK
IRELAND
GREAT BRITAIN
NETH.
GERMANY
POLAND
BELGIUM
LUX.
CZECH REP.
SLOVAKIA
FRANCE
SWITZ.
AUSTRIA
HUNGARY
SLOVENIA
CROATIA
ROMANIA
ITALY
BOSNIA
YUGO.
BULGARIA
MAC.
ALB.
GREECE
TURKEY
PORTUGAL
SPAIN
MALTA
CYPRUS

APPLYING WHAT YOU HAVE LEARNED

Research the Internet or your local library and select a current problem that is facing either the United Nations or the European Union. On the following page, identify the problem, briefly describe the problem, and summarize what the international organization is doing to resolve it.

CONTINUED

★ State the problem: _____

★ Describe the problem: _____

_____

_____

_____

★ Steps being taken to resolve the problem: _____

_____

_____

_____

_____

◆ LEARNING WITH GRAPHIC ORGANIZERS

Complete the graphic organizer below. Give *one* example of a physical factor and one of a human factor or process that influenced where borders were established.

FACTORS INFLUENCING BORDERS

Physical Factors	**Human Factors**
_____	_____
_____	_____
_____	_____
_____	_____
_____	_____
_____	_____
_____	_____
_____	_____
_____	_____

CHAPTER STUDY CARDS

Political Regions / Units

★ Just as each place belongs to more than one physical or cultural region, it can also belong to several political divisions:
- City or Town
- State
- County
- Country

★ **Supremacy of National Government.** A national government is **sovereign**, or supreme, within its own borders.

★ **Sources of National Power.** Many factors influence a government's ability to control territory and influence international events: its size, population, wealth, educational level, military strength, and physical features.

Borders

National boundaries, known as **borders**, are the product of both physical and human processes: rivers, oceans, and mountains often act as borders. These are often modified by history.

★ **United States.** Expansion of lands by purchase, annexation, and warfare.

★ **Mexico.** A country's borders can be determined by conflicts with its neighbors.

★ **Poland.** Faced with no defensible east-west borders, was subject to frequent invasion.

★ **France.** A country's borders can be affected by international political relations.

CHECKING YOUR UNDERSTANDING

Directions: Put a circle around the letter that best answers the question.

Use the map and your knowledge of social studies to answer the following question.

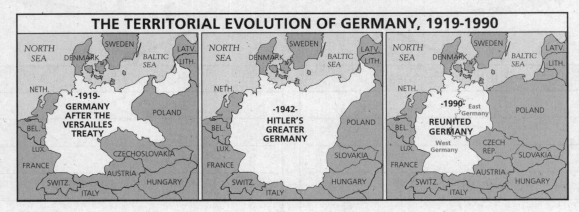

THE TERRITORIAL EVOLUTION OF GERMANY, 1919-1990

1   Based on the information in these maps of Germany, what conclusion can be drawn?
    A   Germany has kept the same borders throughout its history.   [Govt 14(A)]
    B   A country's borders are entirely established by physical geography.
    C   Political events can cause a country's boundaries to change.
    D   After World War II, Poland lost some of its territory to Germany.

Begin by carefully **examining** the question. This question tests your ability to read and compare a series of maps. You should **recall** that physical and human processes influence a nation's borders. Here, the map shows that Germany expanded and contracted at different times in history (1919–1990). **Applying** this information to the answer choices, you should recognize that **Choice A** is wrong since Germany's borders have changed. **Choice B** is wrong since wars and other factors can alter a country's borders. **Choice D** is also wrong since Germany lost territory to Poland, not the other way around. **Choice C** is the best answer.

Now try answering some additional questions on your own:

Use the maps and your knowledge of social studies to answer the following question.

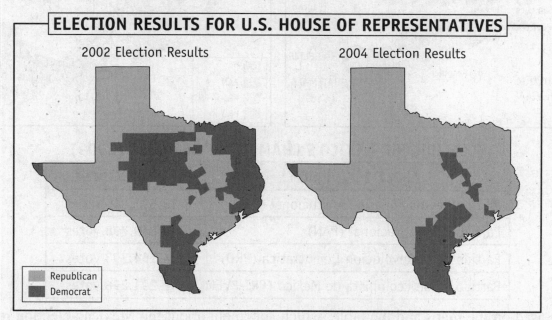

ELECTION RESULTS FOR U.S. HOUSE OF REPRESENTATIVES

2002 Election Results   2004 Election Results

Republican
Democrat

2   Based on the information in the maps above, what conclusion can be drawn?

    F   Few election districts in Texas voted Republican.   Govt 13(B)

    G   Election results can lead to a shift in political power.

    H   The Democratic Party cannot win future elections in Texas.

    J   Redistricting of Texas Congressional districts occurs every ten years.

3   An important effect of mountain ranges, large rivers, and ocean coastlines on a country has often been the —

    A   growth in available fertile land   Govt 14(A)

    B   encouragement of cultural convergence

    C   formation of the country's borders

    D   promotion of a democratic form of government

4   The conflict between Israel and its Arab neighbors since 1948 shows that —

   F   strong leadership often leads to a return of traditional ways

   H   conflicts between neighbors can result in shifting borders

   G   Communism has played a major role in Israel's development

   J   Europe still controls its former colonial territories

Govt 14(C)

Use the maps, table, and your knowledge of social studies to answer questions 5 and 7.

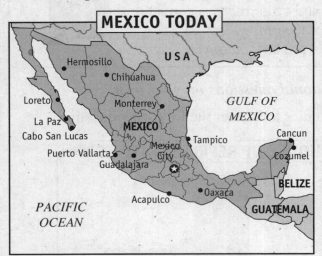

ELECTION FOR MEXICO'S CHAMBER OF DEPUTIES (2009)

POLITICAL PARTY	VOTE COUNT
Partido Revolucionario Institucional (PRI)	12,591,855 votes
Partido Accion Nacional (PAN)	9,549,798 votes
Partido de la Revolucion Democratica (PRD)	4,164,393 votes
Partido Verde Ecologista de Mexico (PRI-PVEM)	2,291,298 votes

5   Based on the maps and the table, which statement about the Mexican election results of 2009 is most accurate?

   A   The Partido Revolucionario Institucional won the election.

   B   The strength of the Partido Verde Ecologista de Mexico came mostly from Northern Mexico.

   C   Partido Verde Ecologista de Mexico was Mexico's largest political party.

   D   Partido Accion Nacional's strength comes mostly from northern Mexico.

Govt 13(B)

6   Which political party received the most votes in Guadalajara?

   F   PRD   **G**   PRI

   H   PAN   **J**   PRI-PVEM

Govt 13(B)

7   Partido Verde Ecologista de Mexico's political strength was found —

   A   in Northern Mexico   **C**   in Central Mexico

   B   Acapulco and La Paz   **D**   throughout Mexico

Govt 13(B)

Political Processes and Citizenship

This chapter looks at how government decisions are made. It corresponds to some of the special skills sections found in HMH's *World Geography*.

❏ *Before Reading:* You might begin your study of this topic by reading the TEKS, *Geographical Terminology*, *Important Ideas* and *Essential Question* on pages 272–273.

❏ *During Reading:* Next you should read pages 273–275 to learn the steps that government officials often follow in making decisions. Read about the same decision-making process on page 739 SK1 of HMH's *World Geography* and then fill in the flow chart on page 276, below. Then read about the importance of considering different points of view, on pages 277–280 below, and compare this information with the skill of evaluating different sources on page 97– SK1 of HMH's *World Geography*. Read about citizenship practices, the impact of cultural beliefs, patriotism and nationalism in both books, and consider the case studies of different viewpoints on international issues — such as Russia and Chechnya, Israel and Palestine, Iran and nuclear energy, the "War on Terror," and the turmoil in the Balkans — using information from both books. Consider how the treatments of these issues in these two books are similar and different. You should complete your study of this unit by conducting the *Acting as an Amateur Geographer* activity on page 285 below. You might use information from both the Internet and from HMH's *World Geography* to complete its "executive summary."

❏ *After Reading:* Reinforce your learning by completing the graphic organizers, reviewing the study cards and answering the test questions at the end of the chapter.

Topics	Mastering the TEKS	HMH's World Geography
Decision-making Process	pp. 273–275	p. 739 SK1
Importance of Different Points of View	pp. 277–280	
Influence of a Variety of Viewpoints	p. 277	p. 97 SK1 (Evaluating the Validity of Sources); Example: Aboriginal Land Claims in Australia, pp. 727–729
Citizenship Practices	p. 278	
The Impact of Cultural Beliefs		
Cultural Beliefs	p. 279	pp. 71–72
Patriotism	p. 279	
Nationalism	pp. 279–280	pp. 83, 297–298, 305
Different Viewpoints on International Issues	pp. 280–284	
Russia and Chechnya	pp. 280–281	pp. 175, 385–387
Israel and Palestine	pp. 281–283	pp. 510–514–515, 527, 532–533
Iran and Nuclear Energy	pp. 283–284	
U.S. War on Terrorism		pp. 173–175
Turmoil in the Balkans		pp. 319–321

Using Multiple Sources of Information

• Use information from both books to write your own answers to the *Essential Questions* on page 272.
• Your teacher should select members of your class to pretend to be citizens debating an important local issue. Use information from both books to guide your discussion.
• Use information from both books to create your own slide show, video, Prezi or PowerPoint presentation on one of the international "hot spots" in this chapter.
• Use information from both books to write a "letter to the editor" on one of the "hot spots" in this chapter.

Name _____ Date _____

POLITICAL PROCESSES AND CITIZENSHIP

CHAPTER 16

TEKS
COVERED IN
CHAPTER 16

■ **Citizenship 15** The student understands how different points of view influence the development of public policies and decision-making processes on the local, state, national, and international levels.
  • **Citizenship 15(A)** Identify and give examples of different points of view that influence the development of public policies and decision-making processes on local, state, national, and international levels.
  • **Citizenship 15(B)** Explain how citizenship practices, public policies, and decision making may be influenced by cultural beliefs, including nationalism and patriotism.
■ **Culture 18(B)** Assess causes, effects, and perceptions of conflicts between groups of people, including ... terrorism.
■ **Social Studies Skills 21(B)** Locate places of contemporary geopolitical significance on a map.
■ **Social Studies Skills 23** The student uses problem-solving and decision-making skills, working independently and with others, in a variety of settings.
  • **Social Studies Skills 23(B)** Use case studies ... to identify contemporary challenges and to answer real-world questions.
  • **Social Studies Skills 23(C)** Use problem-solving and decision-making processes to identify a problem, gather information, list and consider options, consider advantages and disadvantages, choose and implement a solution, and evaluate the effectiveness of the solution.

In this chapter, you will look at how government decisions are made. You will consider how citizens participate in government and how government policies are shaped by cultural beliefs. You will also look at how government decisions and international issues are often influenced by different points of view.

AN ESSENTIAL QUESTION

○— How are government decisions and international issues shaped by different points of view?

GEOGRAPHIC TERMINOLOGY IN THIS CHAPTER

■ **Decision-Making Process**   ■ **Point of View**   ■ **Patriotism**
■ **Government Policy**   ■ **Cultural Beliefs**   ■ **Nationalism**

— IMPORTANT IDEAS —

A. Governments often make decisions. Government officials usually follow a logical **decision-making process** to make them:
- Identify a problem;
- Gather information;
- List various options;
- Consider the advantages and disadvantages of each option;
- Choose and implement a solution;
- Evaluate the effectiveness of the solution.

These are the same decision-making steps that were examined more fully in Chapter 4.

B. A **government policy** consists of a series of decisions and actions on a particular issue or topic.

C. Different **points of view** frequently influence the development of public policies and decisions. This occurs at the local, state, and national levels of government.

D. **Cultural beliefs**, such as **nationalism** and **patriotism**, influence citizenship practices, public policies and decision-making processes.

E. Different points of view also affect policies and decision-making at the international level, between nations.

DECISION-MAKING PROCESSES AND GOVERNMENT POLICIES

Governments frequently have to make important decisions affecting thousands or even millions of people. For example:

Should Texas students have to pass an End-of-Course test in geography?	Should taxes be increased to help reduce the national debt?	Should oil companies be allowed to drill in the Gulf of Mexico?	Should American troops be kept in Iraq or Afghanistan to fight terrorism?

THE DECISION-MAKING PROCESS

Chapter 4 explored some steps for making good decisions. The steps one should follow to make a good decision are known as the **decision-making process**. In order to make decisions, government officials usually follow a similar process.

IDENTIFY THE PROBLEM

First, government officials identify a need or a problem. For example, the government may need to protect citizens against acts of terrorism.

GATHER INFORMATION

Next, government officials must gather and analyze information. They could look at terrorist acts committed in the United States and elsewhere. They could make a list of known terrorist leaders and organizations. A government might use satellite surveillance, undercover agents, exchanges of information with foreign governments, and similar steps to obtain information about these terrorist groups — including their leaders, their goals and activities, and their strengths and weaknesses.

Spy satellites orbit undetected in an attempt to conduct surveillance of other nations.

CONSIDER OPTIONS

Next, government officials will consider different ways of meeting the need or solving the problem. They will think of all their options for dealing with terrorists. At one extreme, they could attack countries where terrorists reside or are protected by the government in power. At the other extreme, they could do nothing and hope the problem will eventually resolve itself.

Usually, government leaders can think of a number of policy options between these two extremes:

| Do nothing. | Politely ask other countries to expel terrorists. | Economic Sanctions: refuse to trade with countries housing or supporting terrorists. | Eavesdrop on conversations of suspected terrorists; freeze their bank accounts in the U.S. | Supply military assistance to foreign governments actively fighting terrorists. | Launch attacks against countries where terrorists are operating. |

APPLYING WHAT YOU HAVE LEARNED

Identify another option not listed on the continuum for dealing with this problem.

_____

_____

_____

_____

CONSIDER ADVANTAGES AND DISADVANTAGES

Government officials now consider the advantages and disadvantages of each option. Every option usually has both benefits and costs. For example, eavesdropping on the telephone conversations and e-mail correspondence of suspected terrorists may yield valuable information about the next possible terrorist threat, potentially saving thousands of innocent lives. On the other hand, this practice may infringe on traditional liberties of American citizens, specifically protected in the U.S. Constitution.

Eavesdropping on citizens' conversations can have both positive and negative consequences.

SELECT, IMPLEMENT, AND EVALUATE THE BEST OPTION

Finally, officials select one policy option or combination of options. Then they apply this approach to the problem and evaluate its effectiveness. They assess whether this proposed solution works and whether it creates new problems of its own.

APPLYING WHAT YOU HAVE LEARNED

Which approach do you think is best for dealing with global terrorism, and why?

_____

_____

_____

_____

LEARNING WITH GRAPHIC ORGANIZERS

Complete the graphic organizer below by identifying and then describing each of the steps involved in the decision-making process:

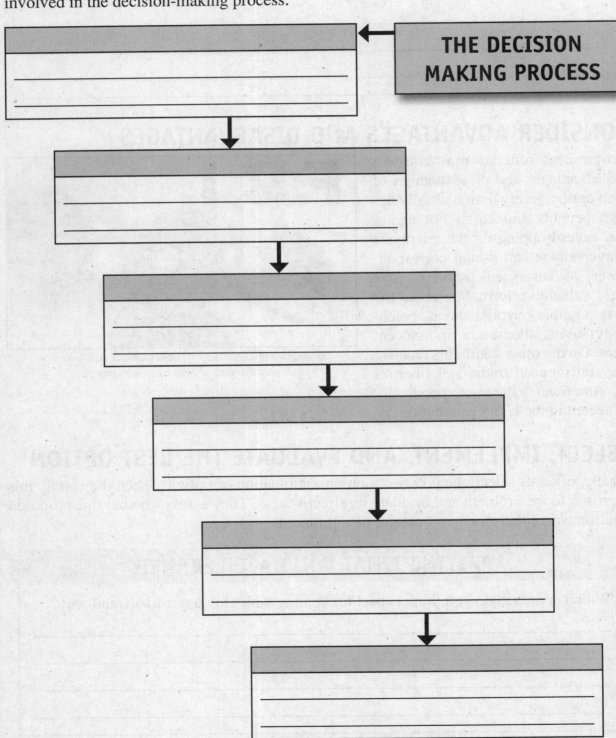

THE DECISION MAKING PROCESS

THE IMPORTANCE OF DIFFERENT POINTS OF VIEW

When government leaders make decisions affecting millions of people, it is important for them to consider different points of view.

Government officials will usually consult with different advisors and experts on the subject. For example, to decide how to deal with global terrorism, U.S. leaders might interview specialists who have studied terrorism. They would also question generals and other officers who have been active in military operations against terrorists. Undercover agents who secretly penetrated terrorist organizations might be

The U.S. President meets with his national security advisers.

asked for their views and ideas on the situation. U.S. leaders might further ask for the advice and suggestions of close allies and other countries. Officials might even decide to approach some international organizations, such as the United Nations.

THE INFLUENCE OF A VARIETY OF VIEWPOINTS

Democratic governments like the United States are generally very open to different points of view. Because democratic government leaders are elected, they need to be able to explain their policy choices to the public. There is usually a lively public discussion on key issues.

Leaders also come to office with special viewpoints based on their own backgrounds and interests. If a lawyer who has defended clients against evidence from wiretapping is elected to public office, she may view the problem of wiretapping differently from someone who was a former prosecutor. When a legislature, such as the U.S. Congress, looks at an issue, it usually reflects many different points of view. These leaders are often subject to a range of influences. Such influences include direct lobbying efforts, corporate political action groups, issue advertising, and pressure from constituents in their home district.

For example, some members of Congress have been elected by farmers or farm equipment makers. They often see issues from the farmers' point of view. Other Congressional members may have been supported by oil companies, labor unions, or other groups. Each representative will look at issues in part from these particular points of view. This variety of viewpoints occurs not just at the federal level, but at the state and local level as well.

APPLYING WHAT YOU HAVE LEARNED

What different viewpoints do you think influenced the Texas legislature in its decision to require students to take an End-of-Course Assessment in World Geography?

_____

_____

_____

_____

_____

Non-democratic forms of government, such as monarchies, dictatorships, and theocracies, are less open than democracies to participation by ordinary citizens. They are less concerned about public opinion than democratic leaders are. As a result, their leaders do not always take into account different points of view.

CITIZENSHIP PRACTICES

Citizenship practices also differ between governments. In a republic or democracy, citizens play an active role in government. They hold their leaders accountable for their actions, and expect that government will be sensitive to the will of the majority. They hold elected office, vote for officials, join political parties, and exchange ideas in free assemblies and through a free press.

In other forms of government, citizens do not usually enjoy the same rights. In a totalitarian dictatorship, citizens can participate in government, but only by joining the ruling party. They cannot lawfully speak out against the dictator.

Dictatorial governments often stage mass rallies, parades and other demonstrations to show that the dictator enjoys widespread support. Participants in these exciting, government-sponsored events may become caught up in waves of mass enthusiasm in support of the government. Government propaganda on television, in news articles, and in schools continuously tells citizens how good their government is, and paint any opposition as being disloyal or unpatriotic. The government may hold elections, but the candidates always follow the ruling party line.

Rally in support of the government in Iran.

THE IMPACT OF CULTURAL BELIEFS

Cultural beliefs can have a tremendous impact on government decision-making. If all the members of a culture share certain beliefs, then those shared beliefs will shape government decisions.

Annual meeting of China's Communist Party, where opposition to official policies is never permitted.

For example, all government leaders in China are members of the Chinese Communist Party. Although China has welcomed free enterprise in its economy, it does not allow rival political parties. Because all Chinese government leaders share the belief that Communist Party rule provides the best government for China, it is unlikely that they will permit opposition parties or dissension in the near future. Their shared political culture thus affects their decision-making.

In another example, the Vietnamese have feared their larger and dominating neighbor, China, as an enemy for most of their history. These fears have been memorialized in many Vietnamese folk songs and legends. These long held cultural beliefs sometimes affect decisions today by the Vietnamese government regarding its relations with China.

PATRIOTISM AND NATIONALISM

Patriotism and nationalism are two particular cultural beliefs that often influence citizenship practices.

Patriotism is loyalty and support for one's country. It is the belief that citizens should obey their country's laws and rally to its defense. People's attitudes often differ about the value of patriotism. Some acts of patriotism produce great admiration even among foreigners. For example, many people admire those Dutch soldiers who died in an attempt to halt the Nazi army from invading the Netherlands in 1940. On the other hand, invading Nazi soldiers also felt that they

were engaged in a patriotic act by fighting on behalf of Germany. Yet few admire these Nazi soldiers because of the brutality of the Nazi regime.

Nationalism is the belief that each people or ethnic group, known as a "nation," should have its own government and nation-state. In established nation-states, nationalism is often the belief that one's country is among the very best countries in the world. Some nationalists feel their nation is so superior that they have the right to take territory from or to even rule over others.

Like other cultural beliefs, patriotism and nationalism can have profound effects on government policies and decision-making. For example, if a country is attacked, patriotic feelings will encourage its people to defend themselves against the aggressor. Nationalist feelings may lead a country to commit acts of aggression, such as attacking weaker neighbors or seizing overseas colonies.

Nationalist feelings may also discourage a country's leaders from cooperating in international associations. Nationalism can be a constructive or destructive force. It can help harness national energies, but in multi-ethnic states, the nationalist feelings of minority groups can tear the country apart.

APPLYING WHAT YOU HAVE LEARNED

Do you see nationalism as mainly a constructive or destructive force? Explain your viewpoint. _____

_____

_____

DIFFERENT VIEWPOINTS ON INTERNATIONAL ISSUES

In dealing with international issues, it is especially important for government leaders to consider other viewpoints. Each side is often influenced by its own cultural beliefs, individual interests, and history. It's difficult to reach a compromise or a solution if the different sides do not understand each other's points of view.

INTERNATIONAL "HOT SPOTS"

Different viewpoints on important issues can best be seen by examining a few of the major "hot button" issues in our world today.

RUSSIA AND CHECHNYA

The Soviet Union was formed after the Russian Revolution in 1917. In 1991, the Soviet Union dissolved into several independent states. The largest of these was Russia. Within Russia, there are still several ethnic minorities.

One such ethnic minority are the Chechens, who live in the region of the southern Caucasus Mountains. Many Chechens sought independence from Russia. In 1991, Chechen separatists declared their independence from Russia. This was followed by a series of terrorist bombings. These terrorist acts led the Russian army to enter Chechnya to restore Russian rule by force in 1999.

The Chechen Viewpoint. The Chechen people have their own language and traditions. They have a long history of fighting against foreign rule. The Chechen population numbers over a million people. Many Chechens are Muslims. Chechen separatists feel that Chechnya has the right to be independent. Chechens accuse the Russian army of committing human rights violations against their people. Thousands of Chechens have been killed or have lost their homes under brutal Russian treatment.

Chechen separatist fighters.

The Russian Viewpoint. Russians point out that every modern nation has some minorities that would like to be independent. Each ethnic minority cannot be given its own state, or modern nations will all disintegrate into a world of mini-states. Even the United State once used force against seceding Southern States to preserve its unity. Russians fear that if they give Chechens self-government, other regions in Russia with minority ethnic groups will also demand their independence. Russians further point out that the Chechens have used terrorism in their efforts at independence. For example in 2004, Chechen separatists seized a school and killed almost 200 children. They fear ethnic Russians in an independent Chechnya would be abused. Finally, the Russians point out that some Chechen separatists have even cooperated with the Al Qaeda terrorist organization.

The Perspective from Ukraine. While Russians have opposed Chechen separatists in their own country, they have supported ethnic Russian separatists in nearby Ukraine. In 2014, Russian President Vladimir Putin precipitated a crisis by supporting ethnic Russians in the Crimea and annexing it. Next, Putin threatened Eastern Ukraine, which also has many ethnic Russians. While opposing separatism in Chechnya, Putin has thus supported pro-Russian separatism in Ukraine. Many fear Putin plans to restore Russian power by annexing more former Soviet territories.

APPLYING WHAT YOU HAVE LEARNED

How is an understanding of both sides of this conflict important for working towards a solution? What solution would you propose?

_____

_____

_____

ISRAEL AND PALESTINE

The modern State of Israel traces its historical and religious roots back to Biblical times. However, it was not until 1948 that Israel was established by the United Nations as a permanent homeland for the Jewish people. At the same time, many Arab Palestinians were also living in that area. Arab nations refused to recognize the creation of Israel. In 1948, they launched an attack on Israel, but were quickly defeated. Some 725,000 Palestinians fled Israel to neighboring Arab countries or were expelled from their homes.

War erupted again in 1967. Israel defeated its enemies in six days and acquired the Gaza Strip and Sinai Peninsula from Egypt, the West Bank from Jordan, and the Golan Heights from Syria. Egypt and Syria launched another surprise attack on Israel in 1973. Israel again repelled Arab forces.

The West Bank and Gaza Strip were later established as a home for Palestinians. Palestinian uprisings in these territories were followed by Israeli military occupations. Both sides accuse the other of atrocities. A Palestinian Authority was established, but Israelis and Palestinians have been unable to agree on the terms for the creation of an independent Palestinian state. Some Palestinian groups still refuse to accept the existence of Israel, while Israel has repeatedly occupied Palestinian territory. Israelis and Palestinians also disagree on many specific issues, such as the future of Jerusalem. For example, conflict broke out there again in 2014 after three Israeli teenagers were kidnapped and killed in Gaza. Israel invaded Gaza to destroy its tunnel system, killing about two thousand Palestinians, while several thousand rockets and mortars were fired from Gaza into Israel.

The Israeli Viewpoint. Many Israelis feel that Israel cannot be secure so long as some Palestinian groups continue to fire missiles at civilian Israeli targets. They believe that only a strong military defense can insure their survival against future attacks. Some Israelis further fear that an independent Palestinian state might be hostile to Israel and provide a home to terrorists or even someday invade Israel. Other Israelis, however, feel that some compromise with moderate Palestinians is vital to Israel's future and is the only way to achieve secure borders.

Military service is mandatory in Israel for all non-Arab citizens over the age of 18.

The Palestinian Viewpoint. Palestinians feel that they were forced to move from Israel in 1948. They contend that this was their land, and that the United Nations had no right to give this land to Israel. Most Palestinians are now willing to accept the independence of Israel, but they oppose continued expansion of Jewish settlements in Palestinian areas. They resent the Israeli occupations, and feel that Israelis have not made a genuine effort to achieve peace. Some Palestinians justify acts of terrorism as the only effective way to resist Israel's superior and highly mechanized military force. Moderate Palestinians hope to reach a compromise with Israel.

Hamas forces continue to challenge Israel's existence.

APPLYING WHAT YOU HAVE LEARNED

How is an understanding of both sides of this conflict important for achieving a solution? What solution would you propose?

_____

_____

_____

_____

_____

_____

_____

_____

IRAN AND NUCLEAR ENERGY

Many world leaders suspect that Iran is developing nuclear weapons under the pretext of building nuclear power plants to supply their nation with electricity. The United States and the United Nations have imposed severe economic and political sanctions against Iran for refusing to halt its nuclear enrichment program. **Sanctions** are strict measures used by a country or group of countries to pressure another nation-state to modify its behavior. For example, an economic sanction might impose a ban on trade with that country.

The Iranian View. Iranians claim they are a major power in the Middle East. They say they need to enrich uranium to build nuclear reactors for peaceful purposes: for example, as a source of future energy, and for radiation therapy to treat cancer patients. Iran's religious leaders have issued a decree banning nuclear weapons. Iran further claims that it is hypocritical for countries like the United States to actually have nuclear weapons and then to criticize Iran for supposedly seeking to develop them.

The View of Iran's Critics. Critics say that Iran is stockpiling refined uranium in order to conceal its own plans to develop nuclear weapons. They say that as a major producer of oil, Iran does not need to develop nuclear energy at this time. They further claim that Iran's government is untrustworthy— for example, it used brutal force against citizens peacefully protesting irregularities in its 2009 presidential election.

In November 2011, U.N. weapons inspectors found new evidence that Iran is enriching uranium to make nuclear weapons. The United States and the European Union agreed to impose additional sanctions on Iran. These sanctions include a nearly total economic embargo banning companies from doing business with Iran, blocking all imports from Iran, and preventing all dealings with Iranian banks. Many fear Iran's government might threaten Israel with its nuclear bombs, or sell nuclear weapons to Islamic terrorists, further destabilizing the region. They point out that Iran has repeatedly violated United Nations rules. Furthermore, if Iran does acquire nuclear weapons, this would pressure its neighbors in the region do the same. Other countries would feel compelled to obtain nuclear arms to prevent Iran from upsetting the current "balance of power" in the Middle East.

Recent Progress. In June 2013, Hassan Rouhani was elected as the President of Iran. Since taking office, Rouhani has worked to improve relations with the West. In November 2013, a temporary agreement was reached between Iran and the permanent members of the Security Council plus Germany ("P5+1") for a partial freeze of Iran's nuclear program and an easing of Western sanctions.

APPLYING WHAT YOU HAVE LEARNED

Do you think United Nations sanctions against Iran are justified? _____

Why or why not? _____

_____

_____

ACTING AS AN AMATEUR GEOGRAPHER

Using the Internet, the library, and your class notes and other resources, select one other current "hot spot" in the world today. For this "hot spot," complete an "executive summary" providing background information and two different points of view on the issue. You might wish to investigate the issue further in a report.

★ What is the issue? _____

_____

★ Location: _____

_____

★ Background information: _____

_____

_____

_____

_____

★ Viewpoint of first side: _____

_____

_____

_____

_____

_____

★ Viewpoint of second side: _____

_____

_____

_____

_____

_____

LEARNING WITH GRAPHIC ORGANIZERS

Complete the graphic organizer below by explaining the significance of different viewpoints.

HOW DIFFERENT POINTS OF VIEW INFLUENCE GOVERNMENT DECISION-MAKING AND POLICIES

Role in Decision-Making	International "Hot Spots"
_____	_____
_____	_____
_____	_____
_____	_____
_____	_____

Complete the graphic organizer below by identifying *two* types of cultural beliefs and providing an example for each.

THE INFLUENCE OF CULTURAL BELIEFS

Patriotism	Nationalism
_____	_____
_____	_____
_____	_____
_____	_____

CHAPTER STUDY CARDS

The Decision-Making Process

To make good decisions, government officials should:

★ **Identify the problem.**
★ **Gather information about the problem.**
★ **Consider a range of different options for solving the problem.**
★ **Weigh the advantages and disadvantages of each option.**
★ **Select the best option.**
★ **Implement the best option.**
★ **Evaluate the effectiveness of the solution.**

The Importance of Different Viewpoints

★ Government leaders often consult with others and consider other viewpoints in order to reach better decisions.
★ Government leaders are influenced by their own backgrounds and views of supporters.

Citizenship Practices

★ Citizenship practices differ among different forms of government.
★ Citizens participate actively in the decision-making process in a democracy.
★ Dictatorial governments stage mass rallies but do not allow free and open criticism.

Cultural Beliefs

★ **Cultural beliefs** often influence decision-making.
★ **Patriotism.** The love of one's country and a willingness to serve and defend it.
★ **Nationalism.** Belief each "nation" deserves their own government and nation-state.
  • Nationalism can be both a destructive and a constructive force in a nation.
  • Nationalism can harness national energies and promote national unity.
  • In a multi-ethnic country, if each ethnic group demands its own nation-state, nationalism can tear that nation apart.

Case Studies of Contemporary Challenges

★ **Terrorism.** Use of terror against civilians to gain concessions.
★ **Russia and Chechnya.** Chechens use terror tactics to gain concessions from Russians.
★ **Israel and Palestine.** Both sides claim acts of violence; Palestinians want an independent state, while Israel wants secure borders and an end to violence.
★ **Iran and Nuclear Energy.** Iranians claim they need nuclear power for peaceful purposes; critics say they are developing nuclear weapons to use against their enemies.

CHECKING YOUR UNDERSTANDING

Directions: Put a circle around the letter that best answers the question.

1 Which type of government allows the greatest participation by ordinary citizens in the process of government decision making?

   A dictatorship
   B monarchy
   C democracy
   D totalitarianism

> • **E**XAMINE **The Question**
> • **R**ECALL **What You Know**
> • **A**PPLY **What You Know**

Citi 15(B)

Begin by carefully **examining** the question. This question tests your knowledge of citizenship practices under different types of government. You should **recall** that citizens participate most actively in a democracy, influencing their representatives in a number of ways — through phone calls, meetings, demonstrations, petitions, and voting. **Apply** this information to the answer choices. You should recognize that in **Choices A, B,** and **D** name governments where there are often strict limits on the flow of ideas by citizens on government decisions. **Choice C** is the best answer because there is a large degree of citizen participation in government decision-making in a democracy.

Now try answering some additional questions on your own:

2 In which example did nationalism most clearly affect public policy?

   F European countries signed the Maastrich Treaty to create `Citi 15(B)` the European Union.

   G British citizens refused to join other European nations in adopting the Euro so that they could continue to use their traditional currency, the pound.

   H Countries around the world donated relief aid when a tsunami struck Indonesia and Thailand.

   J Texas now mandates that an End-of-Course Test be given in world geography.

Use the information and your knowledge of social studies to answer the following question.

In May 2010, the leaders of Iran, Turkey, and Brazil made the following announcement from Iran's capital city of Tehran:

> "We reaffirm our commitment to the Treaty on Non-Proliferation of nuclear weapons and … recall the right of all state parties, including the Islamic Republic of Iran, to develop research, production and use of nuclear energy … for peaceful purposes…."

3 What point of view is expressed in this announcement?

   A Iran has a right to develop nuclear weapons for its defense. `Citi 15(A)`

   B The Nuclear Non-Proliferation Treaty should be overturned.

   C Iran has a right to develop nuclear energy for peaceful uses.

   D Turkey and Brazil will sell nuclear weapons to Iran.

4 Which is a major cause of conflict and discord in present-day Russia?

   F Russian patriots want to expand into Central Asia. `Cult 18(B)`

   G Business owners in Russia object to communism.

   H Chechen nationalists seek independence.

   J In the Baltic states, Russian minorities demand Russian aid.

Use the information and your knowledge of social studies to answer the following question.

- Israeli athletes were taken hostage and killed in 1972 at the Munich Olympic Games by anti-Israeli terrorists.

- The United States embassies in Kenya and Tanzania were bombed in 1998 by a group of radical terrorists.

- In 1998, extremists exploded a bomb on Pan Am flight 103 as it flew over Lockerbie, Scotland, killing all those aboard.

5 What conclusion can best be drawn from these three events?
   A Israel has traditionally been the focus of terrorist activities.   `Cult 18(B)`
   B Some groups feel terrorism is justified to resolve their problems.
   C For more than 100 years, the Middle East has been a troubled area.
   D The use of terrorism is increasing in sub-Saharan Africa.

6 Which is an important cause of terrorism in the Middle East?
   F Iranians use terrorism to collect uranium for nuclear weapons.   `Cult 18(B)`
   G Israelis believe terrorist acts are needed to defend settlements in the West Bank.
   H Many Palestinians believe terrorism is justified against Israeli occupation.
   J Radical groups in Egypt wish to give control of the Suez Canal to Britain.

Use the information in the boxes and your knowledge of social studies to answer the following question.

Russians oppose independence for Chechnya	**Hutus attack and kill Tutsis in Rwanda**	**Israelis and Palestinians disagree on Palestinian statehood**

7 Which important contemporary challenge do these three examples illustrate?
   A How can different ethnic groups get along?   `Cult 18(B)`
   B How can more food be produced to end world hunger?
   C How can atmospheric pollution be reduced to stop global warming?
   D How can people be protected from Chechen acts of terrorism?

8 At a town meeting, the mayor has presented several ways the town could provide childcare to families in which both parents work. What should the participants at the meeting do next?
   F Hold elections for a new mayor.   `Citi 15(A)`
   G Implement each of the ways to see which one works best.
   H Evaluate how well the mayor's proposals work.
   J Consider the costs and benefits of each way before choosing one.

Name _____   Date _____

UNIT 5 REVIEW
PULLING IT ALL TOGETHER

Imagine you are setting up your own government. List *two* things you would do based on what you learned in this chapter.

1. _____

   _____

2. _____

   _____

Select *one* of the *Essential Questions* explored in this unit by checking the box. Then answer it below.

ESSENTIAL QUESTIONS REEXAMINED

☐ What is the best form of government?

☐ What factors determine where boundaries between countries are established?

☐ How do different countries relate to one another?

☐ How are government decisions and international issues shaped by different points of view?

_____

_____

_____

_____

_____

_____

_____

_____

_____

_____

UNIT 5 CONCEPT MAP

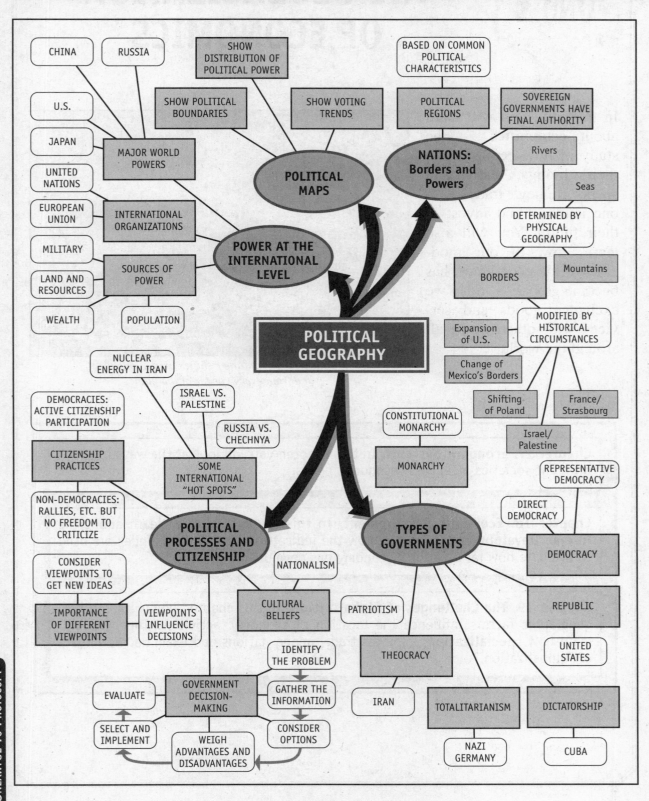

CHINA

RUSSIA

SHOW DISTRIBUTION OF POLITICAL POWER

BASED ON COMMON POLITICAL CHARACTERISTICS

U.S.

SHOW POLITICAL BOUNDARIES

SHOW VOTING TRENDS

POLITICAL REGIONS

SOVEREIGN GOVERNMENTS HAVE FINAL AUTHORITY

JAPAN

UNITED NATIONS

MAJOR WORLD POWERS

POLITICAL MAPS

NATIONS: Borders and Powers

Rivers

Seas

EUROPEAN UNION

INTERNATIONAL ORGANIZATIONS

MILITARY

POWER AT THE INTERNATIONAL LEVEL

DETERMINED BY PHYSICAL GEOGRAPHY

LAND AND RESOURCES

SOURCES OF POWER

BORDERS

Mountains

WEALTH

POPULATION

POLITICAL GEOGRAPHY

MODIFIED BY HISTORICAL CIRCUMSTANCES

Expansion of U.S.

NUCLEAR ENERGY IN IRAN

Change of Mexico's Borders

DEMOCRACIES: ACTIVE CITIZENSHIP PARTICIPATION

ISRAEL VS. PALESTINE

Shifting of Poland

France/ Strasbourg

CITIZENSHIP PRACTICES

RUSSIA VS. CHECHNYA

CONSTITUTIONAL MONARCHY

Israel/ Palestine

NON-DEMOCRACIES: RALLIES, ETC. BUT NO FREEDOM TO CRITICIZE

SOME INTERNATIONAL "HOT SPOTS"

MONARCHY

REPRESENTATIVE DEMOCRACY

DIRECT DEMOCRACY

CONSIDER VIEWPOINTS TO GET NEW IDEAS

POLITICAL PROCESSES AND CITIZENSHIP

TYPES OF GOVERNMENTS

DEMOCRACY

IMPORTANCE OF DIFFERENT VIEWPOINTS

VIEWPOINTS INFLUENCE DECISIONS

NATIONALISM

CULTURAL BELIEFS

PATRIOTISM

REPUBLIC

IDENTIFY THE PROBLEM

THEOCRACY

UNITED STATES

EVALUATE

GOVERNMENT DECISION-MAKING

GATHER THE INFORMATION

IRAN

TOTALITARIANISM

DICTATORSHIP

SELECT AND IMPLEMENT

WEIGH ADVANTAGES AND DISADVANTAGES

CONSIDER OPTIONS

NAZI GERMANY

CUBA

UNIT 6

THE GLOBALIZATION OF ECONOMICS

In this unit, you will learn about **economics** — the study of how people make their livings, earn and spend money, trade with one another, and invest in their future. You will also learn how, in our modern world, economics has become global — today we exchange goods and services with others from all around the world.

Today, large container ships carry goods to and from every corner of the globe.

Chapter 17. Economic Systems. In this chapter, you will look at the ways in which different societies meet their economic needs.

Chapter 18. Economic Development. In this chapter, you will learn about the **Human Development Index** and how the indicators shown on this index are used to evaluate how far a nation's economy has developed.

Chapter 19. The Challenges of Globalization. In this chapter, you will learn how geographic factors influence the location of economic activities. Then you will learn how **specialization** promotes trade among nations and examine the impact of "globalization."

Economic Systems

This chapter tells you what economics is all about. You will learn the three fundamental economic questions and study the characteristics of four major economic systems. You will also learn about the differences between subsistence and commercial agriculture, and between cottage and commercial industries. This chapter corresponds to various sections of HMH's *World Geography*.

❑ *Before Reading:* You might begin your study of economics by reading the TEKS, *Geographical Terminology*, *Important Ideas* and *Essential Question* on pages 294–295.

❑ *During Reading:* Next you should start by learning what economics is. Read pages 295–296 below on "What is Economics?" Then read page 91 of HMH's *World Geography*. Now you are ready to learn about economic systems. Read pages 296–302 below. After reading about each type of economic system in this book, read the corresponding pages in HMH's *World Geography*, as indicated on the chart below. Some of these pages provide examples of how a particular economic system works in practice. For example you can read about the free enterprise system on pages 295–296 of this book, and on page 91 of HMH's *World Geography*. Then you can see how this system works in the United States on pages 140–142 of HMH's *World Geography*, in Canada on page 159, in Latin America on pages 252–253, and in Taiwan on page 645. You can also read how Eastern Europe and China are moving towards free enterprise — or "market" — economies on pages 313 and 637. You should complete your study of economic systems by completing the *Acting as an Amateur Geographer* activity on page 304 of this book. You can use the Internet and HMH's *World Geography* to find information about the current economic systems of Latin American countries.

❑ *After Reading:* Reinforce your learning by completing the graphic organizers, reviewing the study cards and answering the test questions at the end of the chapter.

Topics	*Mastering the TEKS*	HMH's *World Geography*
What is Economics?	pp. 295–296	p. 91
The Problem of Scarcity	p. 295	
What are Goods and Services?	p. 296	p. 91
Types of Economic Systems	pp. 296–298	p. 91
Traditional Economy	p. 297	pp. 91, 582, 644, 707
Subsistence Agriculture	p. 297	pp. 92, 569, 575
Cottage Industries	p. 298	p. 92, 570, 575
Free Enterprise System (Market Economy)	pp. 298–299	pp. 91, 140–142, 159, 252– 253, 637, 645
Supply and Demand	pp. 298–299	p. 91
Role of Government	p. 299	pp. 247, 250, 462, 569, 653
Communism	p. 300	pp. 83, 313, 364, 637, 645
Socialism	pp. 301–302	pp. 232, 306–307
Mixed Economies	p. 302	pp. 91, 313, 388–389
South American Economies (Student Project)	p. 304	pp. 211–213, 234–235, 238, 245–247, 250–255

Using Multiple Sources of Information

• Use information from both books to write your own answers to the *Essential Questions* on page 294.

• Create your own concept map around one of the *Important Ideas* on page 295. Find facts and examples from both books for your concept map.

ECONOMIC SYSTEMS

CHAPTER 17

■ **Economics 10** The student understands the distribution, characteristics, and interactions of the economic systems in the world.
  • **Economics 10(A)** Describe the forces that determine the distribution of goods and services in free enterprise, socialist, and communist economic systems.
  • **Economics 10(B)** Classify where specific countries fall along the economic spectrum between free enterprise and communism.
  • **Economics 10(C)** Compare the ways people satisfy their basic needs through the production of goods and services such as subsistence agriculture versus commercial agriculture or cottage industries versus commercial industries.
■ **Culture 18(C)** Identify examples of cultures that maintain traditional ways, including traditional economies.

TEKS COVERED IN CHAPTER 17

In this chapter, you will learn how societies have different economic systems — traditional, free enterprise, socialist, or communist. Each of these systems goes about meeting its people's economic needs in different ways.

ESSENTIAL QUESTIONS

◯— How do different societies around the world meet their economic needs?

◯— What are the advantages and disadvantages of each economic system?

GEOGRAPHIC TERMINOLOGY IN THIS CHAPTER

■ Economics
■ Economist
■ Economic System
■ Problem of Scarcity
■ Traditional Economy

■ Subsistence Agriculture
■ Cottage Industries
■ Free Enterprise System
■ Capitalism
■ Profit

■ Supply and Demand
■ Commercial Industries
■ Communist* Economy
■ Socialist* Economy
■ Mixed Economy

*A Note about Capitalization: "Communism" and "Socialism" are capitalized when they refer to a specific country or political party, but not when they refer to a general idea, such as "a communist economy."

— IMPORTANT IDEAS —

A. **Economics** is the study of how people meet their basic needs. All societies must answer three fundamental economic questions: (1) What should be produced? (2) How should it be produced? (3) Who gets what is produced?

B. How a society answers these three fundamental economic questions determines its type of **economic system**.

C. In a **traditional economy**, people meet their basic needs much as their ancestors had done. Traditional economies are marked by **subsistence agriculture**, in which families grow just enough to feed themselves. Goods like textiles are produced at home in **cottage industries**.

D. In a **free enterprise economy**, people are free to produce what they want and to buy what they want. In a free enterprise economy, prices are determined by the forces of **supply and demand**. Food is produced through **commercial agriculture** in which farmers grow food to sell to others, while goods are manufactured through **commercial industries**.

E. In a **communist economy**, the government owns and operates all businesses. State managers develop a national plan for the production and distribution of all goods and services. Factory managers are given quotas to meet, based on the national plan.

F. In a **socialist economy**, the government owns and operates many basic industries. Other businesses are privately owned.

G. Specific countries can be **classified** based on the type of economy they have.

WHAT IS ECONOMICS?

Economics is the study of how individuals, businesses, and nations make things, buy things, spend money and save money. People who study economics are known as **economists**.

THE PROBLEM OF SCARCITY

Economists believe that the basic problem of economics is the **problem of scarcity**. Something is scarce when we do not have enough of it. The problem of scarcity involves two basic ideas:

★ People usually have **unlimited wants**. There are many things each of us wants. Even if we had them all, we would most likely find new things that we wanted.

★ A society can produce only a **limited** number of things at any one time. There is only a certain amount of available goods and services. Therefore, a society cannot fulfill all of everyone's wants.

WHAT ARE GOODS AND SERVICES?

★ **Goods** are those things that people make; for example, foods, toys, clothes, cars and houses are all considered goods. Department stores, shoe stores, bakeries and supermarkets all sell goods to consumers.

★ **Services** are those things that people do for others. People who provide services include electricians, teachers, plumbers, barbers, doctors, and auto mechanics.

APPLYING WHAT YOU HAVE LEARNED

Suppose that everyone in the world were given 10 million dollars. Do you think that would end the problem of scarcity? Explain your answer.

_____

_____

_____

_____

_____

THE FUNDAMENTAL ECONOMIC QUESTIONS

Because every society has limited resources, no society has enough goods and services to meet the unlimited needs and wants of all its members. This problem of scarcity forces every society to answer three fundamental economic questions:

| What should be produced? | How should it be produced? | Who should get it? |

TYPES OF ECONOMIC SYSTEMS

The way in which a society answers these three economic questions is known as its **economic system**. There are four types of economic systems you should know:

| Traditional | Free Enterprise | Communist | Socialist |

TRADITIONAL ECONOMY

In a **traditional economy**, the three basic economic questions are answered according to tradition. Generally, people do what their ancestors did. Traditional economies tend to be primarily agricultural. They usually center around the family or tribal unit. Economic decisions are made on the basis of customs and beliefs that have been handed down from one generation to the next. Individuals do not choose what their position in society will be. They are born in a small village and simply do whatever their parents did. Thus, a child's occupation is determined at birth: the child will follow the example of his or her father or mother. Resources are allocated by inheritance, and tools tend to be primitive. Major occupations in a traditional economy consist of hunting, farming, and herding cattle.

A traditional economy relies heavily on customs and traditions of the past.

MAIN FEATURES OF A TRADITIONAL ECONOMY

Economic Decisions. Custom and tradition determine what should be produced, how it should be produced, and for whom.

Production. The production of goods is based on custom and time-honored methods. New ideas are discouraged. Change and growth proceed very slowly.

Private Property. Often there is no private property: things are owned by the family or village in common.

Trade. Goods and services are produced to meet the needs of the members of the family or tribe. Since they are produced and consumed locally, there is very little trade with outsiders.

PRODUCTION METHODS

Traditional economies are generally marked by **subsistence agriculture** and **cottage industries**.

Subsistence Agriculture. In traditional economies, the land usually produces only enough crops to feed the farmer and his family. Almost everything grown is intended for use by the family or village. There is rarely a surplus, so very little is sold or traded. Economic growth is quite slow. In most of Africa, Asia, and many parts of Latin America, a large percentage of people are primarily involved with feeding themselves from their own land and livestock.

Cottage Industries. In traditional societies, people use their spare time in their home to weave cloth, make furniture and clothes, and to produce other goods by hand. These "cottage industries" are quite common in traditional societies where a large portion of the population is engaged in agriculture. Cottage industries help farmers and their families meet their needs, and may give them extra income during the winter months when there is little work on the farm. Typically, cottage industries involve the entire family working together.

A woman bleaches yarn in a cottage industry.

Examples

Throughout history, most economies have been traditional ones. Today, traditional economies are still found in many rural, non-industrial areas. Traditional economies exist among the Bushmen of the Kalahari Desert of South Africa, the Berber tribesmen of Algeria, and the villages in South Asia.

FREE ENTERPRISE SYSTEM

Free enterprise (*also known as **capitalism** or the **free market system***) is an economic system in which people own their own goods and property. Some people invest their money in different ways of producing things (*factories*, *machines*, and *land*) or in distributing goods so that they may gain a **profit** — what remains after the costs of running the business are paid. In a free enterprise system, people are free to produce whatever they wish and to buy whatever they can afford. The three basic economic questions are answered by the interplay between consumers (*buyers*) and producers (*sellers*).

HOW PRICES ARE DETERMINED

Prices in a free enterprise system are established by the interaction of supply and demand. **Supply** refers to how much of a good producers are willing to make and sell. **Demand** refers to how much of a good consumers are willing to buy. As the diagram shows, when the demand for a good is high, the price goes up. If the supply is high but demand is low, the price goes down. If a producer charges too much for an item, other producers will sell the item at a lower price and outsell that producer.

THE INTERACTION OF SUPPLY AND DEMAND

High Demand/
Short Supply

PRICES

PRICES

Low Demand/
Large Supply

This interaction between supply and demand is the force behind how resources are allocated. In a free enterprise economy, supply and demand led to the distribution of resources in the most efficient way possible. In this way, an economy based on free enterprise will eliminate inefficient producers and limit the production of unwanted goods.

THE ROLE OF GOVERNMENT

There is limited government interference in the economy in a free enterprise system. However, government still plays a vital role. Government acts as an umpire, providing and enforcing a set of common rules, maintaining a monetary system, providing for the nation's defense, and protecting people's right to own property. In a free enterprise system, people sometimes look to government to break up or regulate companies that have obtained so much power that they could defy market forces.

MAIN FEATURES OF FREE ENTERPRISE SYSTEM

Private Property. People have a right to own private property (*personal possessions, factories, farms, businesses*) and to use this property as they see fit with limited governmental interference.

Free Enterprise. People are free to take part in any business, buy any product, or sell any legal product. Businesses are also free to do anything they wish in order to attract customers — such as lower prices, provide better quality goods, advertise, etc.

Profit Motive. The ability to make profits is what drives people to risk their money in starting a new business.

Supply and Demand. The interaction of supply and demand determines prices in a free market economy. When demand is high, the price goes up. If the supply is high but demand is low, the price goes down.

PRODUCTION METHODS

Unlike traditional economies, free enterprise economies generally have **commercial agriculture** and **commercial industries**. Farmers grow food not just for themselves, but in order to sell it to others for cash. In commercial agriculture, crop production is intended for distribution to wholesalers and retailers, such as supermarkets and grocery stores. Large-scale commercial agriculture makes production cheaper. Farmers can use tractors and other equipment over large tracts of land. In commercial industries, goods are manufactured in factories for sale throughout the country or overseas.

Examples

The free enterprise system exists in such nations as the United States, Great Britain, France, Chile, Canada, Japan, Germany, and Singapore.

APPLYING WHAT YOU HAVE LEARNED

Think of a good or service you bought recently. Explain how the interaction of supply and demand most likely determined how much you paid for that product.

_____

_____

_____

COMMUNISM

Communism was developed in the 1800s by **Karl Marx** (*1818–1883*). Marx believed that business owners (*whom he called **capitalists***) used their wealth to take advantage of workers by taking away most of the value of what they produced. Marx predicted that the conditions of workers would grow so bad that they would eventually rise up and overthrow their capitalist rulers in a violent revolution. After the revolution, workers would establish an equal society and live in perfect harmony, under what Marx called "communism." In theory, there are no social classes in a communist system. Cooperation is supposed to replace competition, allowing everyone's needs to be met.

Karl Marx

In practice, communism is an economic system in which all important economic decisions are made by government leaders. These leaders decide what, how, and for whom goods and services will be produced. The way goods are produced and distributed is controlled by government leaders for the good of society as a whole. Government officials develop national plans, often for five-year periods, that specify which goods each factory will make.

MAIN FEATURES OF COMMUNISM

Role of Government. All major decisions on production, distribution and the use of resources are made by government planners.

Private Property. Private property ownership is abolished and replaced by national ownership of all land, factories, farms, and major resources.

Cooperation. Communism is based on cooperation, in which all workers should labor together and share equally. The economy is supposed to be run for the benefit of all members. In practice, government leaders run things to prepare for true communism.

Major Goal. The goal is to achieve a classless society — equality among all workers.

Examples

At one time, there were many Communist states, including the Soviet Union, the countries of Eastern Europe, China, North Korea, Vietnam, and Cuba. However, communist economies were unable to keep up with the goods created by free enterprise systems. Government planners were not able to predict all of society's needs. Without incentives to reward workers for harder work or better performance, many workers failed to work hard or to do their best. To get extra goods or benefits, people often bribed government officials. Corruption in most Communist countries became widespread. The Soviet Union and Eastern Europe abandoned communism.

Today, China, North Korea, Vietnam, and Cuba are still Communist countries. China, however, has kept its communist political system but has taken rapid steps towards creating a free enterprise economy.

SOCIALISM

Like communism, **socialism** is an economic system in which the most important businesses producing goods (mines, factories, businesses) are owned by the government rather than by individuals. Socialist governments typically own their nation's railroads, airlines, hospitals, banks, utility companies, mining or oil companies and other major industries. However, unlike communism, socialism encourages private ownership of small businesses (such as shops and small manufacturers). Some economists refer to socialist economies as "free market socialism" because these economies do not involve state planning.

Socialism first began in the 1800s as a political movement in response to the injustices of industry and the exploitation of workers in Europe. Many workers had to work long hours for low wages in unsafe conditions. Socialist reformers believed the best way to protect workers was to have the government control the major means of production. They saw the government as the best protector of the worker.

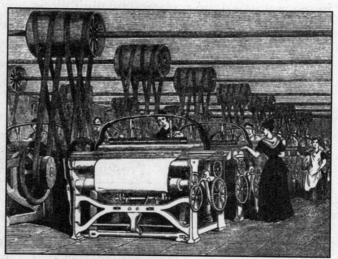

In the early days of industrialization, many workers were taken advantage of.

However, socialists disagreed with the communist belief that workers' lives could only be improved through violent revolution. Socialists believed that workers could improve their own conditions by voting for sympathetic government leaders. The government could then own basic industries and also provide essential services, like free schooling, low-cost housing, public transportation, and a national health program.

MAIN FEATURES OF SOCIALISM

Role of Government. Government should use its power to bring an end to poverty by taking control of the major resources of the nation (*railroads*, *airlines*, *radio stations*) and by providing public services.

Economic Decisions. Many decisions about production, distribution and the use of resources are made by the government. Other decisions are made privately.

Private Property. Major industries are owned by the government. Other property is held privately.

Major Goal. Socialism seeks a fairer distribution of income among all members of society. People's basic needs (*health care*, *transportation*, *education*, *housing*) are met for free or at very low cost.

Examples

Such nations as Sweden and Israel model their economies on the ideas of socialism. After World War II, most countries in Western Europe became Socialist, but many then sold off their public ownership of major industries in the 1980s and 1990s in a wave of "privatization." India was Socialist from its independence in 1947 until 1991, but it is now moving towards free enterprise. In Africa, Ghana was Socialist but it is now also privatizing its state-owned enterprises.

MIXED ECONOMIES

In the real world, no economy totally follows any one economic system. Most countries have economies that blend features of each. Countries can be classified on a spectrum ranging from free enterprise to communist based on how actively the government intervenes in the economy.

APPLYING WHAT YOU HAVE LEARNED

Complete the following chart by filling in the blank spaces.

Economic Systems	What to Produce?	How Is It Produced?	Who Gets It?
Traditional	Set by tradition and custom.		Set by tradition and custom.
Free Enterprise	Interaction of producers/consumers.	Producers decide how to produce.	
Communist	Determined by government planners.		
Socialist			

APPLYING WHAT YOU HAVE LEARNED

Review the graphic organizer below summarizing the types of production.

TYPES OF PRODUCTION

Subsistence Agriculture.
Traditional economies mainly consist of poor farmers engaged in subsistence agriculture — in which they grow only enough food for themselves and their immediate families to eat.

Cottage Industries.
Traditional economies have cottage industries in which goods are made by hand in homes or small workshops largely for family or local use.

Commercial Agriculture.
Free enterprise economies have a market-oriented agriculture — farmers produce goods to sell to others rather than to meet their own needs.

Commercial Industries.
A free enterprise economy has commercial industries — where goods are mass-produced in factories for sale by businesses to consumers, including other businesses.

Now use the Internet or look in magazines in your library to find *one* picture for each of the types of production described in the graphic organizer above. Print or cut out a picture and label each one with an appropriate caption.

ACTING AS AN AMATEUR GEOGRAPHER

★ Countries can be classified based on the type of economic system they have. Select any ten countries on this outline map of South America.

- Use the Internet or other resources to find out the type of economic system each has. Remember that few countries will have a purely traditional, free enterprise, communist or socialist economy. Classify each economy based on the type of economic system it most closely resembles.

- On this map, create a legend with symbols or colors showing each type of economic system. Color in the countries you have researched.

SOUTH AMERICA

★ As you have just learned, countries can be classified on a spectrum from free enterprise to communist. Select *four* countries that you classified in the activity above and place their names along the following spectrum:

| No Government Interference | Some Government Interference | Government Owns Some Businesses | Complete Government Ownership |

FREE ENTERPRISE   **SOCIALIST**   **COMMUNIST**

LEARNING WITH GRAPHIC ORGANIZERS

Complete the graphic organizer below. Describe each type of economic system and provide one example.

Traditional

_____
_____
_____
_____
_____
_____
_____

Example: _____
_____

Free Enterprise

_____
_____
_____
_____
_____
_____
_____

Example: _____
_____

TYPES OF ECONOMIC SYSTEMS

Communist

_____
_____
_____
_____
_____
_____
_____

Example: _____
_____

Socialist

_____
_____
_____
_____
_____
_____
_____

Example: _____
_____

CHAPTER STUDY CARDS

Economics

★ **Economics.** The study of how people meet their basic needs.

★ All societies must answer three fundamental economic questions:
  • What should be produced.
  • How should it be produced?
  • Who gets what is produced?

★ How a society answers these three fundamental economic questions constitutes its **economic system**.

Traditional Economy

★ People meet their basic needs much as their ancestors did.

★ Economic decisions are made on the basis of customs and beliefs handed down from one generation to another.

★ **Subsistence Agriculture.** Farmers grow just enough to feed themselves and their families.

★ **Cottage Industries.** Goods like textiles are produced in private homes by hand, usually by the entire family.

Free Enterprise System

★ People freely produce and buy what they want.

★ The three fundamental economic questions are answered by the interplay between consumers and producers.

★ Prices are set by the interaction of **supply** and **demand**.

★ Producers invest their money in order to make a **profit**.

★ There is little government interference.

★ Inefficient producers are eliminated by going out of business.

Socialist Economy

★ Government owns some basic industries.

★ Private ownership of smaller businesses is allowed.

★ Government provides low-cost or free public services: schools, health care, etc.

Communist Economy

★ Government sets economic goals to be met.

★ Workers labor together and are supposed to share equally in the fruits of their labor.

★ Private property ownership is abolished.

CHECKING YOUR UNDERSTANDING

Directions: Put a circle around the letter that best answers the question.

Use the information in the boxes and your knowledge of social studies to answer the following question.

| The opportunity to make a profit drives people to put their money at risk. | Producers determine the supply, or availability, of a product. | Consumers determine the demand for a product. |

1 The features described in these boxes best describes the workings of a —

    A traditional economy   **C** socialist economy

    B free enterprise economy   **D** communist economy

Begin by carefully **examining** the question. This question tests your understanding of different types of economic systems. You should **recall** what a traditional, free enterprise, communist and socialist economic system are. In a free enterprise economy, people are driven to make profits, producers determine supply, and consumers decide demand. **Applying** this information to the answer choices, you can see that **Choice B** is the best answer. These are all characteristics of a free enterprise economy.

Now try answering some additional questions on your own:

2   In Indonesia, the government owns large industries and sets some prices. However, private businesses are also encouraged and several hundred are actively traded on the Indonesian Stock Exchange. This country's economy system can best be classified as —
  F   traditional
  G   free enterprise
  H   socialist
  J   communist

`Econ 10(B)`

> • **E**XAMINE The Question
> • **R**ECALL What You Know
> • **A**PPLY What You Know

3   Which is a central characteristic of a free market economy?
  A   The government owns the means of production.
  B   All wage earners are paid the same amount.
  C   Labor unions are prohibited.
  D   Businesses are driven by the desire for profits.

`Econ 10(A)`

4   In which economic system would you expect the widest selection of consumer goods?
  F   traditional   **G**   socialist
  H   free enterprise   **J**   communist

`Econ 10(A)`

5   In a traditional economy, information about the way goods are produced is passed from one generation to the next by the —
  A   family   **C**   public schools
  B   legal system   **D**   government

`Cult 18(C)`

6   Which is a major feature of an economy based on subsistence farming?
  F   Most adults work outside the home.
  G   Farmers compete with each other.
  H   Farmers raise just enough crops for their family to survive.
  J   The government decides which crops will be grown.

`Econ 10(C)`

UNLAWFUL TO PHOTOCOPY

Use the newspaper article and your knowledge of social studies to answer the following question.

The Minister of Economics has created a plan for the economy which emphasizes the production of iron, steel, and hydroelectric power. In manufacturing, such goods as tanks and tractors will receive high priority. Consumer goods are regarded as less essential. The people are expected to sacrifice comfort in order to raise the level of industrialization of their country.

---

7   Based on the information in the article, the Minister of Economics most likely lives in a country that has a —

A   traditional economy
B   socialist economy
C   communist economy
D   free enterprise economy

`Econ 10(B)`

---

8   Which group has the greatest influence in determining what goods and services will be produced in a communist economic system?

F   farmers
G   government officials
H   consumers
J   business leaders

`Econ 10(A)`

9   In a socialist economic system, the government —

A   has little say in what goods are made
B   does not influence the distribution of goods and services
C   guarantees all consumers a high income
D   often owns major businesses

`Econ 10(A)`

10   Which heading best completes the partial outline below?

I.   _____

   A.   Interaction of Supply and Demand

   B.   Profit Incentive

   C.   Entrepreneurs

F   Types of Economic Systems
G   Characteristics of a Free Enterprise Economy
H   Structure of a Socialist Economic System
J   Cottage Industries

`Econ 10(A)`

11   Which statement describes an aspect of a traditional economy?

A   Profit motivates individuals to set up private businesses.
B   The interplay of supply and demand regulates prices.
C   Tradition and customs greatly influence economic decisions.
D   Government directs and controls the means of production.

`Cult 18(C)`

Use the information and your knowledge of social studies to answer questions 12 through 14.

Country 1: "In my country, people produce what they need to survive by doing things as they were done by our ancestors. People hunt for food or grow it themselves."

Country 2: "In my country, all key decisions are made by our central planners. They hold complete power over the political and economic life of our nation. Our government directly owns the land, natural resources, and factories for the good of the people."

Country 3: "In my nation, people are free to produce whatever they wish and to consume whatever they can afford. People seek to make or sell goods and services so that they can earn a profit."

---

12 What occupation would most commonly be found in Country 1?

   F subsistence farming   **H** mining

   G computer programmers   **J** commercial agriculture

`Cult 18(C)`

13 Which statement would be true of the economy in Country 2?

   A Many businesses compete to have the lowest prices.

   B Most people follow their parents' occupations.

   C A major goal of the economy is to have a classless society.

   D Few people receive education or training outside the home.

`Econ 10(B)`

14 A supporter of the economic system found in Country 3 would most likely agree with which statement?

   F All nations can benefit from cottage industries.

   G Revolution is the only solution to current economic problems.

   H A planned economy is necessary in order to industrialize.

   J Government should limit its interference in the economy.

`Econ 10(A)`

---

15 Which forces play the greatest role in determining the distribution of goods and services in a free enterprise economic system?

   A court rulings and expert opinions

   B government officials and military needs

   C producer supply and consumer demand

   D village elders and community tradition

`Econ 10(A)`

16 An essential characteristic of a communist economy is the —

   F interaction of supply and demand

   G organization of worker unions

   H privatization of business

   J government ownership of property

`Econ 10(A)`

Economic Development

In this chapter, you will learn about the challenges faced by developing countries. You will learn how economists use various indicators to describe a country's economic development, and you will also learn about the types of economic activities associated with various levels of economic development.

❑ *Before Reading:* You might begin your study of this topic by reading the TEKS, *Geographical Terminology*, *Important Ideas* and *Essential Questions* on page 311.

❑ *During Reading:* Next you might read the text of the first section of this chapter, on pages 312–315, to learn about the Human Development Index and about various indicators of development, such as a country's Gross Domestic Product (GDP), average life expectancy and literacy rate. As you read about each of these indicators, you might turn to HMH's *World Geography* for an additional explanation, especially on pages 94–95. You could then look at the rising GDPs of Eastern European nations on page 313 or the literacy rates of China and other East Asian nations on pages 616–617. As the table below indicates, you can also find this data in HMH's *World Geography* for the countries of each regional group. After you have studied the various indicators using materials from both books, complete the *Acting as an Amateur Geographer* activity on page 315 of this book. Then look at the classification of different types of economic activities on page 316 of this book and page 92 of HMH's *World Geography*. Lastly, you should study the economies of several nations in greater depth. Turn to the pages of HMH's *World Geography* listed on the chart below for "Economic Development/Growth." Each of these sections (after the first) describes the economies of nations in different parts of the world and their problems. For example, pp. 219–220 deal with the economy of Mexico, pp. 225–226 with the Caribbean, p. 292 with the Mediterranean region of Europe, p. 313 with Eastern Europe, pp. 388–391 with Russia, pp. 443–444 with West Africa, pp. 450–451 with Central Africa, pp. 455–456 with Southern Africa, pp. 461–463 with the economic development of Africa in general, and pp. 637–638 with China. Complete your study of this chapter with the *Acting as an Amateur Geography* activity on page 317.

❑ *After Reading:* Reinforce your learning by completing the graphic organizers, reviewing the study cards and answering the test questions at the end of the chapter.

Topics	*Mastering the TEKS*	HMH's *World Geography*
Economic Development	pp. 312–314	pp. 91–95
Indicators of Development	pp. 312–314	pp. 92–93
Human Development Index	p. 312	p. 92
Demographic Indicators	pp. 312–313	pp. 78–79
Life Expectancy	p. 312	
Birth and Death Rates	p. 312	pp. 78–79
Infant Mortality Rate	p. 312	p. 79
Economic Indicators	p. 313	
Gross Domestic Product	p. 313	pp. 92–93
GDP per capita	p. 313	pp. 92–93
Social Indicators	p. 313	
Literacy Rate	p. 313	pp. 616–617
Political Indicators	p. 314	*See regional data files in each
Government's Relation	p. 314	unit for more indicators
to Economic Development		
Types of Economic Activities	p. 316	p. 92
Primary Economic Activities	p. 316	p. 92
Secondary Economic Activities	p. 316	p. 92
Tertiary Economic Activities	p. 316	p. 92
Quaternary Economic Activities	p. 316	p. 92

Using Multiple Sources of Information

• Use information from both books to write your own answers to the *Essential Questions* on page 311.

Name _____ Date _____

ECONOMIC DEVELOPMENT

CHAPTER 18

TEKS COVERED IN CHAPTER 18

- **Geography 5(B)** Interpret political, economic, social, and demographic indicators (*gross domestic product per capita, life expectancy, literacy,* and *infant mortality*) to determine the level of development and standard of living in nations using the terms Human Development Index, less developed, newly industrialized, and more developed.
- **Economics 11(A)** Understand the connections between levels of development and economic activities (*primary, secondary, tertiary,* and *quaternary*).

In this chapter, you will learn how various indicators are used to describe how developed a nation's economy is. These same indicators are also used to measure the level of a country's standards of living.

ESSENTIAL QUESTIONS

- How do economists measure a country's level of economic development?
- Which economic activities are most clearly associated with different levels of development?

— IMPORTANT IDEAS —

A. Various indicators are used to determine the level of development and standards of living of a country, including **Gross Domestic Product** (*G.D.P.*) **per capita, life expectancy, infant mortality,** and **literacy rate**.

B. The type of economic activities in a country influence its level of development.

GEOGRAPHIC TERMINOLOGY IN THIS CHAPTER

- Human Development Index
- Less Developed
- Newly Industrialized
- More Developed

- G.D.P.
- G.D.P. per Capita
- Infant Mortality
- Literacy

- Primary Activities
- Secondary Activities
- Tertiary Activities
- Quaternary Activities

ECONOMIC DEVELOPMENT

Economic development refers to how advanced an economy is. Countries with advanced economies are known as **more developed nations**, while countries with lower standards of living and less advanced technologies are known as **less developed nations**. Countries that are moving from less to more developed economies are known as "**newly industrialized**" or "**emerging economies.**"

INDICATORS OF DEVELOPMENT

The **Human Development Index** was developed by the United Nations in 1990 as a tool for ranking countries based on their level of economic development, gender and social equality, and the quality of life enjoyed by their citizens. This index classifies countries in terms of their human development as "**very high**," "**high**," "**medium**" or "**low**." Other economists, as stated above, classify countries as "**less developed**," "**newly industrialized**" (also known as "middle developed"), or "**more developed.**" They take into account demographic, economic, social, and political indicators to determine the level of economic development and standards of living of the people in a nation.

DEMOGRAPHIC INDICATORS

Demographic indicators relate to population:

★ **Life Expectancy. Life expectancy** is the average number of years an individual in a country is expected to live. Life expectancy is often affected by the country's level of poverty, diet and malnutrition, number of doctors, and the presence of infectious diseases within the population.

★ **Birth and Death Rates.** Birth and death rates are usually measured by how many people are born or die for every thousand people in that nation in a given year. The death rate is also referred to as the **mortality rate**.

Young mothers learn to care for newborn infants in a hospital in Myanmar.

Generally, countries with high birth and mortality rates are often less developed since these reflect the degree of poverty and quality of health care.

★ **Infant Mortality Rate.** The **infant mortality rate** is the number of infants who die for every thousand births. Infant mortality rates are closely related to the level of medical care available when an infant is born. The most common causes of infant deaths in the world have traditionally been dehydration, diarrhea, malnutrition, and malaria.

◆ A more developed nation has a low birth rate, a low mortality rate, a low infant mortality rate, and a long life expectancy.

◆ A less developed nation has a high birthrate, a high mortality rate, a high infant mortality rate, and a short life expectancy.

ECONOMIC INDICATORS

Economic indicators tell how well an economy is performing. The **Gross Domestic Product** (*G.D.P.*) is the total value of all goods and services produced by a nation in a year. The **Gross Domestic Product per capita** (*G.D.P./number of people*) reflects the value of goods and services produced in a year in a nation by an average person. Other economic indicators include the average number of automobiles, telephones, televisions, or computers per person.

◆ A **more developed nation** has a high G.D.P. per capita. There are a greater number of automobiles, doctors, and telephones, reflecting the higher standard of living. Workers are productive because they use machinery, computers, and other high-tech tools.

◆ A **less developed nation** has a low G.D.P. per capita income. Often, less developed nations concentrate on agriculture — many people remain engaged in subsistence farming and use primitive tools to work the land. Less developed nations lack investment, so their workers tend to be less productive and less competitive.

SOCIAL INDICATORS

Because more developed nations are wealthier, they are able to provide more social services to their citizens. People are healthier, better educated, and more productive than the citizens of less developed nations. Some of the social indicators economists consider include **literacy rates** (*percentage of people who can read and write*), the percentage of people attending colleges and universities, and the number of professional people, such as doctors and lawyers. Some of the other social indicators include housing, water supply, and sanitation.

The quality of education plays a key role in determining if a nation is less or more developed.

◆ A **more developed nation** has a high literacy rate and a greater percentage of people attending colleges and universities. There are a large number of doctors and hospitals serving the population.

◆ A **less developed nation** has a lower literacy rate, and a lower percentage of people attending colleges and universities. Only a small number of doctors and hospitals serve the population.

POLITICAL INDICATORS

Another factor economists and geographers look at in determining the level of development of a country consists of **political indicators**. These indicators include the freedoms people enjoy, the degree of democracy and voting rights, the level of human rights, the degree of government oppression, and the tolerance for different points of view.

GOVERNMENT'S RELATION TO ECONOMIC DEVELOPMENT

There is no direct relationship between economic development and a nation's system of government. Some more developed economies have been ruled by dictators, while some democracies are less developed nations.

A South African citizen casts her ballot during elections.

Nonetheless, since the end of the Cold War in 1991, most advanced economies have adopted the free enterprise system along with democratic government. Because a democratic government generally provides a system of laws and gives people the freedom to start their own businesses, it often leads to faster economic growth. Economic development is aided by freedom of expression, which ensures the free flow of information, and the checks and balances found in a democracy prevent the build up of military forces or theft of a nation's wealth often seen in dictatorships. Many newly industrialized economies now have some form of democratic government. On the other hand, the world's fastest growing economy, China, still does not enjoy a democratic government.

Some economists believe a nation's economic system can even help transform its political system. They point to the fact that economic development often leads to the creation of a strong middle class, the basis of a democracy. Economic development also promotes a strong sense of independence and personal freedom. Greater wealth allows individuals and businesses to strengthen their independence from the government. Some experts even predict that China may gradually become more democratic if its economic prosperity continues.

Name _____ Date _____

ACTING AS AN AMATEUR GEOGRAPHER

You can better grasp the differences between less and more developed countries by examining the chart below. How would you classify each of these: as less developed, newly industrialized, or more developed? After you make your own classifications, look up their actual classification on the Internet by searching for the most recent Human Development Index. You will see that the Human Development Index actually uses these terms: "less developed," "middle developed," and "highly developed."

Country	USA (N. America)	France (Europe)	Zimbabwe (Africa)	Bangladesh (South Asia)	Syria (Mid-East)
Population	309 million	65 million	12 million	162 million	21 million
Gross Domestic Product	$14.256 billion	$2.675 million	$4.397 million	$94.507 million	$52.524 million
G.D.P. per Capita	$37,500	$27,460	$2,180	$1,870	$3,430
Infant Mortality	6.4 per 1,000 births	4.2 per 1,000 births	51.1 per 1,000 births	59.1 per 1,000 births	27.7 per 1,000 births
Life Expectancy	78.0 years	79.9 years	39.5 years	62.8 years	70.6 years
Literacy Rate	99%	99%	91%	53%	83%

Country	Your Classification	Human Development Index
USA		
France		
Zimbabwe		
Bangladesh		
Syria		

How accurate was your initial classification of these countries? Explain your answer.

_____

_____

_____

_____

TYPES OF ECONOMIC ACTIVITIES

As you know, **economic development** refers to how advanced an economy is. Economists and geographers have found that a nation's level of economic development is often closely tied to the types of economic activities its people engage in. If economic development can be compared to how far a country has advanced in school, then economic activities can be compared to the "subjects" a country takes. More advanced students usually take more advanced subjects. Economists have classified different economic activities into four main groups:

PRIMARY ECONOMIC ACTIVITIES

The most basic, or **primary**, economic activities in all societies involve the production of foods and the extraction of resources. These include growing crops, raising livestock, grazing, fishing, logging and mining. The smaller the portion of people involved in primary economic activities, the greater the likelihood the country's economy is more developed. For example, about 3% of the U.S. labor force is currently engaged in primary sector activities.

SECONDARY ECONOMIC ACTIVITIES

The manufacture and production of goods, such as the making of textiles and furniture, is considered the next level of economic activity. **Secondary economic activities** add value to raw materials by processing them or by changing their form. For example, logs are cut into wooden planks and then assembled into furniture; iron ore is changed into steel and shaped into railroad tracks.

What type of economic development would you classify this activity as?

TERTIARY ECONOMIC ACTIVITIES

Tertiary, or third-level, economic activities deal with **services**. This sector is identified by a variety of services performed by people and businesses. Services include such occupations as teacher, nurse, doctor, accountant, retailer, truck driver, or musician. In the United States, more than 80% of the labor force are tertiary workers. They perform some service rather than producing a good.

QUATERNARY ECONOMIC ACTIVITIES

Quaternary, or fourth-level, economic activities consist of those involving information processing and management. This level of economic activity is conducted by such occupations as a computer programmer or the general manger of a company.

CONNECTION WITH DEVELOPMENT

Economists have found there is usually a strong relationship between a country's level of economic development and the types of economic activities its population engages in:

★ In a **"less developed"** country, most people will be engaged in primary economic activities, such as agriculture and mining. Most people are engaged in subsistence agriculture, or in forms of commercial agriculture in which a few key crops are grown and sold to buyers in other countries.

★ In a **"newly industrialized country"** like China or Thailand, large numbers of people are engaged in secondary economic activities, such as manufacturing textiles or automobiles for export.

★ In a **"more developed country"** like the United States or France, the majority of workers are engaged in tertiary or quaternary economic activities. They perform services or process information.

ACTING AS AN AMATEUR GEOGRAPHER

★ Choose any country other than the United States. In the space below, describe its main type of economic activities and its level of economic development. Use the Internet, library or your own notes as sources of information.

Country: _____ Economic Activities: _____

_____

_____

_____

_____

Level of Development: _____

★ Why do you think there is often a connection between the types of economic activities in a country and its level of economic development?

_____

_____

_____

_____

_____

LEARNING WITH GRAPHIC ORGANIZERS

Complete the graphic organizer below. Define some of the indicators used in the Human Development Index:

G.D.P. per Capita	Infant Mortality

Life Expectancy	Literacy Rate

Now define the different types of economic activities tied to economic development.

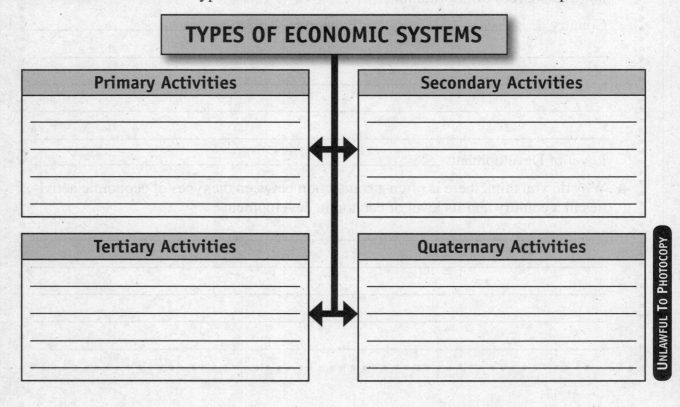

TYPES OF ECONOMIC SYSTEMS

Primary Activities	Secondary Activities

Tertiary Activities	Quaternary Activities

CHAPTER STUDY CARDS

Indicators of Development

The **Human Development Index** was developed by the UN to rank countries based on their level of economic development, social and gender equality, and the quality of life enjoyed by their citizens.

Indicators of development include the following:

★ **Demographic Data.**
  • Size of the population.
  • **Birth Rate.** Births per 1,000.
  • **Infant Mortality Rate.** Infant deaths per 1,000 births.

★ **Economic Data.**
  • **G.D.P.** Total of goods and services made in a nation in one year.
  • **G.D.P. per capita.** G.D.P. per person

★ **Social Data.**
  • **Literacy Rate.** Percentage of people who can read and write.

Levels of Economic Development

★ **Less Developed Nations.**
  • high birthrate and infant mortality rate
  • increasing population size
  • low G.D.P. per capita and literacy rate

★ **Newly Industrialized.**

★ **More Developed Nations.**
  • low birthrate and infant mortality rate
  • stable population growth
  • high G.D.P. per capita and literacy rate.

Economic Activities

★ **Primary.** Agricultural, mining

★ **Secondary.** Manufacturing

★ **Tertiary.** Services

★ **Quaternary.** Management and information processing.

CHECKING YOUR UNDERSTANDING

Directions: Put a circle around the letter that best answers the question.

Use the table and your knowledge of social studies to answer questions 1 through 3.

ECONOMIC CONDITIONS IN LATIN AMERICA, 2009

Nations	Population	G.D.P. (in millions)	Infant Mortality (deaths)	Literacy	Life Expectancy
Bolivia	10 million	$17,627	45.6 per 1,000	90.7%	65.6 years
Brazil	193 million	$1,574,039	23.6 per 1,000	90.0%	72.4 years
Haiti	10 million	$6,558	48.8 per 1,000	62.1%	60.9 years
Mexico	107 million	$874,903	16.7 per 1,000	92.8%	76.2 years
Venezuela	29 million	$337,295	17.0 per 1,000	95.2%	73.7 years

1   Based on the table, which statement is most accurate?

   A   Most people in Venezuela live into their 90s.   `Geog 5(B)`
   B   Haiti has the best schools in Latin America.
   C   The infant mortality rate is similar among these Latin American countries.
   D   Mexico has one of the most developed economies in Latin America.

Examine. This question tests your ability to read a table and to assess the level of development of a nation's economy. **Recall** that a more developed economy has a higher G.D.P. per capita, higher literacy rate, lower infant mortality rate, and higher life expectancy. **Applying** this information to the answer choices, you should see that **Choice D** is the best answer. Mexico's G.D.P., literacy rate, and life expectancy is among the highest in Latin America, while its infant mortality rate is lower than all the other countries listed in the table.

Now try answering some additional questions on your own:

2 Which conclusion can best be drawn from the information in the table? `Geog 5(B)`
   F   Venezuela has the best schools in Latin America.
   G   Most people in Haiti live into their 80s.
   H   Brazil is more highly developed than Haiti.
   J   Mexico has the largest population in Latin America.

3 Based on the table, most people in Haiti probably engage in — `Econ 11(A)`
   A   primary economic activities   **C**   tertiary economic activities
   B   secondary economic activities   **D**   quaternary economic activities

---

4 Which type of economic activities would most likely be found in a newly industrialized country with commercial industry?
   F   primary activities   **H**   tertiary activities   `Econ 11(A)`
   G   secondary activities   **J**   quaternary activities

5 Which is an example of a secondary economic activity?
   A   growing corn on a farm for export   `Econ 11(A)`
   B   working in a plant, manufacturing automobiles
   C   growing just enough food for one's immediate family
   D   managing a large multinational corporation

6 Which characteristic is typical of a less developed country?
   F   Government does not interfere in the economy.   `Geog 5(B)`
   G   Entrepreneurs play a key role in the nation's economy.
   H   There is a high infant mortality rate and a short life expectancy.
   J   There is a high literacy rate and a long life expectancy.

7 As a country moves closer to becoming newly industrialized, it tends to —
   A   develop a more rigid class system   `Geog 5(B)`
   B   move away from traditional beliefs and customs
   C   have population shifts from cities to the countryside
   D   limit technological innovations

Use the graphs and your knowledge of social studies to answer questions 8 and 9.

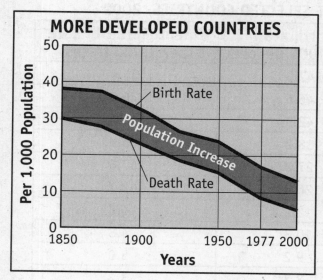

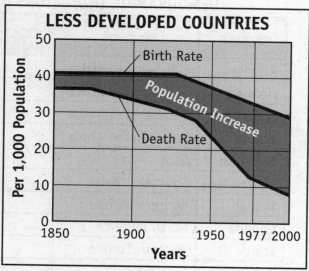

8   Which statement is best supported by the information in the graphs?

   F   Population in both less and more developed countries increases
at the same rate.

   G   By 2000, the world's more developed countries had reached a point of zero
population growth.

   H   Most growth since 1900 has been due to a drop in the death rate.

   J   Most growth since 1900 has been due to an increased birth rate.

`Geog 5(B)`

9   Which conclusion can be drawn from the information in the graphs?

   A   More developed countries have increasing birth rates.

   B   Less developed countries have rising populations.

   C   More developed countries have falling populations.

   D   Less developed countries are marked by sharply rising death rates.

`Geog 5(B)`

10   A newly industrialized nation is usually characterized by having —

   F   a large number of workers engaged in manufacturing

   G   most people engaged in subsistence agriculture

   H   a lack of human resources like skilled and unskilled labor

   J   most of its workers engaged in quaternary economic activities

`Econ 11(A)`

11   Which statement would be true for a country with a large number of people engaged
in quaternary economic activities?

   A   Most people are engaged in subsistence agriculture.

   B   It has a high level of infant mortality.

   C   It has a low level of literacy

   D   Many occupations involve information processing and management.

`Econ 11(A)`

Use the table and your knowledge of social studies to answer questions 12 and 13.

DEMOGRAPHIC INDICATORS OF SELECTED COUNTRIES, 2009

Nation	Region	Birthrate (per 1,000 people)	Infant Mortality Rate (per 1,000 births)
Angola	Sub-Saharan Africa	47.3	131.9
Uganda	Sub-Saharan Africa	46.6	76.9
Somalia	Sub-Saharan Africa	42.9	116.3
Ethiopia	Sub-Saharan Africa	38.2	86.9
Pakistan	South Asia	27.2	67.5
Cambodia	Southeast Asia	26.4	62.7
France	Western Europe	12.2	4.2
Canada	North America	10.3	4.8
Italy	Western Europe	9.2	5.0
Japan	East Asia	8.3	3.2
Germany	Western Europe	8.2	4.3

12 Which is a valid generalization, based on the information in the table?

   F   In more developed nations, infant mortality rates are usually higher than birthrates.   `Geog 5(B)`

   G   More developed nations have lower birthrates and infant mortality rates than less developed nations.

   H   Decreasing infant mortality rates slow population growth in less developed nations.

   J   More developed nations have higher birth rates than less developed nations.

13 According to the table, some of the lowest birthrates are found in —

   A   Western Europe   **C**   Southeast Asia   `Geog 5(B)`

   B   Southeast Asia   **D**   Sub-Saharan Africa

---

14 What conclusion can be inferred from the data presented in the graph?

   F   Most children under 5 are malnourished.

   G   Africa has the most malnourished children under 5.

   H   In Asia, many children under 5 years old are malnourished.

   J   Almost half the children in the world under 5 years old are malnourished.

   `Geog 5(B)`

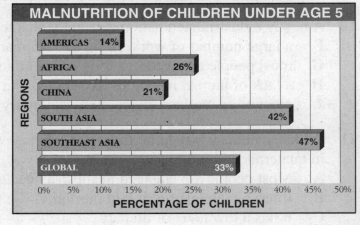

MALNUTRITION OF CHILDREN UNDER AGE 5

AMERICAS 14%
AFRICA 26%
CHINA 21%
SOUTH ASIA 42%
SOUTHEAST ASIA 47%
GLOBAL 33%

REGIONS

PERCENTAGE OF CHILDREN

The Challenges of Globalization

This chapter completes your study of world geography. It explores world trade and the process of globalization, which is transforming our world today.

❑ **Before Reading:** You might begin your study of trade and globalization by reading the TEKS, *Geographical Terminology*, *Important Ideas* and *Essential Question* on pages 325–326.

❑ **During Reading:** Next read pages 326–331, below, on how the location of productive resources, such as fossil fuels, minerals, water and skilled workers, influences the location of economic activities. Turn to HMH's *World Geography* for specific examples of these different types of resources and how they often affect the location of economic activities. For example, read about the location of natural resources in the United States and Canada on pages 121–122 of HMH's *World Geography*, study the map on page 120 (showing these resources), and consider the location of Canada's primary, manufacturing and service industries, summarized on pp. 159–160. Pages 204–205, including the map, similarly describe the location of natural resources in Latin America, while pp. 276–277 describe the natural resources of Europe and how they shape economic life. After looking at these examples, return to this book to read pages 331–332 below. You will learn how changes in climate, resources or infrastructure can lead to changes in the locations of economic activities. Then read several of the corresponding sections of HMH's *World Geography*, as indicated on the chart below, for more detailed examples. In the next section of this chapter, pages 334–336, you will learn how the uneven distribution of world resources leads nations to specialize and to trade with each other to obtain goods they may not produce themselves. Again, look at the corresponding sections of HMH's *World Geography* for more detailed examples. Then you should read the short history of world trade, from ancient times to the present, found on pages 336–339. You can find additional information on the pages of HMH's *World Geography* indicated in the chart below. Since the end of World War II, the barriers to world trade have been falling while transportation costs have also lowered. These circumstances have led to a rapid increase of world trade and contributed to the process now known as globalization. Finally, read pages 341–342 in this book to consider the benefits and costs of globalization, including pandemics and global terrorism.

❑ **After Reading:** Reinforce your learning by completing the graphic organizers, reviewing the study cards and answering the test questions at the end of the chapter.

Topics	Mastering the TEKS	HMH's *World Geography*
Geography and the Location of Economic Activities	pp. 326–331	pp. 88, 141, 159–160, 238, 292, 299, 305, 418–419, 462, 483, 506, 547, 553, 569, 637, 644–645, 666
Role of Productive Resources	p. 327	pp. 299, 313, 637–638
Location of Productive Resources	p. 327	pp. 93, 219–220, 225–226, 238, 292, 299
Natural Resources	p. 327	pp. 93, 120–122, 159–160, 204–205, 238, 245–247, 276–277, 305, 349, 417–418, 450, 456, 462, 554–555, 581, 622–623, 721
Resource Management	p. 328	pp. 348–349, 490, 495–499, 623, 732
Water Resources	p. 328	pp. 33, 149, 347–349, 426–427, 490, 493, 495–496, 623, 628–630
Climate	p. 329	pp. 59–61, 597–599
Human Resources	p. 329	pp. 82, 234–235, 463, 531, 595, 639, 645, 653, 655
Infrastructure	pp. 329–330	pp. 88, 94, 177, 212, 513, 530
Access to Consumers	pp. 330–331	pp. 88

Using Multiple Sources of Information

- Use information from both books to write your own answers to the *Essential Questions* on page 325.
- Use information from both books to make an illustrated chart identifying the different types of productive resources
- Use information from both books to create a chart showing how different geographic factors (such as landforms, climate and natural resources) affect where economic activities are located.
- Use information from both books to create your own video, slide show, Prezi or PowerPoint presentation about the uneven distribution of resources around the world. Your presentation should explain how this inequality in resources actually encourages specialization and promotes trade.
- Use information from both books to create an illustrated timeline, showing the history of world trade.
- Use information from both books to create a chart showing the effects of globalization.
- Use information from both books to hold a panel discussion in your classroom on the main challenges facing young people around the world in the future.

CHAPTER 19

THE CHALLENGES OF GLOBALIZATION

TEKS
COVERED IN
CHAPTER 19

- **Geography 7(D)** Examine benefits and challenges of globalization, including connectivity, standard of living, pandemics, and loss of local culture.
- **Economics 10(D)** Compare global trade patterns over time and examine the implications of globalization, including outsourcing and free trade zones.
- **Economics 11(B)** Identify the factors affecting the location of different types of economic activities, including subsistence and commercial agriculture, manufacturing, and services industries.
- **Economics 11(C)** Assess how changes in climate, resources, and infrastructure (*technology*, *transportation*, and *communication*) affect the location and patterns of economic activities.
- **Economics 12** The student understands the economic importance of, and issues related to, the location and management of resources.
  - **Economics 12(A)** Analyze how the creation, distribution, and management of key natural resources affects the location and patterns of movement of products, money, and people.
  - **Economics 12(B)** Evaluate the geographic and economic impact of policies related to the development, use, and scarcity of natural resources such as regulations of water.
- **Science, Technology, Society 20(A)** Describe the impact of new information technologies such as the Internet....
- **Science, Technology, Society 20(B)** Examine the economic, environmental, and social effects of ... changing trade patterns on societies at different levels of development.
- **Social Studies Skills 23(B)** Use case studies ... to identify contemporary challenges and to answer real-world questions.

In this chapter, you will learn how geography influences economic activities, how economic specialization leads to trade, and how the forces of globalization are "flattening the world," affecting the economies of every country.

ESSENTIAL QUESTIONS

- What factors influence where economic activities are located?
- Why do nations carry on trade with each other?
- How is globalization transforming the world?

GEOGRAPHIC TERMINOLOGY IN THIS CHAPTER

- Globalization
- Outsourcing
- Human Resources
- Capital Resources
- Infrastructure
- Entrepreneurship
- Productive Resources
- Specialization
- Comparative Advantage
- Export / Import
- Protective Tariff
- Free Trade Zones

— IMPORTANT IDEAS —

A. Geographic factors, such as landforms, climate, natural resources, areas of human settlement, and **infrastructure** (*technology*, *communications*, *transportation routes*, and *other human-made resources*), influence the location of economic activities.

B. Changes in climate, resources, and infrastructure can affect the location and patterns of economic activities.

C. The management of scarce natural resources poses special problems.

D. The distribution of natural resources affects trading patterns.

E. Global trading patterns have changed over time.

F. **Globalization**, including **outsourcing** and the creation of **free trade zones**, is changing economies around the world today.

G. Globalization holds great promise but also provides challenges for the future.

In 1492, Christopher Columbus set sail from Spain to prove the world was round. Just over 500 years later, *New York Times* writer Thomas Friedman published his best-selling book, *The World Is Flat*. What Friedman meant by his strange title is that there are now few barriers in getting from one part of the world to another. Goods, information, money, and people flow effortlessly over national borders and across the surface of the Earth in all directions.

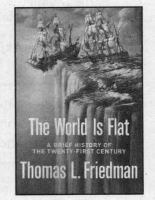

Friedman's book is actually an examination of those forces that have led to **globalization** — the creation of a single global economy and community. Friedman identifies several key forces behind globalization. He calls these the "Ten Forces that Flattened the World." Among them, he mentions the end of the Cold War, the spread of democracy, the creation of the Internet, and the new practices of outsourcing and offshoring. **Outsourcing** is the process by which a company hires other companies to perform some of its work. **Offshoring** is the practice of moving production overseas. In this chapter, you will learn about globalization.

HOW GEOGRAPHY INFLUENCES THE LOCATION OF ECONOMIC ACTIVITIES

We start with location. A variety of geographic factors influence where economic activities are situated — whether within your own community, the United States, or around the world. These include the location of both productive resources and consumers.

THE ROLE OF PRODUCTIVE RESOURCES

Economic activities produce goods or provide services. Economists identify four types of resources that economic activities require:

PRODUCTIVE RESOURCES

Natural Resources. Natural resources are the resources provided by nature that people use to create goods and services. They include air, water, plants, and minerals. Lumber, cotton, iron ore, and fresh water are all natural resources.

Human Resources. Human resources include all the human labor that is required to produce something. They include all the planning, studying, and training, as well as the work that is actually required to produce a good or service.

Capital Resources. Capital resources are goods made, not to consume, but to make other goods and services. Machines and tools are capital goods. For example, a hammer is a capital good used by a builder to make houses. Infrastructure (*technology, transportation routes, communications, networks*) is a capital resource.

Entrepreneurship. People who bring together and organize all the other productive resources are called entrepreneurs. Often they are business owners or managers.

THE LOCATION OF PRODUCTIVE RESOURCES

The location of an economic activity is based in part on where these resources can be found. Physical geography often determines where many of the productive resources that go into making a good or service are located.

NATURAL RESOURCES

Natural resources are the materials from nature — the minerals, plant fibers, animal products, and energy — that go into making a good. They also include the rivers, lakes and oceans that often make it possible to bring these materials together. Manufacturing is often located close to these natural resources. For example, large amounts of coal are needed to make steel. In the United States, western Pennsylvania has valuable coal deposits. For this reason, Pittsburgh

A steel mill in Pittsburgh, Pennsylvania.

became the center of the U.S. steel industry. Similarly, Saudi Arabia has large oil reserves. For that reason, oil companies have invested in drilling and recovering crude oil in Saudi Arabia.

RESOURCE MANAGEMENT

Because the availability of natural resources is essential to many economic activities, it is important for countries to manage key natural resources wisely. Often countries will require companies to obtain licenses or permits before they take and processes valuable resources, such as oil, gas, water, or minerals. Companies have to follow strict regulations to minimize pollution and to restore areas after mining activities. The requirements of natural resource management often affect where businesses are located and where money is invested.

The management of water resources poses special problems. Fresh water is needed as drinking water by ever growing populations. It is essential to farmers in order to irrigate their crops, especially in dry areas.

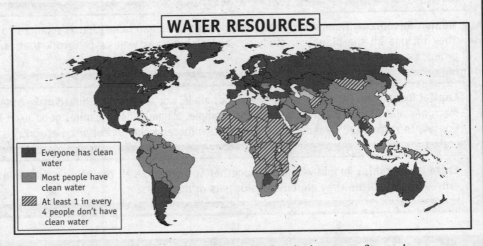

WATER RESOURCES

■ Everyone has clean water

■ Most people have clean water

▨ At least 1 in every 4 people don't have clean water

Factories often use water in their manufacturing operations. Most countries require special permits or licenses to establish facilities that use large amounts of water. They often impose penalties on polluters. This allows regulators to balance competing uses and to control pollution.

APPLYING WHAT YOU HAVE LEARNED

★ In the United States, water use is subject to the **Clean Water Act**. Look up on the Internet the provisions of this act. List *two* of them below. Then explain why water management is so important to our nation's well-being.

_____

_____

_____

_____

★ Research another country to see how it manages its water resources. How is it similar to or different from the United States? Discuss your answer in class.

CLIMATE

Climate is another important factor affecting the location of economic activities. It greatly influences the types of crops that can be grown in a place and therefore is especially important in the location of agricultural activities. For example, many Caribbean islands experience warm temperatures with plentiful rainfall. In the 1700s, these islands became centers for growing sugar cane. In those days, most sugar cane was grown by enslaved workers from Africa. Because it was expensive

Harvesting sugar cane in Cuba.

to ship raw sugar cane, which is heavy and bulky, plantation owners built refineries on these islands to process the sugar cane and turn it into sugar. Another example is Southeast Asia. Because of its warm, tropical climate, it became a center for growing and processing rubber.

HUMAN RESOURCES

Japanese workers on a Toyota production line.

Natural resources are one ingredient in producing a good. **Human resources** and entrepreneurship are just as important. Where they are located also affects the location of economic activities. For example, Japan lacks many natural resources, but its population is highly educated and provides a large supply of skilled labor. Because of its advanced technology and skilled workers, it has become a center of manufacturing. Electronics manufacturers, like Sony, and automobile manufacturers, like Toyota and Honda, are located in Japan.

INFRASTRUCTURE

Infrastructure also plays an important role in the location of economic activities. **Infrastructure** is a type of capital resource. It is the investment that a society makes by building roads, laying railroad tracks, constructing electric power plants, and setting up telephone and Internet lines. Infrastructure also includes the investment a society makes in providing a system of law-and-order, money and banking, hospitals and healthcare, and other essential services. Infrastructure is simply the foundation upon which businesses operate.

Infrastructure is an essential ingredient for economic growth. The available infrastructure makes it possible for different productive resources to come together. It also makes it possible for producers to bring their finished goods to consumers. It reduces a company's costs of production, provides access to modern technology, and reduces workers' time spent on non-productive activities. The existence of infrastructure is a critical factor in the location of farms, manufacturing plants, offices, and other economic activities. For example, if a location lacks electric power, telephone communications, railroad tracks, or paved roads, it cannot become a center of manufacturing.

Electricity is a vital part of the infrastructure that many economic activities require.

ACTING AS AN AMATEUR GEOGRAPHER

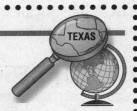

Choose one of the four types of productive resources described on the previous pages. Then discuss how the availability of that resource has influenced the location of economic activities in your own community.

_____

_____

_____

_____

_____

ACCESS TO CONSUMERS

It is not just the location of productive resources, but also the location of consumers that influences the location of many economic activities. Some economic activities provide **services** to consumers. Schools, hospitals, professional services, and retail stores will usually be located directly where consumers are found — especially in large population areas. Even production facilities like factories need access to consumers. Physical barriers — such as mountains, forests, deserts, and rivers — may make it difficult to reach consumers. Flatlands, valleys, and rivers are more likely to bring productive resources and consumers together.

Changes in technology and the creation of infrastructure can sometimes overcome geographic barriers. With recent improvements in communications and transportation, shipping costs have become lower. Many businesses have moved to areas where production costs are lower. This is happening on a global scale, with some businesses moving "off-shore" to countries where the costs of human resources are lower. They then ship their goods to global population centers.

Sneakers being made at a factory in Hanoi, Vietnam. Shoes are among Vietnam's top exports.

THE EFFECT OF CHANGES IN GEOGRAPHY

Because geography influences the location of economic activities, changes in physical or human geography often lead to changes in the location of these activities.

CHANGES IN CLIMATE

Changes in climate, such as global warming, can affect the location of economic activities. For example, the Sahel region in Africa separates the Sahara Desert from the Savannah region. Traditionally, peoples in the Sahel engaged in herding cattle. However, because of climate change, there is less water and grass in the Sahel region for cattle, and people are migrating farther south. Recent changes in climate may also mean that farming activities in the Northern Hemisphere will move northward. The United Nations estimates that for every degree of global warming, farming should move 200 to 300 kilometers northward.

CHANGES IN RESOURCES

Often the discovery of resources, such as precious minerals, leads to a flourishing of economic activity. During the California gold rush, mining towns blossomed in the Sierra Nevada Mountains almost overnight. After the gold ran out, these towns were suddenly deserted and their activities were abandoned.

CHANGES IN INFRASTRUCTURE

Changes in infrastructure also affect the location of economic activities. The construction of new canals, railroad lines, or paved roadways make it possible for producers to obtain resources less expensively or to reach new markets. This can attract new activities.

For example, the completion of the Erie Canal in 1825 made it possible for farmers in the Midwest to ship their goods to the Great Lakes, across the Erie Canal, and down the Hudson River to New York City and the Atlantic Ocean. Now that farmers had access to population centers in the Northeast, they could grow wheat and other crops for sale to Eastern consumers.

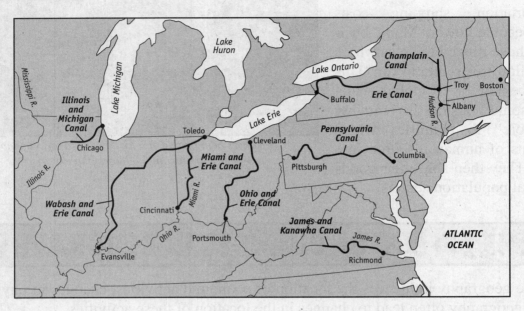

Similarly, the completion of railroad lines after the Civil War linked the Western United States to the East. It became possible for ranchers in Texas to drive their cattle across the open range to railroad lines in Kansas. Railroad cars then carried the cattle to stockyards and slaughterhouses in Chicago. From there, beef could be shipped by railroad to consumers in the East.

APPLYING WHAT YOU HAVE LEARNED

Using the Internet, library or other resources, select one recent change in climate, resources, or infrastructure. Then explain how that change has affected the location of economic activities.

_____

_____

_____

_____

_____

_____

_____

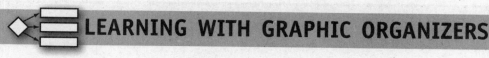

LEARNING WITH GRAPHIC ORGANIZERS

Complete the graphic organizer below by summarizing the factors that influence the location of an economic activity. Define each of the types of productive resources that go into making a good or service. Then describe those factors affecting access to consumers.

Natural Resources/ Climate	Human Resources/ Entrepreneurship	Capital Resources/ Infrastructure
_____ _____ _____ _____ _____ _____	_____ _____ _____ _____ _____ _____	_____ _____ _____ _____ _____ _____

LOCATION OF RESOURCES

LOCATION OF AN ECONOMIC ACTIVITY

ACCESS TO CONSUMERS

Natural Routes/ Physical Barriers	Location of Population Centers	Infrastructure
_____ _____ _____ _____ _____	_____ _____ _____ _____ _____	_____ _____ _____ _____ _____

TRADE

The same factors that affect the location of economic activities in your community, state, or country also affect the location of economic activities in various countries around the world. Different areas tend to **specialize** in specific economic activities. Such specialization leads to trade. **Trade** is simply the exchange of goods and services.

THE UNEVEN DISTRIBUTION OF RESOURCES

Productive resources are not spread evenly around the world. For example, various parts of the world have different climates, landforms, soils, and minerals. This gives rise to diverse ecosystems with very different plants and animals. Farmers can only grow certain crops in each region. In some regions, farmers are unable to grow much food at all.

PETROLEUM

These variations can be seen by looking at one of the world's most important natural resources — petroleum. It is a key source of energy and an essential ingredient in chemical products, ranging from fertilizers to plastics. Petroleum is created by the decay of microscopic animals that once lived in the sea. The oil and natural gas their bodies create are trapped underground. Oil and natural gas are not found everywhere. These resources are unevenly distributed throughout the world. They are located only in those areas where conditions allowed these resources to be trapped. Many countries have almost no oil and gas. A few, such as Saudi Arabia, have a great abundance of these resources.

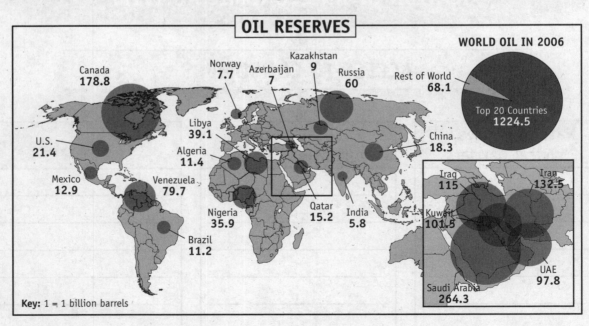

OIL RESERVES

WORLD OIL IN 2006

Rest of World 68.1

Top 20 Countries 1224.5

Canada 178.8
Norway 7.7
Azerbaijan 7
Kazakhstan 9
Russia 60
U.S. 21.4
Libya 39.1
Algeria 11.4
China 18.3
Mexico 12.9
Venezuela 79.7
Nigeria 35.9
Qatar 15.2
India 5.8
Brazil 11.2

Iraq 115
Iran 132.5
Kuwait 101.5
UAE 97.8
Saudi Arabia 264.3

Key: 1 = 1 billion barrels

HUMAN RESOURCES

Not only natural resources, but also human resources are unevenly distributed. Some countries, like China, have large numbers of workers with lower living costs. They are willing to work for lower wages than workers in more developed nations.

In highly developed countries, many workers have strong educational backgrounds. Some have the experience or training to act as entrepreneurs who can organize resources to improve production. Such countries can design new high-tech goods. To do so requires a highly educated work force and costly equipment.

A characteristic of highly developed countries is an educated workforce with high-tech skills.

SPECIALIZATION

The uneven distribution of both natural and human resources around the world encourages **specialization**. Each region tends to make certain types of goods, based on the productive resources it has available. Each region will produce those goods and services it can make at the lowest cost. Economists refer to this as **comparative advantage**. Each region sacrifices less labor and time to make those specialized goods than it would to make other goods. By making just a few kinds of goods or services, producers in a region can become more skilled at making them. Producers learn how to make these goods faster and more efficiently. Producers may even invest in special tools, facilities, and training to produce these goods. This helps to lower production costs even further.

HOW SPECIALIZATION ENCOURAGES TRADE

Because regions specialize, they rarely produce everything they need. Instead, different regions depend on one another to supply many goods and services. They exchange these goods through trade. Countries and regions **export** products they make and **import** products from others.

IMPORTS
Goods from foreign countries brought into a country for use or sale.

EXPORTS
Goods and services sold from one country to other countries.

For example, Japan has very few natural resources. It is especially lacking in oil to meet its energy needs. Japan needs fuel for its factories, electricity, automobiles, and heating needs. On the other hand, Saudi Arabia has an abundance of oil. Because Japan lacks its own oil, it must import oil from other countries like Saudi Arabia. It does this by selling its own products, such as electronics (*cameras* and *televisions*) abroad. With the money it receives from selling electronics, the Japanese are able to buy oil. The Japanese are also able to buy products from other countries, such as agricultural products from the United States.

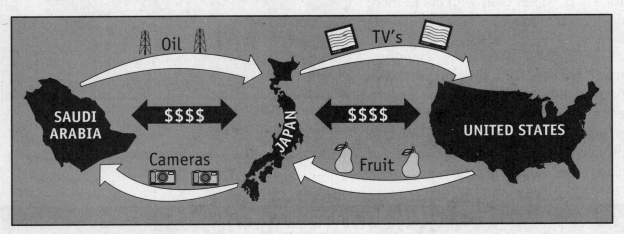

The unequal distribution of productive resources has thus encouraged Japan to trade with others. The Japanese obtain resources they lack by taking advantage of the resources they have — skilled workers, infrastructure, and entrepreneurship.

APPLYING WHAT YOU HAVE LEARNED

Provide your own example illustrating how specialization encourages trade between regions.

_____

_____

_____

_____

_____

A SHORT HISTORY OF GLOBAL TRADING PATTERNS

Trade between different regions has existed throughout history.

THE ANCIENT WORLD

In fact, specialization led to the rise of trade between peoples even before the invention of writing. Trade became quite advanced even in the ancient world.

★ **Ancient Egypt.** Ancient Egypt, for example, had surplus grain and valuable minerals, including gold. Other places in the Mediterranean region did not have the resources that Egypt possessed. Egyptians traded wheat and gold with the Greeks for olives and wine. Egyptians likewise exchanged their wheat and gold with the peoples of the Arabian Peninsula for spices and incense.

★ **Roman Empire.** The ancient Romans also engaged in extensive trade. The Romans exported olive oil and wine from the hillsides of Italy across the Mediterranean Sea. Sicily and North Africa grew wheat, which they shipped to Rome in exchange for this olive oil and wine. Romans even traded along overland routes across the steppes, deserts, and mountains of Central Asia to obtain porcelain and silk from China. They traded through Egypt, the Red Sea and across the Arabian Peninsula to obtain cotton and spices from India.

THE MIDDLE AGES

After the fall of the Roman Empire, trade in Western Europe was disrupted. Local communities in Europe became largely self-sufficient. Merchants displayed their goods in occasional fairs. In other parts of the world, however, trade continued to thrive:

★ **Byzantium.** Constantinople, the capital of the Eastern Roman Empire, was located on the Black Sea where Asia meets Europe. Traders between these two continents exchanged European goods for Chinese silks and Indian incense and spices.

★ **Islamic World.** Alexandria, Aden and other ports were centers of trade for goods from India, Africa, and throughout the Middle East.

★ **West Africa.** In West Africa, Timbuktu arose as a center of the gold-salt trade. Arab merchants crossed the Sahara Desert to bring salt, cloth, and horses. In exchange, they received gold and slaves.

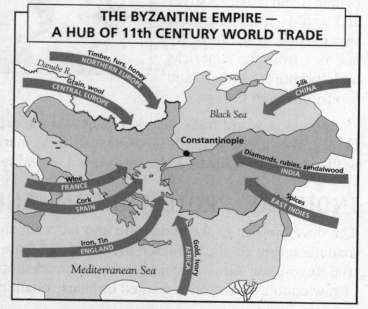

THE BYZANTINE EMPIRE — A HUB of 11th CENTURY WORLD TRADE

★ **The Americas.** In the Americas, the Maya traded their salt, obsidian, cacao, and pottery with the people of Guatemala in exchange for turquoise, jade and bird feathers.

In the later Middle Ages, Europeans developed a new taste for Eastern luxuries after the Crusades. The city-states of Italy began an active east-west trade across the Mediterranean Sea to Constantinople, where they exchanged European goods for spices, silks and other products from Arabia, China, and India.

THE RISE OF ATLANTIC TRADE

After the voyages of Christopher Columbus, Europeans established colonial empires in the Americas and established new ocean routes to India and China by sailing around the southern tip of Africa. Spain established a vast colonial empire, taking new foods and vast amounts of gold and silver from the Americas to Europe. These new trade routes greatly enriched European rulers, and raised standards of living in Europe.

This created a major shift in trade patterns, as trade across the Mediterranean Sea lost its importance. In its place, new Atlantic trade routes emerged. Cities like Lisbon in Portugal, Seville in Spain, and Amsterdam in Holland grew quickly. Merchants exchanged enslaved people from Africa, silver and gold from Mexico, sugar cane, fur, tobacco, and rice from the Americas and furniture, clothes, and foodstuffs from Europe.

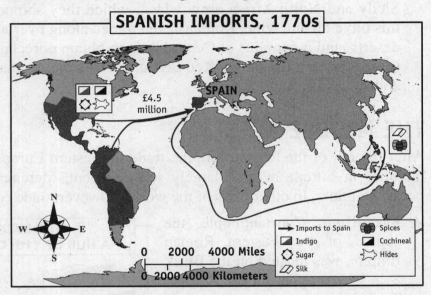

SPANISH IMPORTS, 1770s

£4.5 million

SPAIN

N W E S

0   2000   4000 Miles

0   2000 4000 Kilometers

→ Imports to Spain   🍩 Spices
▨ Indigo   ◪ Cochineal
◇ Sugar   🖾 Hides
⬮ Silk

Increased world trade also led to new wars, especially between Britain, Holland and France. By the end of the 1700s, Great Britain emerged as the world's leading naval power with colonies in Canada, India, and Africa. Britain now dominated world trade.

INDUSTRY, PROTECTIONISM, AND EMPIRE

The development of the steamship and railroad, and the spread of the factory system for manufacturing goods, increased the speed and scale of trade still further. During the Industrial Revolution, Great Britain became the workshop of the world. It imported vast amounts of raw cotton. Its factories created immense quantities of goods, which were sold abroad.

In the 1800s, Britain and other European countries divided Africa and Southeast Asia into colonies. These European powers established plantations and mines in their colonies to obtain raw materials for Europe's factories, and to create markets for Europe's manufactured goods. Britain also established trading posts in China, while the United States opened up trade with Japan.

Ships carrying Chinese tea, Egyptian cotton, and British manufactured and other goods now criss-crossed the oceans. Some countries reacted to the influx of cheap British goods by enacting **protective tariffs**. These tariffs added duties

HOW A PROTECTIVE TARIFF WORKS

In America

In Britain

When shipped to America, a 75¢ tariff is added to the price of British socks

American-made socks sell for $2.00 a pair

British-made socks sell for $2.50 a pair

British-made socks sell for $1.75 a pair

(*taxes*) to imports, making British goods more expensive.

THE COLLAPSE OF TRADE BARRIERS

In the early twentieth century, the world experienced the Great Depression and two world wars. Countries often put up **high tariffs** or **quotas** as barriers to trade. After World War II, leading countries created rules and organizations to promote world trade.

In 1947, the **General Agreement on Tariff and Trade** (*GATT*) was signed by 23 nations to promote world trade and to remove trade barriers. This later led to the **World Trade Organization**, created in 1995. Today, membership in the WTO has grown to over 150 members, representing more than 97% of total world trade. Other WTO functions include overseeing the administration of trade agreements and providing a forum for negotiations and for settling disputes.

Free Trade Zones. Several groups of countries have also created free **trade associations**. In these associations, member countries create **free trade zones** with no tariffs or quotas. For example, in the 1990s, the United States, Mexico and Canada formed the **North American Free Trade Association** (*NAFTA*). Tariffs between these three countries are gradually being eliminated.

European Union. European countries created the European Economic Community, which later became the **European Union** (*EU*). Members of the EU can live and work in any member country without restriction. There are no customs duties or other restrictions on goods moving from one member country in the EU to another member country.

Most members in the European Union also use a common currency, the Euro. Since the **Euro** entered circulation in 2002, it has replaced each of the EU countries' former national currencies. The Euro has grown to become the second most widely held international currency after the U.S. dollar.

The Euro is the currency of the European Union.

APPLYING WHAT YOU HAVE LEARNED

★ What patterns can you see in the expansion of global trade?

_____

_____

_____

★ How does global trade differ today from trade carried on 200 years ago?

_____

_____

_____

THE CHALLENGES OF GLOBALIZATION

Today, the lowering of trade barriers by the World Trade Organization, accompanied by improvements in communications and transportation, has greatly increased the pace and scale of world trade.

OFFSHORING AND OUTSOURCING

Many companies are now moving their production facilities to countries where the costs of labor and other productive resources are lower. This practice is known as **offshoring**. Companies are also hiring other companies, often from overseas, to produce parts or to provide other services. This is known as **outsourcing**. Outsourcing permits companies to focus on other business issues, while freeing up management professionals to focus on more important issues.

A computer assembled in the United States today, for example, may have parts manufactured in Taiwan, China, Thailand and Mexico. The computer may use software designed by computer engineers and programmers in the United States and India. When American customers call customer service, they may be talking to English-speaking representatives half-way around the world in India or the Philippines.

Some American companies now outsource their customer service responses to India.

New information technologies, such as the Internet, make it easier for customers to search for products and to place orders, even from overseas. These technologies also make it easier for manufacturers to track their inventory and to predict future needs. Shipping has also become easier with **containerized** cargo. Goods are packed into large truck-like containers and loaded onto a cargo ship. After the ship lands at its destination, the containers serve as the backs of trucks or as railroad cars, without repacking.

A containerized cargo ship.

THE BENEFITS AND COSTS OF GLOBALIZATION

With a global network of communications, free trade barriers, and lower shipping costs, people, resources, and products can now flow easily across national boundaries. These conditions have created a global market. Economic activities move to wherever they are most efficient on a global scale. Goods and services are then exchanged through trade. This whole process is known as **globalization**.

Benefits. Globalization has provided many benefits. People enjoy goods and services from all around the world. They also enjoy the benefits of greater **connectivity** — ease of communication. We can now reach one another by telephone, Facebook, cell phone, e-mail, or such new services as **skype** — an internet-based video phone call. Advances in information technology, medicine, and engineering spread quickly. Globalization has also speeded up the pace of economic development. Average standards of living are higher than ever before.

Costs. There have been some important costs to globalization. Manufacturing has shifted away from countries where labor costs are higher. Many workers in more developed countries have lost their jobs. While these workers have lost jobs, some workers in newly industrialized countries are forced to work long hours under harsh conditions; many feel exploited. Globalization has also increased pollution and global climate change. Diseases now spread more quickly, creating a risk of **pandemics**. Some elected leaders feel they have lost control over their nation's individual economy. A financial crisis in one country can quickly spread to others. This increases the potential threat of a global recession. Globalization has also created huge trade imbalances. For example, Americans buy far more goods from China than they sell there.

Another disadvantage is that local communities and cultures are losing much of their uniqueness under the impact of globalization. Global phenomena, like American fast-food or '"pop" music, replace local customs and traditions. The wave of globalization can even provoke violent reactions. Muslim Fundamentalists express anger at the spread of contemporary global culture. Despite these disadvantages, globalization has become too deeply ingrained to disappear.

APPLYING WHAT YOU HAVE LEARNED

Your class should debate the following: *"Resolved: The benefits of globalization outweigh its costs."* The affirmative team should argue that globalization is beneficial. The negative team should argue against globalization. One member from each team should give a 4-minute speech supporting their position. Then one member from each team should be given a 2-minute rebuttal against the arguments from the other side. Use the space on the right to outline your presentation.

 LEARNING WITH GRAPHIC ORGANIZERS

Complete the graphic organizer below by identifying some major causes of globalization.

THE CAUSES OF GLOBALIZATION

LEARNING WITH GRAPHIC ORGANIZERS

Complete the graphic organizer below by describing *two* positive and *two* negative the effects of globalization.

THE EFFECTS OF GLOBALIZATION

First Positive Effect	Second Positive Effect
_____	_____
_____	_____
_____	_____
_____	_____

First Negative Effect	Second Negative Effect
_____	_____
_____	_____
_____	_____
_____	_____

CHAPTER STUDY CARDS

Productive Resources

★ **Natural Resources.** Those resources that are provided by nature, such as minerals, plant fibers, or coal for energy.

★ **Human Resources.** All the human labor required to produce something.

★ **Capital Resources.** Goods used to make other goods or services. This also includes infrastructure: technology, transportation routes, communications.

★ **Entrepreneurship.** The people who bring together and organize all of the other productive resources.

How Geography Affects the Location of Economic Activities

★ **Physical Geography.** Determines where many of the productive resources that go into making a good or service are located.

★ **Climate.** Influences the types of crops grown.

★ **Natural Resources.** Where minerals and raw materials are located can affect the location of an economic activity.

★ **Natural Transportation Routes.** Rivers, lakes, oceans.

★ **Infrastructure.** Includes investments in roads, railroads, electricity, and the Internet.

Geography Affects Access to Consumers

★ Physical barriers, like mountains, forests, deserts, and some water bodies, can make it difficult or impossible to bring resources to consumers.

★ Flatlands, valleys, and rivers often help to bring productive resources to consumers.

★ Businesses that are closer to consumers will often be more successful.

★ Improvements in transportation, shipping and communications can lower costs and make areas formerly unreachable more accessible.

Specialization Leads to Trade

★ **Unequal Distribution of Resources.** Regions and countries have different natural resources, human resources, capital resources, and entrepreneurship.

★ **Specialization.** Countries specialize in producing those goods and services that they make best, based on their available resources.

★ **Trade.** To obtain other products, countries exchange the goods they make with other countries through trade.

Global Trade Patterns

★ Since ancient times, peoples have traded goods with distant neighbors.

★ In the Middle Ages, Constantinople, the Islamic world and West Africa were centers of trade.

★ The Columbian Exchange shifted major trade routes from the Mediterranean to the Atlantic.

★ In the 1800s, European colonial empires increased global specialization.

Causes of Globalization

★ The recent lowering of trade barriers.

★ **Rise of Free Trade Associations.**
- GATT
- World Trade Organization
- NAFTA
- European Union (*EU*)

★ Spread of new information technologies.

★ Transportation improvements.

★ **Outsourcing.** When companies hire other companies to do some of their work.

★ **Offshoring.** When companies move operations to countries with lower labor costs.

CHECKING YOUR UNDERSTANDING

Directions: Put a circle around the letter that best answers the question.

Use the map and your knowledge of social studies to answer questions 1 and 2.

1   Company A is thinking about locating its lumbering processing facility on the nation of Islandia. Which new location would be the best place for Company A to build their factory?

    A   Location A
    B   Location B
    C   Location C
    D   Location D

    Econ 11(B)

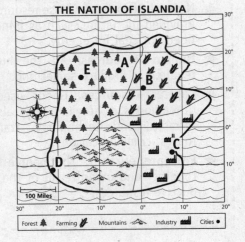

THE NATION OF ISLANDIA

Forest | Farming | Mountains | Industry | Cities

When you **examine** this question you find that it tests your understanding of factors affecting the location of economic activities. You should **recall** that manufacturing is often located close to the natural resources it uses. A lumber processing facility will be closest to the trees it processes into lumber. **Applying** this information to the answer choices, you should realize that **Choice A** is the best answer since it is near where the trees on the nation of Islandia are located.

Now try answering some additional questions on your own:

2   Where on the nation of Islandia would be the best location to build a port for large ships to arrive?

    F   Location A

    G   Location B

    H   Location C

    J   Location D

> • <u>E</u>XAMINE The Question
> • <u>R</u>ECALL What You Know
> • <u>A</u>PPLY What You Know

`Econ 11(B)`

3   Japan has few natural resources, but it has one of the most highly developed economies in the world. What best explains this achievement?

    A   It imported manufactured goods.

    B   It developed technologies that can be exchanged for the resources it needs.

    C   It printed more money whenever living standards started to decline.

    D   It produced goods and services without using natural resources.

`Econ 12(A)`

Use the information in the boxes and your knowledge of social studies to answer the following question.

Because Saudi Arabia has vast oil reserves, it produces and refines oil.	**Because of its climate and soils, Columbia grows coffee beans.**	**Because Japan consists of islands, many of its people engage in fishing.**

4   Which conclusion is best supported by the information in these examples?

    F   Major urban centers are usually found only along rivers

    G   Technology has little effect on economic activities.

    H   The physical geography of an area often affects its economic activities.

    J   Natural resources are more important than climate to economic activities.

`Econ 11(B)`

5   Which statement provides an important reason why countries and regions specialize in their economic activities?

    A   They become more self-sufficient.

    B   They do not wish to compete.

    C   They have different productive resources.

    D   They are unable to overcome trade barriers.

`Econ 10(D)`

Use the flow chart and your knowledge of social studies to answer the following question.

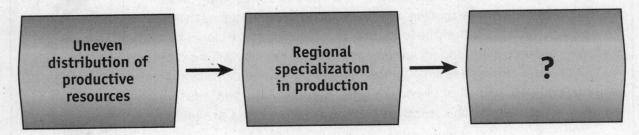

6   Which phrase best completes the flow chart?

F	Higher production costs
G	Growth of global trade
H	Higher tariff rates
J	Decreased use of consumer goods

Econ 10(D)

- **EXAMINE The Question**
- **RECALL What You Know**
- **APPLY What You Know**

7   What goal led to the formation of both the North American Free Trade Agreement (*NAFTA*) and the European Union (*EU*)?

Econ 10(D)

A   to keep communism out of Western Europe
B   to reduce environmental pollution
C   to increase economic cooperation between member nations
D   to eliminate global climate change

8   Countries generally specialize in producing particular goods. What is one result of such specialization?

Econ 12(A)

F   Production and consumption gradually decrease.
G   Countries depend on trade to obtain other goods.
H   Countries become less interdependent.
J   Prices increase as many goods become more scarce.

Use the information and your knowledge of social studies to answer the following question.

> Country A has large deposits of iron and the technology to make cars and trucks. However, it lacks grazing land to raise livestock to create butter. Country B is covered in rolling fields and has a large supply of cows. Its farmers are efficient at making large amounts of butter, but they do not produce trucks to carry this butter to cities and ports.

9   Based on these facts, what is the most likely result?

Econ 12(A)

A   Country A will begin to make its own butter.
B   Country A and B will trade products with each other.
C   Country B will start to manufactures its own trucks.
D   Country B will sell trucks to Country A.

UNIT 6 REVIEW
PULLING IT ALL TOGETHER

Write down *two* generalizations you learned about global economics in this unit.

1. _____

   _____

2. _____

   _____

Select *one* of the *Essential Questions* explored in this unit by checking the box. Then answer it below.

ESSENTIAL QUESTIONS REEXAMINED

- ☐ How do different societies around the world meet their economic needs?
- ☐ What are the advantages and disadvantages of each economic system?
- ☐ How do economists measure a country's level of economic development?
- ☐ Which economic activities are most clearly associated with different levels of development?
- ☐ What factors influence where economic activities are located?
- ☐ Why do nations carry on trade with each other?
- ☐ How is globalization transforming the world?

_____

_____

_____

_____

_____

_____

_____

_____

_____

_____

_____

UNIT 6 CONCEPT MAP

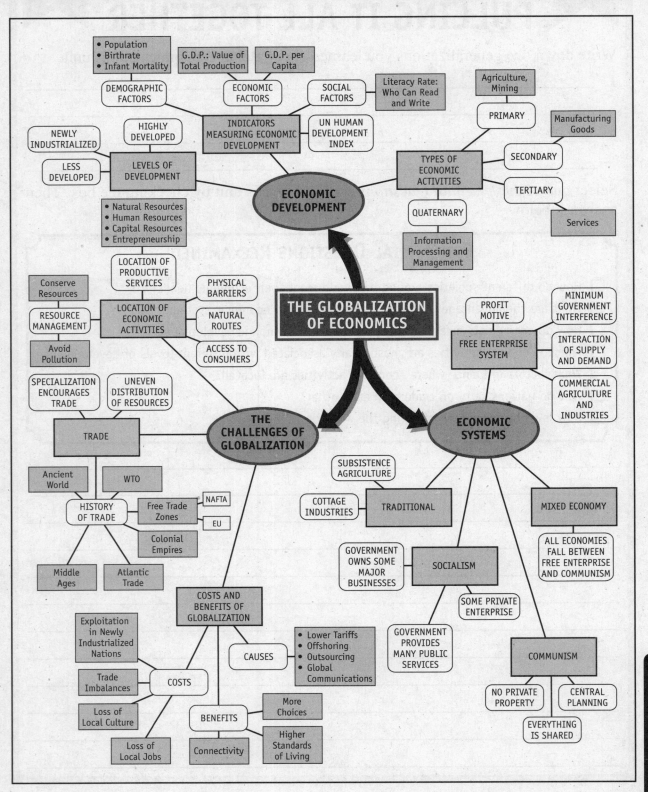

- Population
- Birthrate
- Infant Mortality

G.D.P.: Value of Total Production

G.D.P. per Capita

Literacy Rate: Who Can Read and Write

Agriculture, Mining

DEMOGRAPHIC FACTORS

ECONOMIC FACTORS

SOCIAL FACTORS

INDICATORS MEASURING ECONOMIC DEVELOPMENT

UN HUMAN DEVELOPMENT INDEX

PRIMARY

Manufacturing Goods

NEWLY INDUSTRIALIZED

HIGHLY DEVELOPED

TYPES OF ECONOMIC ACTIVITIES

SECONDARY

LESS DEVELOPED

LEVELS OF DEVELOPMENT

TERTIARY

ECONOMIC DEVELOPMENT

QUATERNARY

Services

- Natural Resources
- Human Resources
- Capital Resources
- Entrepreneurship

Information Processing and Management

LOCATION OF PRODUCTIVE SERVICES

Conserve Resources

PHYSICAL BARRIERS

RESOURCE MANAGEMENT

LOCATION OF ECONOMIC ACTIVITIES

NATURAL ROUTES

THE GLOBALIZATION OF ECONOMICS

PROFIT MOTIVE

MINIMUM GOVERNMENT INTERFERENCE

Avoid Pollution

ACCESS TO CONSUMERS

FREE ENTERPRISE SYSTEM

INTERACTION OF SUPPLY AND DEMAND

SPECIALIZATION ENCOURAGES TRADE

UNEVEN DISTRIBUTION OF RESOURCES

COMMERCIAL AGRICULTURE AND INDUSTRIES

TRADE

THE CHALLENGES OF GLOBALIZATION

ECONOMIC SYSTEMS

Ancient World

WTO

SUBSISTENCE AGRICULTURE

HISTORY OF TRADE

Free Trade Zones

NAFTA

COTTAGE INDUSTRIES

TRADITIONAL

MIXED ECONOMY

EU

Colonial Empires

ALL ECONOMIES FALL BETWEEN FREE ENTERPRISE AND COMMUNISM

Middle Ages

Atlantic Trade

GOVERNMENT OWNS SOME MAJOR BUSINESSES

SOCIALISM

COSTS AND BENEFITS OF GLOBALIZATION

SOME PRIVATE ENTERPRISE

Exploitation in Newly Industrialized Nations

Lower Tariffs
- Offshoring
- Outsourcing
- Global Communications

CAUSES

GOVERNMENT PROVIDES MANY PUBLIC SERVICES

COMMUNISM

Trade Imbalances

COSTS

Loss of Local Culture

BENEFITS

More Choices

NO PRIVATE PROPERTY

CENTRAL PLANNING

Loss of Local Jobs

Connectivity

Higher Standards of Living

EVERYTHING IS SHARED

UNIT 7

CHAPTER 20

A PRACTICE
FINAL TEST
IN WORLD GEOGRAPHY

Now that you have completed all the chapters of this book, you are ready to take a final practice test to evaluate your progress This test will assess your mastery of all the world geography you have learned in this book. Before you begin, let's look at some common-sense tips for taking such tests:

Answer All the Questions. Don't leave any questions unanswered. There is no penalty for guessing. Answer all questions, even if you're only guessing.

Use the "E-R-A" approach. In which you *EXAMINE The Question*, *RECALL What You Know*, and *APPLY What You Know* to answer each question.

Use the Process of Elimination. When answering a multiple-choice question, it should be clear that certain choices are wrong. They are either irrelevant, lack a connection to the question, or are inaccurate statements. You should eliminate these choices, and then choose the best response that remains.

Read the Question Carefully. If a word in the question is unfamiliar, try to break it down into words that are familiar. Look at the prefix (*start of the word*), root, or suffix (*ending*) for clues to the meaning of the word.

Directions: Put a circle around the letter that best answers the question.

1   Which analysis of the effects of Africa's physical geography is most accurate?
   A   Its wide, flat areas led to constantly shifting borders.   Hist 1(A)
   B   Its deserts and forests were geographic barriers that promoted greater
        cultural diversity.
   C   Its many peninsulas provided natural harbors, leading to extensive sea trade.
   D   Its cold climate led to a short growing season, discouraging
        progress in agriculture.

GO ON

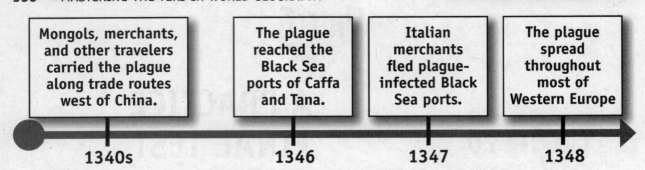

| Mongols, merchants, and other travelers carried the plague along trade routes west of China. | The plague reached the Black Sea ports of Caffa and Tana. | Italian merchants fled plague-infected Black Sea ports. | The plague spread throughout most of Western Europe |

1340s   **1346**   **1347**   **1348**

2   Which conclusion is supported by information in the timeline?

    F   The plague only affected people living in China.   Hist 1(B)

    G   The interaction of these cultures led to a pandemic.

    H   Port cities were relatively untouched by the plague.

    J   The plague originally started in West Africa.

Use the map to answer questions 3 and 4.

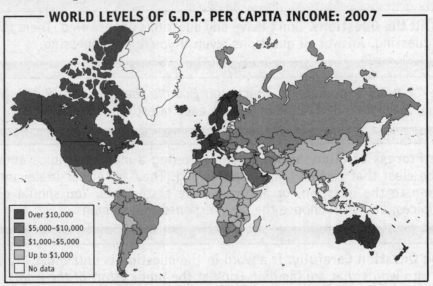

WORLD LEVELS OF G.D.P. PER CAPITA INCOME: 2007

Over $10,000
$5,000–$10,000
$1,000–$5,000
Up to $1,000
No data

3   Which conclusion is supported by the map?

    A   The world communist movement is growing.   Geog 5(B)

    B   More developed nations are found in North America and Western Europe.

    C   Less developed countries are concentrated in Europe and Australia.

    D   Economic self-sufficiency in less developed countries is increasing.

4   Which description could be best applied to those regions on the map now with a G.D.P. per capita of $1,000 or less (*with the exception of China*), back in the 1800s?

    F   They were leading industrial powers.   Hist 2(A)

    G   They were colonies of European powers.

    H   They were countries of Eastern Europe.

    J   They were countries with democratic governments.

GO ON

5 The loss of local traditions, increased levels of pollution, and the risk of pandemics are negative aspects of — `Geog 7 (D)`
  A genocide
  B ethnic cleansing
  C cottage industries
  D globalization

6 Frequent earthquakes and volcanic eruptions occur in an area of the Pacific Ocean called the "Ring of Fire." Which of the following causes such events? `Geog 3 (B)`
  F Earth's rotation on its axis
  G the formation of canyons
  H the movement of tectonic plates
  J a rise in the ocean surface temperature

7 Much of the Middle East is desert. A study of the population distribution of the Middle East would show that most people — `Geog 6 (A)`
  A live near fresh water supplies
  B inhabit mountainous areas
  C live in the center of the desert
  D are evenly distributed throughout the region

8 The daily path of the Sun, as viewed from the Earth, appears to change with the seasons because the —
  F Earth's axis is tilted `Geog 3 (A)`
  G Sun revolves around the Earth
  H Earth's distance from the Sun changes
  J Sun rotates

The vast size of the Atlantic Ocean once protected the peoples of the Western Hemisphere. After 1492, the Atlantic Ocean became a channel for trade. Tobacco, sugar, rice and other products grown in the Americas were carried on ships to Europe. Manufactured goods, tea, and other products were then shipped across the Atlantic from Europe to the Americas.

9 What changes led to these diverse uses of the Atlantic Ocean?
  A Population growth forced Europeans to expand. `Hist 2 (B)`
  B Technological improvements such as the compass and improvements in ship design made ocean voyages possible.
  C Europeans had challenged the views of the Catholic Church on travel.
  D The spread of the plague encouraged Europeans to search for safer areas.

Buddhism is introduced into Japan around A.D. 1200.	Islam extends from the Middle East into Spain by A.D. 732.	Catholic missionaries bring Christianity to Africa in the 1800s

10 What generalization do these examples illustrate?
  F All world religions originated from a single source. `Cult 18 (A)`
  G Most religions are monotheistic.
  H People are more religious today than in the past.
  J Cultural change can result from spatial diffusion.

GO ON

11 Which statement describes an impact of the Columbian Exchange on the lives of Europeans?   Hist 1(B)

  A Cross-cultural contacts between South America and Europe declined.

  B The transfer of new products and ideas encouraged economic growth.

  C New diseases, brought to Europe from the Americas, led to massive deaths.

  D Native Americans migrated to Europe to compete with Europeans for jobs.

12 Mountain-building rock structures, like the one in the photograph, are most often caused by —   Geog 4(B)

  F tectonic plate collisions

  H heavy rainfall in tropical regions

  G the movement of a glacier

  J large deposits of sediment

13 Which biome is paired with its correct climatic zone?   Geog 4(C)

  A heavy rainfall and warm temperatures — tundra

  B moderate rainfall and cold temperatures — desert

  C little rainfall and warm temperatures — tropical rainforest

  D moderate rainfall and warm to cold temperatures — deciduous forest

14 The Amazon rainforest constitutes a region because it —   Geog 9(A)

  F has greater trade within this area than without

  G has a common climate and the same plants and animals

  H is cut off from surrounding areas by mountains

  J is under the rule of a single government

15 The cross-section below shows the prevailing winds that cause different climates on the two sides of this mountain range. Compared to the western side of this mountain range, the eastern side is more likely to receive —

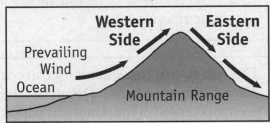

  A frequent hurricanes   Geog 4(A)

  B less precipitation

  C larger snow accumulations

  D heavy rains

16 People live on savannas and mountains, in deserts and rainforests, along river valleys and coastlines, and on islands. What does this diversity in the areas of human settlement demonstrate?

  F People organize   Geog 8(A) similar forms of government.

  G People can adapt to many different physical surroundings.

  H People follow similar occupations in very different regions.

  J People prefer to live in isolation from each other.

GO ON →

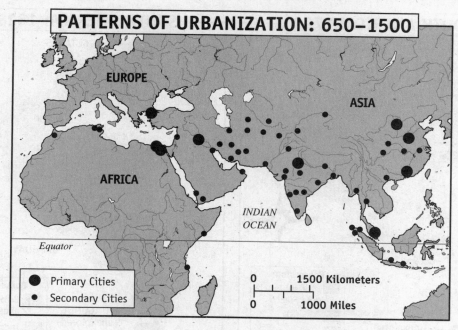

PATTERNS OF URBANIZATION: 650–1500

17 Which conclusion is supported by the map?

  A Urbanization first occurred in Sub-Saharan Africa.

  B Urbanization first took place in cooler climates.

  C Most urban areas before 1500 were located in Europe.

  D Most urban areas before 1500 developed along waterways.

Geog 6(A)

---

18 What is the best explanation for the change in world population shown on the graph between 1950 and 2000?

  F Family planning services became more widespread. Geog 7(C)

  G There were several major wars in Asia and Africa.

  H Improvements in medicine and agriculture were accompanied by rising birth rates in less developed nations.

  J A dramatic increase in the number of famines and natural disasters occurred in the last half of the twentieth century.

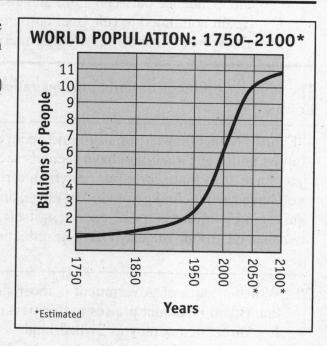

WORLD POPULATION: 1750–2100*

*Estimated

GO ON

19 Which conclusion can be drawn from a comparison of these maps of South America at different time periods?

A All of South America was independent from colonial rule by 1828.   `Hist 2(A)`

B Current boundaries were mainly set when South American countries gained independence between 1790 and 1828.

C Spain continued to rule over colonies in South America after 1828.

D Between 1790 and 1828, South American political boundaries remained unchanged.

The following passage describes the operation of absolute monarchy in France under King Louis XIV.

> "Finally, reflect on what we have said about royal authority. You have seen a great nation united under one man: you have seen his sacred power, paternal [fatherly] and absolute: you have seen that secret reason which directs the body politic, enclosed in one head: you have seen the image of God in kings, and you will have the idea of majesty of kingship. God is holiness itself, goodness itself, power itself, reason itself. In these things consists the divine majesty. In their reflection consists the majesty of the prince."
>
> — *Bishop Jacques-Benigne Bossuet*

20 Which system of government is most similar in operation to the type of government that Bishop Bossuet praises in this passage?

F direct democracy in Switzerland

G theocracy in Iran under Ayatollah Khomeini   `Govt 14(B)`

H socialism in Sweden after World War II

J republic in the United States

Name _____

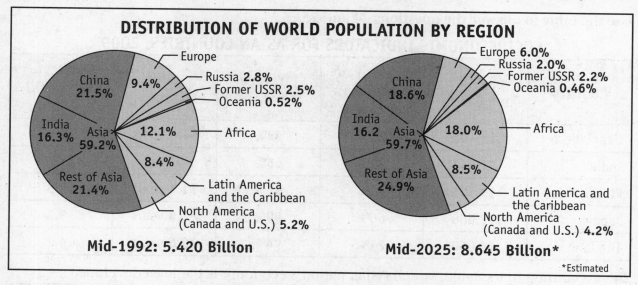

DISTRIBUTION OF WORLD POPULATION BY REGION

Mid-1992: 5.420 Billion

China 21.5%
India 16.3%
Asia 59.2%
Rest of Asia 21.4%
Europe 9.4%
Russia 2.8%
Former USSR 2.5%
Oceania 0.52%
Africa 12.1%
8.4%
Latin America and the Caribbean
North America (Canada and U.S.) 5.2%

Mid-2025: 8.645 Billion*

China 18.6%
India 16.2
Asia 59.7%
Rest of Asia 24.9%
Europe 6.0%
Russia 2.0%
Former USSR 2.2%
Oceania 0.46%
Africa 18.0%
8.5%
Latin America and the Caribbean
North America (Canada and U.S.) 4.2%

*Estimated

21 What prediction about world population in 2025 is supported by the information in these graphs?

A Africa may experience problems with overpopulation.

B Technological improvements will cause a population decline in Asia.

C More developed nations will become home to a majority of the world's population.

D Efforts to curb population growth in less developed nations will be highly successful.

`Geog 7(C)`

---

22 Which is the best example of a perceptual region?

F Sahara Desert, based on shared physical characteristics

G Mississippi drainage basin, based on common functions

H "Old South" of the United States, based on people's attitudes

J ancient Roman Empire, based on its protected political boundaries

`Geog 9(B)`

THE DAILY SENTINEL	**HOUSTON CHRONICLE**	**EL PASO TIMES**
Reliance on Imported Oil Raises Concerns in Europe	Coca-Cola Accused of Wasting Precious Water in India	Competition for Control of Cobalt Mines Leads to Violence in the Congo

23 These newspaper headlines show the importance of —

A developing human resources through education

B avoiding massive deficits from over-borrowing

C managing natural resources through public policy

D responding quickly to natural disasters

`Econ 12(B)`

GO ON

Use the table to answer the questions 24 and 25.

SOCIOECONOMIC INDICATORS FOR ASIAN COUNTRIES: 2009

Country	G.D.P. per Capita	Percent of Population in Cities	Literacy Rate	Life Expectancy	Birthrate per 1,000 People
Bangladesh	$1,465	26%	53%	64.1 years	24.8
India	$2,941	29%	66%	64.7 years	23.0
Philippines	$3,521	64%	93%	71.7 years	25.8
Japan	$32,608	66%	99%	82.6 years	8.3
Thailand	$8,060	21%	94%	70.6 years	14.1

24 According to the table, which Asian nation's economy is the least developed?

    F Bangladesh   **H** India   `Geog 5(B)`

    G Japan   **J** Thailand

25 Based on the information in the table, which type of economic activities would a geographer expect to contribute the most value to Japan's gross domestic product?

    A primary and secondary   **C** secondary and tertiary   `Econ 11(A)`

    B primary and quaternary   **D** tertiary and quaternary

---

26 In recent years, companies from more developed nations have often built new production facilities in less developed nations. This outsourcing has occurred because less developed nations frequently have —

    F a favorable climate   `Econ 10(D)`

    G capital resources

    H a supply of inexpensive labor

    J greater political stability

27 On January 24, 1848, gold was discovered in Coloma, California, in the foothills of the Sierra Nevada Mountains. How did this discovery lead to changes in settlement patterns?

    A People fled from   `Geog 6(B)` these areas to avoid mining operations.

    B Mining towns sprang up almost overnight where gold was discovered.

    C Population in the mountains increased rapidly as farmers arrived to plant crops.

    D San Francisco's population decreased as people moved inland to the Sierra Nevada Mountains.

GO ON ➤

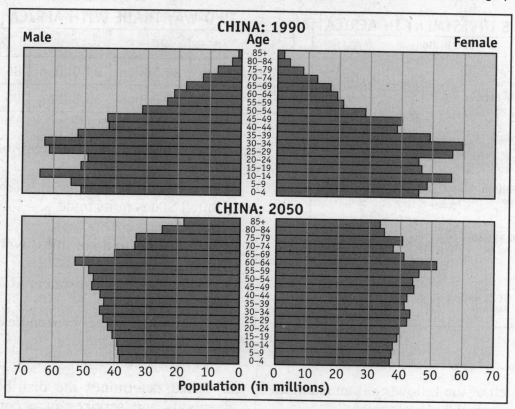

CHINA: 1990

Male   **Age**   **Female**

CHINA: 2050

Population (in millions)

28 By 2050, what concern will China have to address because of changes in the structure of its population?

   F   a greater demand for military spending

   G   the rising health care needs of an aging population

   H   a collapse in the market for consumer goods

   J   a need to build more children's schools

`Geog 7(A)`

TITLE: _____

Push Factors	Pull Factors
Turkish authorities persecuted Christian Armenians in their villages and drove many women and children into the desert.	Armenians with relatives in the United Sates were attracted by stories of economic opportunity and a life without persecution.

29 What would be the best title for the chart?

   A   Reasons Armenians Migrated to America

   B   The Diffusion of Armenian Culture into Turkey

   C   Reasons for the Persecution of Armenians in Turkey

   D   Reasons Armenian-Americans Migrated to Turkey

`Geog 7(B)`

GO ON

CHINA'S INVESTMENT IN AFRICA

$20 Billion Construction

$6 Billion Infrastructure

ALGERIA

NIGERIA

$23 Billion Refineries

DEMOCRATIC REPUBLIC OF CONGO

ANGOLA

$2.5 Billion Offshore oil

$5.5 Billion Banking

SOUTH AFRICA

Source: *The Economist*

TWO-WAY TRADE WITH AFRICA

	2000	2006	2009
United States	38 Billion	99 Billion	86 Billion
China	10 Billion	55 Billion	90 Billion

Source: *China in Africa* by Chris Alden

30 An analysis of this table and map of Africa would show that —

F   China has overtaken the United States in its trade with Africa.   `Econ 10(D)`

G   China refuses to do business with Angola.

H   the United States investment in Africa peaked in 2009.

J   the United States has broken ties with most of Africa.

31 Which of the following is an example of sustainable development?

A   Brazil cuts down sections of the Amazon Rainforest to provide lumber and to create new farms and ranches.   `Geog 8(C)`

B   Oil companies drill in the Gulf of Mexico in an attempt to find new reserves of oil.

C   Central government planners in Vietnam order factories to increase production by 20% over the next two years.

D   Officials in Thailand limit fishing in surrounding waters to give local fish sufficient time to reproduce.

32 What determines the distribution of goods and services in a communist economy like that of North Korea?

F   the interaction of supply and demand   `Econ 10(A)`

G   government officials' guidelines in a five-year plan

H   local elders guided by tradition and custom

J   decrees issued by the nation's religious leaders

GO ON

Use the map to answer the questions 33 and 34.

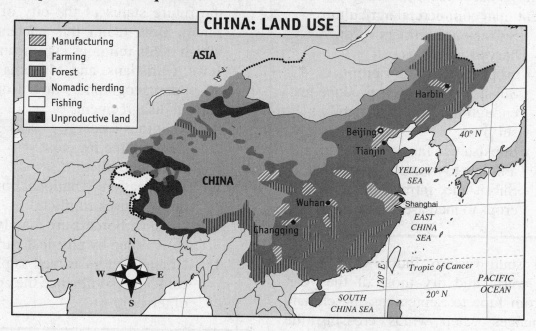

CHINA: LAND USE

Legend:
- Manufacturing
- Farming
- Forest
- Nomadic herding
- Fishing
- Unproductive land

33   Which inference is supported by the map?
  A   China has more people than its land can support.
  B   Most of China's people work in factories.
  C   Most of China's people live in the eastern half of the country.
  D   Much of China's climate is too warm for farming.

  `Econ 12(A)`

34   Why do a large number of people in the western areas of China, as shown on the map, make their livings as nomadic herders?
  F   The climate in the area is too dry for farming.
  G   Herding requires special high-tech equipment.
  H   They can easily ship cattle by sea to foreign markets.
  J   Cattle herds enjoy living in mountainous areas.

  `Econ 11(B)`

35   Agreements such as the North American Free Trade Agreement (*NAFTA*) and associations such as the European Union (*EU*) reflect a movement toward —
  A   national policies of protectionism
  B   free trade zones
  C   a rebirth of command economies
  D   a reliance on social welfare policies

  `Econ 10(D)`

36   In Sweden, the national government owns many enterprises. Other businesses in Sweden are privately owned. The government also provides many public services, including free health care, retirement benefits, and a university education. How should Sweden's economy be classified?
  F   traditional
  H   free enterprise
  G   socialist
  J   communist

  `Econ 10(B)`

GO ON

37 Why is subsistence farming less efficient than commercial agriculture?

   A Subsistence farmers   `Econ 10(C)`
          harvest a surplus of
          crops to be sold for profit.

   B Subsistence farmers produce just
          enough food for their family's
          survival.

   C Subsistence farmers domesticate
          animals to transport goods.

   D Subsistence farmers often irrigate
          crops to increase production.

---

38 In southwestern India, the climate
is warm and dry most of the year.
From June to September, the climate
changes when winds crossing the
Indian Ocean bring heavy monsoon
rains. In contrast, Southern China is
also warm but receives rain throughout the year. What is one effect of
these differences?

   F Indian farmers grow   `Econ 11(C)`
          wet rice, but Chinese
          farmers cannot.

   G India has two growing seasons,
          while China has only one.

   H Both Indian and Chinese farm-
          ers grow rice in the summer, but
          China also has a second growing
          season in the winter.

   J Indian farmers grow rice, but
          Chinese farmers are only able to
          grow wheat.

39 Israelis and Palestinians disagree over
the future status of the city of Jerusalem. Both claim this ancient city,
which holds religious significance for
Jews, Christians, and Muslims alike.
What can geographers infer from this
current disagreement?

   A Religious leaders   `Govt 14(C)`
          are to blame for most
          current conflicts.

   B The location of national borders
          rarely causes conflict.

   C National borders are mainly
          determined by physical barriers.

   D Human factors as well as physi-
          cal features influence the control
          of territory.

---

40 How was the operation of Stalin's
totalitarian dictatorship in the Soviet
Union in the 1940s similar to that of
Ayatolla Khomeini's theocratic rule in
Iran in the 1990s?

   F Free and open   `Govt 14(B)`
          elections were
          permitted.

   G Citizens were not permitted
          to demonstrate, even in favor
          of the government.

   H Supreme power was
          concentrated in the hands
          of a single person.

   J Freedom of the press was
          enthusiastically upheld.

GO ON ▶

In 1980, diamonds were discovered in the Kalahari Game Reserve. Since 1997, the government of Botswana has been removing native Bushmen from this area. Many Bushmen wish to return to their traditional homelands.

> "In a recent court case concerning the Bushmen's right to return to their ancestral lands, government lawyers assured the court that the evictions had nothing to do with diamonds. The Bushmen's lawyers defended the Bushmen's right to live on lands occupied for thousands of years. Yet a government minister admitted: 'Many Bushmen have been removed because of economic interests. In my area, many people were removed because of a diamond mine. Botswana is where it is today because of this [action].' Meanwhile, the Botswana government has been cutting up the area into diamond concessions and dividing them among several companies."
>
> —Adapted from "Why are the Bushmen being evicted?" *The Ecologist*, September 2003

41 Which conclusion is supported by this excerpt?

A Indigenous rights are valued over access to natural resources.   `Econ 12(A)`

B Bushmen are promoting economic progress in Botswana.

C The location of natural resources has an important impact on patterns of economic activity.

D The eviction of Bushmen is unrelated to the presence of diamonds.

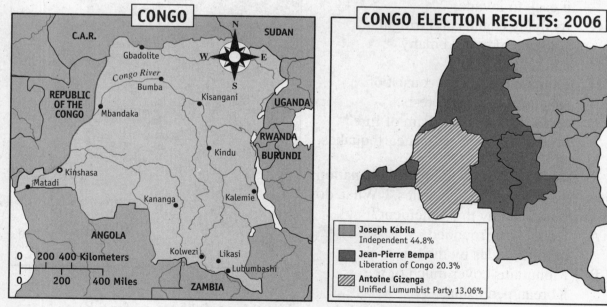

42 Based on the information in the maps, which candidate was most popular in the cities of Kolwezi, Likasi, Lubumbashi, and Kalemie?

F Joseph Kabila

G Jean- Pierre Bempa   `Govt 13(B)`

H Antoine Gizenga

J Cannot be determined

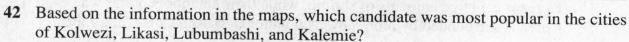

GO ON

> "Because several Christian and Jewish prophets, including Abraham and Moses, are named in the Qur'an [Koran], and because the Jewish Torah and Christian Gospels are recognized as revelations from Allah, the Muslim rulers of Andalusia called Christians and Jews 'People of the Book' and permitted them religious and personal freedom. Jews enjoyed many liberties, and many Jews distinguished themselves in science, the arts, and government."
>
> —Adapted from Lawrence Houghteling, "Al-Andalus: Islamic Spain," *Calliope*, 1995

43 Which thesis statement could be supported by evidence from this passage?

    A The Torah and the Bible were rejected in Islamic Spain.   `Cult 17(D)`

    B Arabs, Jews, and Christians shared places of worship in Islamic Spain.

    C Religious tolerance in Islamic Spain encouraged a successful multicultural society.

    D Islamic Spain was troubled by deep-rooted religious conflicts.

Use the map to answer questions 44 and 45.

44 According to the map, which statement about the geography of Japan is most accurate?

    F Its location has made   `Hist 1(A)` it easy to invade.

    G Its many islands and irregular coastline provided many natural harbors.

    H Its main landforms consist of savannas and rainforests.

    J Its location on the "Rim of Fire" protected Japan against earthquakes.

45 Koreans sometimes refer to their nation as "a shrimp among whales." What do Koreans mean by this statement?

    A Korea is surrounded   `Govt 14(C)` on three sides by the sea.

    B Mountains cover much of the Korean peninsula.

    C Koreans eat large amounts of shrimp, while their neighbors prefer whales.

    D Korea is surrounded by more powerful nations: Russia, China, and Japan.

Map labels: RUSSIA, MONGOLIA, CHINA, NORTH KOREA, SOUTH KOREA, JAPAN, PACIFIC OCEAN

0   400 Kilometers
0   200 400 Miles

GO ON

Name _____

46 Which of the following speakers is most influenced by nationalist beliefs?

F "All South Africans should enjoy the same rights, regardless of their race."   Citi 15(B)

G "Palestinians should be allowed to form their own independent state."

H "As Afghans, we are determined to defend our country against attacks."

J "Individuals in China should be allowed to form their own business enterprises with less government interference."

47 Christianity, Judaism, Islam, and Sikhism are similar in that each religion —

A worships many gods   Cult 17(B)

B practices strict codes of nonviolence

C affirms the existence of one God

D first arose in India

48 Which geographic characteristic do the modern nations of Turkey, Egypt, and Panama share?

F location near strategic waterways   Hist 6(A)

G large deposits of oil and natural gas

H expansion of deserts into regions with fertile soil

J isolation of people caused by mountain ranges

49 Some modern groups justify their use of bombings, violence and other terrorist tactics by arguing that —

A all human life is precious and must be respected   Cult 18(B)

B they lack the strength to challenge their government more openly

C terrorism is necessary to keep group members faithful

D they need to use their superior weaponry to control ethnic minorities

---

The Tuareg people traditionally have a nomadic life-style in the Sahara Desert, where they ride camels and often herd cattle. They eat millet grain and drink goat and camel's milk. Tuareg men cover part of their face with a blue-colored veil.

The Yanomano people live in the Amazon Rainforest in villages of 50 to 400 people. They grow bananas and gather fruits from the rainforest. They hunt animals and fish. Traditionally, the Yanomano also ate insect larvae.

---

50 Based on the information above, which factor best accounts for the cultural differences between the Tuareg and Yanomano peoples?

F The Yanomano do not eat meat for religious reasons.   Cult 17(A)

G The Yanomano are more highly educated than the Tuareg.

H The Tuareg live in a much drier climate than the Yanomano do.

J The Tuareg have larger families than the Yanomano.

GO ON ➡

Use the map to answer the questions 51 and 52.

51 Which letter identifies an area where the Inca once controlled a vast empire by adapting to mountainous conditions? [Geog 8(C)]

   A A

   B B

   C C

   D D

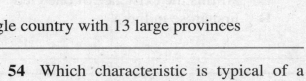

SOUTH AMERICA

CARIBBEAN SEA

ATLANTIC OCEAN

A

B

C

D

PACIFIC OCEAN

52 Which conclusion is supported by the lines on the map? [Govt 13(B)]

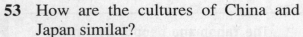

   F South Americans are divided into distinct cultural regions based on different colonizers.

   G South Americans are divided into different countries based on the distribution of political power between different elites.

   H South Americans are divided into different linguistic regions based on different Indian tribes in Pre-Columbian America.

   J South Americas are united into a single country with 13 large provinces

---

53 How are the cultures of China and Japan similar?

   A Both China and Japan are governed by the Communist Party. [Cult 17(A)]

   B People in both cultures speak the same language.

   C Both cultures were deeply influenced by Buddhism.

   D Both cultures quickly adapted to European ways.

54 Which characteristic is typical of a culture with a traditional economy?

   F an international banking system [Cult 18(C)]

   G a currency based on the gold standard

   H family members engaged in cottage industries

   J a tax on all goods imported into the country

GO ON

55 Which example illustrates cultural convergence?

   A People in many countries now enjoy eating American "fast food" and listening to American "pop" music. `Cult 18(D)`

   B In 1991, the Soviet Union divided into separate countries.

   C When the colony of India achieved independence in 1947, it formed the new countries of India and Pakistan.

   D After World War II, the United States and the Soviet Union became rivals in the Cold War.

The Berlin Wall.

56 This photograph of the destruction of the Berlin Wall in 1989 illustrates cultural convergence resulting from the spread of —

   F ethnic cleansing `Cult 18(D)`

   G democratic ideals

   H new information technologies

   J pandemics

"When a group of urban planners was asked to rank the ten most important influences on America in the last hundred years, one of the top advances on the list was the air conditioner. In 1960, air conditioning was found in only 12% of U.S. homes. In the South, only 18% of homes had it. Today, 85% of homes nationwide have air conditioning. The rise of air conditioning has had its most obvious impact on our choice of where to live. Between 1960 and 2009, the population of the Northeast region grew by 23% and the Midwest by 28%. Meanwhile, the South swelled by 96% and the West ballooned by 143%. A mass migration led millions of families to the Sunbelt cities. Air conditioning has made hot, humid and mosquito-infested regions more habitable."

            — Stan Cox, *The Los Angeles Times*, 2010

57 Based on this passage, how did air conditioning affect Americans?

   A It helped people to adapt to hot and humid places. `Sci 19(B)`

   B It had little effect since most American homes still lack air conditioning.

   C Few new homes in the Northeast are built with air conditioning.

   D Between 1960 and 2009, the U.S. population in the South grew by 28%.

GO ON

58 People have lived on savannas, in deserts and mountains, along river valleys, along coastlines, and on islands. This demonstrates that people —

F prefer to live in isolated areas `Geog 8(A)`

G can adapt to varied physical environments

H settle in temperate climatic zones

J adopt different forms of government

59 Which is the best definition of an institution?

A rules for the proper behavior of an individual `Cult 16(B)`

B a set of beliefs about the purpose of life

C an organization developed by societies to take care of social needs

D the things people usually do, such as how they eat and dress

60 How does life in a rural village typically differ from life in an urban setting?

F Villagers travel more often than urban residents. `Cult 16(D)`

G Village residents receive a more formal education than people in cities.

H People in rural villages often engage in subsistence agriculture and cottage industries.

J People in rural villages have greater access to the latest technologies.

61 Which of the following statements best characterizes the treatment of women in the traditional Islamic monarchy of Saudi Arabia?

A Women enjoy equal opportunities with men at work. `Cult 17(C)`

B Special government programs favor schools that educate women.

C Women must cover their bodies in public and have limited educational opportunities.

D When a man marries, he moves to his wife's village and takes her name.

62 Animists generally believe that —

F meditation leads followers to nirvana `Cult 17(B)`

G after death the soul is reborn in another human form

H holy wars must be fought to gain entry into heaven

J spirits inhabit both living and nonliving things in nature

63 What important challenge faces many less developed nations today?

A Due to improved agricultural technology, many farmers have lost their jobs. `Geog 5(B)`

B Social welfare programs have reduced military spending.

C High rates of illiteracy and a lack of infrastructure slow the pace of economic development.

D A high-calorie diet causes widespread obesity and a short life expectancy.

GO ON

INTERNET USAGE IN THE WORLD: 2008

Heavy Internet Usage		
Canada	United States	China
Norway	Sweden	Finland

Medium Internet Usage		
Chile	Argentina	Costa Rica
Britain	France	Ireland
Denmark	Netherlands	Belgium

Little Internet Usage							
Mexico	Peru	Nicaragua	Brazil	Panama	Puerto Rico	Cyprus	Kuwait
Colombia	Jamaica	Ecuador	Senegal	Venezuela	Guinea	Saudi Arabia	Turkey

64 What conclusion about Internet usage can be drawn from the chart?

Sci 20(A)

F Internet usage limits international cooperation.

G Lower standards of living are linked to higher Internet usage.

H More developed nations have greater access to the Internet than less developed nations do.

J Eastern Hemisphere nations use the Internet more than Western Hemisphere nations.

Use the passage to answer questions 65 and 66.

"In the 2001 census, the majority of new immigrants to Great Britain came from Asia (40%) and Africa (32%). The largest three groups came from Pakistan, India and Somalia. In 2004, Poland entered the European Union. It is estimated that by 2007, 375,000 Poles had registered to work in Britain. Many Poles work in seasonal occupations, and frequently move back and forth between Britain and Poland."

— *Report: Immigration to the United Kingdom since 1922*

65 What is the point of view of the authors of this report?

Citi 15(A)

A Great Britain should halt all foreign immigration.

B Polish workers do not perform as well as British workers.

C The opening of borders within the European Union has led to increased European migration.

D Pakistan, India and Somalia halted immigration to Great Britain.

66 Based on this report, what is the main reason for recent Polish migration to Britain?

Geog 7(B)

F Push factor — to escape communism

G Push factor — to escape religious persecution

H Pull factor — for greater economic opportunity

J Pull factor — for a more pleasant physical environment

GO ON

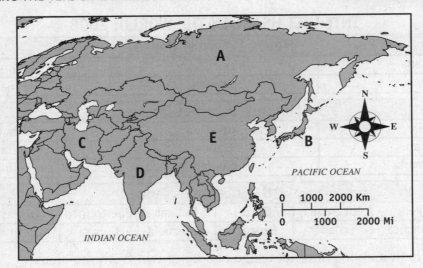

67 Which letter on the map correctly identifies a theocratic state that has caused contro-
versy by its nuclear development program and its anti-American rhetoric?

A A   C C   Govt 14(B)
B B   D E

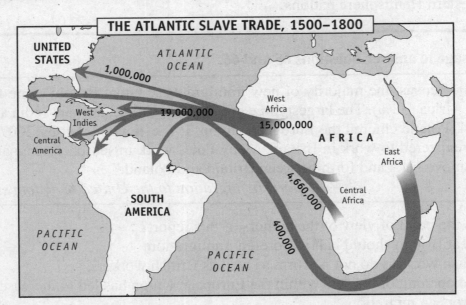

THE ATLANTIC SLAVE TRADE, 1500–1800

68 Which source of information could a researcher most likely use to evaluate the validity
of the information in this map?

F a novel written by a former slave   Cult 17(D)

G a movie about the slave trade

H a student research paper on the slave trade

J a statistical table submitted to a Congressional Committee
investigating the slave trade

STOP

INDEX